Rural Poverty in America

Rural Poverty in America

EDITED BY

Cynthia M. Duncan

FOREWORD BY

Susan E. Sechler

Auburn House
NEW YORK • WESTPORT, CONNECTICUT • LONDON

Library of Congress Cataloging-in-Publication Data

Rural poverty in America / edited by Cynthia M. Duncan ; foreword by
  Susan E. Sechler.
      p.   cm.
   Includes bibliographical references and index.
    ISBN 0–86569–013–8 (alk. paper).—ISBN 0–86569–014–6 (pbk. :
 alk. paper)
     1. Rural poor—United States. 2. Economic assistance, Domestic—
 United States.   I. Duncan, Cynthia M.
   HC110.P6R89   1992
   362.5'0973'091734—dc20   91–18655

British Library Cataloguing in Publication Data is available.

Copyright © 1992 by Cynthia M. Duncan

Library of Congress Catalog Card Number: 91–18655
ISBN: 0–86569–013–8
ISBN: 0–86569–014–6 (pbk.)

First published in 1992

Auburn House, 88 Post Road West, Westport, CT 06881
An imprint of Greenwood Publishing Group, Inc.

Printed in the United States of America

The paper used in this book complies with the
Permanent Paper Standard issued by the National
Information Standards Organization (Z39.48–1984).

10 9 8 7 6 5 4 3 2 1

To
Sue and Don Leavenworth

Contents

PART II. POOR PEOPLE AND POOR PLACES

PART III. POLICIES FOR THE RURAL POOR

Illustrations

TABLES

FIGURES

MAPS

Foreword

The early 1980s brought stagnation and uncertainty to the global economy, and for the United States, once supreme among nations, no prognosis seemed too bleak. In the balance of trade, the national debt, interest rates, the loss of manufacturing, unemployment, the economic explosion of the Pacific Rim, and many other indicators, analysts discerned transformations that pegged the American economy for long-term decline. Industry after industry in which the United States had long enjoyed hegemony seemed suddenly unable to compete at all. And just as suddenly, scholars and pundits were filling the air with all manner of sweeping proposals to arrest the American decline. We need an industrial policy, some proposed, with public investment in key industries, massive research consortiums, and a good dose of Japanese management techniques thrown in for good measure. But what good would that do, other voices argued, without an education policy that took Amercia's kids back to basics, so that they—and we—might survive the high-tech competition to come.

Many of us who study the economy of rural America were preoccupied with two phenomena at that time. First, the tremendous forces that were sweeping the economy as a whole in the early 1980s seemed to be wreaking even greater damage and despair in rural America. And second, no one seemed to be taking much notice of the rural situation.

Study after study emerged cataloging the collapse of U.S. manufacturing and the concomitant rise of a flimsier, blurrier "post-industrial" economy, stuck together with high technology and services. When the question arose of where in America these wrenching changes actually were being played out, the stock answers always included allusions to those contrary but serviceable twins, the Rust Belt and the Sun Belt. For dramatic evidence that international capital markets, high interest rates, export-choking exchange rates, or foreign competition were also taking their toll on rural areas, it seemed that one need look no further than agriculture, at the time in the throes of as harsh and debilitating a recession as has been known in decades.

It was one thing, of course, to encounter these formulaic, incomplete or just plain wrong images of the changing economy, and the fate of rural America within it, again and again in mass media reports. To encounter these same images in the minds of the researchers, policymakers, and elected officials to whom rural communities might turn for explanations and help was something altogether more worrisome. And hard to remedy, it turns out.

In a debate shaped by econometric models of global capital flow, promethean manipulations of the national income and product accounts, super-computed projections of job creation by sector and occupation, and other mega-tools used to fabricate ideas about economic policy in this country, anecdotes do not count for much. Yet, in depicting the economic turmoil in rural America, anecdotes were mainly what we had in the early 1980s. Not that they weren't compelling.

Manufacturing plants, old and new, were closing rapidly in the South and elsewhere. Residents of the Sun Belt, whose "rural renaissance" had moved on to even sunnier climes, were forced to drive hundreds of miles a day to find work. In the mid-Atlantic, laid-off workers were migrating long-distances to urban areas for construction jobs and living in their automobiles. Rural homelessness emerged as a phenomenon, only now barns, railroad cars, or deserted farmhouses formed the backdrop in place of urban grates or city shelters. Forest products and mining also plunged into recession. Hunger among rural children reappeared. Families with two full-time workers were unable to support the family. And, in part because of economic pressures, drug and alcohol abuse and family violence were reported to thrive in rusticity as ever they had in the metropolis.

Gradually, eventually, the disturbing anecdotes begot formal studies, and these documented poverty and economic deterioration in rural America that was every bit as serious as that in population centers in the 1980s. Pick a number, almost any number—unemployment rates, poverty rates, business failures, high school dropouts, households headed by poor black women, rate of job creation—and it seems that problems have been disproportionately rationed to rural areas in the past decade. Looking back now, it appears that the term "rural renaissance" had scarcely been coined before many rural residents, poised at the portal of a long awaited modern age, discovered their prospects to be more nearly medieval.

Yet just when people in rural areas needed it most, researchers and activists were at a loss to explain what had gone wrong or what might come next. Indeed, it was difficult merely to describe recent events coherently across industries or geographic regions, let alone assign causality to the decline when the choices ranged from exchange rates to labor costs to lousy schools. It did not help that research and data collection relevant to the rural economy had atrophied in the preceding decade. Little wonder that when federal funding for traditional rural economic development programs was cut by 70 percent in the 1980s, the rural protest sounded weaker and more fractious than ever. It was probably time to let go of those programs. But it most surely was not the time to put nothing in their place.

In response to the perceived disarray and neglect of rural policy studies, the Ford Foundation in 1985 increased the scale of its Rural Poverty and Resources Program to support a series of related grants for research, analysis, and new thinking devoted to the economic changes taking place in rural America. The causes and manifestations of rural poverty were of special concern. As part of this new emphasis, the Foundation supported the establishment of a small staff and an advisory committee, under the auspices of a Rural Economic Policy Program at the Aspen Institute. Their job has been to help identify promising research projects for Foundation support, and to convene researchers, policy-makers, and activists to examine collectively some of the problems that were besetting rural economies. From the outset, the goal was twofold. First, the program sought out researchers who could significantly enhance the state of knowledge about the rural economy and rural poverty, whether or not they had ever worked on rural issues before. Second, the program aimed to gain public attention as this new knowledge emerged, and to elevate rural poverty on the national policy agenda. Often this strategy involved identifying the best re-searchers and encouraging them to add a rural component that otherwise would have been ignored to an important ongoing study of broader economic phenom-ena. Support also went to detailed, micro-level research on specific problems, areas, or population groups, using survey and interview techniques to lend a measure of ground truth to the remote sensing of the macro-studies.

Much of the work featured in this volume was initiated or supported through Ford Foundation grants. Cynthia Duncan, Director of Research at the Rural Economic Policy Program, deserves much of the credit for attracting researchers of the highest caliber to the project, and for the scope and substance of this collection, which she conceived and edited.

To my mind the book's greatest strength is its blending of historical, social, and economic analysis with political insight and a good measure of empathy. The authors have charted the many dimensions of rural poverty with new and much needed social scientific rigor, and in doing so have brought us a long way from the stroboscopic glimpses found in the literature not so long ago. Even so, they have also managed to people this remarkably varied landscape with men, women, and children whose industry, spirit, and potential belie their grim cir-cumstances, command our respect, and deserve our attention. Although the theme of the collection is clearly the paucity of rural work opportunities that pay a living wage, you will find no grand, unified theory of the cause of rural poverty in these pages, nor any all-encompassing solution to the problem, which after all is many problems. But if awareness, understanding, and empathy are still the raw ingredients of political will, and if political will can yet be mustered to the aid of the less fortunate, this book should inspire both investigation and activism on behalf of the rural poor for a long time to come.

Acknowledgments

Many people have helped put this book together. I want to thank the authors who wrote chapters; Norman Collins and Janet Maughan of the Ford Foundation and Susan Sechler of the Aspen Institute, who provided warm support for the project; Margaret Moore, who read early drafts and cheered me on; Stephen Sweet, who worked with me to bring everything to completion; and Jennifer Bakke, who provided clerical assistance. As part of their commitment to encouraging policy-relevant research on the rural disadvantaged, the Ford Foundation's Rural Poverty and Resources Program and the Aspen Institute's Rural Economic Policy Program funded much of the research described here. I am grateful to John Harney of Auburn House for his encouragement and flexibility. Finally, but most importantly, I thank Graham Duncan and Ian Duncan for cheerfully putting up with the "lack of balance in Mom's life," and Bill Duncan for more than I could ever say. I dedicate the book to my parents, Sue and Don Leavenworth, with love and appreciation.

Introduction: Poverty in Rural America

Cynthia M. Duncan and Stephen Sweet

There are over nine million people living in poverty in rural areas of the United States. This book is about those people—who they are, why they are living in poverty, and what approach to social policy might improve their lives. It is reasonable to ask why we need a book that focuses especially on the rural poor. Are the rural poor that different from other poor people? Does paying special attention to the rural dimension of poverty add to our understanding of poverty? We know that the circumstances of the poor in general are affected by the availability of work, family structure, human capital, and what William J. Wilson (1990) has called the "social context" and culture of the poor. Are these factors somehow different for the rural poor?

To people living in crowded urban and suburban areas, "rural" conveys an image of small towns and open countryside. As Bellah et al. (1985) discovered in their study of American values, middle-class Americans associate small-town living with an idyllic community life. It is commonly assumed that small rural communities offer simple face-to-face relationships, opportunities for civic involvement, and a local economy thriving on small proprietorships and hard work. We imagine a world without social class distinctions, a world in which people know one another, take care of one another, and live out the best of the American Dream. We see the whole community as working right.

In contrast, we think of the rural poor as people outside these well-integrated, supportive communities. Our images have been shaped by literature and journalistic accounts—we see the hardened, hollow faces in Agee and Evans's *Let Us Now Praise Famous Men* (1941), the Okies in Steinbeck's *Grapes of Wrath* (1939), or Caudill's broken, dispirited coal miners in *Night Comes to the Cumberlands* (1963). We imagine "people left behind," as President Lyndon Johnson's Commission on Rural Poverty called them, unable to find work in the modern high-technology economy.

Neither of these images is accurate as we enter the 1990s. The small, relatively self-sufficient communities that we carry in our imaginations disappeared in the late 1800s and early 1900s as industrialization and urbanization swept the nation. Now, as the authors in the first part of this volume show, even communities in which the economy was healthy in the 1960s and early 1970s are losing jobs. Across America young rural workers are struggling to make a living, struggling to earn enough to lift their families out of poverty. However, as the chapters in the second part of this book indicate, not all the rural poor are recent victims of changes in the economy. Poverty and inequality have been a constant feature in many rural people's lives. Rigid distinctions on the basis of class and ethnic background have oppressed poor rural people for generations. The social context in chronically depressed rural communities bears little resemblance to the world we associate with small communities. Rather, these poor rural communities tend to have two social classes—those who have control and those who are vulnerable to that control, the haves and the have-nots.

This book focuses attention on poor rural people and poor rural places. Rural places face increasing economic adversity in the 1990s, and, as a result, rural people face declining opportunities. As the chapters in this volume show, most poor people in rural areas work, and working people in rural areas are very often poor. The contributors to this book seek to better understand the circumstances and characteristics of the rural poor—who is poor and why—in order to help build better opportunities in the future.

A second and related reason to analyze poverty in rural communities is that the small size and face-to-face relationships lay bare social relationships that are often submerged in larger social structures. We can see some of the social and political dynamics that prevent the poor from escaping their poverty in any poor community. The researcher can see, for example, how the scarcity of work and lack of economic diversity give employers control over every aspect of the lives of the poor, and how this control not only limits opportunities for mobility locally, but also can undermine opportunities to escape poverty by moving to find work elsewhere. The evolving understanding of rural poverty presented in these chapters, therefore, has important implications for poverty policy in general and sheds light on the continuing debate about the structural versus behavioral causes of persistent poverty.

Renewed national attention to poverty and concern about growing inequality and dependency make the 1990s a particularly good time to look closely at the conditions of the rural poor. Scholars have documented the growing severity of concentrated poverty in the inner cities (William J. Wilson 1989; Sawhill 1988) and the alarming growth in the number of homeless people (Rossi 1989). Increasing inequality, reflected in the growing numbers of working poor, has also received greater attention from scholars and policymakers (Bluestone and Harrison 1988; Bradbury 1986; Levitan and Shapiro 1987; Children's Defense Fund 1988; O'Hare 1988; Committee on the Budget 1988). Most connect growing poverty with the changing structure of the national and world economy (see Levy 1987; Thurow 1987; Wilson 1987).

The plight of the urban poor is readily apparent to journalists and politicians. Both the media and the research community have written extensively about inner-city poverty in recent years. Journalists have raised public concern through stories and documentaries in the national media. Researchers have come to better understand the dynamics of poverty and dependency in areas of concentrated urban poverty.

The rural poor are less visible in the national press, and their behavior is less threatening to the public on a day-to-day basis. The diverse pockets of chronically poor people—rural Blacks in the South, Appalachians in the coal fields, Native Americans on scattered reservations, migrant workers, low-wage farm and manufacturing workers—appear too disparate to write about as a single social problem. The characteristically rural problems of low-wage and part-time or part-year employment are regarded as the inevitable costs of a changing economy.

The contributors to this volume demonstrate that poverty in rural areas is a serious, troubling national problem and has been for decades. An increased exodus to city jobs after World War II brought a dramatic decline in rural poverty, from twenty-two million (or 33 percent of the rural population) in 1950 to twelve million (or 17 percent) in 1970. Hundreds of thousands of migrants moved from Appalachia and the South seeking better employment opportunities in metropolitan areas (Brown 1972; Levy 1987). These rural migrants went to jobs in the expanding automobile and steel factories or to construction jobs in growing cities, jobs where a strong back could ensure steady employment for a hard worker. The postwar period, between the late 1940s and the early 1970s, was a period of national expansion and growing productivity, and urban economies could absorb the unemployed and underemployed from rural areas.

When the first impact of economic restructuring hit these urban industrial areas in the late 1970s, and unemployment dramatically increased in the "rust" belt, rural economies experienced surprising growth for a few years, and there were new employment opportunities. The brief period of revitalization was stimulated by the convergence of several factors: prices for farm products rose, the Organization of Petroleum Exporting Countries (OPEC) oil embargo spurred growth in domestic energy industries, and more and more manufacturing concerns moved routine assembly plants to rural areas where labor costs would be lower. In addition, some retired people began to move back to their childhood communities or to other quiet, less expensive rural areas.

This rural turnaround meant that people who had reluctantly left rural areas in search of work could return and take advantage of new opportunities in their home communities. Some rural analysts speculated that there might be a kind of "renaissance," as many return migrants brought with them higher expectations of public education and a commitment to civic involvement. Sons and daughters of Appalachian miners and Southern sharecroppers returned to their parents' and grandparents' home places, and the future looked brighter for small communities in rural America.

However, the rural turnaround was short-lived. Growing international competition in goods-producing industries hit rural areas hard in the early 1980s. Manufacturing industries—the chief source of rural jobs in the 1960s and 1970s— laid off workers, closed up shop, or moved overseas. Mining and timber companies introduced changes in management and technology that resulted in dramatic productivity gains, and these in turn prompted substantial reductions in their labor forces. Farm-dependent communities suffered as farmers' debt increased and income dropped.

The rural downturn that began in the early 1980s is now widely accepted as a structural, rather than cyclical, change in the national economy. The goods-producing industries that offered opportunities for stable jobs and upward mobility to high-school-educated young workers are no longer a source of employment growth. The good jobs in service industries that offer steady employment require workers with more education and tend to be located in growing suburban areas, not in remote rural or dense urban communities. Thus remote rural areas, like inner cities, appear to have intractable high unemployment and high poverty. In both areas young people have been hit the hardest.

Today about half of the nine million rural poor live in the South. The poverty rate among the rural population in 1987 was 17 percent, close to the 19 percent poverty rate in central cities and higher than the poverty rate for the urban population overall. Many of the communities described in this book have poverty rates as high as 30 to 50 percent. Economic opportunities have been limited in these areas for decades, and chronic underdevelopment has prevented local investment in the basic human-resource and institutional infrastructure needed both for individual mobility and community development.

For some rural places and groups, persistent stereotypes are obstacles to deeper understanding. Poor Black farm laborers, mountain people, or Native Americans are seen as chronically poor and dependent because they do not share mainstream values about work. Research presented here shows how inaccurate these stereotypes are. Rural poverty has always reflected the limited opportunity structure rather than limited ambitions. Since the mechanization of agriculture, mining, and other natural-resource-based industries, rural areas have had far too little employment available for those who need work. The work that is available tends to be low-paying and volatile—part-time, seasonal, and subject to booms and busts in national and international markets.

In some areas families and workers have always lived on the margin of the nation's economy, scratching a living from the land or subject to the employment fluctuations of primary industries. This is particularly true in the deep South, Appalachia, poor farming areas, and Indian reservations. In other rural areas high poverty rates reflect the lower wages and declining employment in manufacturing resulting from more recent structural changes in the national economy. The aim of the first part of this book is to provide an understanding of the underlying dynamics of rural poverty in the United States. The next part is an in-depth look at the circumstances of particular groups of the rural poor, including African Americans, Appalachians, Native Americans, migrant workers, and those outside the mainstream economy in more prosperous places. We look at how conditions differ among various groups of rural poor—between those who are working and those who are not, for example, or for Indians on the reservation compared to families of agricultural workers following crops. Finally, we consider an overall framework within which to consider public policy alternatives.

The book begins with chapters that present a national overview. The authors describe who is poor, why they are poor, and how long their poverty lasts. Kenneth Deavers and Robert Hoppe provide a comprehensive picture of the rural poor in the 1980s. Although many people still think of rural poverty as synonymous with farm poverty, Deavers and Hoppe show that dramatic improvement in farm incomes has brought a decline in the number of poor farmers. Increases in transfer-payment programs have also helped reduce rural poverty over time. However, the economic changes beginning in the early 1980s have contributed to growing unemployment and poverty. Young workers and the traditionally disadvantaged—minorities, children, and female-headed households—are the hardest hit by these changes. Low educational attainment coincides with low-wage, low-skill manufacturing jobs in rural areas, contributing to high numbers of working poor. The rural elderly are the only group for whom poverty declined between 1973 and 1987, largely because of the effectiveness of Social Security and Medicare. Nonetheless, the elderly in rural areas have higher poverty rates than the elderly in urban areas.

In "The Growing Problem of Low Earnings in Rural Areas," Lucy Gorham analyzes changes in the economic structure over the last twenty years and the effect of these changes on rural workers. Her work shows that declining employment in manufacturing and other relatively high-paying goods-producing sectors during the rural recession in the early 1980s has led to a 20 percent increase in the number of working poor in rural areas. In urban areas the effect of these structural changes has been softened somewhat by the growth of high-wage service-sector jobs, but rural areas have not captured these jobs. In 1987 rural workers were over 45 percent more likely to earn low wages than urban workers. Gorham shows that young workers have fared the worst. Currently nearly three-quarters of all young rural workers earn yearly incomes well below the poverty level for a family of four.

In "The Working Poor in Rural Labor Markets," Ann Tickamyer further elaborates how the limited opportunity structure contributes to these growing numbers of working poor in rural America. Analyzing new data by labor markets (rather than by counties or states), Tickamyer shows that poverty rates vary according to the type of labor market in which workers participate. While the extent of poverty differs between rural and urban labor-market areas, there is even greater variation between different types of rural labor markets. When rural labor markets are relatively diversified, they perform more like urban labor markets, offering wider opportunities for workers. Workers take advantage of these opportunities to earn good wages, and, as a result, poverty rates are lower. Tickamyer also shows that labor-market areas characterized by concentrated resource extraction tend to have fewer jobs overall (but higher wages), while labor markets offering manufacturing jobs offer predominantly low-wage jobs. As a result, these narrowly based labor markets tend to have the highest levels of poverty. Overall, she finds that rural labor markets have more working poor than urban labor markets.

Terry Adams and Greg Duncan examine persistent poverty in their chapter, "Long-Term Poverty in Rural Areas." Their analysis of data in the Panel Study of Income Dynamics shows that long-term poverty is greater in rural than in urban areas. Although there have been improvements since the 1960s, four million people in rural areas—and one-third of all rural Blacks—are still persistently poor. Adams and Duncan point out that the rural long-term poor tend to "live by the rules," participating in the labor force and using welfare for only short periods, but they are still poor because there are few good jobs available. Those who have not completed high school and those far from metropolitan areas are especially vulnerable, and there are growing numbers of female-headed households experiencing long-term poverty in rural areas.

The chapters in Part II give a more detailed picture of who poor people are and of the communities in which they live. First, Bonnie Dill and Bruce Williams, in "Race, Gender, and Poverty in the Rural South," detail the multifaceted disadvantages facing Black single mothers in the rural South. Over the last two decades the proportion of poor rural families in the South headed by women has doubled. Dill and Williams argue that discrimination based on race, gender, and class leaves limited options for African American women in rural areas. To make ends meet, they combine work and welfare. But most importantly, they rely on family members to provide additional help. While this dependence on kin is a valuable survival mechanism, it also prevents them from leaving to find better work elsewhere.

Cynthia Duncan's chapter shows how scarce jobs and a historically oppressive coal industry have created rigidly stratified, patronage-driven communities that prevent the Appalachian poor from escaping poverty. The elite control jobs, and are doling them out to family members and political supporters. Those from poor families are outside the job network and, in small, closed communities, have difficulty escaping the stigma associated with their family background. Schools also have low expectations of the poor and do not provide basic skills. Like the Black women described in Dill and Williams's chapter, the Appalachian poor remain in these poor communities, trapped, working at low-wage, part-time jobs and often partially dependent on welfare.

In "Migrant Farm Workers," Doris Slesinger and Max Pfeffer describe the poverty and vulnerability of the nation's often-invisible 250,000 migrant farm workers. Migrant workers receive low wages for hard labor. They follow the crop seasons, unprotected by basic labor legislation that other American workers take for granted. They live in poor housing and move their children from school to school. Slesinger and Pfeffer review the history of policies affecting farm workers, detailing the ways in which they have been excluded from benefits and left vulnerable to employers.

C. Matthew Snipp and Gene Summers's chapter on "American Indians and Economic Poverty" combines a contemporary portrait of the nation's 1.37 million American Indians with a sociohistorical analysis of federal policies that have failed to eradicate their chronic poverty. Over half of all American Indians and Alaska natives live in rural areas, many on the 278 reservations located within the United States. Federal policies have either ignored or tried to destroy the unique culture of American Indians. This cultural identity has also given poor rural American Indians a strength and a greater community cohesiveness than that of other rural groups. But poverty remains a persistent problem among the Indian nations. Snipp and Summers urge a renewed commitment to traditional economic development and capacity-building programs.

Janet Fitchen's chapter, "Rural Poverty in the Northeast: The Case of Upstate New York," provides a detailed account of the rural poor who live in an area that is more prosperous overall. While pockets of poverty have persisted in these remote rural communities for decades, Fitchen finds evidence that conditions are growing worse as we enter the 1990s. Welfare rolls and Food Stamp applications are up as much as 20 percent in some areas, and the poor are more and more visible in small, run-down clusters of trailers or other forms of low-cost housing. Fitchen describes people who live on the margin, moving from place to place as housing arrangements and personal relationships deteriorate under the pressure of inadequate incomes. She argues that this mobility itself traps families in poverty, since they are unable to build social ties.

Cornelia Flora, in "The New Poor in Midwestern Farming Communities," describes growing poverty in the nation's heartland, especially among wage workers. She argues that the poor in midwestern farm communities not only face the problems of piecing together a livelihood in a declining economy, but also must deal with a lack of concern from the nonpoor. The farmers and other middle-class leaders in farm communities believe that the poor have failed to work hard enough to escape poverty. Flora, like Dill and Williams, finds that elites try to keep wages low, in effect preventing these workers from escaping poverty. Like Fitchen, she finds growing poverty among young families that exist on the edges of the community, neither supported by community structures nor making commitments of their own to the community. These young rural households move from town to town and from job to job in search of a job with reasonable income.

Clearly the rural poor face formidable obstacles to escaping poverty. They have difficulty finding steady work that pays a living wage, the welfare benefits they receive are too low to lift them out of poverty, and receiving benefits further distances them from the nonpoor in their communities. Rural communities are generally either inhospitable or openly oppressive to the poor in their midst. The familiarity that makes small communities less frightening than a big, strange city also means that those from poor families are labeled poor and given few chances to escape poverty. What approach to public policy would hold some promises for widening opportunities for the rural poor? In the final part of the book, we explore this question.

Rural poverty has been a problem for decades. Over that period all levels of government have tried a variety of programs. In "Modernization and the Rural Poor: Some Lessons from History," Alice O'Connor reviews past policies from the New Deal through the Great Society, relating their underlying themes to modernization theory. O'Connor shows how policies to address rural poverty have shifted from an early emphasis among Southern regionalists on bringing remote rural places into the modern era to a subsequent "fix the backward people" approach. The third phase was straightforward economic development built on international development experience. O'Connor's historical analysis demonstrates the policy side of the inequities that have helped perpetuate rural poverty. Her account includes descriptions of proposed programs that would have redistributed power over resources. In each case, however, powerful local elites whose interests would not be served by such broad-based redistribution successfully blocked social change.

In "Empowerment and Rural Poverty," Steve Suitts explores the potential for developing strategies that empower the rural poor by increasing their direct control over economic and political institutions. He reviews past efforts among the rural poor to seize control of their economic institutions, showing how these efforts, like those described by O'Connor, succumbed to the power of local elites. Nonetheless, Suitts describes some cases in which the rural poor did gain control over their lives and communities, and he argues that these successes offer promise for future victories. For example, his analysis of recent antipoverty legislation passed as a result of growing African American representation in the U.S. Congress demonstrates the power that the rural poor can have when their elected representatives support national policies to help the poor.

Recognizing that many of the rural poor are working, living in two-parent families, and elderly, Robert Greenstein and Isaac Shapiro take a pragmatic look at national policies that would help alleviate rural poverty. In "Policies to Alleviate Rural Poverty," Greenstein and Shapiro briefly review those characteristics of the rural poor that are most important for federal policy considerations. Drawing on their experience at the Center on Budget and Policy Priorities, they recommend policies that could raise income in working poor families without diminishing work incentive. They discuss the earned income tax credit, minimum-wage laws, programs to assist the unemployed, benefits for the elderly, and policies to help the rural poor with health, housing, and child-care needs.

Clearly many of the policies needed to assist the rural poor, both workers and nonworkers, are also relevant for the urban poor. Workers need better pay and benefits; those unable to work need programs that provide a decent standard of living. The problems of isolation, limited expectations, and limited resources that trap those in poor rural communities are similar to those that trap the poor in inner-city poverty areas. Commitment to improved education and training—from Head Start to schools to youth service and the Job Corps—would widen their opportunities. From a policy standpoint, the differences in circumstances between the urban and rural poor are more likely to imply different implementation strategies than different approaches altogether. But the rural poor are often forgotten by policymakers and those who develop programs. They are truly invisible. The contributions to this volume try to make them visible and broaden our understanding of who the rural poor are, why they are poor, and what kinds of policies and political strategies might improve their opportunities.

NOTES

Bill Duncan made helpful comments on an earlier draft of this chapter.

1. "Rural" and "nonmetropolitan" are used interchangeably throughout this volume. The reference is specifically to the 1983 classification of counties as "metropolitan" and "nonmetropolitan" by the U.S. Office of Management and Budget for use in presenting statistics by agencies of the federal government. Metropolitan statistical areas usually include an urbanized area with a population nucleus of 50,000 or more, as well as nearby communities or counties that are economically and socially integrated with that nucleus. Nonmetropolitan counties are not linked with large cities nor with communities closely tied to large cities. This distinction is different from that between "urban" and "rural" devised by the Census Bureau. According to Census Bureau usage, an area—in this case a county—is "urban" if it includes a "place" (typically a city or village) of 2,500 or greater population, and "rural" if it contains no such place. Only about 10 percent of the population of "nonmetropolitan" counties live in "rural" counties by this definition. The rest live in counties that include at least one "place" of 2,500 or greater population.

Part I

The Dynamics of Poverty and Mobility in Rural America

Chapter 1

Overview of the Rural Poor in the 1980s

Kenneth L. Deavers and Robert A. Hoppe

This chapter is about poverty in rural America: about who is poor, where the poor live, and what has happened to rural poverty over time. Recent reforms of national poverty policy and discussions of the underclass make it clear that the American public seems generally to perceive poverty as an urban problem (Ricketts and Sawhill 1988; Wilson 1987). However, as Figure 1.1 shows, the overall poverty rate is higher in rural than in urban areas, as it has been throughout the past twenty years, and the rural poor have fared relatively poorly since 1980 as the economic performance of rural areas has lagged behind that of the rest of the nation.

It was only twenty-five years ago that a presidential commission report, *The People Left Behind*, brought the problem of rural poverty into the national limelight.

Rural poverty is so widespread, and so acute, as to be a national disgrace. . . . This Nation has been largely oblivious to . . . 14 million impoverished people left behind in rural America. Our programs for rural America are woefully out of date. (U.S. President's National Advisory Commission on Rural Poverty 1967, p. ix)

The current gap between reality and public beliefs about the incidence of poverty results largely from the close contact between city people and the urban poor and from the prominence given to the urban poor by national broadcast media. In contrast, the rural poor, who live in many small scattered settlements in apparently "picturesque" country surroundings, are relatively invisible.

If the characteristics of the rural and urban poor, and government's capacity to provide each with supporting services, were essentially the same, the identification of U.S. poverty as an urban problem would not matter very much. Since they are not the same, however, we believe that national policies to serve the poor often unintentionally discriminate against the rural poor, who in 1987 numbered more than nine million (U.S. Bureau of the Census 1989b).

Figure 1.1
Poverty Rates by Residence, 1967–88

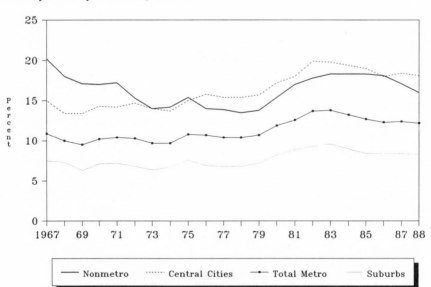

Source: U.S. Bureau of the Census, Current Population Survey, various years.

RURAL POVERTY IS NO LONGER SYNONYMOUS WITH FARM POVERTY

The first published estimates of poverty, for 1961, distinguished between farm and nonfarm poverty and showed the farm family poverty rate (30.1 percent) to be much higher than the nonfarm family poverty rate (17.4 percent) (Orshansky 1963). This interest in farm poverty reflected a tendency to relate the terms "rural" and "farming," a theme that can be traced back at least to the beginning of the twentieth century. When President Theodore Roosevelt established the Commission on Country Life in 1908, more than 60 percent of rural people lived on farms, and farm work and farming incomes were the basis of their well-being. It is not surprising, then, that the commission and the president thought that working to improve farming incomes and farmers' prosperity was the best strategy to improve the lot of rural people.

The well-being of farm people continued to lag in comparison to that of rural nonfarm and urban people until the 1970s. Figure 1.2 shows that the median income of rural farm people was only one-half that of urban people in 1950, and fully three-fourths of all rural farm families and unrelated individuals lived on incomes below the median income of their urban counterparts. Thirty years of change in the technology, scale, and organization of farming, and large federal program payments to farm operators, have changed that situation dramatically.

Figure 1.2
Income by Residence, 1950–80

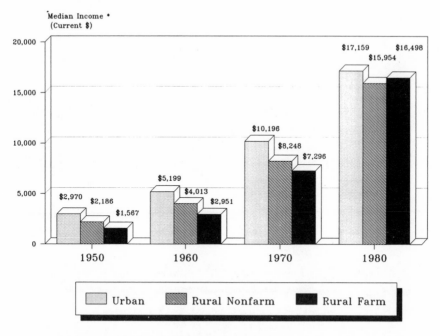

Source: U.S. Bureau of the Census 1953, 1964, 1972b and 1983.
*1950–70 Median Family Income, 1980 Median Household Income.

By 1980 the median income of rural farm people was nearly the same as that
of rural nonfarm and urban people. Between 1970 and 1980 rural farm people
maintained the average real income levels they had achieved at the beginning
of the decade. In contrast, rural nonfarm and urban people were unable to avoid
a decline in average real income during that decade.

Improvements in the incomes of farmers were accompanied by the exit of
large numbers of people from farming, especially in the post–World War II
period. The numbers are really quite remarkable. Between 1950 and 1985 the
farm population declined by 17.7 million people to less than 5.4 million (U.S.
Bureau of the Census 1989c). Most of the people who left farming and rural
areas moved away to take jobs in the cities' expanding factories and services.
Farmers became a relatively small component of the rural population (they now
account for less than 10 percent), and the farm share of rural poverty declined
dramatically. By 1980 the farm share fell to less than 11 percent, slightly more
than one-half of its share in 1970 (U.S. Bureau of the Census 1983, p. 79;
1972b, p. 401). As Figure 1.3 shows, the farm poor now account for only about
2 percent of the nation's poor population.

Most descriptions of the post–World War II revolution in farming and the

Figure 1.3
Farm Poverty, 1959–87

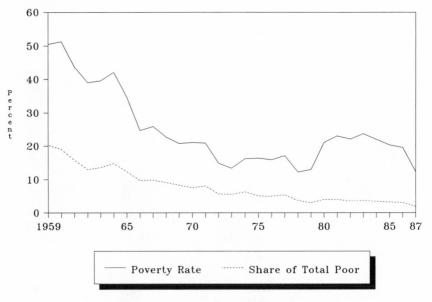

Source: U.S. Bureau of the Census, Current Population Survey, various years.

dramatic improvement in farm incomes leave out an important human and regional dimension of the story, the virtual disappearance of Black farmers. The number of Black farm operators fell by more than half a million between 1950 and 1987 to fewer than twenty-five thousand (U.S. Bureau of the Census 1952, 1989a). They now represent only 1 percent of all farm operators. Their departure, triggered by the collapse of sharecropping agriculture and facilitated by the creation of large numbers of urban blue-collar jobs, contributed significantly to the decline in farm poverty. Most Blacks who remain in rural areas are not involved in farming.

Areas that have retained a dependence on farming are not, on average, low-income areas. In 1985 the Economic Research Service (ERS) published a typology of nonmetro counties (Bender et al. 1985). Three of the county types that ERS identified were dependent on traditional economic sectors as the principal source of income: farming, manufacturing, or mining. As Figure 1.4 shows, the roughly seven hundred counties identified in that study as farm dependent have generally had per capita incomes near or above the nonmetro average since 1969. Farming counties also have fared well when compared with the other counties dependent on one sector (Figure 1.5). Except for the period 1980–83, when mining counties experienced a brief boom due to high energy prices, the farm-dependent counties had higher average per capita incomes than mining

Figure 1.4
Nonmetro and Farming Counties Per Capita Income as a Percentage of United States Per Capita Income, 1969–87

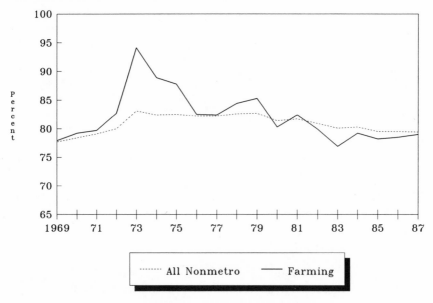

Source: U.S. Dept. of Commerce, Bureau of Economic Analysis, 1989.

counties (Figure 1.5). Only in 1969 and 1983 did farming counties have per capita income substantially below that of the manufacturing counties.

The connection between farming and rural poverty has been broken at both the household and geographic level, but large numbers of rural people remain poor. What do we know about the causes of poverty, and what does this suggest about the persistence of rural poverty even as the importance of farm poverty has declined?

CAUSES OF POVERTY: RURAL DIMENSIONS

Theoretical explanations of the causes of poverty represent two general perspectives (Schiller 1984). One is that poverty results largely from characteristics of the individual that influence his or her likely success in the labor market. Poor people are seen as lacking the personal motivation and/or education and skills to take advantage of available opportunities. In his concept of the culture of poverty, Oscar Lewis (1971) argued that a segment of the poor possessed an attitudinal mind-set, passed on culturally, that served as a barrier to escaping poverty. He characterized about 20 percent of the poverty population as belonging to the culture of poverty. Michael Harrington, in his widely read *The Other America*, wrote:

Figure 1.5
County Types Per Capita Income as a Percentage of United States Per Capita Income, 1969–87

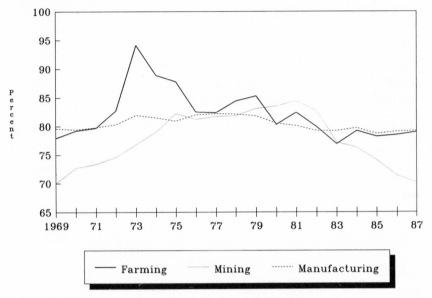

Source: U.S. Dept. of Commerce, Bureau of Economic Analysis, 1989.

The real explanation of why the poor are where they are is that they made the mistake of being born to the wrong parents, in the wrong section of the country, in the wrong industry, or in the wrong racial and ethnic group. . . . most of them would never have had a chance to get out of the other America. . . . The poor are caught in a vicious cycle . . . in a culture of poverty. (1971, pp. 15–16)

Many of the poverty programs begun in the 1960s accepted this culture-of-poverty thesis and attempted to break the cycle of poverty by providing job training, workplace preparation, remedial education, and other experiences focused on enhancing the individual's labor-market attitudes and skills (Plotnick and Skidmore 1975).

The major competing perspective on poverty focuses on external factors as causes of individual poverty—problems with the society or the economy (Schiller 1984). In this view the poor are poor because they do not have fair access to education, health care, adequate housing, or good jobs. Discrimination, labor-market segmentation, or both may be contributing factors. Thus poverty policy must make a concerted effort to remove barriers to educational opportunities, assure equal access to employment, and reduce all institutional barriers to individual achievement, including discrimination.

In our judgment the causes of poverty are so multifaceted and complex that no single theory is entirely satisfactory. More importantly, the failure of the poverty literature to adequately treat rural poverty limits its usefulness in understanding the fundamentally different character and changing nature of rural poverty and thus its value for those designing public programs to serve the rural poor.

For example, the poverty literature largely ignores the important connections between educational attainment, industrial and occupational structure, and rural poverty. Rural education levels, especially in the South and among minorities, lag far behind those of the nation as a whole. According to the Current Population Survey (U.S. Bureau of the Census 1989b), in 1987 the high-school completion rate for adults aged 25 to 64 in the rural South was 68 percent; for rural Blacks in the South it was only 56 percent. (By comparison, the high-school completion rate was 81 percent for the same age group for the nation as a whole.) Clearly, the systematic underinvestment in human capital among rural people with low educational levels has important consequences for rural poverty. At the individual level we know that people with lower levels of education have a higher rate of unemployment, are more likely to experience long periods of unemployment, and are less likely to earn above-poverty incomes when employed. In part, then, we might expect rural people to experience more serious poverty for these reasons alone.

But low educational attainment in the rural South has also affected the structure of the rural manufacturing industry, 50 percent of whose jobs are in that region. Overall, rural areas tend to specialize in routine rather than complex manufacturing activities, having more than 30 percent of all U.S. employment in the former but less than 10 percent in the latter (McGranahan 1988). Similarly, the proportion of nonmetro occupations that are relatively unskilled is twice that of metro areas, while the share of management, technical, and professional jobs is less than one-half that of metro areas. In the rural South the ratio of bottom-of-the-product-cycle manufacturing jobs (e.g., apparel, textiles, leather and leather products) to top-of-the-product-cycle manufacturing jobs (e.g., chemicals, machinery, printing and publishing) is more than two to one, 60 percent higher than for all other rural regions combined (Bloomquist 1987). Within each type of manufacturing the rural South's employment is more heavily weighted toward low-skilled occupations (operators, laborers, and services) than that of any other region. Many factors undoubtedly are at work, but we believe that low educational attainment has played a central role in the evolution of low-wage rural manufacturing industry.

Similarly, the poverty literature has given only passing attention to the persistence of concentrations of areawide rural poverty in a relatively small number of counties, located mainly in the South. There are many rural Southern communities in which the incidence of poverty is so high and of such long duration that we suspect that there is a unique dynamic at work.

RURAL POVERTY: CONCERN, PROGRESS, STAGNATION

When he established the Commission on Country Life in 1908, President Roosevelt said:

But it is equally true that the social and economic institutions of the open country are not keeping pace with the development of the nation as a whole. The farmer is, as a rule, better off than his forbears; but his increase in well-being has not kept pace with that of the country as a whole. While the condition of the farmers in some of our best farming regions leaves little to be desired, we are far from having reached so high a level in all parts of the country. (U.S. Country Life Commission 1975, p. 1873)

Although the narrow reference to farmers is no longer valid, that statement still represents the essence of our national concern for rural people. That is, we care about the well-being of rural people in comparison to the average for the society as a whole and recognize the continuing gap even within the rural population between the situation faced by most of our rural citizens and many others, especially in the rural South. In response to this concern the federal government has occasionally embarked on expensive development programs to overcome perceived disparities. For example, the electrification of rural America was undertaken with massive subsidies from taxpayers, and rural telephone systems were created with subsidies provided by all taxpayers and/or other users of the telephone system. The principal justification for such programs in the 1930s was that rural (at the time, mostly farm) people should enjoy the fruits of society's advancing standard of living, even if the investments were not cost-effective in a purely market sense.

With national development programs playing a part, but changes in transfer programs (especially the expansion and increased benefit levels of Social Security) and overall economic growth playing the more important roles, considerable progress was made in the fight against rural poverty, especially during the late 1960s and early 1970s (see Figure 1.1). The official rural poverty rate declined from over 20 percent in 1967 to 13.5 percent in 1978, interrupted by a noticeable increase during the recession of 1973–75.

Poverty increased sharply after 1979 in both metro and nonmetro areas, and by 1983 the nonmetro rate was 18.3 percent. Because of the severity of the recessions with which we began the decade, the rise in poverty rates was to be expected. But well into the expansion that began in 1983, the nonmetro poverty rate (and that of the central cities) remained stubbornly high. In 1987 the non-metro poverty rate was almost 17 percent. There was some modest improvement from 1986 to 1987. That improvement coincided with evidence from Current Population Survey (CPS) and Bureau of Labor Statistics (BLS) employment and unemployment statistics that suggests that rural areas were growing somewhat faster than urban areas.

Because "in-kind" benefits (such as Food Stamps), not just cash payments, help to ameliorate the condition of the poor, it is useful to adjust the official statistics to include the cash equivalent of benefits received in kind. However, as Figure 1.6 shows, even if in-kind payments are counted as income, poverty rates in both metro and nonmetro areas rose markedly after 1979. This broadened

Figure 1.6
Effects of In-Kind Benefits on Poverty Rates by Residence, 1979–87

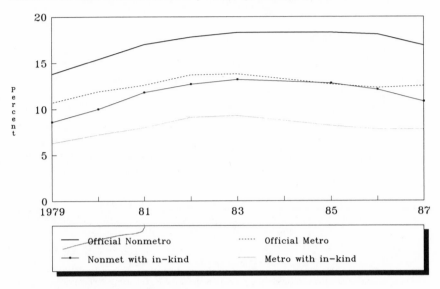

Source: U.S. Bureau of the Census, 1988.

definition of income also shows a small but noticeable improvement in the rural poverty rate between 1986 and 1987.

RURAL ECONOMY: SERIOUS RECESSION, DELAYED RECOVERY

Beginning with a decline in employment between 1979 and 1982, including the loss of nearly 550,000 manufacturing jobs, the rural economy has been undergoing significant economic adjustments (Deavers 1989a). By 1988 urban-area employment had grown by over 18 percent, while rural employment had grown by only about 8 percent since 1979. Rates of urban job growth were higher during the recessions of 1980–82 and throughout most of the recovery. Only recently has rural employment growth been above that of urban areas.

Because of the slow growth of rural employment throughout most of the 1980s, the rural unemployment rate has been above the urban rate since 1979. This pattern prevailed in virtually every region in nearly every year of the 1980s (Deavers 1989). While the national economic recovery has continued, the relative unemployment situation in rural areas has worsened. For example, the rural unemployment rate was 107 percent of the urban rate in 1979, 118 percent in 1982, and 135 percent in 1988. Thus, while the rural unemployment rate has fallen from 11.1 percent in 1982 to 6.9 percent in 1988, the slower rate of job growth in rural areas has continued to cause stress. This is at least part of the reason for the sustained high rate of rural poverty during the 1980s.

OTHER REASONS

Three factors besides the severe recessions of 1980–82 and the poor performance of the rural economy during the recovery contributed to the increase in poverty rates early in the decade.

1. Inflation was very high during the period from 1979 to 1982, and average earnings of individuals were not rising nearly as fast (U.S. President 1989). Because poverty thresholds are adjusted for inflation, they also rose rapidly, causing people whose incomes had been just marginally above the poverty level in 1979 to fall into poverty when their incomes grew slowly.
2. Benefit levels for Aid to Families with Dependent Children (AFDC), an important component of the national network of poverty programs, are not indexed for inflation, so the real value of benefits has declined markedly in the past several years. For example, the median decline in real AFDC benefits for a family of three was 37 percent between 1970 and 1989 (U.S. Congress 1989, p. 545).
3. There was also an effort to tighten eligibility requirements for some government transfer programs, which may have removed people from the cash transfer-payment welfare rolls (Levitan 1985).

In 1984 a number of nonmetro counties were reclassified as metro. The reclassified counties were more likely to be prosperous than the areas that remained nonmetro, and they were more likely to continue to prosper during the expansion while the nonmetro areas languished. Since CPS data show no significant change in the rural poverty rate immediately before and after 1984, however, reclassification alone was not a major factor in the sustained high rural poverty rate of the 1980s.

CHARACTERISTICS OF THE POOR: AGE, RACE, AND HOUSEHOLD STATUS

Poverty rates among population subgroups are markedly different in rural and urban areas (Table 1.1), and the increase in the rural poverty rate since 1973 has not been evenly distributed across all groups of the poor. For example, the rural elderly were the only group among the rural poor with a lower poverty rate in 1987 than in 1973. Despite the substantial decline in poverty among the rural aged, they still have a higher poverty rate than the urban aged and are a somewhat larger share of the poverty population in rural areas. Two federal programs that serve the elderly have had a major impact in reducing their poverty: Supplemental Security Income (SSI) and Social Security. SSI was established in 1974 to provide a nationally uniform basic federal benefit to needy elderly,

Table 1.1
Selected Characteristics of the Poor by Residence, 1973 and 1987

Item	United States		Metro		Nonmetro	
	1973	1987	1973 [1]	1987 [2]	1973 [1]	1987 [2]
	Thousand poor					
Total number of poor	22,973	32,546	13,759	23,423	9,214	9,123
	Percent					
Poverty rate for total population	11.1	13.5	9.7	12.5	14.0	16.9
People in families with a female						
householder, no husband present [3]	37.5	38.3	36.9	36.7	39.2	44.8
Householder	32.2	34.3	31.2	32.6	35.3	41.2
Related children	52.1	54.7	51.8	53.2	52.9	60.3
People in all other families [3]	6.0	7.4	4.3	6.4	9.6	10.6
Householder	5.5	6.3	3.9	5.3	8.6	9.4
Related children	7.6	10.9	5.5	9.6	11.6	14.7
Whites	8.4	10.5	6.9	9.6	11.2	13.7
Blacks	31.4	33.1	28.2	30.7	41.1	44.1
Hispanics [4]	21.9	28.2	20.3	27.6	29.1	35.6
Aged	16.3	12.2	12.7	11.1	22.5	15.6
Percentage of the poor who are [5]						
People in families with a female						
householder, no husband present [3]	35.6	37.1	43.3	39.6	24.1	30.7
Householder	9.5	11.2	11.5	11.8	6.7	9.4
Related children	22.5	21.7	27.7	23.3	14.8	17.7
People in all other families [3]	44.1	39.6	35.1	36.3	57.5	48.1
Householder	11.5	10.5	9.2	9.4	14.9	13.4
Related children	18.6	16.5	15.1	15.4	23.9	19.2
White	65.9	65.8	61.4	63.6	72.6	71.3
Blacks	32.2	29.8	36.3	31.6	25.9	25.0
Hispanics [4]	10.3	16.8	12.9	21.2	6.3	5.6
Aged	14.6	10.7	12.1	10.0	18.4	12.6

Source: U.S. Bureau of the Census, Current Population Survey.

1/ Based on metro/nonmetro designations from the 1970 Census. (See text.)

2/ Based on metro/nonmetro designations as of June 1984. (See text.)

3/ The 1987 family data are based on the "householder" concept, while the 1973 family data are based on the older "head" concept. Changing from the head to the householder concept had minor effects on poverty statistics. Also, families exclude unrelated individuals who do not live with relatives. Therefore, the poor living in the two family types do not add up to the total poor.

4/ Hispanics may be of any race.

5/ The percentages in the various groups sum to more than 100 percent because an individual may be in more than one group.

disabled, or blind people (Hoppe and Saupe 1982). Many states also supplement the basic federal payment. SSI replaced state programs serving the same clientele, and benefits from the program are indexed for inflation. Congress increased Social Security benefits in the late 1960s and early 1970s, and these benefits are also indexed for inflation (Getz and Hoppe 1983).

Nonmetro Blacks and Hispanics had very high rates of poverty in 1987, over 44 percent and 35 percent, respectively, several times the rate for Whites (U.S. Bureau of the Census 1989b). Current poverty rates for Native Americans are not available, but the 1980 census reported that the poverty rate for rural Native Americans was as high as the recent rate for Hispanics (U.S. Bureau of the Census 1983). Nevertheless, most of the rural poor are White. Even in the South, where nearly 95 percent of rural Blacks live, over half of the nonmetro poor were White. This predominance of Whites in the rural poverty population reflects the fact that they make up 90 percent of the nonmetro population overall.

A much smaller share of the rural poor live in female-headed families with spouse absent than in metro areas. Almost 50 percent of the nonmetro poor lived in "other" families, largely married-couple families. However, poverty is more common for those rural people who do live in female-headed families. In these families over 40 percent of the householders and 60 percent of the children were poor. For Black female-headed families, the poverty rate among householders was over 65 percent, and for their children, nearly 77 percent. The very high poverty rates among children in both urban and rural areas is especially worrisome. Nearly two-fifths of all poor people in the United States are children. In rural areas the problem of poor children is about equally divided between female-headed families and other families.

We know from longitudinal analyses of the poverty population that poverty is typically a transitory problem at the individual level. That is, people move into and out of poverty as a result of events in their lives, but relatively few people are persistently poor. Previous work by ERS (and Chapter 4 in this volume) shows that persistent poverty is more common in rural areas (Ross and Morrissey 1989). The persistent rural poor are more likely to be elderly, Black, female, or living in a female-headed family than the temporary rural poor. Many of the temporary poor experience recurrent bouts with poverty since they never are far removed from it even when they are employed.

THE WORKING POOR: GREATER WORK EFFORT AMONG THE RURAL POOR

One of the distinguishing characteristics of the rural poor is their work effort. In both 1973 and 1987 the share of the nonmetro poor who worked was 10 percentage points higher than that for the metro poor (Table 1.2). Nearly one-fifth of poor rural householders worked full-time, year-round.

Reasons for not working were also different for the rural and urban poor. Many more of the rural poor who did not work reported that they were ill, disabled, or unable to find work. One of the dramatic changes between 1973 and 1987 was the share of the nonmetro poor who reported that they were not working because they were unable to find work, which increased by more than 13 percentage points. More than any other single statistic, this may explain the difficulty of reducing poverty even during periods of economic expansion. Apparently, in many of the labor markets in which the rural poor live and seek work, they have been unable to find jobs. In fact, we know that job growth in many of the more remote rural counties has been very slow.

Focusing exclusively on the work of the householder may understate the work effort of the poor, because other family members may also work (Getz and Hoppe 1983). The number of workers per poor family is probably a better gauge

Table 1.2
The Working Poor by Residence, 1973 and 1987

Item	United States		Metro		Nonmetro	
	1973	1987	1973 [1]	1987 [2]	1973 [1]	1987 [2]
			Percent			
Poor householders who worked [3, 4]	51.6	47.2	47.6	44.0	57.3	54.9
Poor householders who worked full-time [3, 4, 5]	18.3	14.6	15.5	12.8	22.2	18.8
Poor householders who did not work [3, 4]	48.4	52.9	52.4	56.0	42.7	45.3
Main reason for not working: [3, 4]						
Ill or disabled	32.2	23.4	25.0	20.6	44.8	31.9
Keeping house	43.0	41.0	51.6	44.7	27.8	30.1
Going to school	3.4	5.7	4.2	6.3	2.0	4.1
Unable to find work	3.6	11.2	4.6	9.9	2.0	15.1
Retired [6]	N.A.	16.6	N.A.	16.3	N.A.	17.5
Other	17.8	2.0	14.6	2.2	23.3	1.3
Total	100.0	100.0	100.0	100.0	100.0	100.0
Poor families with [3, 7]						
No workers	38.1	42.8	42.4	45.9	32.1	35.4
One worker	41.9	39.1	42.0	38.2	41.8	41.3
Two or more workers	20.0	18.1	15.7	15.9	26.1	23.4
Total	100.0	100.0	100.0	100.0	100.0	100.0

Source: U.S. Bureau of the Census, Current Population Survey.

N.A. = Not Available. (Not on the public use tape.)

1/ Based on metro/nonmetro designations from the 1970 Census. (See text.)

2/ Based on metro/nonmetro designations as of June 1984. (See text.)

3/ The 1987 family data are based on the "householder" concept while the 1973 family data are based on the older "head" concept. Changing from the head to the householder concept had minor effects on poverty statistics.

4/ Restricted to families with civilian householders.

5/ Full-time work is defined here as working at least thirty-five hours per week for at least fifty weeks per year.

6/ Retired included in "other" in 1973.

7/ The 1973 data include families whose householders are in the armed forces. The 1987 data exclude such families.

of work effort by the poor. Nearly two-thirds of nonmetro poor families had one or more workers in 1987; almost one-fourth had two or more workers. In part, this reflects the large number of the rural poor who are in married-couple families and families where grown children work and contribute to the family income.

People can work and still be poor for two reasons. First, they may not work the entire year due to the loss of a job, the part-time nature of their job, or illness or disability. Second, even full-time workers may not earn enough to keep a family, particularly a large family, out of poverty. For example, a family of five with only one full-time, year-round worker who earned the average wage paid in the apparel and other textile products industry would be poor. We know that the rural occupational structure is heavily weighted toward such low-wage, low-skill jobs even within manufacturing.

GEOGRAPHIC CONCENTRATION OF
RURAL POVERTY

Rural poverty is heavily concentrated in the South. The 1987 nonmetro poverty rate in the South was 21.2 percent, compared to 13.6 percent for the rest of the country. Over half of the rural poor lived in the South in 1987. A more detailed picture of the geography of poverty can be obtained by examining state-level data concerning nonmetro poverty from the 1980 census. The South had all seven states with a rural poverty rate of 20 percent or more, and all eight states with at least 300,000 rural poor people (U.S. Bureau of the Census 1982a). Only four states outside of the South had rural poverty rates over 15 percent—Arizona, New Mexico, South Dakota, and Missouri. A few populous states have large numbers of rural poor, even though their overall rural poverty rates are relatively low. For example, Michigan, New York, Ohio, and Illinois each had over 200,000 nonmetro poor people, but poverty rates in the 11 to 13 percent range.

Three recent studies by ERS also identify persistent problems of low income among nonmetro counties, especially in the South (Morrissey 1985; Hoppe 1985; Bellamy and Ghelfi 1989). One pattern of persistently low-income counties is shown in Map 1.1, which indicates nonmetro counties that have consistently ranked in the lowest quintile on per capita income since 1950. Given the relatively high poverty rates among rural Blacks that we noted earlier, and the concentration of rural Blacks in the South, it is not surprising that the proportion of Blacks in these persistently poor counties is nearly three times that of all nonmetro counties. Whereas over two-thirds of all nonmetro adults in the South were high-school graduates, less than half of the adults in these counties had a high-school education.

The overall employment structure of the persistent-poverty counties is not much different from that of other rural counties, although they are somewhat more dependent on goods production, especially manufacturing. During the economic restructuring of the 1980s their economies performed somewhat below those of other nonmetro counties. For example, their rate of employment growth was only about 85 percent that of other rural counties between 1979 and 1988, and their 1988 annual average unemployment rate was still nearly 10 percent, almost half again the rate in other rural areas.

Because of their low incomes and high poverty rates, these counties depend much more on transfer payments as a source of personal income. Transfer payments amount to over one-half of the level of earnings in these counties, while they are only slightly above one-third in all nonmetro counties. Transfer payments were a slower-growing share of personal income in nonmetro areas during the 1980s than they were in the 1970s. Thus market forces and public policy shifts seem to have combined in this decade to leave the persistent-poverty counties even farther behind.

Map 1.1
Persistently Low-Income Nonmetropolitan Counties in the United States

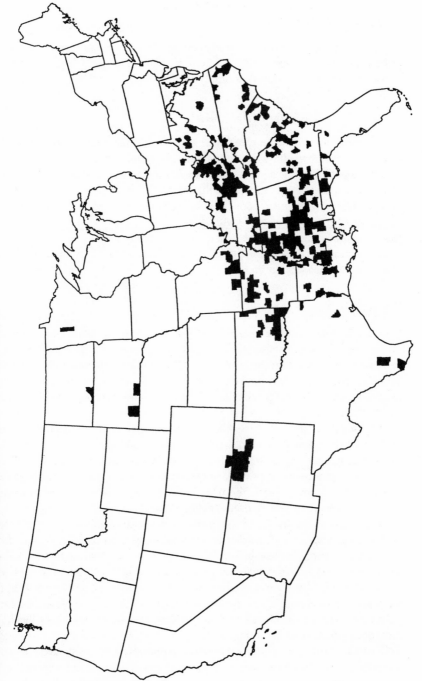

Source: Bender et al. 1985.

POVERTY POLICY: DIFFICULT AND
EXPENSIVE CHOICES

As our description of rural poverty makes clear, there are many dimensions to be considered in formulating public policy strategies to help the rural poor. These dimensions are discussed briefly here.

Personal and Family Characteristics

The rural poor need to be recognized as part of the national poverty population and need to be served by whatever national programs we choose to adopt in our commitment to meet the needs of the poor. The major question is whether federal programs and delivery mechanisms that have the urban poor as the model can adequately serve the rural poor, whose characteristics and residential settings are quite different. For example, AFDC is targeted largely at children in female-headed families. Because 65 percent of central-city children live in such families, AFDC is critical to their well-being. But fewer than one-half of rural poor children live in female-headed families.

Equity among the Poor

In our judgment simple questions of fairness argue for some changes in the framework of federal, state, and local poverty assistance. One test of equity in national programs is that the poor who are in similar situations receive similar benefits. By this criterion the current wide variations in payment levels among various programs are not acceptable. For example, the maximum monthly AFDC payment for a family of three is $629 in Vermont but only $118 in Alabama (U.S. Congress 1989, pp. 546–47). Clearly this cannot be a reflection of cost-of-living differences alone. Similarly, the maximum SSI benefit levels in 1987 for people with no income were sufficient (when combined with Social Security) to lift aged couples out of poverty in eleven states and aged individuals in four states (U.S. Congress 1989, pp. 681–84, 689). Are the aged poor in the remaining states really less deserving of assistance?

Since many of the rural poor live in states that have established relatively low AFDC benefit levels and provide lower state supplements to the basic federal SSI benefits, reform in these programs is of special significance to them. Another aspect of reform is its regional dimension. Large numbers of the rural poor live in a handful of Southern states, and persistent very low income is a problem for a couple of hundred rural counties in that region. In such areas state and local governments are hard pressed to fund services that other states and localities routinely provide to help the poor.

Over the past several years numerous proposals have been made to shift responsibility for programs among different levels of government. For example, the Committee on Federalism and National Purpose proposed in 1985 that nationally uniform minimum benefit levels be established for AFDC and Medicaid, and that the federal government provide 90 percent of the funding necessary to provide these benefits. In return, states and localities would assume full responsibility for many community-development, infrastructure, and social-service programs. But the committee recognized that financial resources vary widely among states, with some unable to afford these new responsibilities. Thus the dozen or so poorest states would receive special grants with which to fund these programs. Such interstate transfers to account for differences in financial capacity are central to any effort to redress the existing inequity in payment levels of national poverty programs.

The Working Poor

Another knotty problem is the appropriate strategy to redress poverty among those who work, especially full-time, year-round workers. There has been a reluctance to help the working poor based on a fear that such aid would reduce their work effort. However, experimental evidence suggests that assistance causes only moderate reductions in work by the poor (Munnell 1987), and efforts to assist the nonworking poor through transfers while ignoring the working poor may actually create disincentives for the poor to work. As Schiller says:

Public assistance programs are particularly inequitable in their disregard of the needs of poor families with working fathers. These working poor are excluded from assistance due to a misplaced concern for work motivation and a general desire to contain public expenditures. (1984, p. 188)

Because a substantial number of the rural poor work, any national effort directed toward the working poor would prove very beneficial to rural areas.

The National Economy

The severe recessions of the early 1980s demonstrated that the overall performance of the national economy has large and direct effects on the level of poverty in the United States. Efforts to reduce poverty while the national economy falters will fail. Likewise, despite strength of the economic expansion in the late 1980s, rural areas have lagged, and rural poverty rates remained high. This suggests that many rural areas and the rural poor are at a disadvantage in competing for new jobs and higher incomes even in a growing economy. Public programs, carefully targeted, can improve the competitive position of lagging rural areas, upgrade the skills and education of the rural poor who can work, and provide adequate transfers to those who cannot.

CONCLUSIONS

Public policy currently seeks to place the principal responsibility for solving poverty problems on the poor and the private marketplace, for example, by requiring work by many of the adult AFDC recipients. It may, however, be extremely difficult to achieve much progress against poverty with such a narrowly conceived strategy. Recent research indicates that as many as six people would be seeking every existing suitable rural job (Bloomquist, Jensen, and Teixeira 1988). Such a high ratio of applicants to available jobs suggests strongly that work requirements must be tied to job creation if they are to be effective.

It is also important to recall that many of the rural poor belong to groups who cannot reasonably be expected to work—the aged, the ill, the disabled, and children. Ameliorating poverty among these people requires effective transfer-payment programs. Any effort to significantly reduce poverty among these groups would be expensive. For example, raising the federal SSI benefit level to elim-inate poverty among the elderly would cost at least $3.9 billion; that was the gap between poverty and income received by elderly poor households in 1987 (U.S. Congress 1989, p. 970). However, that is a relatively small increment in total public aid spending as of fiscal year 1986, which totaled about 2.5 percent of gross national product (GNP) (Bixby 1989).

Finally, an acceptance of markets as a way to organize economic activity does not require unquestioning acceptance of the distribution of income that results. We share the view that markets generally work, and that prices provide appro-priate signals to allocate resources among competing uses in both the short and long run. The challenge for poverty policy is to redress perceived inequity in the income distribution without unduly impairing the essential allocative and organizational roles played by the market. Whether 2.5 percent of GNP is an adequate commitment of national resources to problems of the poor is ultimately a political question.

Chapter 2

The Growing Problem of Low Earnings in Rural Areas

Lucy Gorham

One consequence of the profound economic restructuring of the past two decades appears to be that a growing share of workers are earning poverty-level wages, even if they work the equivalent of a year-round, full-time job. Nowhere has this been more true than in rural America,[1] and in rural America nowhere has this been more dramatic than in farming. In 1987 roughly three out of ten American workers had hourly earnings that, on an annualized basis, were too low to lift a family of four out of poverty (Gorham and Harrison 1990). In rural areas four out of ten workers earned below the poverty line, and among those living on farms more than three out of four received poverty-level earnings (Gorham and Harrison 1990).

Moreover, the percentage of workers with low hourly earnings grew dramatically between 1979 and 1987. For example, in 1979, 32 percent of rural workers were low earners, while by 1987 this figure had leapt to 42 percent. This represents an increase of over 30 percent in the share of low earners in just eight years. While these figures on the share of workers earning low wages are disturbing, perhaps even more distressing is the fact that the growth of low earners during the 1980s reversed the trend of the previous decade, during which the percentage of low earners declined (Gorham and Harrison 1990).

This increase in the share of low-wage workers has contributed to the growth in the population of working poor in rural, as well as urban, areas. It has also played a role in the emergence of the "new poor." The remainder of this chapter will explore how and why the distribution of earnings has changed for workers in rural areas and what we can learn from examining both industry and regional differences. In order to provide some background to this discussion about earnings, however, first we consider who the rural new poor are, and what it is that makes them "new."

THE RURAL NEW POOR

In order to understand the emergence of the rural new poor over the past decade, we have to explore what changed in rural areas in the 1980s compared to the previous two decades. During the 1960s and 1970s a largely unanticipated level of economic growth and population expansion took place in rural America (Henry, Drabenstott, and Gibson 1987; Fuguitt and Beale 1984; Till 1981; Garnick 1984, 1985; Summers and Branch 1984). A combination of fortuitous economic trends contributed to an unprecedented surge in rural prosperity. Manufacturing employment moved from urban to rural areas at an accelerated pace, resource-based industries such as agriculture, mining, and energy boomed, the infrastructure for transportation and communications improved, and rural areas became an increasingly attractive place to live, especially for the retired.

As a result, employment opportunities both expanded and diversified. This contributed to an increase in the earnings and family income of rural residents, both absolutely and relative to workers in cities (Hoppe 1987; Garnick and Friedenberg 1982; Henry, Drabenstott, and Gibson 1986). Rural women, who had lagged behind their urban counterparts in joining the labor force, began to work in record numbers. For the first time since the start of the industrial revolution, the historic trend of migration from country to city halted.

But just as the boom in rural America was not anticipated by many, neither was the sudden decline of rural growth starting in the late 1970s and continuing into the 1980s. While the traditional rural industries of farming, mining, and energy (particularly oil) experienced a simultaneous expansion in the 1970s for a variety of reasons, they all underwent sharp contractions in the 1980s. The new economic prosperity of the 1970s suddenly evaporated for many rural communities. Commodity prices plummeted, real interest rates remained high, the high value of the dollar discouraged foreign exports and encouraged imports, and international economic stagnation and third-world debt dampened the demand for U.S. products, including both food and manufactured goods (Henry, Drabenstott, and Gibson 1986; Brown and Deavers 1987; Galston 1985; Reimund and Petrulis 1987).

Related rural industries such as farm machinery and wood products came under severe strain, resulting in even fewer opportunities for rural workers. Plant closings in traditional manufacturing industries that had migrated from the cities in previous decades, such as textiles and furniture, left many small towns reeling as their major source of jobs disappeared. Job losses in one sector often had far-reaching consequences. For example, with roughly 60 percent of farm family income derived from nonfarm sources, declining opportunities for off-farm employment added yet another source of instability to the farming sector (Goodwin and Jones 1986).

While many rural communities continued to prosper during the 1980s, rural America as a whole has been hard hit by the level and intensity of economic restructuring that the past decade brought. The new rural poor, then, include those who have lost farms or farm jobs, those who have lost a well-paying factory or mining job and must now struggle to support families on lower wages, or those who began their working lives in poorly paid services jobs and expected to move on to something better, but can now find no alternatives. Predictably, this kind of economic turmoil has bred instability in family relationships that in itself has contributed to the growth of rural poverty.

Thus the new poor are "new" because they have only recently moved into poverty as a result of the economic disruption of the past decade. But their poverty is also new in the sense that the turmoil that has created it is the result, at least in part, of heightened competition that in itself is new. This competition, both global and domestic, has spawned new forms of economic adjustment. These adjustment strategies include firms moving production to low-wage sites overseas, automating domestic production to cut labor costs, demanding lower wages from their U.S. employees, and, in some instances, moving from a product with a mass-market appeal to a more specialized market niche. Both rural and urban areas have felt the impact of these changes.

While economic transformation is nothing novel in and of itself, the exact form it takes changes from one decade to the next, benefitting some groups, industries, regions, and countries at the expense of others. One indicator of how well the rural United States has fared during this latest period of economic turbulence is whether the earnings of its workers have improved. In the following section the impact of the economic shifts of the past decade on the distribution of earnings in rural areas will be explored.

THE CHANGING DISTRIBUTION OF EARNINGS OF RURAL WORKERS

The economy of the rural United States experienced some devastating shocks over the 1980s, but we know little about how these changes have affected the distribution of earnings. As farm and other natural-resource-based industries have declined, what has been the impact on the earnings of different groups in the rural labor force? How has this varied by region? How does this compare to what has happened in urban areas, often themselves going through major structural transformations such as the shift from manufacturing to services?

My analysis of earnings trends (conducted with Bennett Harrison of Carnegie Mellon University) uses the March Current Population Survey (CPS) for the years 1979 and 1987.[2] I define "low earners" to be individuals whose hourly wage and salary incomes (WSI) would leave them below the official poverty line for a family of four persons, even though they worked the equivalent of a year-round, full-time job. By this definition, in 1987 a low earner made $11,611 or less in annual earnings.[3]

One problem in comparing workers' wages is that people's work experience varies enormously over the course of the year. Some people work year-round and full-time, others only part-time or part-year. How can these differences in work time be incorporated into an analysis of wages that gives an indicator that can be meaningfully compared across labor-force groups?

The procedure is straightforward. From the CPS tapes, each individual's annual wage and salary income (WSI) is known. This is divided by the number of weeks the respondent worked and then again by the number of hours the respondent "usually" worked per week. The resulting figure of hourly earnings is then multiplied by 2,080 (52 weeks × 40 hours) to yield a work-experience-adjusted estimate of "annualized" WSI, what I referred to earlier as the equivalent of a year-round, full-time job. Such an indicator allows seasonal, occasional, and part-time workers to be incorporated into a comprehensive count of how many workers are low earners and to compare their earnings to an annual poverty level.

To begin, we consider how rural workers were doing compared with urban workers in 1979, the start of our 1979 to 1987 time period. In 1979, 31.9 percent of rural workers earned below the poverty level for a family of four, compared with 23.4 percent of urban workers. Thus, despite the economic prosperity experienced by many rural areas in the 1970s, rural workers were still 36 percent more likely to be earning low wages than urban workers. By 1987 the rural/urban gap had widened considerably. The percentage of rural low earners in 1987 had risen to 42.1 percent, an increase of over 10 percentage points. While urban workers also experienced a rise in the percentage of low earners, the increase was just over half that for rural workers—an increase of 5.5 percentage points from 23.4 to 28.9 percent. Thus in 1987 rural workers were over 45 percent more likely to be earning low wages than urban workers.

Why have rural areas been harder hit generally than urban areas? One answer, discussed earlier, is that during the 1980s nearly all the major industrial sectors found in rural areas—agriculture, mining, manufacturing, timber, and other natural-resource-based industries—experienced almost-simultaneous recession and loss of employment. Because rural local economies are usually less diverse than the economies of cities, a downturn in even one of these sectors could have a major impact on rural employment and earnings. The cities that have felt the biggest shocks—Detroit, Flint, Youngstown, Houston, and so on—are also cities where the economic base is heavily tied to one industry.

A second answer lies in the different roles that services play in rural and urban economies. The services sector was the big growth sector of the 1980s, providing an engine of economic renewal for cities such as Boston and Chicago. While the services sector has also grown in rural areas, by and large this growth has been in industries such as retail sales or food and entertainment—industries that are at the lower end of the wage spectrum. Thus services rarely provide the same stimulus to development in rural areas that they do in cities, and they are not as likely to offer the same opportunities for replacing better-paying jobs at a comparable wage.

DIFFERENCES BETWEEN MEN AND WOMEN

The disparity in job opportunities between urban and rural areas emerges plainly when one examines differences in the earnings of men and women. While the gap in the percentage of low earners between men and women widened slightly in rural areas over the past decade, it actually narrowed in urban areas. Is this because the opportunities for urban women have improved, because those for rural women have deteriorated, or for some other reason?

To answer this question, we begin by looking at how job-market opportunities changed for rural men and women between 1979 and 1987. First, it is necessary to keep in mind how important women are to the rural economy. In spite of the stereotype of the rural worker as a male farmer or lumberjack, our CPS sample indicated that in 1987 women comprised almost half (47 percent) of the rural labor force. Women's labor, both paid and unpaid, has always been of vital importance in maintaining the living standards of rural families. With economic opportunities narrowing and many women becoming the sole source of support for their families, this is more true today than ever.

Have rural men and women been affected equally by the economic turmoil of the past decade? The answer is yes and no. For women, the share of workers with low hourly earnings rose 10.2 percentage points between 1979 and 1987, whereas for men it rose by 9.4 percentage points. By this measure, then, women have fared somewhat worse than men, but the difference is not dramatic. However, whereas the share of low earners rose from 22.2 percent to 31.6 percent for men, it rose from 43.7 to 53.9 percent for women. Thus in 1987 less than a third of rural men workers were low earners, compared with over half of all women workers. Rural women have always been at a disadvantage in the labor force vis-à-vis rural men. In spite of two decades of affirmative action and rural women entering the labor force in record numbers, this continues to be true.

In urban areas, in contrast, the male/female gap in the percentage of low earners actually narrowed slightly between 1979 and 1987, declining from 16 to 13.4 percentage points. To keep this in perspective, however, in 1987 urban women were still over a third again as likely to be earning low wages as men. Also, as with their rural counterparts, for both urban men and women the percentage of low earners increased between 1979 and 1987 (from 16.2 to 22.6 percent for men and from 32.2 to 36.0 percent for women). The answer to our earlier question about why the gap had narrowed between urban men and women, then, is that men did relatively worse than women over the decade, not that women did better.

Not only did the gap between rural men and women widen between 1979 and 1987, but so did the gap between rural and urban men and between rural and urban women. The widening of the rural/urban gap was not nearly as dramatic for men as for women. For men, the gap increased from 6 to 9 percentage points, whereas for women it increased from 11.5 to 17.9 percentage points. Thus in 1987 the rural/urban gap for women was nearly twice that for men.

These differences in urban and rural opportunities for women are reflected in the percentage of women who received high hourly wages (equal to $35,000 on a year-round, full-time basis in 1987) in 1979 and 1987. In 1979 only 2.9 percent of rural women were high-wage earners, compared with 5.0 percent of urban women. By 1987 the share of women high-wage earners had dropped to 2.3 percent in rural areas, but had risen to 6.3 percent in urban areas. Unfortunately for rural women workers, there appears to be little on the horizon in the way of employment growth trends that would diminish these differences in the near future.

While my focus has been on the low-wage end of the earnings distribution, let me say a little more about the high-wage end, lest anyone feel that he or she is only getting half of the picture. The problem of a decline in the percentage of high-wage earners is not confined to rural women. In fact, urban women (whether White, Black, or Hispanic) are the one exception to the rule that the percentage of high earners has declined in both urban and rural areas among all labor-force groups (divided by race, age, and education). Thus whatever forces are driving the share of low-wage earners up is also driving the share of high-wage earners down.

GROWING RACIAL INEQUALITY

If the past decade did little to boost the earnings prospects for rural men and women, it did even less for rural Blacks and Hispanics. Rural areas have never offered great job opportunities to minority workers, and this was even more true in 1987 than it was in 1979. In 1979, 30 percent of rural Whites, 40 percent of rural Hispanics, and almost 50 percent of rural Blacks earned below the poverty level for a family of four. By 1987 these percentages had increased to 40 percent for Whites, 57 percent for Hispanics, and over 60 percent for Blacks. Thus all three race groups showed a dramatic increase in their percentage of low earners in rural areas—9.9 percentage points for Whites, 11.5 percentage points for Blacks, and an incredible 16.5 percentage points for Hispanics. Whereas rural Hispanics had a considerably lower percentage of low earners in 1979 than Blacks, by 1987 the position of Hispanics had deteriorated to the point where it almost matched that of Blacks.

The percentage of low earners not only increased for all race groups in rural areas from 1979 to 1987 but in urban areas as well. The largest increase was among urban Hispanics (from 30.3 to 41.0 percent), followed by Blacks (from 30.0 to 36.8 percent) and Whites (from 22.1 to 26.4 percent). For all three race groups, the rural/urban gap has also increased significantly, again because the position of rural workers has deteriorated so dramatically. In 1987 rural workers of each race group were roughly 50 percent more likely to be earning low wages than their urban counterparts.

Taking the analysis one step further, I divided each rural and urban racial group into men and women (Table 2.1). Here again, an increase in the percentage

Table 2.1
Percentage of Low Earners, Rural and Urban Workers, by Race and Sex, 1979 and 1987

RURAL LABOR FORCE GROUP	1979	1987
White Men	20.2	29.2
Black Men	41.5	52.3
Hispanic Men	29.5	48.5
White Women	42.1	52.1
Black Women	58.4	69.0
Hispanic Women	58.0	69.8
URBAN LABOR FORCE GROUP		
White Men	14.8	19.4
Black Men	23.1	32.9
Hispanic Men	22.5	36.6
White Women	11.2	17.9
Black Women	21.7	28.5
Hispanic Women	16.4	22.6

Source: Author's estimates from Bureau of the Census data.

Note: Annual earnings are adjusted for weeks and hours of work.

of low earners between 1979 and 1987 for all groups, a growing rural/urban gap, and a greater increase in low earners among rural workers than among urban workers are evident. However, some important differences between Black and Hispanic men and women emerge out of these results.

For White men and all racial groups of women, the percentage-point increase in low earners in rural areas was two to three times that for urban areas. For Black and Hispanic men, however, the percentage-point increase in low earners in urban areas between 1979 and 1987 was much closer to that for rural areas (10.8 compared to 9.8 percentage points for rural and urban Blacks, respectively, and 19.0 compared to 14.1 percentage points for rural and urban Hispanics). This is an indication that Black and Hispanic men have not only fared poorly in rural areas, but are also being left behind by the new urban economy. In spite of this, however, the percentage of low earners among urban Black and Hispanic men was still significantly lower in 1987 than for urban Black and Hispanic women.

REASON FOR CONCERN? WHAT DIFFERENCES BY AGE AND EDUCATION TELL US

While the distribution of earnings has clearly slumped downward over the past decade in rural areas (as it has to a lesser extent in urban areas), we must

Table 2.2
Percentage of Low Earners, Rural and Urban Workers, by Age, 1979 and 1987

Rural Labor Force Group	1979	1987
Age 16-24	51.0	72.6
Age 25-34	23.5	38.5
Age 35-54	23.1	29.8
Age 55 and over	31.9	38.4
Urban Labor Force Group		
Age 16-24	44.8	59.6
Age 25-34	15.8	23.0
Age 35-54	14.8	17.7
Age 55 and over	19.4	25.0

Source: Author's estimates from Bureau of the Census data.

Note: Annual earnings are adjusted for weeks and hours of work.

now ask, should we be worried? Could this be a short-term aberration that will soon correct itself?

One such argument is that the growing percentage of low-wage workers is due to the entrance of large numbers of baby-boom workers into the job market. This influx of new workers results in an "oversupply" of workers. With the pressure off to compete for workers, employers can afford to offer lower wages. If this argument is correct, we should not see an increase in the percentage of low earners in older groups of workers who are past the baby-boom bulge, nor in the very youngest groups of workers, whose absolute numbers were actually declining in the 1980s, even creating labor shortages in some areas.

Contrary to the baby-boom argument, all age groups of rural workers showed an increase in the percentage of low earners between 1979 and 1987 (Table 2.2), as did all age groups of urban workers. In fact, rural workers aged 16 to 24 (the post-baby-boom group) showed an increase in low earners of an overwhelming 21.6 percentage points. In 1987 nearly three-quarters of all young rural workers earned less than the poverty level for a family of four, compared with just half in 1979. We would expect young workers to have a higher percentage of low earners than older workers, both because we expect experience to be rewarded and because of seniority provisions. However, this does nothing to explain the huge increase in the share of young low earners between 1979 and 1987. At a time when it is essential to convince youth that the traditional labor market—as opposed to the underground economy—has something to offer, these earnings

Table 2.3
Percentage of Low Earners, Rural and Urban Workers, by Education,
1979 and 1987

Rural Labor Force Group	1979	1987
High School Dropout	47.3	57.1
High School Graduate	29.2	43.4
Some College	22.4	33.6
Four Yrs College or More	17.8	25.5
Urban Labor Force Group		
High School Dropout	39.9	53.7
High School Graduate	22.3	30.7
Some College	16.8	21.4
Four Yrs College or More	14.1	16.2

Source: Author's estimates from Bureau of the Census data.

Note: Annual earnings are adjusted for weeks and hours of work.

trends for young workers are particularly distressing. Rural areas will have a difficult time holding on to their most talented young people, a problem that will only hobble their efforts to revitalize their economies.

The earnings trends for workers with different levels of education provide another reason to be concerned about the ability of rural areas to revitalize their economies. Not only did rural high-school dropouts and high-school graduates show a sizeable increase in their percentage of low earners, but workers with some college or with four years of college or more did so as well (Table 2.3). In 1987 over a quarter of all rural workers with four years of college or more earned less than the poverty level for a family of four, up from 17.8 percent in 1979. While urban workers in all four education categories also experienced an increase in the percentage of low earners over the past decade, the absolute levels were much lower to begin with, and, with one exception I will return to in a moment, the percentage-point increases were not nearly as dramatic as those for rural workers. Clearly, the earnings trends of the past decade are not providing better-educated rural workers with an incentive to stay.

The one exception to the general rule that rural workers have experienced a greater increase in the percentage of low earners than their urban counterparts concerns high-school dropouts. Unlike the other three education groups (and in fact unlike our results for any of the other groups we have examined so far), for high-school dropouts the percentage-point increase in low earners was greater

Table 2.4
Percentage of Low Earners, Rural and Urban Workers, by Region, 1979 and 1987

	Rural		Urban	
Region	1979	1987	1979	1987
New England	26.8	31.0	24.7	23.0
Middle Atlantic	26.3	37.3	20.8	23.9
East North Central	27.6	39.0	21.3	29.2
West North Central	32.8	45.0	25.8	28.7
South Atlantic	33.4	43.1	26.2	31.0
East South Central	35.4	46.4	27.4	38.0
West South Central	38.6	47.0	26.8	34.1
Mountain	32.6	43.9	26.6	31.8
Pacific	26.8	36.4	21.8	27.6

Source: Author's estimates from Bureau of the Census data.

Note: Annual earnings are adjusted for weeks and hours of work.

in urban areas than in rural areas. The difference is sizeable—a 13.8 percentage-point increase for urban high-school dropouts, compared with a 9.8 percentage-point increase for those in rural areas. Also, unlike any of our other results so far, between 1979 and 1987 the rural/urban gap for high-school dropouts actually declined, a result of the deteriorating position of urban high-school dropouts.

The fact that the percentage of low earners among urban high-school dropouts is fast approaching that in rural areas brings us back again to a consideration of industrial change. The loss of manufacturing jobs in cities has eliminated a major source of better-paying jobs for urban workers with less education in the same way that the loss of agriculture, mining, and manufacturing jobs has hurt the earnings of rural workers. In both urban and rural areas, services may provide a replacement job, but high-paying services jobs are not plentiful for workers in this education group.

THE REGIONAL PICTURE

A final way that we can gain perspective on how concerned to be about the trend toward an increasing percentage of low earners is to consider how universal it is geographically. We know that in rural areas nationwide each labor-force group we have examined based on sex, race, age, and education has shown an increase in the share of workers earning below the poverty level. If we divide the country into nine subregions, do we find the same trend?[4]

Each region in the country showed an increase in the percentage of low earners among its rural work force between 1979 and 1987 (Table 2.4). The biggest increase occurred in the West North Central region—the traditional farm-belt states of Iowa, Minnesota, Missouri, Kansas, Nebraska, North Dakota, and South Dakota. Somewhat surprisingly, however, the urban work force in this same farm region showed the second-smallest increase in the share of low earners. While the farm belt's rural work force has been hard hit by the troubles of farming and other natural-resource-based industries such as mining and timber, its urban work force appears to have emerged relatively unscathed.

If we look at which regions have the highest absolute share of rural workers earning below poverty, the West South Central (Texas, Oklahoma, Arkansas, and Louisiana) and the East South Central (Kentucky, Tennessee, Mississippi, and Alabama) regions topped the list in 1987, as they did in 1979. Historically, these regions have had high concentrations of rural poverty, and the last decade has done little to change that. The region with the lowest percentage of low earners in 1987 was New England, although even this region of extraordinary economic growth showed a sizeable increase in its share of rural low-wage workers.

Have urban workers in different regions fared better than rural workers? With the exception of New England, the urban work force of each region increased its share of low-wage workers. However, workers in urban areas in every region also showed a considerably lower percentage of low earners than did workers in rural areas. The position of rural workers also declined more dramatically between 1979 and 1987 so that in each region the gap between rural and urban areas widened. The region showing the largest increase in its rural/urban gap was the West North Central—again the traditional farm belt. Because of the declining fortunes of its rural areas, this region also had the largest rural/urban gap of any region in 1987.

THE ROLE OF INDUSTRIAL CHANGE

We now examine more specifically what role industrial restructuring has played in changing the distribution of rural wages. Is the growth in the percentage of rural low earners between 1979 and 1987 due to shifts of employment between industries, for example, the decline of manufacturing and the growth of services?

From the evidence presented in Table 2.5, which analyzes employment categorized into eight major sectors, the answer to this question would have to be no. The distribution of rural employment among these eight sectors remained remarkably constant between 1979 and 1987 (columns 2 and 3 in Table 2.5). While the share of workers employed in both durable and nondurable manufacturing declined slightly and the share of workers employed in both business and distribution (B & D) services and consumer and social (C & S) services increased slightly, these shifts were not great enough to account for the 10.2 percentage-point increase in the overall share of rural low earners. Instead, we find that the share of low earners increased in all eight industry sectors. Thus the growing problem of low earners is more the outgrowth of changes within industries than of employment shifts between industries.

Table 2.5
Rural Low-Wage Employment by Industry, 1979 and 1987

	% Rural Employment		% Low Earners in Industry		% of all Rural Low Earners	
Industry	1979	1987	1979	1987	1979	1987
Agric	4.1	4.5	71.2	76.2	9.3	8.1
Nat'l Res	2.0	1.7	9.6	18.7	0.6	0.8
Construc	7.0	6.4	21.6	30.2	4.8	4.6
Dur Mftg	13.9	12.0	14.2	22.0	6.2	6.3
Nondur Mftg	11.8	10.9	25.3	36.5	9.3	9.5
Bus/Dist Serv	14.3	15.9	20.3	32.3	9.1	12.2
Cons/Soc Serv	41.9	43.9	43.8	53.7	57.7	56.0
Public	4.9	4.8	19.2	22.0	3.0	2.5

Source: Author's estimates from Bureau of the Census data.

Note: Annual earnings are adjusted for weeks and hours of work.

Again looking at the results presented in Table 2.5, we see that the percentage of low earners working in agriculture (71.2 percent in 1979, rising to 76.2 percent in 1987) exceeded that in any other sector by some margin in both years. Thus, for those workers able to remain employed in agriculture in 1987, more than three out of every four attained only poverty-level earnings. The consumer- and social-services sector had the second-highest percentage of low earners (53.7 percent in 1987). Since this is one of the few sectors with expanding employment in rural areas, this does not bode well for rural areas being able to reduce their dependence on low-wage jobs. While business and distribution services, the other sector of employment expansion, had a lower percentage of low earners in 1987 than did consumer and social services, still close to one out of every three workers were low earners, up from one out of five in 1979. Compared to the other seven sectors, the public sector appears relatively stable—an increase in the percentage of low earners between 1979 and 1987 of less than 3 percentage points.

The growth in the percentage of low earners within industries is not peculiar to rural areas, but is found in urban areas as well.[5] Except for very slight declines in the share of low earners in the natural-resources and public sectors, all urban industrial sectors also showed a growing share of low-wage earners between 1979 and 1987.

The real difference between rural and urban industry wage trends lies not in whether the share of low earners increased between 1979 and 1987, but rather in how much it increased and in how high the levels were in both years. All rural industrial sectors showed a substantially higher level of low earners than urban industries in 1987, and the increase in low earners over the eight-year period was on the order of 50 percent higher in rural than in urban areas. In fact, in 1979 the percentage of low earners in the natural-resources sector was lower in rural areas than in urban areas. By 1987, however, it had climbed to a level in rural areas approximately 80 percent higher than that in urban areas.

The last two columns of Table 2.5 show the share of all rural low earners found in each industry. For example, while the durable-goods sector accounted for 12 percent of rural employment in 1987, it was responsible for only 6.3 percent of rural low earners. The consumer- and social-services sector, on the other hand, employed just under 44 percent of all rural workers but was responsible for 56 percent of all low earners. Thus low earners are "underrepresented" in durable-goods manufacturing but "overrepresented" in C & S services.

A development strategy based solely on minimizing low-wage work should concentrate on expanding employment in those sectors where low earners are underrepresented—natural resources, construction, durable-goods and nondurable-goods manufacturing, business and distribution services, and the public sector. With the exception of a small increase (1.6 percentage points) in the share of rural workers employed in B & D services, however, each of these sectors accounted for a declining share of rural workers between 1979 and 1987. Since the services sector is the growth sector in both rural and urban areas, at least at present, a development strategy that would result in a higher share of better-paying jobs must either emphasize the expansion of higher-wage B & D services industries or increase the percentage of better-paying jobs in all services industries. The latter could be accomplished by greater unionization, raising the minimum wage substantially, and improving the education and skills of the work force to improve productivity.

The data in Table 2.6, which shows high-wage employment by sector, confirm the importance of the business and distribution services sector in providing better jobs to rural workers. Unfortunately, as shown in columns 4 and 5, all of our eight industry sectors experienced a decline in the percentage of high earners between 1979 and 1987 (roughly $35,000 or more in 1987 dollars). However, the B & D services sector increased its share of rural employment over the same period to 15.9 percent of all rural employment and had the second-highest percentage of high-wage workers (10.8 percent). As a result, by 1987 this sector accounted for more than 25 percent of all rural high-wage workers.

The consumer- and social-services sector employed an additional 25 percent of all rural high-wage workers in 1987. This is not because it is a relatively high-wage industry like B & D services, but simply because it employs such a large number of rural workers. However, because the percentage of high earners is so much lower in this sector, to get the same number of high-wage jobs would require creating three times the number of consumer- and social-services jobs as business and distribution services jobs. Since the B & D services sector is linked to other industries, of course, it is not as simple as choosing to encourage

Table 2.6
Rural High-Wage Employment by Industry, 1979 and 1987

Industry	% Rural Employment		% High Earners in Industry		% of all Rural High Earners	
	1979	1987	1979	1987	1979	1987
Agric	4.1	4.5	2.7	2.7	1.1	1.8
Nat'l Res	2.0	1.7	30.9	19.1	6.2	5.0
Construc	7.0	6.4	16.4	8.2	11.6	7.9
Dur Mftg	13.9	12.0	13.1	7.9	18.3	14.4
Nondur Mftg	11.8	10.9	9.4	7.4	11.1	12.2
Bus/Dist Serv	14.3	15.9	15.2	10.8	21.8	26.1
Cons/Soc Serv	41.9	43.9	5.7	3.8	23.9	25.5
Public	4.9	4.8	12.0	9.6	6.0	7.0

Source: Author's estimates from Bureau of the Census data.

Note: Annual earnings are adjusted for weeks and hours of work.

the development of this sector over others. But being aware of the consequences of growth in one sector versus another in terms of wages (and thus family incomes) can only enhance local planning efforts.

THE IMPACT ON SEX AND RACE INEQUALITY

In an earlier section I discussed the growing percentage of low earners among rural men and women and among rural Whites and Blacks, as well as the widening gap between White and Black workers. What insight into these trends can we gain by examining industrial change?

Beginning with an examination of the earnings trends among men and women, we look at how the distribution of employment by industry differs for these two groups (Table 2.7).[6] The first thing to note is the concentration of women in the consumer- and social-services sector, an industry with a high percentage of low-wage workers. The C & S sector employed over 60 percent of rural women workers in both 1979 and 1987, over twice the percentage of rural men. Not only were rural men more evenly distributed across industries in both years, they were much more likely to find jobs in the higher-paying sectors of durable manufacturing and business and distribution services.

From Table 2.7 it is clear that for both men and women, the composition of employment between industries has not undergone dramatic change. Both durable-goods and nondurable-goods manufacturing showed a small drop in their share of rural workers among both men and women, while both services categories showed small increases. However, these shifts between industries are not

Table 2.7
Distribution of Rural Employment by Sex, 1979 and 1987

	% in Industry			
	Women		Men	
Industry	1979	1987	1979	1987
Dur Mftg	8.2	7.1	18.5	16.3
Nondur Mftg	12.2	10.8	11.4	11.0
Bus/Dist Serv	11.1	12.6	16.9	18.9
Cons/Soc Serv	60.8	61.1	26.5	28.4
Public	3.9	4.5	5.8	5.0

Source: Author's estimates from Bureau of the Census data.

Table 2.8
Percentage of Rural and Urban Low Earners, by Industry and Sex, 1979 and 1987

	% Low Earners							
	Rural Men		Rural Women		Urban Men		Urban Women	
Industry	1979	1987	1979	1987	1979	1987	1979	1987
Dur Mftg	10.0	18.4	25.8	31.3	7.0	10.5	18.6	22.4
Nondur Mftg	13.1	23.0	39.1	51.9	11.7	14.4	30.4	36.0
Bus/Dist Serv	16.0	23.5	28.4	47.1	12.4	17.5	21.8	25.9
Cons/Soc Serv	31.7	42.4	50.2	59.6	26.1	34.5	38.5	42.9
Public	15.0	15.2	26.8	30.5	6.8	7.7	20.8	17.1

Source: Author's estimates from Bureau of the Census data.
Note: Annual earnings are adjusted for weeks and hours of work.

large enough to account for the large growth of low earners among both rural women and men.

As was the case for all rural workers, the key to understanding the growth in the percentage of women and men low earners lies more in changes within industries, rather than in changes between them. Table 2.8 shows the change in the percentage of low earners within industrial sectors for rural and urban men and women. Within each industry the share of rural women low earners grew substantially between 1979 and 1987, the most dramatic increases being found in B & D services (18.7 percentage points) and in nondurable manufacturing (12.8 percentage points). Rural women workers also had a much higher absolute

Table 2.9
Distribution of Rural Employment by Race, 1979 and 1987

	% in Industry			
	Whites		Blacks	
Industry	1979	1987	1979	1987
Dur Mftg	13.8	12.0	16.9	13.8
Nondur Mftg	11.6	9.7	14.5	23.3
Bus/Dist Serv	14.8	17.0	9.6	7.5
Cons/Soc Serv	42.1	44.1	40.5	41.5

Source: Author's estimates from Bureau of the Census data.

level of low earners in each of these five sectors than did rural and urban men or urban women.

Turning now to a discussion of differences between Blacks and Whites[7], we again start by looking at where both groups were employed in rural industries (Table 2.9). A larger share of rural Blacks were employed in the durable and nondurable manufacturing sectors, while Whites were more heavily concentrated in business and distribution services. Roughly an equal share of both Blacks and Whites worked in consumer and social services.

As was true for both men and women, the distribution of employment among these four industries between 1979 and 1987 did not change dramatically for either Blacks or Whites, with one exception. The share of Black workers employed in the nondurable manufacturing sector increased 8.8 percentage points over this period, at the same time that the share of White workers employed in the industry declined slightly. If nondurable manufacturing were a high-wage sector, this shift would bode well for improving racial equality in wages. However, as we can see from Table 2.10, nondurable manufacturing had a high percentage of low earners, particularly for Blacks. Moreover, the likelihood of earning low wages in the industry if a person were Black increased substantially from 1979 to 1987—from 45 to 55 percent. While the share of White low earners in the industry also increased, still less than a third of Whites in the industry were earning low wages in 1987.

A second disturbing trend for rural Blacks is that the share of workers finding employment in the business and distribution services sector showed a slight decline of 2.1 percentage points between 1979 and 1987, while the share of Whites rose 2.2 percentage points over the same period. This is troubling not only because this is a relatively high-paying sector, but also because it is one showing growth in rural areas. For both Blacks and Whites, the share of low earners in the industry rose substantially—by roughly 12 percentage points for

Table 2.10
Percentage of Rural Low Earners by Race, 1979 and 1987

| | % Low Earners | | | |
| | Whites | | Blacks | |
Industry	1979	1987	1979	1987
Dur Mftg	12.4	19.7	27.5	39.4
Nondur Mftg	23.1	32.0	45.2	55.0
Bus/Dist Serv	18.9	31.1	40.1	52.4
Cons/Soc Serv	42.1	51.8	61.5	73.9

Source: Author's estimates from Bureau of the Census data.
Note: Earnings are adjusted for weeks and hours of work.

both groups. But for Blacks who were employed in this sector in 1987, over half were low earners, compared with less than a third of Whites.

While the shift of Blacks out of durable manufacturing and business and distribution services and into nondurable manufacturing is certainly responsible for some of the increase in the growing gap between Black and White workers, I would argue that changes within each of these sectors are equally, if not more, important. Again in Table 2.10 we see that in each sector the percentage of low-wage Black workers increased and that these increases matched or exceeded the increases for Whites.

These industry wage trends for Blacks and Whites carry a number of implications for efforts to reduce racial wage inequality in rural areas. First, efforts to increase the share of Blacks earning better wages need to place equal emphasis on strategies for changing where Blacks are employed both within and between industries. Strategies within industries include more vigorous implementation of affirmative action, training and education programs that are tied to specific ladders for upward mobility within firms and industries, and increased employee organizing and unionization.

Improving higher-wage opportunities could also mean doing an assessment of the industrial structure of a specific area and identifying which segments of an industry's activities provide better-paying jobs. Opportunities for expanding these activities can then be pursued, such as export promotion or assisting local firms to produce goods and services that are currently being imported from outside the area. Of course, such a strategy must be coupled with a strong affirmative-action program if it is to benefit Black (and women) workers.

In addition to these within-industries strategies, increasing employment opportunities for Blacks in the better-paying segments of the services sector should be a priority. Barring a major reversal in the decline of manufacturing employment in the United States, services will continue to be the area of employment growth for both rural and urban areas. This means increasing the share of Blacks employed in the business and distribution services sector. In 1987 only 7.5 percent of Blacks worked in the B & D services sector, compared to 17 percent of Whites.

CONCLUSION

The economic turbulence of the 1980s has created terrible difficulty for rural America. This is reflected clearly in the tremendous growth in the share of rural workers earning too little to raise a family of four above poverty, regardless of their region, sex, race, age, or educational attainment. Equally disturbing is the fact that we appear to be moving farther away from the goal of economic equality. The rural/urban gap in earnings has widened, as have those between rural men and women, between Whites, Blacks, and Hispanics, between age groups, and between those with and without any college education.

One expected consequence of these developments is that more rural workers lived in poor families in 1987 than in 1979—9.4 percent of all rural workers in 1987, compared to 6.6 percent in 1979. This represents a 20 percent increase in the number of rural workers living in poor families in less than a decade. As disheartening as this statistic is, it significantly understates the extent of the problem because it excludes all those rural workers who are unemployed or who have left the labor force altogether.

The broader economic changes that have contributed to this turmoil in rural America do not show signs of a reversal in the short term, though the longer-term prospects are impossible to predict. Eventually the United States will have to balance its huge trade deficit, which may bring some manufacturing employment back to rural locations. Global overproduction of oil and other natural-resources commodities such as copper is not likely to abate in the near future, which will continue to depress domestic production in these industries.

Certainly having global economic trends swing back in favor of the rural economy would help. But rather than wait for such uncertain developments, we would be better off to assist rural workers and communities to make whatever adjustments they can make now. A later chapter outlines a thoughtful agenda for action that can help in this process. But first we must acknowledge that creating a society of growing inequality runs counter to our deepest aspirations as a nation and that active intervention is called for.

NOTES

The research that forms the basis of this chapter was undertaken in collaboration with Bennett Harrison, Visiting Professor of Urban and Public Affairs at Carnegie Mellon University. The research was made possible by a grant from the Ford Foundation's Rural Poverty and Resources Program and the Aspen Institute's Rural Economic Policy Program, whose support I gratefully acknowledge.

1. All of the analysis in this chapter uses data from the Current Population Survey, published by the U.S. Census Bureau. For the examination of rural/urban differences, I followed the convention of using the CPS geographic classifications of "metropolitan" and "nonmetropolitan." However, within the body of the chapter I use the terms rural and urban for ease of understanding. The CPS has the limitation that the boundaries of rural and urban areas, that is, the official definitions of metropolitan and nonmetropolitan, were changed by the U.S. Office of Management and Budget in the 1985 CPS. This means that the metro/nonmetro data can be compared from CPS years 1963 to 1984, but only with (unknown) error to any year after that. Data from the years 1986 onward can be compared, but only with error to any previous year. Because 1985 was a transition year in the definition, its data cannot be compared to any year before or after without error. Accordingly, I have had to exercise caution when comparing metro/nonmetro results from 1979 to 1987.

2. In an effort to minimize distortions caused by the business cycle, the year 1979 was chosen as a starting point because it was the last business-cycle peak. The year 1987 was the latest year of continued economic growth for which CPS data were available at the start of the research project.

3. The poverty-line standard for both 1979 and 1987 was adjusted for inflation by the now-standard CPI-X1 deflator of the U.S. Census Bureau.

4. The nine census subregions of the United States consist of New England (Maine, New Hampshire, Vermont, Massachusetts, Rhode Island, Connecticut); the Middle Atlantic (New York, New Jersey, Pennsylvania); the East North Central (Ohio, Michigan, Indiana, Illinois, Wisconsin); the West North Central (Minnesota, Iowa, Missouri, Kansas, Nebraska, North Dakota, South Dakota); the South Atlantic (Maryland, Delaware, District of Columbia, Virginia, West Virginia, North Carolina, South Carolina, Georgia, Florida); the East South Central (Kentucky, Tennessee, Alabama, Mississippi); the West South Central (Arkansas, Louisiana, Oklahoma, Texas); Mountain (Montana, Wyoming, Idaho, Colorado, Utah, Nevada, New Mexico, Arizona); and Pacific (Washington, Oregon, California, Alaska, Hawaii).

5. See Gorham and Harrison 1990.

6. Because of the limitation of sample size, the agriculture, natural-resources, and construction sectors could not be included in the analysis.

7. Due to inadequate sample sizes, it was impossible to compare Blacks and Whites in all eight industrial sectors or to include Hispanics in the analysis.

Chapter 3

The Working Poor in Rural Labor Markets: The Example of the Southeastern United States

Ann R. Tickamyer

Rural areas have always had a disproportionate share of poor people, but, as the previous chapters indicate, the economic transformation in local, regional, national, and international economies during the 1980s had a particularly devastating effect in rural America, exacerbating old sources of inequality and deprivation. This chapter uses information about labor markets, households, and individuals to define opportunity structure and show how labor-market opportunities and other aspects of social life combine to affect the likelihood of being poor.

The analysis focuses on the southeastern portion of the United States, the region that currently has and historically has had the highest concentration of rural poor. My detailed analysis of the southeastern region shows how rural and urban labor markets differ, how different labor markets influence the incidence of poverty, and how the characteristics of the working poor vary across these labor-market areas. I argue that the differences in the behavior of the poor in these labor markets is largely the result of differences in the opportunity structure in their communities. This analysis suggests that an understanding of the differences in labor-market opportunities can help policymakers better address rural poverty.

LABOR-MARKET THEORY AND RESEARCH

The Rural Working Poor

Previous research has shown that persons and families residing in rural and nonmetro areas of the United States whose incomes fall below or near the poverty line have much higher labor-force attachment than their urban/metro counterparts. More than two-thirds of nonmetro poor families had at least one worker in 1984, and more than one-quarter had at least two workers. In comparison, in metro areas only half the poor families had even one worker. Since 1978 there has been a 50 percent increase in the full-time, year-round working poor and a 35 percent increase in part-time working poor (Levitan and Shapiro 1987).

As chapter 2 indicates, rural areas are dominated by low-wage employment in the agriculture, service, and manufacturing sectors. The prevalence of these low-wage sectors is an important cause of rural poverty. The few sources of high-wage employment are found largely in highly volatile industries such as mining and other types of resource extraction (Tickamyer and Duncan 1984). Many other jobs, such as those in agriculture and construction, are part-time or seasonal. Good stable employment, such as a job in the school system or local government, is often controlled by local elites through patronage politics (Duncan 1987). Thus work in rural labor markets tends to be low-paying, unstable, or unequitably available to all members of the community.

Minorities and women are especially vulnerable to tight labor markets and limited opportunities. Counties with large Black populations were more likely to suffer plant and employment losses in the decade between 1970 and 1980 (Colclough 1988), and in the subsequent decade nonmetro Southern Blacks continued to have the highest levels of employment hardship (Lichter 1989). Women have much more limited employment opportunities and much lower earnings in rural counties and labor-market areas where agriculture and mining dominate (Tickamyer and Bokemeier 1988). These industries traditionally provide few jobs for women, exacerbating high levels of female-headed poverty (Tickamyer and Tickamyer 1988). Multiple labor-market disadvantages (e.g., being Black and female) clearly intensify hardship.

These disadvantages are compounded by social welfare policies that are punitive or inequitable. In the United States one's prospects in the welfare system parallel one's opportunities in the labor market. Persons who are privileged in the labor market also fare better when they are unemployed (Pearce and McAdoo 1981). Because women frequently are not employed in the formal labor force, have part-time and intermittent employment, or have jobs in peripheral industries and in secondary occupational labor markets, they are often not eligible for entitlements such as unemployment compensation. More often they must rely on a secondary welfare system where coverage is stigmatized, is uncertain, and varies from place to place (for example, levels of assistance made available to households eligible for Aid to Families with Dependent Children vary widely from state to state). The same observation applies to Blacks, Native Americans, and other disadvantaged minorities whose lack of opportunity in the labor market prevents them from being caught in the "safety net" of social welfare programs. Again, multiple disadvantages increase the difficulties for these already-hard-hit rural workers.

Labor Markets and Labor-Market Areas

The term "labor market" is used by economists and other social analysts to describe the push and pull of labor supply and demand. While it evokes the image of an arena where buyers (employers) and sellers (workers) of labor come to bargain and exchange their wares, in fact (if not in principle), it is conceptualized in a highly abstract manner as a process that operates outside normal constraints of time and place. In part this is because the operation of the labor market is in reality the aggregate of immense numbers of seemingly private transactions between workers and employers that do not actually take place in a central marketplace. There is an important conceptual distinction between labor markets and labor-market areas. The aggregation of transactions between employers and employees is a set of relationships, and it is this set of relationships that is defined as a labor market. Since the transactions composing a labor market occur in actual time and space, they are situated in a labor-market area.

This distinction has important implications for the study of labor-market operations and outcomes. Much standard labor-market theory and research is wrong in assuming perfect labor and capital mobility, that is, that workers and employers can move as necessary to maximize their own interests, impervious to the forces that constrain the activities of living human beings. Real people do not and cannot pick up and go to wherever jobs may be, even if they should become aware of their existence. People are constrained by a variety of factors, including, but not limited to, their family and community ties, their lack of knowledge, their lack of means to make a move, or their customs and tastes. Constraints or costs also apply to employers—although these differ from those experienced by employees—and there may be vast differences in the relative power exercised by the two groups over such decisions.

Thus, even in a society as mobile as the late twentieth-century United States, most people's daily lives occur in a circumscribed area. With the exceptions of those relatively few privileged individuals who enter national labor markets, this locale is circumscribed by where the individual lives. For most people, a local labor-market area is a location bounded by residence and employment that also defines potential residential and employment opportunities. In other words, economic opportunity for the individual is determined by what is available in the area in the form of amount, type, and wages of employment. Other socioeconomic characteristics of the area, such as population composition, educational facilities, and cultural traits, also may influence the availability of employment and the likelihood different groups of people have for obtaining it. Together, these characteristics comprise opportunity structure, a concept that summarizes these factors for a particular locale. Locations will differ in these characteristics, and these differences will have an impact on people apart from their own characteristics that may also enhance or limit their ability to prosper. While there may be variation in how likely or how able people are to expand the circumference of the area where they live and seek employment, it seems likely that persons with limited access to resources will be the most confined by local horizons and the most affected by the nature of the opportunity structure defined by a local labor-market area.

RESEARCH DESIGN AND ANALYSIS

To understand the way labor markets structure opportunity, it is necessary to provide geographical delineation of a labor-market area (Horan and Tolbert 1984; Tolbert 1989; Tolbert and Killian 1987; Tickamyer and Bokemeier 1989). Some researchers do so by analyzing characteristics of the counties or metropolitan statistical areas. While in some cases it may be reasonable to define these as equivalent to labor-market areas, for the most part it cannot be assumed that these boundaries, devised quite long ago for other purposes, currently correspond to a modern-day labor market. This is especially the case with rural counties where workers may have to travel great distances to their jobs, including across state and county lines. Other approaches are even more crude, using information about whether a person lives or works in a rural or urban area or in a region of the country such as the South as a substitute for labor-market information. In recent years, however, a better approach has been developed by a consortium of researchers affiliated with the Economic Research Service in the Department of Agriculture.[1] The labor-market areas developed by this approach are based on commuting information that shows where people actually live and work (Tolbert and Killian 1987). Labor markets defined on this basis approximate the type of area required by theoretical arguments for the importance of labor-market area described earlier.

This study uses the data in these new local labor-market areas (LLMAs) to show how important labor markets and their opportunity structures are to the level of poverty in rural areas. I examine three basic questions: (1) How do rural and urban labor markets differ? (2) How do different rural labor markets influence the incidence of poverty? (3) How do the characteristics of the working poor vary across different labor markets?

Local labor-market areas in Kentucky, North Carolina, Tennessee, Virginia, and West Virginia are analyzed here. Since labor markets are not constrained by state boundaries, contiguous counties in surrounding states that have commuter exchanges are also part of these LLMAs. There are 68 local labor-market areas formed from a total of 584 counties and county equivalents in the region under scrutiny. LLMAs are categorized as rural or urban, with urban defined as a city of at least 50,000 people and the surrounding suburban area. There are 29 rural and 39 urban LLMAs in the region of study.

Two types of data are used in this research. The first type gives the characteristics of labor-market areas that are reported on summary tape files of U.S. counties from the 1980 census. County figures are aggregated across counties within the LLMAs to construct measures appropriate for the entire LLMA. Therefore, for each LLMA we have measures of poverty and near poverty, race, sex-specific employment and unemployment, and industrial and occupational locations of employment.

Second, I select individual-level data from the public use microdata set (PUMS-D) one-in-one-thousand sample to examine characteristics of households and householders (persons classified as head of household). There are four types of households: married couples, female-headed, male-headed, and nonfamily. Only working-age (16–65) householders are included since the focus is on labor-market activity of the rural poor. Poverty level, employment status, and other relevant socioeconomic characteristics for individual householders are examined. The individual-level data are also aggregated across households to provide descriptions of the entire household and not just its head. Individual-level householder and aggregated household data are linked with LLMA-level data to determine how labor-market factors influence poverty status and opportunity for different types of households.

These two types of data allow us to look at aggregate data as well as data concerning individual families in each type of labor market. For the sake of simplicity and reference, the measures used in this chapter are briefly summarized in Table 3.1.

FINDINGS

Rural/Urban Differences in Labor Markets

There are significant differences between rural and urban labor-market characteristics (see Table 3.2). Those in rural LLMAs have higher poverty and near-poverty levels, lower educational attainment, higher levels of male unemployment, and higher levels of both males and females not in the labor force. There are also differences in the distribution of employment across most industrial and occupational categories. Not surprisingly, the largest industry difference occurs in resource industries (agriculture and mining), where rural areas have higher employment levels. Urban LLMAs have more employment in executive/professional/technical and sales/clerical occupations.

While we might have predicted that rural and urban labor markets would differ in these ways, it comes as a surprise that there are large differences within rural areas. As it turns out, there is virtually as much variation within rural LLMAs as between rural and urban LLMAs. Table 3.3 compares the same descriptive characteristics described in Table 3.2, but for rural labor markets only, categorizing them by type of economic base. LLMAs with concentrated, undiversified employment patterns generally have worse socioeconomic conditions than those with more diversified economies. The highest poverty levels occur in resource-based markets; the lowest levels are found in the nonconcentrated LLMAs. In fact, the poverty rate for this latter group is close to the urban level.

Interestingly, however, the percentage of the population in near poverty (1.5 times the poverty level) does not vary across rural labor markets. Even in the nonconcentrated markets that generally perform more like their urban counterparts, the percentage of the population near poverty is relatively high. This suggests that the diverse rural labor markets offer only a fairly small rise in

Table 3.1
Measures Used in Analysis of Poverty in Local Labor-Market Areas

ALL DATA

POVERTY:
Total 1979 pretax family income falls below the official government poverty threshold for the family size and composition.

NEAR POVERTY:
Total family income falls between the poverty line and 1.5 times poverty income.

OTHER POVERTY:
Other income categories defined in relationship to the poverty threshold are 1.5–2.0 times poverty income and > 2.0 times poverty income. In the LLMA data, poverty measures are reported as percentages of all persons for whom poverty status is determined. In the householder data, poverty status is reported only for working-age persons.

RACE:
White, black, other minority reported either as percentage of population or for individual householders.

LLMA DATA
(Local labor-market areas defined as
county groups based on commuter flows)

UNEMPLOYMENT:
Percentage of the working-age civilian labor force who were unemployed in the week prior to the census, shown separately for men and women.

NOT IN LABOR FORCE:
Sex-specific measures are defined in the same way.

INDUSTRY:
Percentage of employment in five industrial categories: resources, construction, manufacturing, producer services, and consumer services.

OCCUPATION:
Percentage of employment in six occupational categories: executive/professional/technical, sales/clerical, services, skilled labor, operative, and agriculture.

ECONOMIC BASE:
Categories of LLMA based on employment levels in different types of industries. Bases include resource industries (agriculture, forestry, fishing, and mining), manufacturing, both resource and manufacturing, and nonconcentrated economies.

RURAL LLMA:
County group with no urbanized areas.

URBAN LLMA:
County group with at least one urbanized area (≥ 50,000 population).

HOUSEHOLDER DATA:
Working-age household "head" comprised of four types— couple containing both husband and wife; male head, no wife; female head, no husband; nonfamily.

EDUCATION:
Four categories: less than high school, high school, some college, and a college degree or more. (Highest degree completed is used in multivariate analysis.)

Table 3.2
Characteristics of Rural and Urban Local Labor-Market Areas (LLMAs) in the Southeastern United States

% of Population:	Rural LLMAs (N – 29)		Urban LLMAs (N – 39)	
	Mean	S.d.	Mean	S.d.
In Poverty***	18.5	4.3	13.9	3.3
Near Poverty***	13.4	4.3	10.9	2.2
Race: White	89.0	13.9	83.6	11.4
Black	10.5	13.9	15.3	10.7
Other*	0.5	0.5	1.1	1.7
Less Than High School				
25+***	52.1	6.4	42.4	5.9
18-24***	32.3	7.3	26.9	4.7
Male Unemployment**	5.6	1.2	4.6	1.3
Female Unemployment	3.5	0.8	3.3	0.7
Male Not in Labor Force***	30.6	3.8	26.6	3.0
Female Not in Labor Force	56.2	6.6	51.7	6.7
Employment:				
Industry				
Resources***	9.7	7.3	4.6	3.9
Construction*	7.1	1.3	6.5	1.1
Manufacturing	28.3	9.9	27.0	9.2
Producer Services***	17.4	2.5	21.7	4.1
Consumer Services*	37.5	4.7	40.1	1.0
Occupation				
Executive/Prof/Tech***	18.4	2.3	22.4	4.1
Sales/Clerical***	20.0	1.9	24.0	3.0
Services	12.0	1.5	12.4	1.3
Skilled Labor	15.8	3.5	14.5	2.5
Operator***	28.4	4.6	23.8	5.7
Agriculture***	5.5	2.8	2.8	1.7

---

  * t test of rural-urban differences significant at $P \leq$ .05.
 ** t test of rural-urban differences significant at $P \leq$ .01.
*** t test of rural-urban differences significant at $P \leq$ .001.

income compared to the nondiversified ones. As expected, there are fairly large differences in the distribution of employment across industries and occupations.

Community Economic Base and the Working Poor

Having firmly established differences in labor markets both between rural and urban areas and within rural America, we want to determine what these results actually mean for people's chances of being poor. Since this study is specifically concerned with the working poor, the next step is to examine the poverty status

Table 3.3
Characteristics of Rural LLMAs with Different Economic Bases

% of Population:	Resources (N = 5)	Manufacturing (N = 15)	Resources & Manufacturing (N = 3)	Non-Concentrated (N = 6)
In Poverty*	21.1	18.7	20.9	14.5
Near Poverty	13.2	13.8	13.8	12.6
Race: White	97.0	86.0	86.3	91.1
Black	2.6	13.5	13.5	8.0
Other	0.4	0.5	0.2	0.9
Less Than High School				
25+**	56.1	53.7	52.5	44.6
18-24	37.1	31.9	32.8	28.9
Male Unemployment	6.4	5.2	5.7	6.1
Female Unemployment	2.7	3.6	3.9	3.8
Male Not in Labor				
Force**	35.8	29.6	29.4	29.1
Female Not in Labor				
Force***	67.5	52.1	56.1	56.9

Employment:

Industry

Resources***	22.2	6.1	12.4	6.8
Construction*	6.4	6.8	6.9	8.5
Manufacturing***	12.9	35.7	28.9	22.3
Producer Services**	18.4	16.2	16.7	19.8
Consumer Services***	40.0	35.2	35.0	42.6

Occupation

Executive/Prof/Tech*	19.0	17.8	16.4	20.2
Sales/Clerical*	20.7	19.3	18.9	21.5
Services***	11.6	11.4	11.9	14.0
Skilled Labor***	21.4	14.5	13.8	15.2
Operator	24.8	14.5	27.7	23.9
Agriculture***	2.5	5.5	11.3	5.1

---

  * t test of LLMA differences significant at P ≤ .05.
 ** t test of LLMA differences significant at P ≤ .01.
*** t test of LLMA differences significant at P ≤ .001.

of individual working-age householders. Table 3.4 depicts various householder characteristics that affect poverty levels in rural and urban labor markets. In both types of LLMAs, female-headed households have the highest poverty and near-poverty levels, but those who live in rural areas are more likely to be poor. All race categories are more likely to be poor in rural areas. Blacks have the highest poverty rates in both locations. Persons with the lowest levels of education are more likely to be poor. Poor rural householders are both more likely to be employed and more likely not to be in the labor force than their urban counterparts. They are equally likely to be unemployed.

Table 3.4
Incidence of Poverty Status and Income Levels among Householders in Rural and Urban LLMAs[1]

	Rural LLMAs Percent:					Urban LLMAs Percent:				
	Below Poverty Level	Near Poverty 1.0-1.5	1.5-2.0 x Poverty	Above 2.0 x Poverty	N	Below Poverty Level	Near Poverty 1.0-1.5	1.5-2.0 x Poverty	Above 2.0 x Poverty	N
Household*										
Couple***	10.8	9.8	11.8	67.7	9,946	5.6	6.5	8.5	79.5	44,768
Male***	19.6	12.4	11.2	56.8	322	10.4	9.5	10.1	70.1	1,606
Female***	39.0	18.6	14.4	28.0	1,299	32.1	14.0	14.1	39.9	7,515
Non-family***	27.9	12.0	13.1	47.0	1,844	16.6	8.3	9.5	65.6	12,538
Race*										
White***	14.5	10.6	12.0	63.0	12,210	8.2	6.9	8.7	76.2	55,281
Black***	32.9	15.4	14.9	36.8	1,142	24.1	12.0	12.4	51.6	10,399
Other	25.4	10.2	10.2	54.2	59	15.5	11.0	11.1	62.4	747
Education*										
None	45.6	8.8	22.8	22.8	57	35.1	14.6	13.5	36.8	171
Less Than High School***	24.8	14.5	13.4	47.3	6,216	19.7	12.1	12.7	55.5	21,515
Less Than College***	9.4	9.0	12.3	69.4	5,753	7.7	6.9	9.4	76.1	31,996
College or More***	3.7	4.0	5.9	86.5	1,385	3.0	2.4	3.5	91.2	12,745
Labor Force Status*										
Employed***	8.7	9.5	11.9	70.0	10,154	6.0	6.3	8.8	78.9	53,888
Unemployed**	28.8	13.8	16.0	41.5	727	27.0	13.1	11.8	48.1	2,347
Armed Forces	6.1	17.4	20.0	56.5	115	5.3	15.5	17.2	62.0	1,406
Not in Labor Force***	43.9	16.4	12.1	27.7	2,415	36.7	13.5	10.6	39.1	8,786

Table 3.4 (continued)

Level of Employment***[2]	Rural LLMAs Percent:					Urban LLMAs Percent:				
	Below Poverty Level	Near Poverty 1.0-1.5	1.5-2.0 x Poverty	Above 2.0 x Poverty	N	Below Poverty Level	Near Poverty 1.0-1.5	1.5-2.0 x Poverty	Above 2.0 x Poverty	N
0 Not Employed***	48.1	16.5	11.6	23.8	2,090	42.5	13.7	10.5	33.3	7,715
1 Employed Part Time***	43.4	13.1	11.2	32.3	601	34.6	11.8	10.7	42.9	2,650
2 Employed Part Time**	33.5	19.1	11.7	35.8	565	28.7	16.0	13.7	41.7	2,322
3 Employed Part Time***	20.9	18.9	14.6	45.6	834	16.1	16.2	14.4	53.4	3,353
4 Employed Full Time	10.5	15.6	17.5	56.4	646	10.7	13.8	13.0	62.5	2,594
5 More Than Full Time Employment***	5.3	7.9	11.8	74.9	8,675	3.1	5.2	8.3	83.4	47,793

* Chi square significant at P ≤ .05.
** Chi square significant at P ≤ .01.
*** Chi square significant at P ≤ .001.

Notes: 1. Chi square tests for underlined variables indicate significance for householder differences in poverty levels controlling for labor market type. Chi square tests for categories of variables indicate significance for labor market differences in poverty levels controlling for householder characteristics.

2. Level of employment combines both hours and weeks worked in the preceeding year. Intermediate categories represent increasing amounts of part-time employment.

Similar patterns are followed for those in near poverty and, conversely, for the upper end of the income distribution. Not surprisingly, in both types of labor markets, the places with the highest levels of employment have the lowest poverty rates and vice versa. In rural areas, however, poor persons tend to exhibit a higher level of work effort than their urban counterparts.

Table 3.5 provides the same information for the different types of rural LLMAs, but only shows figures for householders who fall into one of the two poverty categories: poor and near poor. The largest numbers of householders in poverty in rural labor markets occur in resource-based LLMAs—both in those that are only resource-based and in those that have a combination of manufacturing and resource-based economies. The lowest poverty levels occur for LLMAs that are not dominated by any one type of industry. Nonconcentrated LLMAs have the lowest poverty rates for employed householders; all other types of rural LLMAs have substantially higher poverty rates as well as larger numbers of working-age householders who have dropped out of the labor force entirely.

Resource-based LLMAs not only have the highest poverty rates overall, but also the highest level of poverty for traditional households that include a husband-wife couple. The pattern is not as clear for employment levels. On the one hand, householders in all resource areas (both alone and combined with manufacturing) have the largest percentages of householders who are not employed. On the other hand, combined resource and manufacturing LLMAs have the highest levels of full-time or more employment. Making further sense of these results requires analysis that looks at employment levels in conjunction with household and individual characteristics, as well as labor-market area. First, however, it will be useful to examine more closely what workers with poverty and near-poverty incomes do for work.

Occupations and the Working Poor

We have already seen that families in resource-based labor markets tend to fare worse than those in more diversified labor markets. However, it does not necessarily follow that those employed in resource occupations are those who make up the working poor in the resource-based labor market. This section will explore exactly where the working poor tend to be employed in each type of community economic base.

Table 3.6 shows the industrial and occupational categories of employment for poor and near-poor householders in all types of LLMAs. The highest poverty figures for householders in rural LLMAs are found among those in producer service employment (business, banking, communications, utilities, insurance, transportation, and wholesale services) in rural LLMAs. Poverty for workers in this category is also high in urban areas, but not to the same degree as is found among rural householders. Consumer services (education, social, entertainment, health, personal, public administration, repair, retail, and household services), construction, and resources have the next-highest poverty levels. The lowest

Table 3.5
Poverty Status of Householders in Rural LLMAs with Different Economic Bases[1]

	Nonconcentrated Percent:		Resource Percent:		Manufacturing Percent:		Resource and Manufacturing Percent:	
	Pov	Near Pov	Pov	Near Pov	Pov	Near Pov	Pov	Near Pov
Household*								
Couple***	7.2	8.6	14.3	11.5	9.9	9.4	14.2	9.6
Male	12.6	14.7	22.4	9.4	23.3	13.2	15.4	7.7
Female	32.3	18.7	44.7	18.2	38.3	18.5	41.9	20.4
Non-family**	23.4	10.6	33.3	11.4	27.7	12.0	29.5	18.7
Race*								
White***	10.6	9.5	19.5	12.2	12.9	10.1	16.1	11.1
Black*	26.9	15.1	35.7	8.6	34.3	15.9	41.6	17.8
Other	23.1	11.5	33.3	16.7	24.0	8.0	50.0	--
Education*								
None	55.6	--	50.0	7.1	41.9	12.9	33.3	--
Less Than High School***	20.9	14.2	28.9	15.8	23.4	13.7	27.2	14.8
Less Than College	8.3	8.9	11.0	9.0	8.6	9.0	11.8	9.4
College or More	2.4	3.2	5.2	4.5	3.9	3.9	2.3	5.6
Labor Force Status*								
Employed	6.0	6.3	8.8	10.2	9.4	9.0	10.6	10.2
Unemployed***	27.1	12.9	33.2	9.4	24.3	19.9	34.3	12.9
Armed Forces*	5.4	15.7	--	20.0	--	--	--	--
Not in Labor Force***	36.8	13.4	47.3	18.0	43.1	16.7	48.9	18.1

52

Level of Employment***[2]

0 Not Employed**	43.1	13.5	51.0	17.3	49.1	17.0	56.3	17.9
1 Employed Part Time	37.4	10.4	44.0	16.5	44.2	10.3	50.0	19.4
2 Employed Part Time	28.7	14.7	38.8	21.7	34.8	19.7	23.5	19.6
3 Employed Part Time	12.4	17.9	22.6	17.2	22.8	20.1	24.6	21.5
4 Employed Full Time	11.0	15.6	8.8	15.3	10.2	16.9	16.1	10.7
5 More Than Full Time Employment***	4.2	8.1	4.4	8.0	6.1	7.7	6.9	8.3

* Chi square significant at P ≤ .05.
** Chi square significant at P ≤ .01.
*** Chi square significant at P ≤ .001.

Notes: 1. Chi square tests for underlined variables indicate significance for householder differences in poverty levels controlling for labor market type. Chi square tests for categories of variables indicate significance for labor market differences in poverty levels controlling for householder characteristics.

2. Level of employment combines both hours and weeks in the preceeding year. Intermediate categories represent increasing amounts of part-time employment.

Table 3.6
Industrial and Occupational Categories of Poor and Near-Poor Householders in Rural and Urban LLMAs

	Nonconcentrated Percent:		Resource Percent:		Manufacturing Percent:		Resource and Manufacturing Percent:		All Rural Percent:		All Urban Percent:	
	Pov	Near Pov	Pov	Near Pov	Pov	Near Pov	Pov	Near Pov	Pov	Near Pov	Pov	Near Pov
Industry* **												
Resources***	11.1	16.9	11.9	7.8	25.1	13.5	22.4	19.1	16.3	11.4	16.2	9.8
Manufacturing***	7.4	9.2	15.7	15.2	9.2	10.0	13.1	5.4	9.9	9.9	6.2	6.6
Construction	12.1	8.3	17.3	12.8	14.3	12.3	17.5	12.3	14.8	11.4	9.8	9.6
Producer Services*	16.6	10.2	30.4	14.1	21.7	11.3	24.7	12.0	23.2	11.9	14.2	8.0
Consumer Services*	12.3	9.9	16.9	12.5	14.3	9.5	15.8	14.9	14.5	10.7	10.4	7.7
Occupation* **												
Exec./Prof./Tech.	3.7	3.3	4.2	3.9	4.6	5.7	4.6	3.3	4.3	4.6	3.3	2.9
Sales/Clerical	7.4	8.7	8.7	11.6	7.5	9.1	8.1	9.2	7.8	9.6	7.3	6.1
Service*	19.4	21.3	30.2	19.0	25.7	12.9	30.1	20.6	25.5	17.1	20.8	13.1
Skilled Labor**	18.1	4.5	10.6	8.8	9.3	8.1	9.5	9.5	9.5	7.6	5.8	6.5
Operator***	19.5	13.6	30.1	15.4	21.1	13.8	27.0	11.7	23.8	14.0	17.9	11.4
Agriculture***	12.4	16.3	44.1	16.2	28.8	13.8	22.2	20.8	25.7	15.8	25.5	13.7

* Chi square significant at P ≤ .05.
** Chi square significant at P ≤ .01.
*** Chi square significant at P ≤ .001.

poverty levels are found in manufacturing industries for both rural and urban LLMAs. Among occupational categories, service and agriculture have the highest poverty levels.

These results provide an interesting contrast with the LLMA-level analysis. The highest poverty rates were found in rural labor-market areas with high levels of employment in resource-based industries. However, individual householders are less likely to be poor when employed in resource industries in resource LLMAs. On the other hand, householders employed in resource industries in LLMAs with high levels of manufacturing are among those most likely to be poor.

The percentage of householders in poverty also varies by occupation within and across labor markets. As expected, the highest poverty rates are found among those in less skilled occupations. Within occupational categories, however, a rural householder is more likely to be poor than his or her urban counterpart, and this is especially the case for those living in resource-dominated LLMAs.

Sources of Income for the Working Poor in Different Labor Markets

Central to the thesis of this chapter is the assertion that people are often poor because there are limited opportunities to work and receive wages in their own labor market. If the rural South offers the same types of opportunities to the poor no matter what type of labor market they are in, there should not be much variation in the portion of total family income earned by the poor. If, however, the poor in different labor markets have different amounts of work and wages available to them, we should see variations in the proportion of family income that is earned rather than obtained through other sources such as Social Security and public assistance.

When we look at income according to poverty levels, we put a "ceiling" on the amount of variation in income for each level of the poverty-status variable. That is, our households are all making poverty or near-poverty incomes at the most. Nevertheless, within these categories, there is still variation in actual amount of income as well as source of income between the poor and the near poor. Tables 3.7 and 3.8 show average incomes for poor and near-poor householders in rural and urban labor markets and in the different types of rural economic bases. There are significant differences between types of labor markets for most sources of income. Again, differences between householders within rural labor markets are larger than those between householders in urban and rural LLMAs. In both rural and urban areas, wages of poverty-level householders make up just over 50 percent of total householder income from all sources. In rural LLMAs, wage income varies from a low of 38 percent in resource-based areas to 62 percent in manufacturing labor-market areas. Poverty income is slightly higher for rural than for urban householders. However, this may be a function of household size, which is not controlled for in these tables. Sources

Table 3.7
Mean Poverty and Near-Poverty Householder Income for Rural and Urban LLMAs (in nearest dollars)

| | Rural** | | Urban** | |
| | | Near | | Near |
Income Source**	Poverty**	Poverty**	Poverty**	Poverty**
Wages*	1,384	4,380	1,378	4,686
Self-Employment				
Nonfarm	118	362	64	349
Farm*	20	189	9	64
Interest*	28	97	48	110
Social Security*	441	544	347	485
Public Assistance*	410	121	485	160
Other*	290	569	249	483
All Sources*	2,694	6,262	2,580	6,336

* F tests of rural-urban differences significant at P ≤ .05.
** F tests of all LLMA, Poverty and Income source models significant at
   P ≤ .001.

of income clearly differ by type of LLMA. Rural residents receive greater proportions of income from farming, self-employment, and Social Security, but receive less of other forms of public assistance.

Sources of Income by Household Type and Labor Market

Table 3.9 aggregates individual-level data within households to create household measures of income and its sources for different types of households with working-age heads. It compares poor Black and White couples', male-headed, and female-headed households' heads in rural labor markets with different economic bases and in urban areas. At first glance, this table appears to show that for all but male-headed households, Black household income is consistently higher than White income. However, this pattern reverses quite often when household income is divided by number of persons in the household to determine per capita household income. In other words, Black households are larger, and when income is averaged among all household members, Whites are often somewhat better off. (Male-headed households vary, but in rural areas there are too few cases for reliable analysis.)

Table 3.9 also shows the percentage of household income coming from wages and from combined Social Security and public assistance sources, or transfer

Table 3.8

Mean Income of Poverty and Near-Poverty Householders in Rural LLMAs with Different Economic Bases (in nearest dollars)

Income Source**	Nonconcentrated		Resource		Manufacturing		Resource and Manufacturing	
	Pov**	Near Pov**	Pov**	Near Pov**	Pov**	Near Pov**	Pov**	Near Pov**
Wages*	1,495	5,028	1,072	4,055	1,580	4,460	1,373	3,510
Self Employment								
Nonfarm	118	302	144	440	105	317	93	472
Farm*	--	52	29	80	--	196	231	844
Interest	53	104	25	138	22	75	21	44
Social Security*	443	435	605	737	339	460	331	572
Public Assistance*	428	137	533	132	316	105	373	131
Other*	304	505	388	1010	207	313	298	523
All Sources*	2,841	6,564	2,796	6,591	2,569	5,927	2,720	6,097

* F tests of economic base differences significant at $P \leq .05$.

** F tests of all economic base poverty and income source models significant at $P \leq .001$.

Table 3.9

Sources of Income for Households below the Poverty Line with a Working-Age Householder in LLMAs with Different Economic Bases

| | Rural LLMAs | | | | | | | | Urban LLMA | |
| | Nonconcentrated | | Resource | | Manufacturing | | Resource & Manuf. | | LLMA | |
Household Type	Black	White	Black	White	Black	White	Black	White	Black	White
Couple:	(N = 28)	(N = 184)	(N = 9)	(N = 463)	(N = 86)	(N = 523)	(N = 24)	(N = 136)	(N = 773)	(N = 2519)
Household Income	$5,271	$3,925	$5,062	$4,133	$4,973	$3,942	$5,406	$4,214	$4,461	$3,931
Per Capita Income	1,249	1,213	1,162	1,087	1,113	1,242	1,144	1,237	1,144	1,192
% Wage Income	.58	.51	.41	.41	.51	.41	.65	.24	.53	.46
% Transfer Income	.32	.35	.44	.41	.43	.38	.36	.37	.37	.31
Household Work Effort	.84	.69	.54	.46	.77	.76	.86	.76	.72	.76
Worker Effort	.47	.52	.54	.37	.45	.52	.39	.57	.47	.55
Male Head:	(N = 4)	(N = 10)	(N = 3)	(N = 24)	(N = 10)	(N = 27)	(N = 3)	(N = 2)	(N = 126)	(N = 303)
Household Income	$4,449	$4,017	$2,657	$3,444	$2,553	$3,360	$1,855	$4,190	$4,515	$3,602
Per Capita Income	1,318	1,182	1,130	1,281	993	1,186	927	1,171	1,288	1,303
% Wage Income	.34	---	.00	.15	.50	.38	.00	.14	.47	.47
% Transfer Income	.53	.16	1.00	.63	.48	.51	1.00	.15	.43	.41
Household Work Effort	.60	.94	.00	.14	.44	.45	.00	1.19	.63	.62
Worker Effort	.45	.65	.00	.14	.31	.31	.00	1.19	.45	.44
Female Head:	(N = 50)	(N = 66)	(N = 17)	(N = 171)	(N = 124)	(N = 133)	(N = 19)	(N = 26)	(N = 1523)	(N = 1287)
Household Income	$5,502	$3,662	$3,893	$3,511	$4,579	$3,515	$4,715	$3,205	$4,060	$3,906
Per Capita Income	1,296	1,168	1,100	1,065	1,082	1,180	1,282	1,044	1,089	1,256
% Wage Income	.54	.36	.23	.24	.53	.47	.44	.25	.41	.38
% Transfer Income	.43	.48	.67	.63	.42	.38	.44	.58	.51	.44
Household Work Effort	.62	.41	.14	.22	.56	.47	.50	.28	.42	.40
Worker Effort	.38	.33	.14	.18	.43	.41	.29	.21	.33	.32

income. Poor Blacks consistently have a higher proportion of their income from wages than poor Whites. The two groups have similar proportions of transfer income. For all but male-headed households, Black income is higher in all rural LLMAs than it is in urban areas, but this is not true for White households, which in many cases have equal or higher incomes in urban LLMAs. Both poor Black and White couple income is higher in rural than in urban areas. Black and White female-headed households reverse their position in rural and urban LLMAs, however. Black female-headed households have higher income in urban areas, whereas White female-headed households have higher income in most rural areas. Poor White female-headed households in resource-based LLMAs have the lowest household income, whereas there is much less variation among the different rural LLMAs for Black female-headed households, whose income is uniformly low. The biggest Black/White discrepancies occur in nonconcentrated LLMAs, followed by areas with both resource and manufacturing employment.

Since a quarter to well over half of income for all households is earned in the labor market, we should also look at measures of work effort. For most households, all the work effort of all workers combined does not equal the equivalent of one full-time worker. On the other hand, virtually all households have some labor-market activity, and, contrary to stereotype, poor Black households have greater household work effort. When we look at total household work effort according to the number of workers in the household, we see a smaller gap between races. This finding of higher "household work effort" but similar or lower "per capita work effort" suggests that poor Black households are larger and that they may employ different forms of household labor-market strategies than comparable White households.

DISCUSSION AND CONCLUSIONS

Rural labor markets have both greater poverty and more working persons whose incomes cannot lift them out of poverty than urban labor markets. They also have different industrial and occupational structures and employment opportunities. Differences between rural and urban areas appear to be the result of a combination of local economic activity and the characteristics of the people who live there. Local labor-market areas provide a means for assessing how different types of employment opportunity and industrial structure impact on poverty populations. In addition, they permit analysis of differences across different types of rural areas as well as between rural and urban areas. There is great variation in rural areas, with resource-based economies performing the worst.

These results show a high level of work effort by those in poverty, and this is important for dispelling damaging stereotypes about who is poor and why. The results also underscore the importance of moving beyond crude rural/urban distinctions to specify the particular forms of labor-market differences that influence economic opportunity. Spatial and multilevel analyses demonstrate diversity within rural areas and suggest the need to refine strictly ecological models of socioeconomic activity.

The results also show how individual characteristics intersect with opportunities in different types of labor markets. Race and household composition are clearly major factors influencing poverty status, but they cannot be understood apart from the forms of economic activity and opportunity available to individuals, households, and families. Poor Blacks generally have higher work effort than Whites, but this varies over household type and labor-market area. Differences in Black and White household composition and income-generating strategies are apparent, but these also must take into account the economic context. Similarly, household and worker work efforts in female-headed households vary widely across labor-market types. This analysis strongly suggests that these variations result from differences in the opportunities for work available within the different labor-market areas rather than from characteristics of the individuals who are poor.

This study also has implications for policy aimed at alleviating poverty. Most current debate about poverty and welfare reform focuses on how to make poor people work and how to make work pay adequately. The first part of this prescription is clearly simplistic. Many poor people already work, although they do not work enough or at high-enough wages to bring them out of poverty. While these data cannot demonstrate whether they are working to the maximum level of available employment, given studies that show a shortage of jobs in many rural areas and given the variation between types of labor-market areas found in this study, it is reasonable to assume that there is only limited room for efforts to force people to work more. Certainly there is little hope for the success of this approach without policies that deliberately create additional and more rewarding employment in areas with low opportunity.

Paying people more appears more reasonable, given these high levels of labor-market activity. Many of the policies and programs currently under scrutiny, such as raising the minimum wage, extending the earned income tax credit, and dealing with child-care problems, address this issue and may well have a discernible effect on the fortunes of poor and low-income persons. But their success will also be contingent on regional and local labor-market variation in employment opportunities for different types of persons and households. If these differences are not taken into account, there are likely to be serious problems of mismatch between programs and the needs of the populations they are designed to assist.

For example, it is quite likely that raising the minimum wage will be of greater help to households with high levels of labor-force attachment and with a reasonable number of available jobs. In the most depressed resource-based areas, raising the minimum wage may have minimal impact since the larger problem is the lack of employment, especially for women. Even if the processes producing poverty are the same for both rural and urban areas, the programs designed to deal with them may have to be different. For example, training programs for rural and urban residents will have to consider the special needs found in different locations, such as child-care facilities necessary to enable persons to take advantage of programs. Indeed, all poor workers with children may need assistance in paying for child care. Rural residents also may need greater assistance in finding or even creating child-care facilities.

In summary, it seems clear that headway against high poverty rates must take into consideration spatially based economic factors that shape individual circumstances. The impact of local labor-market factors is evident in 1980 data. It is fair to predict that this impact will become even more apparent as economic restructuring and the global reach of an increasingly international economy affect the fortunes of even the most remote rural areas.

NOTES

Portions of this chapter were presented at the Annual Meetings of the American Sociological Association, Atlanta, Georgia, August 24, 1988. This research was made possible by a grant from the Ford Foundation's Rural Poverty and Resources Program and the Aspen Institute's Rural Economic Policy Program. Thanks are due to Cecil Tickamyer for computation assistance, Melissa Latimer for research assistance, and Dwight Billings for comments.

1. Local labor-market areas are defined in a version of the public use microdata set (PUMS-D). These data are a specifically selected 1 percent sample of the 1980 U.S. Census of Housing and Population, using 382 empirically defined local labor-market areas as the primary sampling units. These local labor-market areas (LLMAs) are a new set of county groupings developed by the U.S. Department of Agriculture Southern Regional Research Project S–184, sponsored by the Economic Research Service, Agricultural and Rural Economic Division. PUMS-D redraws the 1980 census 1 percent sample and adds labor-market-area identification to each file (for details see Tolbert 1989; Tolbert and Killian 1987).

Local labor-market areas were constructed from 1980 census data on commuting patterns of U.S. workers. Matrices arraying county of residence with county of work were analyzed using hierarchical cluster analysis and grouped into areas characterized by flows of workers and residents. County groups represent empirically defined labor-market areas that come closer to specifying the location of the exchange of labor and employment than previously used geographic proxies, because they define an area where residents actually work.

While a major drawback of these data is their age, this is a unique cut from the census that currently cannot be duplicated with any other data. Comparable new census data will not be available until well into the 1990s. Interestingly enough, the patterns described here for the 1980s may well be similar to patterns in the 1990s. After a large increase during the decade, poverty rates at the end of the 1980s looked very similar to 1980 figures. These analyses using the 1980 decade show the utility of the approach and the nature of relationships for this historical period and lay the foundation for future comparative analysis.

Chapter 4

Long-Term Poverty in Rural Areas

Terry K. Adams and Greg J. Duncan

Rural poverty is all but invisible to the average American. The rural poor rarely come into contact with most urban residents, and media stories about poverty focus almost exclusively on the urban "underclass." More systematic information about the rural poor is generally limited to either case-study accounts or snapshot surveys such as the Current Population Survey. While case-study accounts such as Caudill's (1963) depiction of Appalachian poverty create vivid pictures of their subjects, they may focus on individuals who are quite unrepresentative of the rural poor in general.

Snapshot surveys conducted by the Census Bureau provide rich and representative (although decidedly less vivid) information about the characteristics of the over nine million nonmetropolitan Americans who live in poverty. Above all, they show how the nonmetropolitan poor differ from the more visible metropolitan poor (Duncan and Tickamyer 1988; O'Hare 1988). The incidence of poverty is higher outside than inside the nation's metropolitan areas. Compared with metropolitan poverty, nonmetropolitan poverty is more prevalent among intact families and families with considerable labor-market activity. Furthermore, the nonmetropolitan poor do not seem to have benefitted as much as their metropolitan counterparts from the economic growth of the 1980s. These differences, reinforced by differential trends in labor-market phenomena such as unemployment and earnings, suggest that different processes are at work in nonmetropolitan and metropolitan areas to produce and perpetuate poverty.

A weakness of Census Bureau snapshots, however, is that they fail to distinguish between shorter and longer periods of poverty—a major drawback when one remembers that longitudinal studies of economic status reveal many poverty experiences to be short-term (Bane and Ellwood 1986) and that more than half of the poor in large metropolitan areas in a given year are not "persistently" poor (Adams and Duncan 1988). Single-year poverty counts include as poor otherwise well-off households that may have a temporarily low income (owing, say, to a bad year experienced in farming or other self-employment or to a brief spell of unemployment). There are clear policy-relevant differences between persons and families who are poor for shorter and longer terms, and policymakers should develop different strategies and priorities to reflect such differences (Hoppe 1988; Ross and Morrissey 1987). Our focus in this chapter on persons who are poor for longer periods is not intended to minimize the difficulties encountered by those who experience short-term poverty. Rather, we are motivated by the greater urgency in public policy to address the problems of the longer-term poor.

A growing body of literature suggests that long-term poverty has intergenerational consequences. Studies with reliable measures of family income during childhood have found that low parental income is related to lower levels of schooling and less successful careers for children (Sewell and Hauser 1975; Hill and Duncan 1987). The intergenerational study by Corcoran et al. (1987) found that long-term parental poverty had a variety of detrimental effects on the schooling and early career attainments of children, despite controls for an elaborate set of measures of the economic and demographic status of the family of origin. Thus long-term poverty produces effects that may persist across generations. This chapter uses information collected over a nineteen-year period from a representative sample of Americans—poor and nonpoor, metropolitan and nonmetropolitan—to describe the incidence and characteristics of long-term poverty in nonmetropolitan areas of the United States.

IMPORTANT ISSUES

Our look at long-term poverty will be largely descriptive, aimed at developing a set of useful facts about the incidence of long-term poverty in nonmetropolitan and metropolitan areas to provide some perspective on more qualitative accounts of such poverty. Our description is geared to the following set of issues:

How widespread is long-term nonmetropolitan poverty? Census Bureau snapshots show that the incidence of single-year poverty has typically been much higher outside of metropolitan areas than within them. The extent to which the incidence of long-term poverty differs by geography depends upon the mixture of long- and short-term poverty in nonmetropolitan and metropolitan areas. Short-term spells are pervasive overall, as shown by Bane and Ellwood (1986), who estimate (with no distinction between metropolitan and nonmetropolitan areas) that as many as three-fifths of all poverty spells end within three years and that only one-seventh last as long as eight years. If, as Duncan et al. (1984) seem to find, nonmetropolitan poverty is more persistent than metropolitan poverty, then the single-year figures will understate the relative nonmetropolitan/metropolitan differential in long-term poverty.

Has long-term poverty become more pervasive in nonmetropolitan areas? Explanations of the economic fortunes of nonmetropolitan areas based on the "restructuring" of economic forces over the last twenty years yield the grim prospect of an increase in long-term poverty. Data on changes in the incidence of long-term poverty in the last twenty years are used to examine this issue.

Who are the long-term nonmetropolitan poor? While there are some well-known qualitative accounts of persistently poor people living in nonmetropolitan areas (e.g., Caudill 1963; Agee and Evans 1941), there is—with the exception of the work of Ross and her colleagues (e.g., Ross and Morrissey 1987, 1989)— little quantitative evidence from representative samples. Our look at the characteristics of the long-term poor will focus on individuals living in households where the head is neither disabled nor elderly and will contrast the characteristics of the long-term poor living in nonmetropolitan areas with those living in metropolitan areas.

How connected are the long-term nonmetropolitan poor to the labor market? When we restrict our look to the able-bodied, issues of labor-market involvement assume primary importance. We examine the work effort, labor supply, and earnings of the long-term poor and simulate how the incidence of long-term poverty would be affected by a minimum-wage floor and the elimination of unemployment.

How connected are the long-term poor to private help networks and public transfers? Conventional income statistics tell nothing about links between the nonmetropolitan poor and potential sources of help, such as time and money from friends and relatives. This issue, as well as the use of public transfers such as Food Stamps, can be explored with the available data.

To what extent do the long-term poor exhibit "deserving" and "undeserving" characteristics? A recurrent question in the debate over poverty policy, recently rekindled in current discussions of the "underclass," is the extent to which the poor exhibit "deserving" characteristics such as working for pay or being aged or disabled and "undeserving" characteristics such as lacking a high-school diploma or receiving welfare. We will examine the connections between long-term poverty and various behavioral characteristics suggested by the value-laden terms "deserving" and "undeserving."

DATA AND METHODS

Data used in this chapter come from the Panel Study of Income Dynamics (PSID), a nineteen-year longitudinal household study that has conducted annual interviews with a representative sample of U.S. households since 1968. To facilitate our focus on trends, we drew two ten-year subsamples from the PSID: a "recent" sample of individuals living in households during the period from 1976 to 1985 and an "early," comparable sample covering the period from 1967 to 1976. Most of the information we present is based on a further restriction to individuals living in households headed by a nonelderly, able-bodied adult. Except for immigrants since 1968, the design of the PSID provides representative data on the economic experiences of the U.S. population during these two ten-year periods (see the Appendix to this chapter).

As with official poverty data, our measure of long-term poverty is based on a comparison of the total incomes of household members with whom each sample member lived and the official poverty threshold. (Poverty thresholds vary with family size and totalled about $12,000 for a family of four in 1988.) Individuals for whom the sum of ten-year family incomes was below 125 percent of the sum of ten-year official poverty thresholds were considered "long-term poor." More details are provided in the Appendix.

Our definition of "nonmetro" is based on the 1983 classification of counties as "metropolitan" and "nonmetropolitan" by the U.S. Office of Management and Budget. Nonmetropolitan counties can be further classified according to whether or not they are adjacent to metropolitan counties.

Our choice of the "early" and "recent" time periods, 1967–76 and 1976–85, was based on the availability of data—we had information for a nineteen-year period, 1967–85, and we wanted to split the period in half. The result was two ten-year periods, with 1976 data included in each period. Of course, any choice of historical periods is to some extent arbitrary, since there are few discontinuities in economic or other historical statistics, and it can always be argued that any given period is "unusual." Our choice places the boundary in 1976, a year that was near the bottom of the U-shaped curve of Current Population Survey (CPS) annual poverty rates over the entire nineteen-year period, so that our two periods appear to be mirror images, the early period showing declining single-year poverty rates and the recent period showing increasing rates. In this sense, our choice was a fortunate one, since the average annual rates and year-to-year variations in rates within the periods are similar. Since trends within the 1976–85 period are of some interest, we perform some calculations for the 1981–85 period and compare our results with those from the entire 1976–85 period.

A DEMOGRAPHIC PROFILE OF LONG-TERM POVERTY IN NONMETROPOLITAN AREAS

Temporal Aspects of Poverty

Using longitudinal data from the PSID on the annual family incomes and family sizes of individuals living within and outside of metropolitan areas, we can develop many measures of multiyear poverty. In Figure 4.1 we show estimates of the sizes of various poverty groups defined over the decade from 1976 to 1985 with a poverty line set at 125 percent of the official line, including (1) the ever poor, that is, individuals with annual incomes below 125 percent of the official poverty line at least once; (2) the one-year poor, that is, individuals with incomes below 125 percent of the poverty line in a single year (in this case, the middle year of our ten-year period); (3) the long-term poor, the concept used throughout the remainder of this chapter defined by the incidence of ten-year total incomes below 125 percent of the ten-year poverty lines; and (4) the per-

Figure 4.1
Temporal Aspects of Poverty, 1976–85

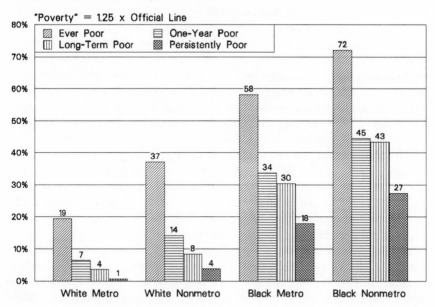

"Poverty" = 1.25 x Official Line

Legend:
- ▨ Ever Poor
- ▤ One-Year Poor
- ▥ Long-Term Poor
- ▦ Persistently Poor

White Metro: 19, 7, 4, 1
White Nonmetro: 37, 14, 8, 4
Black Metro: 58, 34, 30, 18
Black Nonmetro: 72, 45, 43, 27

sistently poor, that is, individuals with incomes below 125 percent of the official poverty line in at least eight of the ten years.

As all other examinations of the temporal nature of poverty have shown (e.g., Ross and Morrissey 1987), we found that people were much more likely to have been "ever poor" than to be poor in a given year, persistently, or long-term (see Figure 4.1), and this holds true for both Blacks and Whites as well as within and outside of metropolitan areas. Blacks were very likely to experience poverty at least occasionally, with 72 percent of nonmetropolitan and 58 percent of metropolitan Blacks poor in at least one year in the decade. By all four measures people were more likely to be poor if they lived in nonmetropolitan than in metropolitan areas.

INCIDENCE OF LONG-TERM POVERTY

Balancing a need to focus on individuals with the greatest long-term deprivation and a concern for adequate sample size, we concentrated on individuals for whom the sum of ten-year family incomes was below 125 percent of the sum of ten-year official poverty thresholds—a group we call the "long-term poor." Despite economic mobility among the poor and nonpoor alike, the incidence of long-term poverty was disturbingly high.

While less pervasive in the 1980s than earlier, long-term poverty still characterized about one in twenty Whites and one in three Blacks. The incidence of long-term poverty among households with able-bodied heads was much higher outside of the nation's metropolitan areas than within them, and among Blacks than among Whites. More than one-third of nonmetropolitan Blacks in households with able-bodied heads experienced long-term poverty.

Taking the decade from 1976 to 1985 and placing no geographic, age, or health restrictions on the sample, we found that only about one in twelve persons (8.3 percent) met our definition of "long-term poor." As in more conventional poverty statistics, Black people suffered a disproportionate long-term poverty, with more than one-third of Blacks but only about 5 percent of Whites living in households considered long-term poor during the 1976–85 period (Table 4.1, row 1, columns 2 and 3).

Also shown in the first row of Table 4.1 (and in Figure 4.2) is a comparison of the incidence of long-term poverty in the "recent" decade of the PSID panel period (1976–85) and the "early" decade (1967–76). Long-term poverty declined substantially for Blacks but changed little for Whites.[1] However, a more careful look at the distribution of long-term economic status, detailed later, shows quite different patterns of change in metro and nonmetro locations.

Most of our subsequent analysis will focus on the so-called able-bodied long-term poor, defined to be individuals living in households in which the household head was neither disabled nor above the age of 64 at any time during the ten-year period. Significantly, only about half of the long-term poor, both Black and White, fall within our definition of the "able-bodied" poor (Table 4.1, rows 3 and 4).

Poverty and Geographic Location

Our primary focus is on long-term poor people living in nonmetropolitan areas. As the bottom half of Table 4.1 shows, people living in households with an able-bodied head were much more likely to be poor if they lived in nonmetro-politan than in metropolitan areas. For the 1976–85 period, the incidence of long-term poverty was more than 50 percent higher for Blacks in nonmetro areas (37 versus 24 percent) and more than twice as high for Whites in nonmetro areas (5 versus 2 percent).

But Table 4.1 also shows falling rates of long-term poverty in nonmetropolitan areas for both Whites and Blacks, a result that is apparently inconsistent with the view that economic "restructuring" has hurt nonmetropolitan as much as metropolitan areas. Since this result may be sensitive to our definition of long-term poverty, we sought more complete information about the changing nature of the long-term income distribution in nonmetropolitan areas.

We did this by refining the definition of "long-term" poverty. Recall that our definition of long-term poverty includes instances where ten-year household incomes were under 125 percent of the ten-year poverty lines. To provide more information, we divided the long-term poor into subsets with (1) severe poverty (i.e., with ten-year incomes less than 75 percent of the poverty line); (2) ten-

Table 4.1
Incidence of Long-Term Poverty by Metropolitan and Nonmetropolitan Residence, Time Period, and Ethnicity

	Recent: 1976-85			Early: 1967-76		
	All*	Black	White	All*	Black	White
Fraction of total population who are long-term poor	8%	34%	5%	9%	43%	5%
Number of long-term poor (in millions)	13.1	6.0	6.8	14.8	7.2	6.6
Composition of long-term poor						
Able-bodied (head never aged or disabled)	46%	48%	43%	53%	50%	53%
Head ever aged or disabled	54%	52%	57%	47%	50%	47%
Fraction of non-metro able-bodied population who are long-term poor	8%	37%	5%	11%	60%	7%
Number of non-metro able-bodied long-term poor (in millions)	2.3	0.9	1.3	3.4	1.3	2.0
Fraction of metro able-bodied population who are long-term poor	4%	24%	2%	5%	26%	2%
Number of metro able-bodied long-term poor (in millions)	3.7	2.0	1.6	4.4	2.3	1.5

Source: Panel Study of Income Dynamics.

*Includes persons other than Black or White. Table reads: 8 percent of the entire population was estimated to be living in long-term poverty between 1976 and 1985.

Figure 4.2
Incidence of Long-Term Poverty among Individuals Living in Households with
Able-bodied Heads by Location, 1967–76 and 1976–85

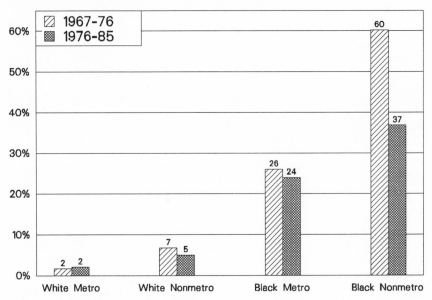

year incomes between 75 and 100 percent of the poverty line; and (3) near poverty (i.e., ten-year incomes between 100 and 125 percent of the poverty line). For Whites living in households with an able-bodied head, these categories showed similar trends; there were modest reductions in the size of all three groups outside of metro areas and small increases within them.

As shown in Figure 4.3, the differences for Blacks were much more dramatic. Severe long-term poverty used to be much more pervasive among able-bodied Blacks outside than inside metropolitan areas. By the 1980s conditions had improved sufficiently in nonmetro areas and worsened in metro areas to produce near parity in these rates. In the "early" decade, from 1967 to 1976, the fraction of Blacks who could be described as living in severe long-term poverty (i.e., with incomes less than 75 percent of the poverty line) was four times as high outside as inside metropolitan areas (24 versus 6 percent). By the "recent" decade (1976–85) the incidence of severe poverty in nonmetropolitan areas had been cut nearly in half (to 13 percent). However, severe poverty within metropolitan areas almost doubled (to 10 percent), producing near parity in the incidence of severe poverty for metro and nonmetro Blacks. If the fact that there was only a small proportion of very badly off Blacks in big cities was ever an incentive for poor nonmetropolitan Blacks to migrate, it is clear that that incentive had vanished by the 1980s.

The rather dramatic improvement we find in the economic position of low-in-

Figure 4.3
Distribution of Ten-Year Total Income/Needs for Blacks Living in Households with Able-bodied Heads by Location, 1967–76 and 1976–85

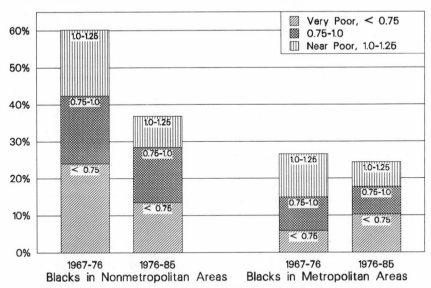

come Black families living in nonmetropolitan areas seems to conflict with more pessimistic assessments often found in the literature. There are several things to remember here. First, one should not confuse findings about changes in the incidence of long-term poverty with conclusions about the incidence itself. Although we find improvement in the long-term position of low-income households living in nonmetropolitan areas, the incidence of long-term poverty among all groups we examined remains higher in nonmetropolitan areas than in metropolitan areas, and one in three nonmetro Blacks experienced long-term poverty.

Second, some optimism is warranted even when one consults "official" data sources such as the Current Population Survey and the decennial census (Jensen 1987). For nonmetropolitan Blacks, the group with the greatest improvement, Current Population Surveys in 1970 and 1981 (near the middle years of our ten-year windows) show a drop in the incidence of one-year poverty from 50 to 42 percent. (Single-year figures from the PSID on nonmetropolitan Blacks living in households with able-bodied heads in 1971 and 1981 are 53 and 42 percent.) While these poverty figures are very high, they do reflect improvement. In contrast, poverty rates for nonmetro Whites in those two years rose somewhat (from 13 to 14 percent in CPS data); since there are larger numbers of Whites than Blacks, this increase dominates the rather pessimistic poverty data for nonmetropolitan areas. The converging family economic situation of metro and nonmetro Blacks parallels a convergence in various unemployment indicators in CPS data found by Lichter (1989).

Figure 4.4
Demographic Characteristics of Individuals Living in Nonmetro Households with
Able-bodied Heads by Race, 1967–76 and 1976–85

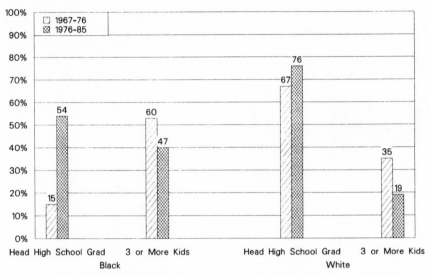

Third, a pessimistic assessment of the demand side of nonmetropolitan labor markets must be balanced against more optimistic changes in the characteristics of nonmetropolitan workers and their families. In particular, schooling levels have risen steadily, especially among Blacks, as older, less educated household heads have been replaced by a younger, better-educated cohort. In addition, family sizes have fallen dramatically for both Whites and Blacks.

The fraction of the heads of Black, nonmetro households who had completed high school more than tripled between 1972 and 1982, while the fraction of nonmetro Blacks living in households containing three or more children fell from 60 to 47 percent during that same period (Figure 4.4 and Table 4.3). Increased schooling should mean that workers have the skills and/or credentials required for a wider range of jobs, many of which would offer higher wages. Smaller families produce less pressure on limited household income. So while both CPS and, as detailed later, PSID data show growing unemployment among the non-metropolitan poor, other, more favorable changes were associated with less long-term poverty in the late 1970s and 1980s than in the late 1960s and early 1970s.

Tempering our optimism about the economic situation of nonmetro Blacks is the fact that our use of the ten-year accounting period between 1976 and 1985 averages together years that were relatively favorable to nonmetropolitan areas (i.e., the late 1970s) with years that were decidedly less favorable (i.e., the early to mid–1980s). During the 1980s trends in labor-market characteristics such as unemployment and wage rates were considerably gloomier outside of metropolitan areas than within them (Shapiro 1989; Majchrowicz and Ghelfi 1988). Thus the picture gained from a decade-long accounting period may hide important changes taking place within that period.

To investigate this possibility, we computed a measure of long-term poverty for the 1981–85 period. For Whites, the 1981–85 measure differs little from that for the entire 1976–85 period. However, for both metropolitan and nonmetropolitan Blacks, overall long-term poverty and severe long-term poverty were somewhat greater in 1981–85 than in 1976–85 taken as a whole.[2]

In summary, it appears that long-term poverty in nonmetropolitan areas remains higher than in metropolitan areas, although the gap narrowed substantially during the nineteen-year period we examined. This is true for both Blacks and Whites and reflects improvements in the situation of nonmetro Blacks and Whites as well as a deterioration in the situation of the poorest metro Blacks.

Demographic Characteristics of the Long-Term Poor

Census Bureau snapshots show that poverty is more prevalent among Blacks, in Southern states, among children, in households headed by women, and in households in which the head has completed little schooling. Based on rather small numbers of observations, our data on long-term poverty for individuals living in households headed by an able-bodied person and in nonmetropolitan areas generally reflect these patterns.[3]

Nearly half of the long-term poor living in nonmetropolitan areas are Black, the majority are children, and most live in households where the head did not complete high school, a picture that has changed little since the late 1960s. Female headship has become much more common among nonmetro poor Blacks. Most nonmetropolitan Blacks, especially the long-term poor, live far from metropolitan areas. Ethnic differences in long-term poverty rates are dramatic and disturbing: Blacks comprise nearly half of the long-term nonmetro poor but only one-tenth of the overall population in these areas.

The first and fifth columns of Table 4.2 show various characteristics of the long-term nonmetropolitan poor in the "recent" decade (1976–85). Comparable information on the entire nonmetropolitan population is provided in Table 4.3.

Geographic characteristics highlight the isolation of Blacks living in long-term poverty. Nonmetro Blacks living in long-term poverty were concentrated in the South and in counties not adjacent to metropolitan areas, a situation that has changed little since the late 1960s. In contrast, poor Whites were evenly divided between the South and the Midwest and were somewhat more likely than poor Blacks to live in counties adjacent to metropolitan areas.

Although constituting only a minority of the overall population, children accounted for the majority of people living in households with able-bodied heads but experiencing long-term poverty. This held for both Blacks and Whites, both within and outside of metropolitan areas, and in both the recent and early periods.

Compared with the urban poor, the poor in nonmetropolitan areas are generally

Table 4.2
Demographic Characteristics of Long-Term Poor Persons Living in Households with Able-bodied Heads

	Black				White			
	Nonmetro		Metro		Nonmetro		Metro	
	Recent	Early	Recent	Early	Recent	Early	Recent	Early
Region*								
Northeast	7%	0%	19%	17%	2%	4%	24%	34%
Midwest	4	0	37	31	48	50	46	7
South	90	100	40	46	42	39	21	44
West	0	0	4	6	8	7	9	15
Adjacent to metropolitan area*	24	18	N.A.	N.A.	34	18	N.A.	N.A.
Age of individual*								
Under 18	59	52	56	71	57	56	61	63
18-34	32	32	34	19	24	22	29	24
35 or older	9	16	10	11	19	22	9	15
Female head								
No years	32	55	13	21	59	78	34	46
Some but not all years	15	19	28	33	32	17	42	27
All years	54	26	60	46	10	5	25	28
Head completed high school*	41	10	31	25	45	34	51	24
Three or more children in household*	58	77	51	78	54	62	49	62
Unweighted number of observations	184	296	763	892	78	103	124	82

Source: Panel Study of Income Dynamics.

*In middle year of ten-year period: 1972 or 1982. Table reads: 7 percent of long-term poor Blacks lived in nonmetropolitan areas of the Northeast in the "recent" (1976–85) period.

Table 4.3
Overall Population Distributions for Demographic Characteristics of Persons Living in Households with Able-bodied Heads

	Black				White			
	Nonmetro		Metro		Nonmetro		Metro	
	Recent	Early	Recent	Early	Recent	Early	Recent	Early
Region*								
Northeast	3%	1%	19%	12%	8%	9%	30%	32%
Midwest	7	3	27	32	44	45	27	30
South	89	97	43	47	37	36	23	19
West	1	0	10	9	12	10	21	19
Adjacent to metropolitan area*	37	26	N.A.	N.A.	43	38	N.A.	N.A.
Age of individual*								
Under 18	49	47	38	50	34	42	30	41
18-34	36	31	37	25	34	32	37	28
35 or older	15	22	25	25	32	26	34	31
Female head								
No years	53	66	42	52	81	82	78	80
Some but not all years	21	17	28	27	16	16	17	16
All years	26	17	30	21	3	2	5	4
Head completed high school*	54	15	63	45	76	67	86	77
Three or more children in household*	47	60	25	48	19	35	19	37
Unweighted number of observations	571	458	2,635	2,285	1,607	1,346	4,367	3,642

Table 4.3 (continued)

	Black				White			
	Nonmetro		Metro		Nonmetro		Metro	
	Recent	Early	Recent	Early	Recent	Early	Recent	Early
Years head and wife employed at least half-time								
No years	5%	2%	6%	5%	1%	0%	0%	0%
Minority of years	9	14	17	14	3	1	3	2
Majority of years	27	26	23	21	19	17	18	16
All years	59	58	54	61	79	82	80	81
Years head unemployed at least 10% of year								
No years	39	43	48	56	63	72	68	73
Minority of years	53	55	46	44	33	27	30	26
Majority of years	8	3	6	1	4	1	2	1
All years	0	0	0	0	0	0	1	0
Years wage rate of head less than $3.35 (1986 dollars)								
No years	57	38	66	70	69	74	86	89
Minority of years	35	45	33	28	29	22	14	10
Majority of years	8	16	1	1	2	4	1	0
All years	0	0	0	0	0	0	0	0

Source: Panel Study of Income Dynamics.

*In middle year of ten-year period: 1972 or 1982.

Figure 4.5
Percentage of Long-Term Poor Living in Families with Female Heads All or Some of the Time by Race and Location, 1967–76 and 1976–85

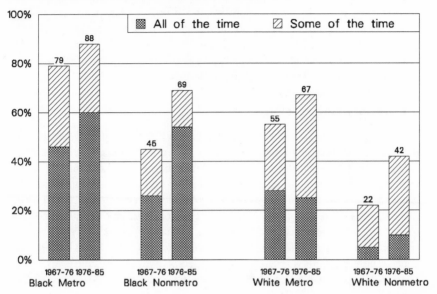

thought to be much more likely to live in two-parent families. Table 4.2 shows that while this is still true for both Black and White families in long-term poverty, the metro/nonmetro differences narrowed substantially between the two decades covered by the data. The proportion of White long-term poor families with a female head throughout the years of the recent decade was still more than twice as high in metro as in nonmetro areas (25 and 10 percent), while the metro/nonmetro difference for Blacks was much smaller (60 percent as against 54 percent).

The multiyear data on female headship in Table 4.2 and Figure 4.5 (as well as for the entire population, as shown in Table 4.3) also show that female headship, like poverty itself, is often transitory, especially among Whites. Much larger fractions of Whites who spent time in female-headed families did so for only part of the period than for all of it. These findings are consistent with more detailed examinations of the dynamics of single-parent families (e.g., Duncan and Rodgers 1987). Blacks were much more likely to continue to live in a female-headed family.

In addition, it is noteworthy that about half of all poor households with able-bodied heads had three or more children, a substantially greater proportion than in the general population (compare Table 4.2 with Table 4.3). Although these proportions declined from the early to the recent period, they were still large enough to have a marked effect on the amount of income needed to raise the family to the poverty line, as well as on the proportion of family members able to obtain that income in the labor market. Differences in family size between Black and White long-term poor families narrowed dramatically between the two decades, so that by the recent decade the differences had nearly disappeared.

The proportion of long-term poor families with heads who had graduated from high school increased considerably between the two periods, and particularly dramatically for nonmetropolitan Blacks. Black/White differences in level of education narrowed correspondingly in nonmetro areas.

Labor-Market Attachment

Single-year poverty statistics from the Current Population Surveys show that the nonmetropolitan poor are more likely to work than the metropolitan poor (Shapiro 1989). When we examine the labor-market involvement of the long-term able-bodied poor in our PSID sample, we find a very similar picture. We also examine evidence of effects of the economic "restructuring" that has taken place in the last two decades. The extent and consequences of the loss of manufacturing jobs and other adverse economic changes that swept through cities like Chicago, Detroit, and Philadelphia during the 1970s and 1980s have received considerable publicity (Wilson 1987). A number of writers have argued that parallel changes have taken place in nonmetropolitan areas. For example, Tickamyer and Duncan (1990) write:

[S]tructural changes in the 1980s have intensified chronic economic instability in rural areas where industries have always been volatile, unstable and vulnerable to cyclical trends. . . . During the 1960s and 1970s, manufacturing jobs provided some stability for rural workers, but this ended with the upheavals created by restructuring. Substantial numbers of "new poor" joined the chronically poor in remote, depressed areas. (p. 78)

Our look at the labor-market dimensions of long-term poverty begins with data on labor-market attachment and supports much of the evidence from single-year snapshots (Shapiro 1989). In contrast to the situation of the metropolitan poor, substantial labor-market work is the rule rather than the exception for both Blacks and Whites living in long-term poverty in nonmetropolitan areas. Consistent with discussions of the importance of economic restructuring in nonmetropolitan areas, unemployment was found to be more pervasive among the nonmetropolitan poor during the late 1970s to mid–1980s than it had been a decade earlier, and work at very low wage rates was less prevalent.

Figure 4.6 and the first four rows of Table 4.4 document the extensive work effort among the long-term poor people living in nonmetropolitan areas. Two-thirds of the long-term nonmetro poor in families with able-bodied heads—both Black and White—lived in families where the head and/or his spouse (if present) worked a combined total of at least 1,040 hours in most of the ten years from 1976 to 1985. (A 40-hour-per-week job worked 52 weeks per year results in 2,080 hours of work.)

Figure 4.6
Percentage of Heads of Able-bodied Long-Term Poor Households with Substantial Employment and Unemployment by Location and Race, 1967–76 and 1976–85

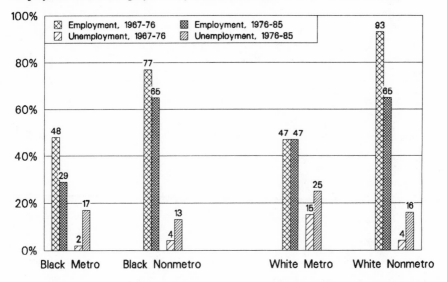

Blacks and Whites living in nonmetro areas and in long-term poverty were equally likely to have substantial labor-market involvement during the recent decade. But labor-market involvement among the long-term poor was much higher in nonmetro than in metro areas and has declined somewhat in both locations over time. For Blacks, the fraction of long-term poor working at least 1,040 hours in all or most of the years was more than twice as high outside of metropolitan areas as inside them (65 and 29 percent), while for Whites the metro/nonmetro differences were smaller (65 and 47 percent). The decline in substantial labor-force involvement between 1967–76 and 1976–85 was larger for nonmetro Whites (dropping from 93 to 65 percent) than for nonmetro Blacks (77 to 65 percent).

One possible effect of economic restructuring on the poor is increased unemployment, as low-skill jobs are increasingly performed by machines or in third-world countries. A count of the number of years in which the head of the household had experienced substantial unemployment (i.e., at least 208 hours, or 10 percent of a full year) confirmed that lengthy periods of unemployment were at least as common among the nonmetro long-term poor as among the metropolitan long-term poor, and that the increase in such unemployment between the two decades was just as striking in nonmetro as in metro areas. (Somewhat smaller increases show up in Table 4.3 when the able-bodied poor and nonpoor are combined into a single sample.) Regardless of ethnicity, more than two-thirds of the long-term poor had substantial unemployment at least once

Table 4.4
Labor-Market Characteristics of Long-Term Poor Persons Living in Households with Able-bodied Heads

	Black				White			
	Nonmetro		Metro		Nonmetro		Metro	
	Recent	Early	Recent	Early	Recent	Early	Recent	Early
Years head and wife employed at least half-time								
No years	14%	2%	25%	16%	6%	4%	8%	16%
Minority of years	21	20	46	36	30	2	45	38
Majority of years	26	33	19	23	25	25	29	30
All years	39	44	10	25	40	68	18	17
Years head unemployed at least 10% of year								
No years	25	32	25	46	33	42	21	32
Minority of years	62	64	59	53	51	55	55	54
Majority of years	13	4	17	2	16	4	24	15
All years	0	0	0	0	0	0	1	0
Years wage rate of head less than $3.35 (1986 dollars)								
No years	29	16	34	37	31	38	27	30
Minority of years	51	58	65	59	54	35	65	67
Majority of years	20	26	2	4	16	28	7	3
All years	0	0	0	0	0	0	0	0

Source: Panel Study of Income Dynamics.

Table reads: 14 percent of long-term poor Blacks living in nonmetropolitan areas were in households in which the combined work hours of the household head and wife totaled less than half-time (1,040 hours) in every one of the ten years in the "recent" period (1976–85).

during the 1976–85 period, although only about one in six had substantial un-employment in most of the years.

As a gauge of the overall importance of unemployment in causing long-term poverty among people who would not otherwise be poor, we simulated how much higher household incomes would have been in the 1976–85 period if unemployment hours of the household head could have been converted into work hours at the head's usual wage rate. To do this, we multiplied the reported number of hours unemployed by the average wage rate while employed and added the result to total family income. (Since we were unable to separate unemployment compensation from workers' disability compensation during the early years, our simulations included both in total family income and doubtless overstated the poverty-reducing effects of eliminating unemployment.)

Reductions in poverty from the elimination of unemployment during the 1976–85 period were modest for nonmetro Blacks, falling by about 12 percent (from 36.8 to 32.7 percent). The relatively small size of the drop is undoubtedly due in part to the weaker labor-force attachment of the large number of Black mother-only households, whose time outside of paid employment is more likely to be time "out of the labor force" than "unemployed." (Recall from Table 4.2 that less than one-third of the nonmetro long-term poor Blacks lived in male-headed households all the time.) The proportionate reduction in long-term poverty among Whites—from 5.1 percent to 3.6 percent—was much larger than for Blacks, although smaller in absolute terms.

Apart from unemployment, a second important link between work and poverty is a low wage rate for the hours worked. When we look at the distribution of wage rates (in 1986 dollars, not shown in Table 4.3) among heads of long-term poor households who worked in the middle year (1981) of the recent ten-year period, we see that substantial numbers worked at very low rates of pay. In nonmetropolitan areas roughly one-third of both Black and White household heads in poor families earned less than the 1986 minimum wage ($3.35 per hour). For Blacks, fully eight in ten earned less than $5.00 per hour—a wage rate insufficient to lift a family of four above the poverty line even with full-time work.

However, when we measured the frequency of wages less than $3.35 per hour (in 1986 dollars) among the heads of long-term poor households over the two ten-year periods, we found that virtually no one, Black or White, metro or nonmetro, had wages below this level for all years in which they worked (Table 4.3, bottom row). Interestingly, there were large metro/nonmetro differences in the incidence of low wages, although in the recent period there were only small differences between Blacks and Whites. In the recent period more than two-thirds of nonmetro poor households had a head earning less than $3.35 in at least one year, a fraction roughly comparable to that of metro poor households. But heads in nonmetro areas were much more likely than those in metro areas to earn less than $3.35 in the majority of years.

The incidence of low-wage work fell dramatically for the entire able-bodied

Black population in nonmetro areas, not just for those in poor families (Table 4.3). This fact undoubtedly contributed to the big drop in severe long-term poverty among nonmetro Blacks.

As we did for unemployment, we performed a simple simulation on wage rates to gauge the effects of higher wage rates on the prevalence of long-term poverty. In particular, we took all long-term poor able-bodied household heads earning less than $4.21 per hour (in 1986 dollars) in any given year and simulated an increase in their wage rates to $4.21 for all hours actually worked in that year. (We chose $4.21 because it is equivalent to the 1986 poverty line for a family of three when divided by 2,080 hours [40 hours per week × 52 weeks per year; see Shapiro 1989 for a similar computation using single-year data] and is likely to be somewhat larger, in inflation-adjusted dollars, than the newly enacted minimum wage of $4.35 per hour that will take effect in 1991.) Our simulations did not take into account the apparently modest disemployment effects that higher wages might occasion (Brown 1988). We also assumed universal coverage of the minimum wage, although actual federal and state statutes exclude about one-sixth of all workers (probably more in nonmetro areas).

Reductions in rates of long-term poverty with the simulated $4.21 minimum wage were slightly larger than with the simulated elimination of unemployment. The incidence of long-term poverty among nonmetropolitan Blacks during the 1976–85 period fell from 36.8 to 32.1 percent, a 13 percent reduction. The comparable figures for nonmetropolitan Whites went from 5.1 to 4.2 percent. (For metro residents the reductions were from 24.4 to 22.5 percent for Blacks and 2.2 to 1.6 percent for Whites.) Thus neither the elimination of unemployment nor an increase in the minimum-wage floor for able-bodied heads of long-term poor households would bring many of them out of poverty.

Although the no-unemployment and $4.21-minimum-wage simulations did not greatly reduce the proportion of persons below our long-term poverty line (125 percent of the official line), the effects were somewhat more pronounced for persons in severe long-term poverty (below 75 percent of the official line). For nonmetro Blacks, severe long-term poverty in the recent period would have been reduced from 13.5 to 11.7 percent by the elimination of unemployment and to 10.6 percent by a $4.21 minimum wage. For metro Blacks, the comparable figures were 10.2, 7.3, and 8.1 percent. There was virtually no change for Whites, less than 1 percent of whom were severe long-term poor in this period. The changes for Blacks in severe long-term poverty are proportionately larger than those obtained using a 125 percent threshold, but still quite small in absolute terms.

Clearly the extent of nonmetropolitan poverty would not be reduced very much by either an increased (and full-coverage) minimum wage of the magnitude currently politically feasible or the elimination of unemployment for heads currently seeking work. This rather disheartening conclusion appears to be due to two facts noted earlier: average family sizes of the long-term poor are sufficiently large that even full-time, year-round work by the head does not produce a poverty-level income unless the wage is considerably higher than we simulated here; and there is substantially more time "out of the labor force" than "unemployed" among heads of long-term poor families, especially when those heads are women.

It should be kept in mind that our simulations involved only the heads of our sample households. We did not attempt to simulate the effects of minimum-wage changes and eliminating unemployment for wives or other family members. This seemed to us a reasonable simplification, since most long-term poor families appear to have only one adult present most of the time (nonmetropolitan Whites are the exception). But it is possible that for a significant minority of households, these policies would increase the incomes of wives and teens sufficiently to raise the family out of poverty. On the other hand, we did not subtract unemployment compensation when we computed the postsimulation poverty rates, so the effects of the no-unemployment simulation are probably overestimated. Nor did we subtract in either simulation any means-tested income such as Food Stamps or Aid to Families with Dependent Children (AFDC) income, even though such benefits would have been reduced substantially as employment earnings rose. Our results are similar to those obtained by Hill and Hartmann (1988) using data from the Survey of Income and Program Participation on female heads.

Emergency Help from Friends and Family

At any given level of income, help from friends or relatives, whether in the form of money or time, can be crucial in an emergency. In 1980 the PSID asked whether respondents had friends or relatives who could provide "several hundred dollars more than they had available or could borrow from an institution." About three in five of the long-term poor responded affirmatively—a fraction that varied little between Blacks and Whites or within or outside of metropolitan areas (see Table 4.5). Even greater proportions of the long-term poor said that they had friends or relatives on whom they could count for spending "a lot of time helping out" if an emergency arose. Interestingly, poor Blacks were just as likely as nonpoor Blacks to say that emergency help was available (data not shown on Table 4.5), corroborating Stack's (1974) conclusions in her study of urban Blacks. In contrast, nonmetro poor Whites were considerably less likely than nonmetro poor Blacks to have such help available.

Public Transfers

The two largest transfer programs for the able-bodied poor are Aid to Families with Dependent Children (AFDC) and the Food Stamp program. Although during the study period AFDC technically provided benefits to two-parent families in about half the states, the majority of AFDC families are headed by a single mother. Transfer receipt among our sample of long-term poor, summarized in Table 4.5 shows that the vast majority of the long-term poor in families with able-bodied heads in both metropolitan and nonmetropolitan areas received Food

Table 4.5

Emergency Private Help Available and Transfer-Income Receipt for Long-Term Poor Persons Living in Households with Able-bodied Heads

	Black				White			
	Nonmetro		Metro		Nonmetro		Metro	
	Recent	Early	Recent	Early	Recent	Early	Recent	Early
Emergency loan available*	60 %	N.A.	71 %	N.A.	60 %	N.A.	60 %	N.A.
Emergency other help available*	95	N.A.	80	N.A.	79	N.A.	84	N.A.
Years received food stamps								
No years	7	24	6	11	18	43	10	5
Minority of years	31	59	23	36	37	53	29	57
Majority of years	48	15	40	46	39	4	45	29
All years	15	3	31	6	5	0	16	9
Years received AFDC								
No years	47	60	24	26	56	86	21	38
Minority of years	24	35	27	35	13	12	50	30
Majority of years	20	6	26	26	28	1	24	25
All years	9	0	22	13	3	0	6	7
Years received any cash transfers or food stamps								
No years	6	11	4	7	17	35	10	4
Minority of years	27	57	10	25	35	61	26	40
Majority of years	40	23	40	40	35	4	38	31
All years	27	8	46	29	14	0	27	25

Source: Panel Study of Income Dynamics.

*Question asked only in 1980 interview. **"Cash transfers" include AFDC, other welfare, SSI, or RSDI.

Table reads: 60 percent of long-term poor Blacks living in nonmetropolitan areas were in households that reported the availability of emergency loans from friends or relatives.

Stamps, AFDC, or some other form of public transfer payment at least once between 1976 and 1985. Receipt of benefits from both the AFDC and Food Stamp programs was much higher than in the previous decade, and the transfer-income receipt was much more prevalent within than outside of metropolitan areas.

The final rows of Table 4.5 show that at least five in six long-term poor persons (in households with nonelderly, never-disabled heads) were in a household that received Food Stamps, AFDC, other welfare, or Social Security benefits at least some of the time. Blacks were especially likely to have benefitted from one of these transfer programs. Both Blacks and Whites made increased use of these programs between the two decades, both within and outside of metropolitan areas. This is attributable in part to the higher percentage of female-headed families among the long-term poor during that period. Receipt of Food Stamps was more common than any other benefits for all groups and for both periods, and Food Stamp receipt dominated the ''All Programs'' results. (Food Stamps are available to two-parent families, but AFDC is not in many states, so it is not surprising that Food Stamp usage is much more widespread.)

The Long-Term Poor: An "Underclass" or "Deserving Poor"?

Popular discussions often equate the ''underclass'' with the long-term poor. For example, although Auletta (1982) focused on the deviant behavior of individuals he observed in both metropolitan and nonmetropolitan job-training programs, he based his estimate of the size of the nation's ''underclass'' on an analysis of individuals whose incomes, not including government transfers, were below the poverty line in at least three of five years. While certain behavioral indicators of ''underclass'' membership (e.g., welfare receipt, female headship, little schooling) are undoubtedly correlated with low incomes, we know that a substantial number of intact, working families (especially in nonmetropolitan areas) also risk long-term poverty, as do the elderly and disabled.

We explored the linkages between long-term poverty and both ''underclass'' and ''deserving'' characteristics by classifying the long-term poor according to the number of years in which they lived in households displaying either ''underclass'' or ''deserving'' characteristics. We used the following indicators of ''underclass'' characteristics: (1) AFDC income was more than half of total family income, (2) the household head was female, (3) the household head was employed less than half-time, and (4) the household head had no high-school diploma. In composing this list, we were guided by a rough consensus among researchers writing about ''underclass'' characteristics rather than by our personal views of what ought to constitute ''underclass'' or ''deserving'' behavior.

Our list of ''deserving'' scenarios included the following: (1) the household head was aged 65 or older, (2) the household head reported a severe disability, (3) the household head or wife was employed more than half-time, and (4) the household head was married, with the spouse present. Since this list includes two characteristics—age and disability status—excluded from our "able-bodied" subsample of long-term poor, we present data on "deserving" characteristics for the entire sample of long-term poor.

A look at the distribution of "underclass" and "deserving" characteristics (Table 4.6) shows that the sample of long-term poor displays both "deserving" and "underclass" characteristics. A majority of all groups of able-bodied long-term poor had at least one "underclass" characteristic in every one of the ten years. But at the same time, all groups of the long-term poor also had at least one "deserving" characteristic in a majority of the ten years, although this proportion declined from the early to the recent period, particularly in metro areas.

That nonmetro poor families displayed both "underclass" and "deserving" characteristics is hardly surprising, given the information we have already presented. Among the "underclass" characteristics, female headship has become much more prevalent for both Blacks and Whites. While substantial work is more the rule than the exception in nonmetro poor families, most experienced at least some years in which work hours fell short of the half-time mark. Among the "deserving" characteristics, the prevalence of disabilities or old age among the heads of long-term poor families was quite high, as was substantial work among the able-bodied heads of poor households.

We are left with a conclusion that reinforces doubts about the conceptual utility of attempts to categorize the poor as "underclass," "undeserving," or "deserving." Our data clearly show the futility of attempts to provide empirical content to these conceptual categories, especially when the data are based on an observation window of several years.

SUMMARY

Our investigation of long-term poverty in nonmetropolitan areas gives cause for both hope and pessimism. Most encouraging are the experiences of nonmetro Blacks, almost all of whom live in the South. Although they are still much more likely to be poor than are Whites, the incidence of long-term poverty, and especially of severe long-term poverty, among Blacks living in households headed by an able-bodied person has fallen dramatically since the late 1960s. In fact, the combination of improvement in economic conditions for nonmetro Blacks and deterioration for Blacks living in metropolitan areas has all but eliminated the metro/nonmetro gap in the incidence of severe long-term poverty among Blacks.

More generally, for several measures of poverty and family characteristics associated with poverty, there was a tendency for the less well off groups— nonmetropolitan Whites and both metro and nonmetro Blacks—to become more like the best-off poor group, metro Whites. For most poverty and other measures, the pattern was one of little change among metro Whites, while the other groups

Table 4.6
"Underclass" and "Deserving" Characteristics of Long-Term Poor Persons

	Black				White			
	Nonmetro		Metro		Nonmetro		Metro	
	Recent	Early	Recent	Early	Recent	Early	Recent	Early
Years with any of four "underclass" characteristics*								
No years	2 %	0 %	1 %	1 %	10 %	19 %	8 %	3 %
Minority of years	3	5	2	8	27	8	19	3
Majority of years	4	14	16	13	13	13	19	18
All years	92	82	81	79	51	61	55	76
Years with any of four "deserving" characteristics**								
No years	6	1	11	7	2	2	4	5
Minority of years	20	15	31	30	16	7	26	21
Majority of years	30	27	30	24	13	18	22	21
All years	44	57	29	39	69	73	48	53

Source: Panel Study of Income Dynamics.

*(1) More than half of cash income derived from AFDC; (2) female head; (3) head employed less than half-time; (4) head completed less than twelve years of school. Sample is restricted to long-term poor persons living in households with able-bodied heads.

**(1) Head age 65 or older; (2) head severely disabled; (3) head or spouse employed more than half-time; (4) head married with spouse present. Sample includes all long-term poor persons.

Table reads: 2 percent of long-term poor Blacks living in nonmetropolitan areas were in households that failed to exhibit at least one "underclass" characteristics in at least one of the ten years in the "recent" period (1976–85).

moved more or less dramatically toward the levels of metro Whites. The major exception to this pattern was the continuing rise in the proportion of households headed by women in all groups.

The improvements for nonmetro Blacks occurred despite an increase in the number of single-parent Black families in nonmetro areas and despite increased unemployment, stemming perhaps from economic "restructuring" in nonmetro areas. Two factors appeared critical: higher wages, possibly related to dramatically higher schooling levels for recent cohorts, and smaller family sizes.

Unfortunately, continuing improvement for Blacks does not appear likely. Economic conditions during the 1980s were not as favorable as in the 1970s, and this led to an increased incidence of poverty in nonmetro areas. But even a growing nonmetro economy may not produce improvements like those seen in the 1970s, since so much more poverty among nonmetro Blacks now occurs in female-headed families with lower levels of labor-force participation and fewer work hours among participants. Our simple simulations involving the elimination of unemployment and of very low wages produced disappointingly small reductions in poverty.

Long-term poverty in nonmetropolitan areas is much less pervasive among Whites than among Blacks. Like Blacks, nonmetro Whites were not as disadvantaged relative to their metro counterparts in the 1980s as they had been in the late 1960s and early 1970s. Rising schooling levels and falling family sizes probably helped some nonmetro White families to avoid poverty. In addition, higher and fairly stable rates of two-parent families and labor-force participation have made prospects for nonmetro Whites somewhat brighter than for nonmetro Blacks.

Despite these improvements, we estimate that more than four million people— half of them children, and one-third of all nonmetro Blacks—live in long-term poverty in nonmetropolitan areas. Two million of the long-term nonmetro poor live in families where the head is neither aged or disabled. Few of the issues arising in the urban "underclass" debate are relevant here: labor-force participation is extensive among the able-bodied nonmetro poor, while long-term welfare receipt is not. Most of the long-term poor are "living by the rules," in that they work at least part-time most years, and yet the combination of low earnings when they do work and low transfer benefits when they do not means that their family income falls short of the poverty line.

While our simulations of "no unemployment" and "higher universal minimum wage" showed discouragingly small effects on poverty, employment and training policies may still hold the key to reductions in nonmetro poverty among families headed by "able-bodied" adults. However, labor-market approaches to reducing poverty must be undertaken with an awareness of the problems faced by the nonmetro poor.

First, especially for the increasing numbers of women raising families by themselves, the relatively low number of hours they spend in the labor force limits the effectiveness of programs that assume that trainees will be available for full-time, year-round work. It will be crucial to ensure adequate child care and to encourage employers to provide jobs with flexible hours to accommodate parenting activities if single mothers are to increase their work hours. Second, again with the increasing number of female-headed families with children in mind, we must address the persistent gender gap in wage rates, a gap that is largely inexplicable on the basis of education, work experience, and other qualifications.

Third, despite recent improvements, schooling attainments in nonmetro areas continue to lag behind those in metro areas. Given the likely importance of increased schooling in reducing long-term poverty during the last twenty years, there is a strong case for increased investments in schooling. Fourth, for Blacks, the deteriorating economic conditions in the cities make rural-to-urban migration strategies much less promising than before.

Fifth, we should recognize that there are families, especially those with large numbers of children, whose earnings alone are unlikely to raise them to a decent standard of living, even given the successful implementation of the employment and training policies noted earlier. For these families, we need to consider some form of earned income supplement such as an enhanced earned income tax credit, perhaps combined with a child's allowance.

Finally, let us underscore a point made briefly earlier: More than half of the long-term poor lived in families headed by persons who were elderly or disabled at some time during the decade, and, if anything, that proportion has grown. Surprising numbers of children—one-sixth of all children and 42 percent of long-term poor children—live in such households. Labor-market policies can be expected to have even less impact on these poor families than on those with "able-bodied" heads. Clearly the increases in Social Security benefits and the adoption of the Supplemental Security Income program during the 1970s have not eliminated poverty among families headed by the elderly and disabled.

NOTES

This research was supported by the Ford Foundation's Rural Poverty and Resources Program and the Aspen Institute's Rural Economic Policy Program. We are grateful to Deborah Laren for her research assistance and to Dorothy Duncan and Isaac Shapiro for helpful comments.

1. The poverty estimates for Blacks and Whites presented in the first row of Table 4.1 are based on fairly large samples and are therefore quite precise. Differences in the incidence estimates for Blacks between the two periods of at least 2.5 percentage points are statistically significant at the 5 percent level; for Whites, differences of 1 percent or more are statistically significant. (These confidence intervals take into account the design effects induced by the clustered PSID sample.) Corresponding significant differences of poverty estimates for the able-bodied samples presented at the bottom of the table are about 9 and 3 percent for Blacks and Whites in nonmetro areas and 4 and 2 percent for Blacks and Whites in metro areas.

2. Specifically, the percentages of nonmetro Blacks with size-adjusted family incomes

below 125 percent and 75 percent of the poverty line were 36.8 and 13.5 percent, respectively, during the 1976–85 period. (These percentages are shown in Figure 4.3.) The corresponding percentages for the 1981–85 period were 39.8 and 14.7 percent. The corresponding figures for metropolitan Blacks during the 1976–85 period were 24.4 and 10.2 percent, and during the 1981–85 period, 24.5 and 13.8 percent.

3. As shown at the bottom of Table 4.2, the number of able-bodied long-term poor, especially among nonmetro Whites, is quite small, making the sampling errors much larger for these estimates than for those presented in Table 4.1. For Whites, differences between "recent" and "early" periods or between metro and nonmetro subsamples need to be at least 12 to 20 percentage points to attain statistical significance at the 5 percent level. (Proportions close to 50 percent have larger confidence intervals than proportions closer to 0 or 100 percent.) For nonmetro Blacks, corresponding differences between recent and early periods must be at least 11 percentage points. For metropolitan Blacks, corresponding differences between recent and early periods must be at least 6 percentage points. In comparing nonmetro and metro Blacks, differences must be at least 9 percentage points.

Appendix

Description of Sample and Poverty Measure

SAMPLE

Our analysis is based on data from the 1968–86 waves of the Panel Study of Income Dynamics (Survey Research Center 1984), to date, a twenty-two-year longitudinal study that has conducted an annual interview with a sample of about 5,000 families since 1968. The study's original design oversampled low-income households; therefore, all of the analyses presented here use sample weights to adjust for both differential initial sampling fractions and differential rates of nonresponse. A number of investigations of the quality of PSID data (e.g., Becketti et al. 1988; Duncan and Hill 1989) suggest that they provide representative estimates of the U.S. population.

To facilitate our focus on trends, we analyzed two separate subsamples from the PSID: one for individuals covering the period from 1976 to 1985, and a comparable sample covering the period from 1967 to 1976. These two ten-year periods overlap in a single year (1976). Requiring that individuals be present in all ten years in either period was undesirable, since it would have eliminated individuals for whom poverty status was measured in most but not all years, in particular, children born soon after the beginning of the ten-year period. We settled on the rule that an individual had to be present in at least five of the ten years.

Frequent changes over time in the composition of families create a number of potential problems for analysis. This led us to use the individual as our unit of analysis. Individuals remain unique over time, even though the "household" in which they reside may contain a very different collection of individuals in two different years. Our estimates of household characteristics are based on a definition of household that includes cohabitors and other economically dependent members, but excludes economically independent members such as roomers and employees. The household-level characteristics of individuals (e.g., sex, age, and schooling of the head) are usually those of the household in which the individual resided in the middle year (i.e., 1982 or 1972.)

However, two of the characteristics that define our major subgroups in each period—metropolitan/nonmetropolitan residence and ethnicity—were based on data from the most recent year of the period in which the individual was present in the sample. We examined the extent of movement between metropolitan and nonmetropolitan areas for individuals in families with "able-bodied" heads in each of our decades and found it to be small but growing somewhat. In the early period, 1967–76, 97 percent of metro Blacks and 89 percent of metro Whites (characterized at the end of the period) spent the entire period in metro areas (although not necessarily the same one). For nonmetro residents in 1967–76, 94 percent of Blacks and 92 percent of Whites spent the entire decade in nonmetro areas. In the recent period, 1976–85, 88 percent of Blacks and 83 percent of Whites who ended the decade in metro areas had spent all of it in such areas. Among those who ended the "recent" decade in nonmetro areas, 91 percent of Blacks and 74 percent of Whites spent the entire decade there. It appears, therefore, that some metro Whites in households with able-bodied heads moved to nonmetro areas, primarily in the late 1970s and 1980s.

The third defining characteristic—whether the head of the family was aged 65 or more, or disabled, at any time during the period—is based on the entire period. (A person is "disabled" for this purpose if he or she says that he or she has a disability that limits "a lot" the amount of work he or she can do).

Finally, a note on ethnic terminology: We have used the terms "Blacks" and "Whites" throughout rather than the more precise "African Americans" and "European Americans" both for the sake of brevity and because the former have been more commonly used in the past twenty-five years.

DEFINITION OF LONG-TERM POVERTY

The concept of "poverty" as used in this chapter is that known as "income poverty" and compares a family's cash income with a defined "standard of need" based on family size and composition. That need standard is based, in turn, on estimates of the amount of expenditures necessary to maintain a given material standard of living.

The selection of the accounting periods over which to accumulate income and needs standards and to measure poverty is no mere technical matter. The proportion of the population said to be below the poverty line declines as the accounting period is lengthened. David and Fitzgerald (1988) found that poverty counts based on calendar quarters were about 30 percent higher than those for the same families based on calendar-year accounting periods; Ruggles (1989) found that poverty counts based on calendar months showed poverty rates more than double those based on calendar years. We find in our current analysis that a ten-year accounting period, the basis for our measure of long-term poverty, produces poverty rates 25 to 30 percent lower than those based on a single calendar year.

Our choice of a ten year accounting period to represent long-term poverty should not be taken as implying that income poverty (and the associated material hardship) experienced for a year, a quarter, or even a month is somehow illusory or otherwise less "real" than the long-term variety. There may indeed be a few self-employed persons who have very low incomes for a large part of a year but who are able to draw on savings and borrowed money to maintain a comfortable standard of living. But the great majority of low-income households have few or no such resources to draw upon and probably begin to feel very real financial hardship after a few weeks of subpoverty income.

Poverty is usually defined by a comparison of total before-tax annual household income and a poverty threshold set by the U.S. government based on the number and ages of household members. The official poverty threshold for a family of four in 1988 was about $12,000 per year; the line is adjusted for inflation each year on the basis of the Consumer Price Index. Since household members are presumed to share the household's total income, a household's poverty status is taken to apply to each member of the household.

We can view the definition of poverty as a special case of a more general "income-to-needs" measure of household economic status, which is obtained by dividing each household's income by its corresponding poverty threshold. In 1988 members of a four-person household whose income totaled $36,000 would have an income-to-needs ratio of about 3.0 and be designated as nonpoor in that year; members of four-person households with a total household income of only $6,000 would have an income-to-needs ratio of about 0.5 and be designated as poor. Poverty statistics collected and published by the U.S. Census Bureau use an annual calendar-year accounting period and simply divide the one-year income-to-needs distribution at 1.0.

Our measure of "long-term" poverty is based on the ratio of an individual's n-year aggregate household income to his n-year aggregate poverty threshold, where n is the number of years in ten when a particular sample individual was observed to be living in a sample threshold. For example, if n were equal to three and a person's income-to-needs ratios in the three years were $7,000/$10,000, $9,000/$10,000, and $24,000/$12,000, then his or her ratio of three-year total income to needs would be 1.25 ($40,000/$32,000). (In fact, most sample individuals were observed for all ten years, and we required that individuals be observed for at least five of the ten years.) Our definition of "long-term" poverty is based on income-to-needs ratios of 1.25 or less, although we also present data based on lines drawn at 1.0 and .75. Given our division of the sample by ethnicity and the restriction to households headed by able-bodied, nonelderly persons, the 1.25 figure was chosen to maximize the number of observations of "long-term" poor.

Part II

Poor People and Poor Places

Chapter 5

Race, Gender, and Poverty in the Rural South: African American Single Mothers

Bonnie Thornton Dill and Bruce B. Williams

It is an inescapable fact of life in the rural South today that single mothers are overwhelmingly African American and that African American single mothers are overwhelmingly poor. The growing presence of single mothers in the rural South reflects a national trend, one that has received greatest attention as a Northern, urban "ghetto" phenomenon. Nevertheless, data show that this is a widespread pattern that is currently increasing in all segments and regions of the society. Wherever it occurs, it is strongly associated with poverty. The conflation of race, gender, and poverty among single mothers in the rural South is rooted in factors related to the historical treatment of Blacks, women, and the poor.

The American South has a unique history with regard to race. Unlike other regions of the country, the history of slavery and racism plays a dominant role in the lives of most Southerners, urban and rural, White and African American. Joe Feagin stated that "Southern culture has perhaps been the most distinctive regional culture, because of the racial oppression of Black Americans and the subsequent rationalizations for that thoroughgoing racial discrimination" (1989, p. 79). Lewis Killian observed that "for a Southerner, the salient fact was and is whether he was White or Black; all else is secondary" (1970, p. 16).

Gender has also taken on its own particular form in the South. A strong patriarchal and conservative culture continues to define women as second-class citizens whose primary role is as keepers of culture, family, and kin (Dillman 1988).

The South has undergone considerable change in recent years, and many of the practices that were openly discriminatory toward Blacks and women have been eliminated. Nevertheless, African American women remain concentrated in poverty and low-wage jobs, and this fact suggests that discrimination still structures their life choices and chances. This chapter focuses specifically upon African American single mothers in the rural South today and attempts to shed light on their circumstances as Southern women, as African Americans living in the rural South, and as single Black women who live, work, and raise their families in a Southern rural political economy.

FAMILY STRUCTURE AND POVERTY IN THE RURAL SOUTH

Most research on family structure and poverty has focused upon low-income Blacks in urban settings. In the 1960s researchers pointed out a pattern of growth in female-headed households among this population that was linked to poverty and to indicators of social disorganization (Moynihan 1965; Clark 1965). Some of this research stirred considerable controversy because of its emphasis upon cultural factors, including family structure, as primary sources of poverty. Debates ensued over the relative importance of cultural and racial characteristics versus economic and social structural factors as sources of low-income status. Within the last several years there has been a resurgence of this debate. On the one hand, studies suggest that economic conditions are a major factor explaining the relationship between family structure and poverty. These include such things as the weakening economy of the 1970s and the increased marginalization of Black males in the labor force (Baca Zinn 1987; Wilson 1987). On the other, a public discussion emphasizes social and cultural patterns—identified as the disintegration of traditional family structure, an acceptance of female-headed families in low-income Black culture, and the presence of social programs that foster dependency—as primary forces responsible for the maintenance of poverty and the rise in female-headed households among the urban poor (Lemann 1986; Moyers 1986). The new dimension in the current discussion is the suggestion that the increasing availability of social welfare and income-transfer programs—specifically Medicaid, Aid to Families with Dependent Children (AFDC), Food Stamps, and the Anti-Poverty Program—have fostered an increase of female-headed families in this population (Murray 1984; Moynihan 1986). In contrast to this perspective, most research argues that there are multiple factors associated with the rise in female-headed families, poverty, and dependency. They include demographic changes, low wages, and increased male joblessness, as well as changing social and cultural trends (Wilson 1987; Bane 1986; Ellwood 1988).

Although social science research and public debate have focused primarily upon urban Black populations, it is widely acknowledged that female-headed families are now a persistent pattern in American society. In 1985, 23 percent of all children lived in single-parent families. Of these, 54 percent were Black, 29 percent were Latino, and 18 percent were White. Overwhelmingly, the one parent is the mother. Feminist scholarship has contributed to efforts to understand this phenomenon by identifying the importance of gender in the relationship between family structure and poverty. Sociologist Diana Pearce (1978) noted that in 1976 two-thirds of the poor in the United States were women with dependent children, and she projected that this proportion would continue to increase through the 1990s. She labeled this phenomenon "the feminization of poverty," calling attention to the fact that gender was an important determinant of poverty status. Discussions of the feminization of poverty have appropriately criticized the framers of this concept for neglecting the fundamental effects of race and class on the production of a low-income population. These critiques have pointed to the long-term impoverishment of both women and men in the African American community and the different causes of poverty for White and Black women who are single parents (Burnham 1986; Wilson 1987). Black women are more likely to be poor before they become single parents, but White women are more likely to become poor as a result of becoming single parents (Baca Zinn and Dill 1990). Although the concept of the feminization of poverty must be modified in its explanation of the relationship between family structure and poverty, it is still quite clear that there is a strong relationship between gender and poverty. Tickamyer and Tickamyer (1988), for example, identify three basic reasons why women are more likely to be poor than men: the low wages of women in the work force; the high participation of women in unpaid labor; and state policies toward women's paid and unpaid work. These factors distinguish women's poverty from that of men, and an awareness of them is essential to any effort to understand the causes and consequences of impoverishment among female single parents.

In rural America the proportion of female single-parent households is smaller than in urban areas, but this family form is growing. Families in nonmetropolitan areas are more likely to have two parents. They are also more likely to have at least one of those parents in the labor force, although that status does not keep the family out of poverty. In contrast to the urban underclass, which is largely Black and Hispanic, the rural poor are more likely to be White. Yet among African Americans, those who live in rural areas have higher poverty rates and a more persistent pattern of poverty than those living in urban areas (Greenstein 1987). Nationally, rural areas are characterized by lower rates of female-headed households; yet among rural communities in the South, the proportion of poor families headed by women has almost doubled in the last two decades. Twenty-seven percent of poor Black families were headed by single mothers with children in 1960. By 1980 that percentage had risen to 59 percent. For Whites, the proportion rose from 16 percent in 1960 to 27 percent in 1980. In addition, in the rural South the long-standing impoverishment of the Black population is seen most starkly among female-headed families. For example, Allen and Rexroat (1989) reported that the 1984 poverty rate in the nonmetropolitan South was 79.7 percent for families headed by never-married Black women and 60.4 percent for those headed by formerly married Black women. The result is a much higher concentration of African American women and children in poverty than Whites (Southeast Women's Employment Coalition 1986).

THE RURAL SOUTH TODAY

The contemporary South is a patchwork quilt of rural, urban, and suburban communities that are being reshaped at a rate and in forms that were previously unheard of in the region. The civil rights movement, feminism, and the migration of Northerners to the Sunbelt are just a few of the factors that contribute to the rapid social change taking place in the region. Nevertheless, as Dillman (1988) argues, Southern culture is "quite formidable," and new ideas and values confront traditional ones that emphasize the importance of church, family, community, kinship networks, genealogical connections, and "a strong individual and collective commitment to maintain differences in sex-role behavior and attitudes toward men and women" (Dillman 1988, p. 10). The three most important elements that maintain the traditional values that affect contemporary life chances of rural women in the South are the Bible Belt, the Black Belt, and the color line.

The Bible Belt

The Bible Belt is a term used to define a region of the country where religion, particularly fundamentalism with its emphasis on the literal interpretation and authenticity of the Scriptures, is dominant. According to Charles R. Wilson (1989), H. L. Mencken, who coined the term in the 1920s, identified the rural Midwest and South as the primary geographical locations of the Bible Belt and called Jackson, Mississippi, "the heart of the Bible and Lynch Belt." Religion is conservative and paramount. A recent Gallup Poll study on religion in America concluded that "the Bible Belt is real, not just a political saying" (*Commercial Appeal* 1987, p. A11).

Southern religion is uniquely different from religion in other areas of the country. This difference is well summarized by Samuel Hill:

(1) The forms that are common in the region are relatively homogenous. The range of popular options is narrow. (2) The South is the only society in Christendom where the evangelical family of Christians is dominant. . . . (3) A set of four common convictions occupies a normative southern religious position. Movements and denominations in the South are judged for authenticity in the popular mind by how well they support these beliefs: (a) The Bible is the sole reference point of belief and practice; (b) direct and dynamic access to the Lord is open to all; (c) morality is defined in individualistic and personal terms; and (d) worship is informal. (1989, p. 1269)

The result, according to Hill, is that the Bible Belt South is a "limited-options" culture. Hence organizational and institutional activities and responsibilities and individual roles and statuses are narrowly and rigidly prescribed.

In many instances roles and statuses are defined and sanctioned by Scripture. For example, according to fundamentalist Christianity, God created woman as helpmate for man; as a helpmate she has a secondary role of low status and power, even if she works outside the home (Flora and Johnson 1973). Although the church eventually served as the primary avenue for African American and White women to enter into the public life of politics and social activism, with rare exceptions, its dominant orientation is still the sanctioning of patriarchal domination in all aspects of Southern life. The sense of communalism incorporated into African American churches did not modify the patriarchal religious convictions as much as might be expected. Hence African American women have traditionally been excluded from positions of authority and control.

There is an intimate connection between the conservative religion of the South and its conservative politics, its economic development strategies, its race relations and social-change orientations, and the plight of rural African American women. As Sessions observed, "The White Southern church has mainly been a conservative, reinforcing agent for traditional values of White Southern society" (1989, p. 1282).

The Black Belt

The Black Belt refers to that geographical part of the South that historically is associated with cotton production, large plantations, and a large number of African Americans. This territory extends from Virginia into North Carolina, reaches through mid- and lower Georgia into mid-Alabama, traverses the length of Mississippi along the Mississippi River basin, and culminates in Arkansas and several Louisiana counties bordering the great river.

Today the counties comprising the Black Belt are essentially rural, poor, and still heavily populated by African American residents (Falk and Lyson 1988). These 147 counties contain the bulk of the rural African American population, and all of these counties are classified as "persistently low-income counties" by the Department of Agriculture. It is here that the life chances of African American women are most drastically affected by the legacy of the old South.

The Color Line

The South has a long and sordid history of racial oppression. A distinctive feature of that oppression has been the desire to maintain a color line to permanently separate Whites and African Americans at most levels of interaction. This tradition flows out of the history of slavery and the desire to maintain political and economic control over a free African American population.

A sense of ethnic group honor combines with religion in the South to create an overpowering sense of White racial group identity. This sense of White group identity helps to maintain the color line between racial groups and the class line within the White community. It allows the poorest of White Southerners into an exclusive club that sets them apart from any and all African Americans (Light 1972). It also keeps these same poor souls from allying with their African American counterparts to improve their mutual lot in life. Individual options remain few because of the social control inherent in the belief system.

This desire to maintain African Americans at the bottom of the social status hierarchy is most evident in the rural South, where traditional plantation culture has its roots. It manifests itself in the fact that the rural South is the most disadvantaged sector of the country and rural African American women one of the most destitute of populations.

Women in the South

The definitions of women's place in this region of the country are even more distinctive because of the historical practice of miscegenation and the use of race in defining femininity. The association of White women with leisure, purity, and sexual repression and Black women with work and sexual permissiveness created a polarity among women while it maintained their dependence on one another. Southern women writers and activists, including the Grimke sisters, Jessie Daniel Ames (Hall 1979), and Lillian Smith (1949) have argued that the pedestals on which White women were placed rested, in essence, on the labor and sexual availability of African American female slaves. At the same time, the idealized image of the Southern lady served to control White women, to offer them protection in exchange for good behavior, and to maintain their status as private property. During the nineteenth century patriarchal control laid the groundwork for the conservative and limited definitions of women's roles that characterize the region today. Fannie Lou Hamer, who worked to establish the Mississippi Freedom Democratic party and to register Blacks to vote in Mississippi during the 1960s, captured the tensions and ties between Black and White women in the South in one of her speeches:

You thought that you was more because you was a woman, and especially a White woman, you had this kind of angel feeling that you were untouchable. You know that? There's nothing under the sun that made you believe that you was just like me. . . . But coming to the realization of the thing, her freedom is shackled in chains to mine, and she realizes for the first time that she is not free until I am free. (Lerner 1972, p. 609)

Slavery, along with the institutionalization of the color line, provided the framework in which African American women developed definitions of women's place that are distinctive, yet exist within the larger constraints that define women's roles within the region. African American women in the South, then, must be understood as a distinctive group whose treatment is a product not simply of the treatment of women alone, or of African Americans alone, but of a combination of two oppressed statuses that resulted in a unique category for African American women in the South (J. Jones 1985; Collins 1990).

These historical patterns have shaped the life chances and choices of African American women in the region for over 350 years. This legacy is seen today in the policies, practices, and attitudes that shape the employment opportunities for Black women and that define the social welfare programs that most frequently affect their lives. Low-income African American women who are single mothers are most vulnerable and therefore most likely to live their lives within the deepest shadows of the slave tradition.

JOBS AND EMPLOYMENT

One of the primary reasons that rural African American women are in such dire straits is that they are concentrated in the worst-paying jobs, are more isolated than other workers from any collective-action forums, or have no job at all. They tend to have fewer options than other groups in this limited-option environment. A recent study by Falk and Lyson (1988) found that more than 90 percent of rural African American women were employed in these kinds of "bad" jobs. They concluded that "the figures become so pronounced that in Black Belt counties, it is nearly a truism to say that if a Black woman is employed at all, it will be in a bad job" (1988, p. 112). Indeed, the largest single employment category for African American women is "unemployed." They noted that the model job categories for employed Southern White women are secretaries or clerks, while those of African American women are maids, cooks, or low-skill machine operatives (1988, chap. 5).

The fact that since the 1980s African American women have held over 50 percent of the operative positions in many Southern factories (Frederickson 1989) is of little consolation when most of these jobs are minimum-wage, dirty, hazardous, and nonunion. These conditions characterize the textile industry, the South's largest industrial employer, and the tobacco and catfish industries—all concentrated in rural areas.

In describing the tradition of employment in the tobacco industry in North Carolina, the Southeast Women's Employment Coalition provided a normative description of rural industrial employment in the South:

The vast majority of Black women were employed as unskilled and semi-skilled workers in the hot, dirty, and labor-intensive prefabrication division of the production process (e.g. in removing the leaf from the stems). White women were employed as semi-skilled machine operators or assistants to male operatives in the manufacturing departments. Skilled and supervisory positions were reserved for white men. (1986, p. 25)

The same scenario is played out across the South in traditional and new industries. For example, the new near-billion-dollar catfish industry in the Mississippi Delta employs a work force in which the overwhelming majority of workers are African American females. However, these women are concentrated on the low-wage, unskilled processing assembly lines. All who tour the processing plants cannot help but notice the lack of White men or women working the assembly lines and the absence of African American supervisors throughout the facilities. Recent unionization and a strike that was supported by an impending national boycott of Mississippi-produced catfish have only recently (December 1990) resulted in a salary increase above the minimum wage and safer working conditions.

It is important to emphasize that neither lack of human capital nor the geographical location (that is, rural or urban) are the major reasons for the dire employment conditions of rural African Americans; racial discrimination is (Cobb 1984; Lichter 1988; Wright 1986). It is no accident that employment opportunities for rural African Americans have not changed significantly since 1970 and are not expected to change in the foreseeable future (Lichter 1988). Louis Swanson, in "The Human Dimension of the Rural South in Crisis," focuses on the key issue:

An unsavory dimension of the rural South in crisis is the persistence of overt and subtle racism. . . . The historical patterns of Southern apartheid continue to occur for those areas with a high proportion of Black residents . . . racism is still a formidable foe to the vitalization of the rural South and an important dimension of the current crisis. (1988, p. 96)

Two notions must be emphasized here: (1) the Delta and the Black Belt economies, as they exist today, are the conscious construction of the rural White elite (Lyson 1989; Cobb 1990); and (2) the class structure of the rural South is organized to maintain the "master-slave" past, relative to race (James 1988). This means that economic development will be controlled by the White elites through their efforts to keep human development needs of new businesses at a minimum. Low-wage jobs keep poor Blacks "in their place."

Under a system of selected economic development, local White elites accumulate large profits that are then invested in small amounts in their own communities and in much larger amounts outside their communities. For example, in one Mississippi county we found that many rural elites have large portions of their wealth invested in North Carolina. The system supporting development of low-wage jobs is reinforced at the state level by state policies that discourage unions, maintain low property income, and depend on high, regressive taxes, such as high gas, food, and auto-license taxes.

State and local officials are also known to informally steer potential foreign and Northern business and industrial investors away from heavily populated African American rural counties (Cobb 1984; Lyson 1988; Timberlake et al., 1991). This informal practice is called the "30 percent solution" because it is applied to counties with 30 percent or higher African American residency.

Existing within this environment, rural African American women find their options limited to a life of low-wage employment and welfare assistance. Although Brown and Warner (1989) present an excellent account of the totality of control that the rural White elite exert over African Americans, it cannot be truly appreciated until one sees it firsthand. From banking, wholesale, and retail to the legal, educational, and political systems, elite-group control remains nearly absolute in the Delta and Black Belt counties, with only slight inroads occurring in the political and educational domains in recent years.

To further complicate the problem, the transfer payments from the welfare system that hold many rural African American families together have been integrated into the formal system of local control and exploitation. Local employers routinely lay off African American workers in seasonal industries. Sometimes workers are laid off as they become eligible for raises or promotions. These workers then are forced to seek welfare for several months, at the least. If they are lucky, they are eventually recalled to work at their old salary and position levels. This can be expected several times a year, every year.

Another informal tactic used by employers to help maintain low wages in rural counties is to refrain from hiring a worker who is currently employed by another local businessman. In one Black Belt county an employer described to us a "gentleman's agreement" among businesses not to consider hiring an employee who was already working for another local company. Additionally, African American women are more likely to be hired as part-time workers—where status and security are lower than for White workers. Part-time work reduces the worker liability of the employer while it increases the need of the African American worker for social welfare support.

The employment and economic needs of rural African American women are not being addressed by the Southern Black Belt states in which they reside nor by any other of the major community institutions. While they operate at the bottom of the hierarchy of limited options, their needs increase daily, but their voices are ignored.

WORK, KIN, AND WELFARE

The organization of work is a key element not only in explaining the relationship between poverty and welfare among single mothers, but also in its influence on the nature of everyday life among low-income African American women in the rural South today. Of particular interest is the relationship between work, welfare, and family support networks. The literature on third-world development stresses the importance of understanding how the structure of the local labor force is a direct reflection of the structure of occupational opportunities available to the local population. This orientation emphasizes the relationship between poverty in peripheral regions, such as the South, to low-wage agricultural jobs, limited industrial opportunities, underemployment, and unemployment.

Our preliminary findings from research in rural Mississippi and Tennessee suggest that, as in the third world, low wages and underemployment in the South are made possible by laborers' reproductive costs being born by subsistence enclaves made up primarily of kin and informal-sector work (Portes 1985)—work that is disproportionately the burden of women (see, for example, Beneria and Sen 1981). Low wages and seasonal employment, when combined with child-care burdens and other gender-specific factors, tend to keep poor women poor. As pointed out earlier, employment in these near-minimum-wage jobs rarely provides for unemployment insurance, medical benefits, or retirement. Thus even those who acquire a decent living through work are vulnerable to poverty as periods of unemployment follow or are interspersed with periods of employment. Allen and Rexroat (1989) have pointed out that "economic growth in Southern metropolitan areas is associated with declining poverty among Black female-headed families. . . . In contrast, economic stagnation in the non-metro South is associated with increased levels of poverty among Black female-headed families" (1989, p. 2).

Given all these limitations, how do these women manage? How do African American single mothers living in the rural South survive and feed and care for their children and themselves? These are the questions we are seeking to answer in our current research project in selected counties in Mississippi and Tennessee (Dill 1988). Our early findings suggest that survival is a process of constantly struggling to acquire resources from three primary sources—work, welfare, and kin. The women that we have interviewed use different strategies, make different arrangements, and have different needs, but it is clear that without their kinship networks they would be extremely hard pressed to provide for themselves and their children.

An example is the case of Alfrenell. She is a divorced mother of two sons, employed at a retail store in a small town in a rural county. She works six days a week, from 8:30 A.M. until 4:00 P.M. on Mondays and Tuesdays, until 6:00 P.M. on Wednesdays and Fridays, and until noon on Thursdays, and from 7:30 A.M. until 6:00 P.M. on Saturdays. She earns $4 per hour and brings home $165 per week. Though divorced, she receives no child support or other money from her ex-husband, who has remained unemployed. Her wages make her ineligible for welfare; however, she does receive about $80 to $100 per month in Food Stamps. After work on Mondays, Tuesdays, and Thursdays, Alfrenell drives to a trade school about forty miles from her home for classes in cosmetology that begin at 5:00 P.M. She is confident that her trade-school training will provide her with a marketable skill that could raise her earnings and her standard of living. She has a relative who owns her own business in a midwestern city and has encouraged her to come and work with her when she completes her training. However, Alfrenell is reluctant to leave this community even for the prospect of a better standard of living. When one looks closely at how she manages to care for her children, work, and attend school, her reluctance to leave is quite understandable.

Alfrenell lives in a small apartment complex containing approximately twenty apartment units. Her brother and his wife also live in the complex. Her older son and her brother's son attend a parochial school within a block of their apartment. Her younger son is in Head Start. Because their uncle lives nearby, her sons see their uncle's house as a second home. Every day after work Alfrenell's sister or mother comes to her home to take care of the boys until Alfrenell gets home. On the days that she has trade-school classes, her sister helps the children with their homework, prepares their dinner, and stays until 10:00 or 11:00 P.M. when Alfrenell returns from school.

One of the things that makes it possible for Alfrenell to attend school in another town is her car. Although a car is a necessity for travelling to work, shopping, and obtaining other services in a rural community, most of the low-income women whom we have interviewed do not have one. Those few who do have difficulty maintaining it on their own. However, Alfrenell's father and brother are mechanics. Her dad has a small auto-repair business, and he and her brother keep her car running.

Services and resources provided by kin are the glue that holds Alfrenell's small family together. By combining her income from long hours of work at low pay with the noncash assistance she receives from her siblings and parents, along with government grants in the form of Food Stamps, Alfrenell keeps her family going. She has been able to make some choices to improve her children's education and her own and, therefore, holds on to the prospect that her life will indeed get better.

Another example of the ways in which kinship networks become essential elements in some of these women's survival strategies is apparent in the case of Ada Sue Flours. Ada is a 25-year-old mother of two children, ages 4 and 2. She complains bitterly about the lack of job opportunities in her community and the fact that she is unemployed despite her consistent efforts to find a job. Although she did not complete high school, she took up a trade at a local junior college as a cashier/clerk and completed the course, but has never been able to get a job. Ada receives Food Stamps and $120 per month from Aid to Families with Dependent Children (AFDC). She lives in a house with her brother and three other sisters and their six children. The brother is the primary breadwinner for the group, earning approximately $250 per month at a seasonal job that lasts about three months per year. Two of the sisters have three children each and receive $144 per month from AFDC. One sister is employed part-time in a fast-food restaurant in a nearby town, and her earnings are deducted from her monthly AFDC allotment. The third sister is unemployed and has no income and no children. The Food Stamp allotment is combined for the entire family of thirteen people and comes to $991 per month. Living together is a strategy this kinship group adopted in order to facilitate the survival of each subfamily within it. While pooling resources has helped, the group still faces a number of problems. Income from earnings is unsteady since those who work only do so seasonally or part-time. Taxes on the home are high ($500 to $800 per year), and they have been unable to pay these. In addition, they have at times had difficulty paying the utilities and have had them cut off. Ada Sue also indicated that they ran out of food at the end of almost every month. She says that she is looking for other living arrangements, even though it means that she will have to separate from her siblings. However, the reality is that options for low-income housing in their community are quite limited. Since she does not receive a housing allowance from AFDC, she will have to pay for housing out of her $120 per month allotment and whatever money she receives from her boyfriend, who is currently unemployed after working seven weeks in a local seasonal industry. In this case, the kinship network has become a means through which subfamilies pool and re-distribute resources from both work and welfare in order to raise, feed, and care for themselves and their children.

Barbara Porter has no kinship network to supplement her income. After years of conflict and problems, she ran away from the home of her stepfather and stepmother at the age of 14. She has lived on her own ever since, and although she sees her father and siblings occasionally, their relationship is strained and distant. Barbara married and had her first child when she was 16 years old. By the time she was 23 she had had all six of her children. She stayed with her husband for two years. When he left her for another woman, she got involved with an older man. As she describes it, they were together, off and on, for five years. During that time she had two children by him and two more by other men. He would drink, verbally abuse her, and often put her and the children out of the house. After five years she decided that she had had enough of that and left. It was only after she left him and had her youngest child that she learned about welfare. She applied and began receiving public assistance six years ago. That was also when she got her own place. This was an important transition for Barbara because it marked the beginning of some real stability in her life. Though she is very dissatisfied with her house, she is no longer dependent on a man, and that means a lot to her. She described those early years in the following way: "Mostly what I was doing was trying to keep a place to stay. And then had a child." Without family or a kinship network to draw on, Barbara turned to her relationships with men to find a source of support.

Today five of her children live with her. She receives $160 to $215 in child support for three of the children, AFDC of $192 per month, and between $450 and $475 in Food Stamps. In addition, she babysits for neighbors, sells cans, and has a boyfriend who "helps out" when he is working. She also has a close girlfriend with whom she trades all kinds of things including food, clothing, and furniture, and she participates in a social-service program that provides household and other goods to supplement her income. She estimates that her income is between $2,500 and $5,000 per year.

Barbara has never held a job, but she talks about how much she would like to have one, how much she would like the routine, and the importance of a weekly paycheck. However, what is apparent from all of these cases is that neither low-wage work nor welfare in the rural counties that we have studied provide enough money to support a woman and her children. Thus she is forced to find a variety of ways to supplement her income. For some women, this means living in their parents' house. For others, it involves combining resources with siblings. In Barbara's case it has meant that relationships with men as cohabitants or just boyfriends required some kind of financial exchange. Probably two-thirds of the women we have interviewed have boyfriends, and in every case the men are expected to provide financial help to the woman and her children.

CONCLUSION

Race, gender, and poverty intersect in the rural Black Belt South to create limited opportunities and options for African American women and their children. Low wages in the workplace and limited opportunities for African American women are complemented by low welfare payments for those who do not work. Kin and friends become essential elements in helping these families survive. Men participate in all of these networks as fathers, paying child support, as kin members, and as boyfriends "helping out." Their earnings, from whatever sources and however intermittent, are part of the resource pool.

In a 1978 study of urban ghetto poverty, Valentine concluded: "Work, welfare, and hustling must be combined in order to secure a minimum level of income for poor Black families" (p. 124). In the rural communities that we are studying, racial and gender discrimination, historical factors, Southern traditions, and a slow economy combine to make the primary task of low-income African American women one of survival. Like their urban sisters, they must "hustle" to bring together resources from a variety of people and places in order to care for their children and themselves. In the rural South they struggle to survive in a world that sets up obstacles because they are African American, because they are women, and because they are from poor families.

NOTE

The research reported here is part of a larger study on female-headed households in the mid-South that is supported by the Ford Foundation's Rural Poverty and Resources Program and the Aspen Institute's Rural Economic Policy Program.

Chapter 6

Persistent Poverty in Appalachia: Scarce Work and Rigid Stratification

Cynthia M. Duncan

Times have always been hard in Appalachia. During the early 1800s mountaineers scratched a living from the hillsides, supplementing subsistence farming with hunting and occasional trading. The region was sparsely settled and economically isolated, and the family was the center of every aspect of life (Blee and Billings 1986). After the Civil War Appalachia was drawn into the national economy. Speculators and businessmen from the Northeast came into the region to purchase the rich timber and mineral resources, and within a short time the region had shifted from its preindustrial dependence on relatively isolated family-based subsistence farms to an industrial wage economy (Blee and Billings 1986). For families in the mountains, this meant trading the uncertainty and hardships of making a livelihood with small farms for the uncertainty and vulnerability of seeking work in a volatile and oppressive industry (Eller 1982).

Over time the structure of work in the region—its scarcity, volatility, and control by a domineering industry—has created a community context that is both unstable and oppressive. Limited opportunity for steady work and income means that control over jobs is a source of wealth and power. Jobs are a kind of currency. Private employers give jobs to family members, friends, and, frequently, political supporters. The valuable, steady public-sector jobs and, in some instances, the benefits and opportunities available through welfare programs are part of an entrenched patronage-driven political system. In many Appalachian communities a few powerful families have control over most of the desirable opportunities in the private and public sectors.

Finding work often depends either on your family's reputation and network, "who you know," or on playing the patronage system right. Employers, workers, and those seeking work in Appalachian communities recognize that one does not get a given job based primarily on one's qualifications. Those from poor families are least likely to have either the reputation or political connections necessary to find steady work in this social structure. The corruption and favoritism that drive who gets opportunities to work or receive opportunities in public-sector programs undermine the quality of public institutions. Schools and other public programs that we expect to be open to everyone instead become part of a spoils system and fail to fulfill their role as support systems for poor people. Opportunities to escape poverty through work are blocked, and the public institutions that we expect to give people the education and skills they need to find work elsewhere are co-opted by a system of political patronage. The "social buffers" (see Wilson 1987) on which poor people depend when resources are limited in their own families do not work in these depressed communities.

Poor Appalachians live precarious lives in unstable, unpredictable communities, vulnerable to individual setbacks such as a job loss, illness of a family member, or even a broken-down car, as well as to the pervasive arbitrary control of those in power. They become trapped in poverty because there are few opportunities for steady work and income in their own communities and few opportunities to develop the skills and educational background necessary to find work elsewhere. They piece together a livelihood with intermittent work, help from family members, and various public assistance programs that can supplement too few hours of work and too low wages. They have little control over their lives.

"BROKEN IN SPIRIT AND BODY"?

Persistent poverty, high welfare dependence, and corrupt local officials in Appalachia were featured in lawyer Harry Caudill's *Night Comes to the Cumberland* (1963), clergyman Jack Weller's *Yesterday's People* (1965), and journalist John Fetterman's *Stinking Creek* (1967). These authors concluded that the Appalachian poor have given up trying to escape poverty and are resigned to living on welfare. They attributed continued poverty and welfare dependence to the "broken spirit" of the people. In a review in the *New York Times*, Harriette Arnow described Caudill's book as "the story of how this rich and beautiful land was changed into an ugly, poverty-ridden place of desolation, peopled mainly by the broken in spirit and body, the illiterate, the destitute and morally corroded" (1963). By emphasizing defeated individuals who have come to accept welfare dependency, Caudill, Weller, and Fetterman contributed to a widely held stereotype of lazy, dependent hillbillies who do not share American values about work. Sociologist Herman Lantz (1964) described coal communities as thoroughly resigned, with apathetic, hopeless people "largely dependent upon miners' pensions, Social Security, and public assistance." In 1968 sociologist Richard Ball summed up "the resignation to the welfare syndrome" in the "Appalachian folk subculture" as analgesic—feeling no pain. More recently, journalist Ken Auletta concluded that poor Appalachians in West Virginia, the "White underclass," were no different in the 1980s than the people Fetterman had described in the 1960s: "As was true of the rural Appalachian mountain community brought to life in John Fetterman's powerful book about rural poverty,

Stinking Creek, much of 'the rural populace in the countless hollows have adopted the welfare rolls as a way of life' '' (1982, p. 159).

These writers emphasized how the poor use welfare, without fully examining their economic opportunities and the social context in poor Appalachian communities. Robert Coles and Kai Erikson presented a more complex picture. In *Everything in Its Path: Destruction of Community in the Buffalo Creek Flood* (1976), Erikson basically accepted Caudill and Weller's accounts of the Appalachian poor as accurate descriptions for the 1960s. However, he argued that those he studied had just begun to overcome "the poverty and insecurity of their parents" and to move beyond "that numbed and dispirited creature shuffling off to welfare offices of one kind or another" when the flood hit and destroyed their community (1976, p. 132).

But even in the 1960s Robert Coles found people who argued that poor Appalachians were trapped by the community's social and political structure, not resigned to accepting the welfare rolls. In *Migrants, Sharecroppers, Mountaineers* (1971), a small coal company operator described the intertwining of lack of jobs, people taking welfare, and a corrupt welfare system:

The poor here . . . who live up the hollows won't take handouts. I mean, they will, of course, because they're desperate; but they don't like the idea. . . . What we need here is factories, lots of them, to give jobs to our people . . . but there's nothing left for people but scratching what they can from the land—or turning to the county welfare system, which is full of rotten, dishonest politics. Welfare is a business here, not the right of a citizen who needs help and is entitled to it. No wonder a lot of people have contempt for welfare, even if they'll accept the money. They know that the county officials use welfare to stay in power, to buy votes and to punish enemies. (p. 283)

The people whom Coles interviewed described how too few jobs and a corrupt local political structure stripped poor people of their opportunities to escape poverty, including the children who were the focus of his study. He saw and related the vulnerability of the poor:

In some counties of Kentucky and West Virginia one or two families run everything; they control the judge's office and the sheriff's office and they have their man as the superintendent of schools. It is impossible for those who live scattered up the hollows and creeks to defy such "authorities" without paying one or several harsh penalties. (1971, p. 297)

It was neither Cole's intent nor style to analyze the social dynamics he had discovered. His purpose, as a child psychologist, was to shed light on "how those children live, how their parents live, and what they are likely to have on their minds" (1971, p. xi). But he recognized the importance of the social context in poor Appalachian communities and knew how deeply it affected Appalachian children.

The same rigid social context that trapped the poor in Appalachia in the 1960s traps them today. The "broken spirits" of poor individuals do not explain persistent poverty in the mountains. The entrenched system of political patronage and the rigidly stratified social structure characteristic of depressed economies have created a community context that blocks every path out of poverty.

This chapter presents preliminary observations from a comparative study of social mobility in remote rural communities, some depressed and some relatively prosperous. In in-depth interviews with poor young adults, local welfare administrators and workers, civic leaders, organizers, and business and political elites, we examine how opportunities to escape poverty vary in different social contexts.[1] The Appalachian case is presented here, with emphasis on how poor people in the mountains see their opportunities and assess the workings of their communities' social and political structures. The early history of social relationships in the coal industry established the setting for today's rigidly stratified and tightly controlled Appalachian communities. Today the continued scarcity and volatility of work perpetuate a local sociopolitical system in which the arbitrary power of the elite over the few opportunities that exist creates a social context that blocks poor people's mobility out of poverty.

EARLY COAL DEVELOPMENT: "ACUTE POVERTY AMONG MINERS"

When coal mining began in the mountains in the late 1800s, politicians and industrialists claimed that coal development would bring wealth and prosperity to the region. In 1913 the *Manufacturers Record*, a leading business journal of the period, argued that "they [outside investors] have been turning these mountains, largely inhabited by an undeveloped and uneducated people, who because of the lack of employment, have been stagnant for generations, into centers of activity and life and civilization's progress" (1913, p. 52). But these claims were not borne out. The coal industry did not bring improved conditions to the mountains, and even when production was expanding, times were hard in coal communities. There was fierce competition in the bituminous coal industry until the 1950s (Baratz 1955; Graebner 1974; Johnson 1979; Simon 1981; Seltzer 1985). Since coal reserves were geographically dispersed, were widely available, and required relatively little capital to mine, it was easy to enter the business. The result was constant overcapacity and overproduction (Seltzer 1985). Throughout the early 1900s coal operators vied for markets provided by railroads, steel companies, and other industrial customers, and these powerful monopolistic industries played operators against each other (Balliett 1978; Simon 1981). Even during years when markets and production were expanding for the industry as a whole, coal companies faced tight competition. Operators were oriented toward short-term gain, and profitable mining was only possible if costs were held at an absolute minimum. Thus wages were kept low, and companies made only minimal investments in coal-camp infrastructure. In 1937 Justice William Douglas observed that "labor and capital alike were the victims. Financial distress among the operators and acute poverty among miners prevailed during periods of prosperity'' (quoted in Balliett 1978, p. 28).

Most miners lived in coal-company towns legendary for their poor conditions and the absolute control wielded by coal operators (Seltzer 1985). Since there was virtually no other economic activity, coal operators provided not only employment, but also housing, utilities, and whatever health and education and recreation were available. Operators molded their company towns, as they did their mining operations, to achieve maximum control and profits (Parker 1940; Corbin 1981; Seltzer 1985). When a company's markets shrank, it would lay people off or cut wages to keep the business going. Business conditions were sometimes so bad that coal companies made their only profits in their company stores (Simon 1981).

Miners and their families were always vulnerable to arbitrary layoffs, and with job loss came the loss of housing and everything else they had. Most miners had difficulty supplementing wages with gardens or keeping small livestock— as they might have before moving to a coal town—because the surrounding wooded lands were owned by coal companies (U.S. Department of Agriculture 1935). Local economies were wholly dependent on the volatile coal industry for income and employment, and this dependency thwarted investment in noncoal private-sector ventures as well as public infrastructure. Indeed, in these hard-pressed one-industry towns, the only potential source of revenue for community investment was the coal companies, and they had the power to block any taxation efforts community leaders might propose. A pattern of absolute control by the coal operators was established, and those who resisted were run out of town.

While the result of this fierce competition in the bituminous coal industry was cheap energy to fuel industrialization in the Northeast and Midwest, the costs were severe for miners and their families:

The blessings of cheap coal were less obvious to the men who mined it. Constant downward pressure on wages—and the ever present threat of unemployment in a highly unstable industry—meant lives of grinding poverty for many coal miners and their families. It also resulted in minimal expenditures on health and safety measures by the operators in the most hazardous occupation of the industrial age. (Miernyk 1979, p. 8)

In 1935 the U. S. Department of Agriculture (USDA) examined the Appalachian coal industry's potential contribution to regional development. The USDA concluded that although the prospect of coal employment drew thousands of families into the region and discouraged the emigration of thousands more by offering an alternative to subsistence farming,

on the whole, the development of coal mining has not made for a satisfactory economic organization. The coal mining camps, usually erected and owned by the owners of the mines, have often been unwholesome. The work in the mines has usually been irregular, and even before the present economic depression, most mines were closed from one to several months each year. (USDA 1935, p. 40)

Seltzer's comprehensive study of miners and managers in the coal industry (1985) showed how labor and management relationships in the industry were characterized by distrust and exploitation from the beginning. Over the years bloody and violent labor struggles further contributed to a community context of suspicion and oppression (e.g., Corbin 1981; G. C. Jones 1985; Seltzer 1985). Both the violent labor struggles and ruinous competition were finally formally addressed by the industry in the 1950s. John L. Lewis of the United Mine Workers and George Love, representing the Bituminous Coal Operators Association, the largest producers, reached an agreement to raise wages and force many marginal producers out of business (Seltzer 1985). But the agreement also depended on sudden mechanization, and this meant massive layoffs and permanent unemployment (Miernyk 1979; Seltzer 1985). In the five-year period between 1949 and 1954 alone, eastern Kentucky coal employment declined from 60,000 to 27,000. Similar job losses occurred in West Virginia and southwestern Virginia. Between 1950 and 1960 over a million and a half people emigrated from central Appalachia (Brown 1972). Those who stayed but did not have jobs lived in deep poverty.

HARD TIMES IN THE 1980S AND 1990S: "YOU CAN'T BUY A JOB"

The scarcity and volatility of work and the absolute, arbitrary control of coal-industry employers during the first half of this century set the stage for conditions in coal communities today. In the early coal-company towns there were two social classes—miners and managers—and the large gap between them was rigidly maintained. Over time the lack of economic diversity, the lack of numerous different employers and different options for employment, has perpetuated the basic system of haves and have-nots. When those miners who kept their jobs after mechanization gained better pay in the 1960s, they became part of the "haves."

The region's high poverty rates indicate that income and jobs are distributed unequally in the mountains. Coal miners who work fairly steadily earn $30,000 or more a year, but a much larger group lives on the margin, scrambling for the few low-paying, part-time jobs in the fast-food industry or odd-job opportunities. My 1980 study of the distribution of work and income in rural Kentucky found significantly greater inequalities in coal-dependent counties than in counties dependent on farm, manufacturing, or government and service economies (Duncan 1985). There were fewer workers, but those who worked in wage and salary jobs earned high wages. Average earnings in coal counties were almost 40 percent higher than in other types of counties, but 23 percent of coal-field families had no worker at all. An astonishing 36 percent of coal-field teenagers were "hanging out," not in school, not working, and not looking for work—compared to an average of 22 percent in other counties. Despite these dramatic differences in average earnings and proportion of adults working, coal-field counties did not differ greatly in their relative dependence on earned income versus transfer-payment income. Sixty-six percent of total personal income was earned at work in coal counties, compared to an average of 65 percent in other counties. Twenty-four percent of total personal income in coal counties came from transfer payments (including black-lung benefits), compared to an average of 21 percent in the other types of counties.[2] These 1980 statistics indicate high inequality in coal areas compared to areas dependent on other economic activity (Duncan 1985). Declines in coal employment during the 1980s would suggest that these inequalities have probably been exacerbated rather than minimized over the last decade. The lack of economic and social diversity means that those few families who have control over jobs and other opportunities wield great power over those who need them and have no other options.

Coal is still the lifeblood in mining areas. In coal-producing counties of eastern Kentucky over 40 percent of income comes from coal employment, and in many areas the percentage is even higher (Duncan 1985). Like many other core industries in the United States, the coal industry has introduced changes that make coal production more efficient. Through a combination of better management and new technology, coal companies produce more and more coal with fewer and fewer miners (Mountain Association for Community Economic Development [MACED] 1986). Although new health and safety and environmental regulations in the 1970s meant that companies added workers to deal with new rules, today companies meet these requirements efficiently without adding great numbers of workers to their payroll (MACED 1986). Less efficient small mines are going out of business, while larger mines are introducing new machinery such as long-wall miners that dramatically improve efficiency (MACED 1986). These improvements in productivity mean that the industry increased coal production 70 percent between 1950 and 1984 while at the same time reducing employment from 416,000 to 178,000 (MACED 1986). Production continues to go up, and employment continues to go down. In Kentucky alone, coal employment declined from 39,700 in 1984 to 31,500 in 1988. In 1984 Appalachian coal fields produced 1.86 tons per miner per hour. By 1987 that figure had increased to 2.3 tons per miner per hour (Kentucky Coal Association 1989). Most Appalachian coal miners today are skilled, highly paid workers in larger companies that tend to have at least some stable, long-term contracts with utility customers.

Even in an era of relative stability and good wages in the coal industry, however, there are not enough of these jobs for would-be workers in the region. Employment is steadier and safer in the larger mines today, but these opportunities are contracting, not expanding. When there are openings, the jobs require sophisticated skills, and companies advertise in a national labor market. Poor Appalachian youth who are not well educated are unlikely to find work in the coal mines in the 1990s. One industry manager put it this way in 1985: "We are at the point of saturation in the mining industry [here]. . . . The youngsters who were getting out of high school in the early 1970s have now been working for my company for ten years. They were the fortunate ones. . . . The jobs aren't there now'' (MACED 1986).

Although in the past Appalachian residents who had experienced coal's boom-and-bust cycle might have expected a new boom, today nearly everyone recognizes that coal employment will not expand. Over and over, young people say that there is no work in coal: "Everywhere he's asked, they don't need nobody. He's asked down at the coal yard I don't know how many times, and they don't need nobody. As a matter of fact, the mines is laying off instead of hiring, so there ain't no jobs here.'' It is generally understood that there are no longer openings for the unskilled who want to be rock pickers or rock-truck drivers for the mines: "You need experience to get a job with a big operator . . . so instead [people] end up at, you know, McDonalds, for 20 hours. It's hard to put together a living that way.''

Even though it is hard to make a living in the low-wage, part-time jobs in fast-food restaurants or grocery stores, young workers trying to support a family struggle to get these jobs and struggle to keep them. To avoid paying benefits, fast-food restaurants structure the jobs so that people do not get full-time work, and as a result, workers are always hoping to get more hours. While teenagers and, in some cases, retired people use this kind of job for extra spending money in many parts of the country, young adults in depressed communities must depend on jobs like these to support their families.

One young man's story was representative of many in his predicament. With a baby and teenage wife to support, he had fixed up an old trailer on his uncle's property, had bought a car for $75 that he coaxed into running, and was now trying to buy food and gas and pay utilities on what he could make working part-time in a fast-food restaurant. He had dropped out of school and had tried finding work in Florida, but there were few options in the mid-1980s for a mountain boy with no education, and he returned home. Now he needed this fast-food job to hold his young family together.

Workers like this young man do anything they can to get "hours." A young woman working in a fast-food restaurant described how much she liked to close up, even though it meant staying late and more drudgery work cleaning pots and pans. Closing assured her of more hours:

If you're in a restaurant, 'bout the only time you make your money is if you work "closin.' '' That's where all the hours are. You don't get sent home early or anything like that when its slow. You can automatically get six and a half hours, whether it's slow or not slow. . . . You clean the pots, shine everything down for the next day.

She was worried that the following week would bring too few hours to pay for the gas it took to get to work:

Right now it's up and down. Ten hours I've worked [all week]. I don't know if I can stay around, 'cause for the next five days I only get two days and I can't make it. You don't get no hours like that. That's it. I'd only be with 20 hours. . . . I may as well just stay home, saving my gas 'cause I'm just making it for gas to come out here and back.

When business is slow, workers are sent home or told not to come in, and thus every week income is uncertain. One manager cut his workers' hours, keeping costs low relative to profits, in order to achieve the margin he needed to make his bonus:

He has to get all the costs down and sales so much above the costs, so he would work *our* jobs. That's dirty. People that need the money—there's a lot who need the money badly—women who had kids, no husbands, no help whatsoever. . . . But there isn't anything anyone can do about it.

But business demand is not the only force determining a low-wage worker's income in a restaurant in these communities. The arbitrary control of managers also affects how many hours workers get and even whether they keep their jobs. Managers frequently have the authority to change rules to benefit themselves or members of their families. A worker in another community described how a rule was developed preventing two siblings from being in management at the same place in order to remove a worker who stood in the way of the manager's own wife's advancement. The storyteller was amused by the obvious ethical contradictions this represented, but not surprised. On the one hand, this kind of power for managers and lack of power for workers is the accepted way of operating in these poor communities. On the other hand, many managers are said to be tightly connected to those few families who make up the elite power structure. Their connections implicitly permit them to exercise the same kind of arbitrary power over workers that elites exercise over the communities.

People from the poorest families have trouble getting these low-wage jobs in the service sector. Managers prefer high-school students and college students from the "good families," in part because they only want the part-time work available, and in part because they have the appearance and habits that suggest that they will be good workers. Workers who are supporting families complain that students, who need the money less, get more of the hours. One fast-food manager explained:

The main reason we have a lot of high school students and college students—most of the time it's your best applicant. When they come in for an interview, they're ready for it. They know the answers, and a lot of people just come here and want a job, they don't want to work. The college students just want part-time 'cause their parents are putting them through anyways.

There are so few jobs available in these communities, and so many who need work, that people seek fast-food and other part-time retail work in order to support their families. But the jobs are set up for those who do not need them to offer a living wage. When household heads do get these jobs, their hours are always uncertain and unpredictable, always subject to change.

Those who cannot get the fast-food jobs and other retail or service jobs do "odd jobs" such as babysitting, carpentry, grass cutting, and plumbing jobs, often for older people who may have a small pension coming in and can pay a few dollars to get a small job done. An economy characterized by great inequality generates more "odd jobs"—those who have good work and incomes can pay very little to have jobs done for them that they otherwise might do themselves.

In this way the informal sector of a depressed rural economy in the United States is comparable to that in a developing country that still has remnants of a colonial system. The relatively small number of upper and middle class households have substantial resources compared to the large number of poor needing any kind of work, and so the poor can pick up a little painting or plumbing job here and there, or some hauling or clearing. The work and the income are uncertain, but people go out to get what they can day after day. Of course, when unemployment grows, and more miners are laid off, even this work becomes hard to find. One unemployed coal miner said that "anymore, even the odd jobs are hard to find."

One coal miner who had been unemployed for three years ran a used-car business in the daytime and cleaned school rooms in the evening. He said,

It's getting back to worse as it's ever been . . . if you don't work in the coal mines here, there's nothing else to do. During the coal boom there was a lot of work available. . . . Now, you know, people around just can't *buy* a job. If you work for somebody, you're going to have to pay them.

"WHO'S YOUR DADDY?"

Opportunities to Work

When jobs are scarce in a small, closed community, whom you know makes all the difference in whether you find any work at all. Even during the coal boom, when thousands of new miners were hired in large, multinational energy companies, the hiring process was largely filtered through connections. Companies with headquarters in the Northeast and the Midwest bought Appalachian companies or opened new mines to take advantage of the coal boom, but many relied on local managers to hire the work force. Thus, even in a period of relative job growth, those with the best connections get the "best" jobs. A miner explained:

If you're not tight with the people that own it, you're not going to get a job. The people that have the authority to hire will make sure that their friends or their families get the jobs because they know there are none anywhere else. I know if I had the authority, I'd hire my brother before I'd let him work in a "scab mine."

Steady jobs of any kind are always at a premium, but there is not much turnover. Those who have the jobs keep them, and when they retire, they try to get their family members in to replace them. One young man said:

'Bout all the long term jobs around here are took. The only thing would be to go into the coal mines—but they is layin' so many off right now. . . . You have to know somebody, have somebody put in a good word fer your father, something like 'at, you know.

In a small community with few jobs and a well-established elite, there is little opportunity for jobs that offer mobility. The fundamental reality is that there just are not enough jobs. In addition, however, one's potential to get work and have opportunities depends to a large extent on one's family background. People are assigned the reputation of their families. One young woman described how there were two classes in school—the "upper class that was going somewhere" and the "lower class, who, you could see, would never go anywhere." People distinguish between the ones who are "dirty and nasty—unshaven, hair unkept, you can tell they aren't workin' " and those who are neat, are clean-cut, and work. One member of the elite put it this way:

There's the people who work and do well and have a lot of money, and there's the poor. And you don't have an in-between . . . the people who are just regular coal miners can bring home thirty to forty thousand—they're all in that bracket. And then you go from that, and the transition's like a cliff's edge, and it drops off and you got people who are very very poor.

The inequality is apparent to people on both sides of the spectrum; they agree that your family's name—and which side of that divide your family has historically been on—is of the utmost importance in determining your opportunities. One upper-class person said:

You know, we was talkin' about the classes and the distinctions and how you can tell. This sounds silly, but with generations of people bein' this way, and the last name—a lot of times you can hear somebody's last name and before you even meet 'em, you already got the idea. They're either a good person or they're sorry as can be.

If someone from a poor family cleans up and wants to get work, what are his or her prospects?

No [you can't overcome the disadvantages of a bad family name]. I knew this fella, I was fixin' to go out with him, but his last name happened to fall into one those lists, and even though he wasn't from the crowd I knew, I couldn't go out with him, you know. It would look bad. You have to be extremely careful here.

For the poorest of the poor, whose "daddy's never amounted to anything," this reliance on family reputation often means that they are not given a chance to work:

Everybody around here knows everybody, and they know what family you come from. Now my family, they've been always a bad family . . . there are places they can't even rent a house, because of their last name. And it's just the way it is . . . you can't change it. You just have to live with it.

A young woman summed up her household's predicament: "Way I see it, poor people 'round here can't git a job. My boyfriend tried and tried 'fore he ever got his social security. He couldn't git a job."

In small communities where the labor market is tight, getting a job generally depends on family members' reputations for being good workers or on performing direct political work, ensuring votes, for those who control the jobs. In any case, you need to have someone who is well established with the employer "speak for you." If you are not in the network of those who have work, it is difficult to break into the limited steady-job market. If in addition you come from a poor family and your father or mother are generally regarded as never having "done any good," you have a much more difficult time breaking into the job market: "You have to come from the right family around here. You gotta know people. It depends on what your name is, if you got a last name that is a rich name, they'll take you, [otherwise] you can't find no work."

Opportunities at School

The bias the poor face when they seek jobs, either because of their family reputation or their "nasty" appearance, extends to the classroom. Children from poor families are not expected to do well in school. One young mother complained:

These kids walk in the door and they are categorized by 90 percent of the teachers. "This is so-and-so over there; his mommy and daddy never did amount to a hill of beans. They don't know how to read and write. There's no point in my wasting time on Johnny here."

Another bitter parent from a poor family said:

Whatever a child has got on his back and no matter how ticky his hair is, no matter how nasty it is, no matter what hole it comes out of, it deserves the same chance as Sally sitting over here in a ruffled dress.

The children themselves are acutely aware of school personnel's discrimination against those from poor families. Comparing teachers' treatment of "upper-class" students with that of "lower-class" students, one young person said:

They make their picks on the people that's got the most money up here, and they try to say it's 'cause they achieve more, but it's not. It's 'cause they got more money. . . . The teachers treats them with respect, treats them right, like they're supposed to be, like a human being. And the principal treats them right, they don't direct them in the office for blinking their eyes the wrong way. Now for me, when I was going to school, I went to the office every day, even if I didn't do nothing, and I got paddled. And they did my brother the same way, whether he did anything or not, he got paddled every day. And that's why kids quit school.

The patterns that lead to dropping out are repeated over and over as personal problems intersect with school problems. Many who dropped out said that things were "real rough" at home; or they fought a lot in school (both men and women), pushing and instigating scuffles every day until school authorities kicked them out; some with problems with learning failed again and again, until they said that they just got too old and big for the grades they were in (17 or 18 in the eighth and ninth grades); many got in with a "rough crowd" and drifted out of school. One young woman, born to a teenage mother and brought up in a broken family, described how she became involved with a wild group:

I just kinda got up with the wrong crowd, you know—it was like this gang of bad kids. And I started skippin' school and runnin' around. It took me a long time to realize how bad I'd gotten my life messed up. When I was goin' to school there was two crowds. There were the good rich kids and there were the bad poor people. And they were segregated, you know. I felt like I needed to be with somebody like me, and I wound up in the wrong crowd. I experimented with drugs. I ran away and stayed out. I was out with people you couldn't trust. I was out all night gettin' drunk. I didn't think nobody cared what happened to me, and I didn't care what happened to me.

Now this young woman is herself the unwed mother of a four-year old. She is working on her general equivalency degree, and she has a part-time waitressing job. She lives with her aunt, who also has a part-time job in the service sector, in a small house with bad plumbing. She is doing all she can to "make something" of herself—getting her high-school degree, working as many hours as she can get, and providing whatever opportunities she can for her child.

Both "upper-" and "lower-class" people describe how the poor children receive less attention and have less expected of them. They have trouble with "learnin'," but they do not get help:

I liked goin' to school but I wasn't that good on learnin'. I couldn't git through the third grade. And, you know, it didn't seem like the teacher had concern, you know, ta learn. Take time with ya. So I was the one that didn't have no teachin'. Somebody to teach for me to learn . . . 'cause the teacher didn't give me no time, and, I wanted to learn, but seemed like I couldn't learn.

So those from poor families start to "skip" school, and the school and public authorities condone it. One young woman who had lived elsewhere saw a real difference in her Appalachian school:

They just let you go and let you do whatever, they let you skip. They don't care, that's why I was failing. In Illinois, if you got caught skippin', you were in big trouble. I got straight A's in Illinois. But here it's easy [to skip].

One adult explained how little control teachers have when authorities in the community tolerate "skippin' ":

My sister-in-laws are teachers, and they say there's not much they can do in the school system. They talk about punishing kids, and—well, around here kids don't have to go to school . . . sometimes they take families to court, but they don't make them do anything about it.

Those teachers who try to teach seriously and who try to treat students equally are undermined by the prevailing atmosphere that favors those from "upper-class" families and ignores or discriminates against those from poor families. They are pressured by the parents of the nonpoor to give their children privileges and condone transgressions. One man described the pressure on earnest teachers:

If teachers try to enforce discipline, they get calls at night, parents calling and hollering and stuff if little Janie doesn't get on the honor roll, if they try to take any privileges away from their children—oh no, their parents won't have it: "My little child wouldn't do that." . . . there's not much the teachers can do. It's the wealthier families. The poor people, they don't hardly go into the schools, you know. They don't say too much about it. But the wealthier ones, well, they think they should be able to buy everything that child needs, including its education.

The problems of the schools, and the schools' failure to teach poor children, have become part of a cycle of low standards and low expectations. Few take school seriously as a place of learning—not the parents, not the students, not the teachers, and not the administrators. Students describe chaotic classrooms, with fights in the hallways, students climbing in and out of windows during class periods, and a general lack of order. Many teachers are untrained or ill suited for their jobs, but have them because of their participation in the patronage system.

Schools are at the heart of the corrupt patronage system that drives these poor communities. In many Appalachian counties schools provide the majority of jobs, and these jobs—from schoolteachers to aides, kitchen workers, and bus drivers—are doled out by elected school-board members to political supporters or family members. Some parents described the biggest obstacle facing their communities as corruption in the schools:

The biggest problem you get into with the school board is the fact that they control more jobs and more people and more people's lives than any other thing in this county. They have the employees, and any time you have that type of situation in a low economic area, you have a beautiful setup for bribery, corruption, and political power plays. And that is what happens.

People whose fathers had worked in elections, delivering hollows, expected to get on as teachers, even though they freely admitted that they would rather "be a secretary, really," or that "hangin' drywall is what I like." As one young person put it:

There's a lot of teachers who went into teaching because it's a job, and there's a lot of problems in the school system. I'd say we have a lot of teachers who don't need to be teaching, who hate kids, who do not care what the kids do.

Even those who do graduate have not learned to read or write. One businessman observed:

We have got so many . . . that cannot read their name, can't recognize it if they see it on paper. They can't write their names. Now that's what kind of graduates we got—that's went through high school and graduated, and they can't read their name.

Coal-industry employers say that they cannot risk hiring an illiterate worker in a dangerous job. One described how he dealt with applications from people who could not read and write:

People would come in here to apply for a job, and the secretary would read their application, and they would give the answers, and she would write them in because they couldn't read and write. I let them do this, because I didn't want them to feel rejected, but I would never hire anybody like that. I just put an X on the application and filed it away. I figure if they can't read a warning sign, then they just would not be safe in our jobs.

Thus the poor in Appalachia often arrive at the age to work without even the most elementary education and training. Students who cannot read, write, or "do figures" are suited for very few jobs in the mountains or elsewhere: " 'Bout the only thing you can find around here without an education is cuttin' grass, or odd jobs here and there."

PUBLIC JOBS AND PUBLIC PROGRAMS IN APPALACHIA: "HONEY, EVERYTHING HERE IS POLITICS"

This patronage system extends well beyond the school system. The corruption that characterizes school-board races and school personnel hiring extends into every aspect of community life. Whether it is access to free government food, access to slots in youth training programs, jobs in state government offices, or referrals to openings at a new fast-food restaurant or a good security job with a private firm, having an opportunity depends on whom you know or whom you supported in the last election. Those who have lived and worked elsewhere are struck by the lack of meritocracy in these depressed communities:

There's just types of things that you see that go on. You can see it in the paper and you can see it in who's talking. The political games that go on. It's there. And it's not necessarily you get things on merit—it's on who you know. And I've lived away from here and I know what's on merit. Other places it can be merit—qualifications, your education.

Scarcity of jobs means that control over jobs is a source of wealth and power, and volatility of jobs means that steady work in the public sector—in the schools, in the welfare or employment office, on the road crew—is the biggest prize. Often young people who were hoping to get a public job soon, or who had just gotten one, would describe the political activity of their disabled fathers. "Oh, he stays real active—politickin' mainly." Their fathers are men in their forties and fifties who receive disability payments and then use their time to work as middlemen, delivering votes for the politician who hired them. They get paid with money and with jobs for their relatives. One political middleman told us how he worked:

The way I work is I pick the families, and I'll get 30 people working for me over there. So I've got 30 people working for, say $40 a piece. They're all working for the same thing. They all have families. You get them out of big families, you know. I had families I relied on, whom I had taught how to do this.

The system and who runs it are clear to everyone in the community. When asked, "Who runs things around here?" most people in Appalachian communities name the same small group of powerful families in their community. "They have a lot of pull," one young woman said, "and everybody's kind of afraid of them 'cause they know what they can do." Another commented, "We have a system right here that just cannot be fought. . . . There's too much money and too much power where they are at. And you just can't win." Running unsuccessfully against a corrupt school board in Appalachia in an effort to bring about reforms means that your daughter and nephew are likely to lose their jobs or be moved to a less desirable one: "If you're not careful you'll make enemies. And you don't want to make enemies. Especially if you don't have importance."

There appears to be widespread consensus that the few families that run things have control over jobs in both the private and public sectors and can ensure their control by having those who challenge them under any circumstances fired, no matter where they work. To illustrate the long reach of the elite, one well-placed group of young people whose families had supported the ruling elites and who therefore had good public-sector jobs told me that if the political stories they were telling me ever "got out," none of them could ever "flip a hamburger" in their town again. This concentrated power that comes with control over jobs in both the private and the public sector means that one cannot challenge the local elite without losing one's own job or having one's relatives lose theirs. It is a complete system in which jobs are awarded on the basis of whom you know and whom you support. People throughout the area take the system for granted, and even those who want community change in the region feel that the system is too entrenched to fight.

Social welfare programs play an important role in maintaining the status quo in these poor communities. They provide crucial support for the poor, both those who are unemployed and those who have jobs that neither pay enough to support a family nor offer health benefits. They also contribute substantial dollars to the local economy, dollars that go to local grocers, landlords, health-care providers, and even employers who hire people eligible for training and wage subsidies. Finally, by providing a safety net of sorts for the low-wage workers in the area, welfare programs maintain a local work force for local industries.

There are some family members who "lay around" and will not get work, but most welfare recipients whom we interviewed use welfare programs to make up for what they cannot get through work. For low-income individuals, welfare supplements low wages and too few hours and provides a source of medical coverage, protecting poor people living on the margin in these communities. For poor people in a depressed community, the two biggest worries are "payin' the bills" and "makin' sure we can git a doctor if we need one for the baby." Often it is public assistance programs that can alleviate these worries.

Elites tend to group all welfare recipients into the "generations of welfare dependence," those families "that just don't care to work." But federal welfare programs also directly benefit the elites in these communities in several ways. First, in a general sense, the programs subsidize rural industries and employers that depend either on low wages or seasonal labor. Wages can be too low to live on, hours can be too few to count on, and jobs can expand and contract with the volatile movement of markets far from these communities. But workers can stay and survive and be available when employers need them because Food Stamps, Aid to Families with Dependent Children (AFDC), Medicaid, and unemployment benefits carry them, making up for lack of benefits or for low wages or providing a base during seasonal layoffs.

Second, as Robert Coles's informants pointed out in the 1960s, welfare benefits represent another source of political, economic, and social power and control for local elites (Coles 1971). In fact, public programs that offer special opportunities are often doled out to supporters, just like jobs. Those who are known to "deliver" the votes of families in certain hollows for the politicians are rewarded when their children get federally funded summer job opportunities, the special training a new program offers, a special scholarship, or a position managing a new federal program. Just as families who voted right will get their roads graveled, those who play the right side often will get that valuable public housing slot, a summer job training opportunity for their child, or free "meals on wheels"—whether or not they technically qualify for the programs—while officials look the other way. When resources are so scarce, the small benefits that come from public programs represent real wealth, to be manipulated and dispensed to political supporters.

These ways of allocating jobs and public program benefits give the community and the lives of the people living in it a disorganized, unpredictable character. The powerful, and those who do their bidding, have extraordinary and arbitrary control over the lives of those who need work and need public assistance. Poor people live precarious, violent, and unstable lives, vulnerable not only to economic vicissitudes, but also to the power of elites who keep them in their place.

PRECARIOUS LIVES

The poor in Appalachia live on the edge, unsettled, tossed from one day to the next, from one disaster to another. The lack of work and the constant anxiety about money and bill paying, combined with the general disrespect accorded those who are poor, mean that people feel powerless in their everyday lives. Their lack of control over their lives produces tension and instability in relationships. Personal lives are stormy, mirroring the soap operas that men and women watch on television day after day—jealousies, shootings, and men and women "going out on each other."

Women are most vulnerable. One young woman described a situation we heard from many women:

Whenever he's laid off from work and it's sorta hard, you don't know if you gonna meet your bills from one month to the next. And my little girl wantin' things I can't afford at the time, you know. It just makes me feel real bad, you know. . . . If we had, you know, if he had a good job, you know, and I had a good job, I guess he would, you know, be a lot better to me then, than he would be now. 'Cause now it's so hard, you know, trying to get by. It's real hard . . . it's so hard now, it makes you really disappointed.

Violent relationships and the possessiveness men feel over women came up over and over again:

He was real jealous. He shot at me. . . . Men down here, they just use a woman. He can be good to me, but then again, he can be so mean. It's just, I don't know. . . . He don't want me to go out . . . he don't want me to dress nice. . . . Men back here, they like to live on a woman. I just wished I could be a man for a day.

Women avoid new relationships long after they split up with a husband or old boyfriend, fearful of renewed abuse. One young mother explained:

You get divorced, but they still won't let you live in peace . . . they still want to bother you or something. That's the reason I don't see nobody else—when I tried it he hollered and threatened me, and I'm scared of him . . . skiddish.

But the violence is not just between men and women. Often we encountered young men who had been beaten by their fathers when they were little, whose refrain was "I depend on myself really. I'm independent. I don't need nobody."

A number of young men described how they were kicked out of the house for protecting their mothers from their fathers' or their stepfathers' physical assaults.

This violence and uncertainty in individual lives permeate neighborhoods and community life. Personal disagreements and battles over lovers or children or property spill into others' lives. Family members watch out for one another, and bars and clubs frequently erupt in fights. Time and time again we encountered people who had lost close friends or relatives to a fight or a showdown between two or more young men.

In this atmosphere of violence and "settling of scores," young people cannot count on the public sector for fair and impartial protection. Both the members of the "upper class" and the poor describe corrupt and unpredictable police forces and systems of law. Police tend to be those rewarded for political support, and they are perceived as either incompetent or themselves involved in illegal behavior. One small-business owner said: "I reckon we got a police chief can't read or write or hold a gun, not even allowed to shoot a gun." Poor people do not trust the law to protect them, and uncertainty about how they might be treated in an encounter with the law is one more tension in their lives. A young man described how his father had gotten on the wrong side of a local official, and as a result, that policeman pulled this teenager into jail on a trumped-up charge. These stories come up over and over, indicating that law enforcement is widely perceived to be unfair. The authorities in poor Appalachian communities are part of the overall system in which control is concentrated and rewards and punishments are dispensed arbitrarily. As one young man put it:

There's just no law here, it's not like any place in the world. It's just, a few people run things the way they see fit. I mean, if somebody commits a crime and they know him, or is a cousin's brother or somebody's sister or such crap like that, then he's free. But you can't say nothing, you can't do nothing.

The everyday lives of the poor in depressed Appalachian communities are filled with uncertainty and vulnerability. They have little control over their economic situation in a world of favoritism and patronage. Economic uncertainty creates tension in personal relationships, and lives are violent. Living poor in a poor community is to be trapped, denied access to work, denied access to good educational opportunities, denied the chance to fulfill the American Dream and "make something of yourself."

CONCENTRATED POVERTY IN URBAN AND RURAL COMMUNITIES

Social Isolation in the Inner Cities

Urban poverty scholars have been focusing increasing attention on the way poor people are trapped in inner-city poverty areas. Many of the dynamics are similar to those in poor Appalachian communities. Deepening poverty in the inner cities during the 1970s and 1980s reignited concern about concentrated poverty and stimulated debates about whether an urban underclass has developed there (e.g., Kornblum 1984; Wilson 1987; Sawhill 1988; Harris and Wilkins 1988; William J. Wilson 1989). Wilson (1987) and Kasarda (1989) argued that the changing job opportunity structure of the 1980s effectively denied inner-city residents access to employment.

But, in addition, there has been growing attention to the cultural and social consequences of living in poor communities (Wilson 1990). Several studies in Wilson's special *Annals of the American Academy of Political and Social Science* (1989) volume on the ghetto underclass pursued this theme. For example, Wacquant and Wilson (1989) discussed "the high cost of living in the ghetto," showing how traditional avenues for social mobility are undermined in areas of concentrated poverty. Extreme poverty areas, by definition, have proportionately more very poor households—people who are either jobless and welfare dependent or in very low wage or part-time jobs—and proportionately fewer working and middle-class households. The result is social isolation for the very poor and the absence of what Wilson called "social buffers," or those social mechanisms that both soften the effect of individuals' poverty and facilitate escape from it. In a discussion of mobility among mother-only families, McClanahan and Garfinkel (1989) considered the impact of social isolation: Social isolation may occur because the community no longer functions as a resource base for its members, as when a neighborhood has no jobs, no networks for helping to locate jobs, poor schools, and a youth culture that is subject to minimal control" (p. 99). The studies in *The Ghetto Underclass: Social Science Perspectives* (1989) emphasized how joblessness and concentrated poverty create a social context in which the expected avenues to escape poverty, the expected social supports for the poor that can facilitate mobility, do not exist. Clearly, a similar dynamic occurs in poor Appalachian communities, but here potential community resources, possible "social buffers" to help the poor escape their poverty, are co-opted by a corrupt community power structure that effectively maintains a rigid stratification system to benefit the families with "good names" who make up the "haves."

Vulnerability in Remote Rural Communities

Despite the widely accepted stereotype of coal-field residents as lazy and contentedly welfare dependent, we found that young Appalachians value work and independence and do all they can to achieve it. Their hope for the next five or ten years is to have a good job, be married, and be independent:

Well, hopefully, I'll have a pretty good job and I'd say, the time I'm thirty, I'll be married and hopefully living somewhere on my own. . . . I would prefer to make my own money and not draw food stamps and stuff like 'at. I want to live off myself.

When everything necessary for a good life is scarce—jobs, housing, clothing, and transportation—individual anxiety eats away at civic generosity, and a tension infuses the community. Even the kinds of activities that represent civic commitment in other places, like food pantries and secondhand clothing outlets, are compromised—people who are with the right crowd reportedly "get the best things," and "you have to pay to get that food." Families look out for their own relatives and friends. Elites seem to vie with one another for position and prestige and keep their own lives separate and private. There is little civic activity and few community improvements or charitable functions. The community is sharply divided, with families looking after their own members and the poor left to rely on their own limited resources, isolated in a world of tension, failure, and dependency.

It is harder to be poor and harder to escape poverty in depressed communities. As Wilson (1987) and Williams and Kornblum (1985) have pointed out, poor youth in poor places have few role models and few public institutions that can buffer the lack of jobs and opportunities. They are isolated from the mainstream, and their families do not have the resources to help them do well in school or find a job. These are the young people for whom public programs are the only mechanism of escape. Where youth from middle- and upper-income families depend on their own families for support, young people from poor families must look for help from special education programs, youth recreation programs, and federal job-training and job-placement programs.

The rural poor in the Appalachian mountains live in concentrated poverty, much like those in the nation's troubled inner cities. These poor young people do not have access to public programs and institutions like schools, parks, youth recreation programs, local transportation, and child-care programs that help the poor in more diverse communities. In the poor coal communities of Appalachia, these programs are part of a corrupt patronage system, and the poor have been assigned permanent places at the bottom of the social structure. The rigid stratification system, a small world of haves and have-nots, means that there is no public-sector investment that buffers the inequalities and offers opportunities for those who want to work hard and escape poverty.

This outcome appears to confirm findings of urban researchers that suggest that those poor who can escape poor places are more likely to escape poverty themselves. Studies show that poor young people who move from the depressed inner-city neighborhoods to communities with more workers and better schools do better in school and work (Rosenbaum and Popkin 1989; Wilson 1990; Osterman 1990). Expectations, like class boundaries, are less rigid, and those from poor families can improve themselves. In poor rural communities this is not the case, and the poor only move up by moving out.

In past decades one could move out, hope for a job in a steel or auto plant, and become a member of the blue-collar middle class. Briefly, during the 1970s, when high energy and farm prices stimulated employment growth in rural areas, one could stay home and make a life. But now there are no "good jobs" for the unskilled and barely literate from poor schools and poor communities. They stay home, piecing together incomes from "odd jobs," part-time work, illicit activities, and whatever welfare benefits they can qualify for. As economic conditions deteriorate, communities and schools become more violent and the social context itself deteriorates.

These are not hardened criminals or desperate crack addicts. The best times in their lives were "when I had that job, and didn't owe anybody. I was makin' my own." The people they admire are their aunts, uncles, mothers, and fathers who "made it, you know, worked hard, even when it was so rough." They buy the American Dream: they sit on the falling-down porch of the house with no plumbing for which they pay $80 a month rent—and they say that their dreams are to own their own place, have a wife or husband and two kids, and, most importantly, have a good steady job. They work as many hours as they can get at the fast-food restaurant, rebuild a car they bought for $75, and hope no one gets sick.

Most blame themselves for not escaping. "Oh I messed up," they will say, "I should have . . . finished school, not gotten pregnant" (although their children are also the best parts of their lives now). They are living on the margin, struggling, "messing up," moving from place to place to find work, a steady family life, a new start, then returning home for the protection and familiarity of family members in a place they know. These poor young men and women are trapped by mistakes they made as teenagers that prevented them from finishing school or learning skills and by being born to poor families in depressed communities where there is too little work and one does not escape one's poor background. They are only in their twenties, and they want a better life for themselves and their children. They want steady work, not welfare.

Poor people in Appalachia work hard under trying conditions to get jobs, finish their education, acquire training, and improve their lives. But in chronically poor Appalachian communities they not only struggle to overcome the disadvantages of their family's poverty, but also to overcome a debilitating corrupt social system that makes jobs, education, and training part of a patronage system that perpetuates the status quo. A rigid two-class system in which elites have control over work and public programs perpetuates poverty in depressed, remote communities.

NOTES

This chapter is part of research on youth and opportunity in a restructured economy, a project funded by the Ford Foundation's Rural Poverty and Resources Program and the Aspen Institute's Rural Economic Policy Program. I am grateful for Bill Duncan's insightful comments on early drafts of this chapter

1. Julie Ardery, doctoral candidate in sociology at the University of Kentucky and editor of *Welcome the Traveler Home: Jim Garland's Story of the Kentucky Mountains*, conducted many of the Appalachian interviews. Her thoughtful, sensitive, and deeply

intelligent participation has been critical to the research project and to the development of this chapter.

2. The Gini coefficient of household income concentration, a common measure of inequality in development literature, was 440 in coal areas, compared to an average of 419 in other areas.

Chapter 7

Migrant Farm Workers

Doris P. Slesinger and Max J. Pfeffer

Migrant farm workers are among the most underprivileged groups in our society. Typically, they receive low wages from irregular employment and live in poverty with access only to substandard housing and inadequate health care. Perhaps what is most disturbing about migrant-farm-worker poverty is its persistence over time. Farm labor has never commanded much more than a subsistence wage, and migrant farm work, where individuals and families follow the planting and harvesting of crops, has usually been compensated at the lowest of wages available for hired farm workers.

Migrant farm workers have been an important part of the agricultural economy in the United States for more than a century, and during that time many of the conditions of their lives have not improved. As noted by a Washington State Employment Security Department report (1990), seasonal and migrant farm workers can be viewed as a "contingency" work force, since they are needed in large numbers for temporary work at certain times of the year. These workers have special needs, since they typically have little security and fewer benefits than do permanent workers. This state of affairs is in stark contrast to the advances made by workers in other sectors of the economy during the twentieth century.

Official agencies differ in their definitions of "migrant." The U.S. Department of Agriculture (USDA) definition of a migrant farm worker is "someone who temporarily crosses state or county boundaries and stays overnight to do hired farm work" (Oliveira and Cox 1988, p. 8). Other federal agencies use slightly different definitions. The U.S. Department of Education divides migrant families into two categories: "currently migrant," meaning that a member of the family was employed in agriculture and stayed overnight away from home within the past two years; and "formerly migrant," meaning that the family member was engaged in migrant agricultural work within the past six years. Some federal agencies, such as the U.S. Department of Labor, regard work in meat processing or in canneries as not "agricultural"; thus migrant work forces working in these

Map 7.1
Migrant Farm Worker Streams in the United States

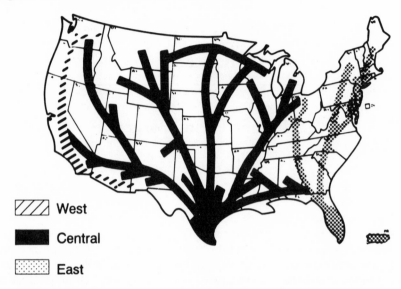

West

Central

East

Source: Map provided by National Migrant Resource Program, Inc., 1987, Austin, Texas

industries are not considered migrant agricultural workers; even sheepshearers who travel on contract are not considered "migrant" workers. On the other hand, the U.S. Public Health Service considers all workers and family members who fit any definition of "migrant" by any one or another of the federal programs as eligible for the health services specifically provided for migrant and seasonal farm workers (Slesinger and Cautley 1988). For our purposes, USDA's fairly general and inclusive definition is the most useful.

As Map 7.1 indicates, there are three primary streams of migrant workers in the United States: the western, central, and eastern. In the West migrants travel north from northern Mexico, southern Texas, and southern California up the West Coast. Northern Mexico and southern Texas are also the sending areas for the migrants who travel in the Midwest. Both these streams are made up primarily of people of Mexican heritage. The third or eastern stream is ethnically more varied. Blacks living in rural Florida often migrate northward up the coast, working in Georgia, the Carolinas, New Jersey, Pennsylvania, and New York State. However, the East Coast also attracts Puerto Ricans, Haitians, Mexicans, and Southeast Asians, some of whom spend the winter in major cities. Some migrants in each stream are citizens of the United States; others are recently arrived immigrants under refugee status; still others are under contracts with foreign governments for specific harvest (e.g., apples or sugar beets); and others are illegal workers, who never have obtained work permits. It also should be noted that over 40 percent of the migrants are likely to work within the state in which they reside, especially in the states of California, Florida, and Texas (Martin 1988, p. 54).

Little is yet known about the effects of the new "amnesty" Immigration Reform and Control Act of 1986 on the quantity of agricultural workers in the United States. This law permitted workers to apply for citizenship who could prove that they had been employed in agricultural work in the United States for the past six years, but who did not have legal work permits. Preliminary evidence indicates that substantial numbers of migrant workers who have filed for citizenship have not yet left agricultural work for urban-based employment. However, there was some concern that providing legal citizenship would deplete the agricultural work force. Apparently this has not yet happened. Approximately 1,300,000 to 2,000,000 farm workers are estimated to have applied for citizenship. To date, no figures are available as to the number that have been approved (Mines 1990).

Migrant agricultural workers are employed in tasks that require hand labor from early spring to just before Christmas. In early spring they are typically employed in nurseries and seedling companies. They then may be employed to prepare the ground for planting. Often they do hand weeding and hoeing; for example, they "walk the beans" (weed the soybean rows) in Nebraska, hand weed the mint farms in Wisconsin, or plant strawberries in California. Next are the early harvests of peas, followed by the detasselling of corn and the back-breaking work of cutting cabbage and picking cucumbers, tomatoes, and strawberries. They are found in packing sheds in or near the fields, stuffing plastic bags with carrots, celery, onions, and other vegetables. After the harvest is completed in most states, they can be found spraying and shaping Christmas trees to make them green and perfect pyramids.

Some migrants work in slaughterhouses and meat-packing plants, while others work in canneries, canning fruits and vegetables. These are not field workers and so may or may not be counted as migrant farm workers. However, almost all of these workers also usually receive the minimum wage and rarely receive any fringe benefits. Today the USDA estimates that out of a work force of about 2.5 million hired farm workers, approximately 250,000 (or one in ten) fit the Oliveira and Cox definition as described earlier (Martin 1988, p. 52).

HISTORY

U.S. agriculture has used migratory labor since before the turn of the century, and racial and ethnic minorities have been and continue to be the sources of workers for migrant work. In California Chinese of the 1880s were followed by Japanese in the early 1900s and then by Filipinos in the 1920s. Immigrants from Europe provided hand labor throughout the United States in the 1920s. They included immigrants who came directly to farms from Europe, as well as immigrants who settled in major cities such as New York, Chicago, and Philadelphia and then supplemented their incomes by picking up seasonal farm work as needed. During World War II prisoners of war were put to work planting and harvesting to make up for shortages of migrant workers. For example, in the early 1940s Wisconsin counted over 3,500 prisoners of war who worked on farms (Sorden, Long, and Salick 1948). Since the late 1940s Mexicans have streamed across the Rio Grande Valley border in search of agricultural work. In addition, many Mexican Americans living in Texas also become migratory workers every spring, returning to Texas after the harvest season in the fall. People of Mexican heritage have become the mainstay of long-distance migratory workers in the West and Midwest. However, Blacks from Florida, Louisiana, and other Southern states and Puerto Ricans and other Caribbean Islanders have also been involved in migratory agricultural work since before World War II. They, however, usually work the crops up and down the East Coast.

When domestic labor shortages occurred, such as during and after World War II, or in times of high urban employment, when rural residents flocked to cities, the United States attempted to find agricultural workers through contracts with other countries. Formal agreements with Caribbean countries such as Haiti, the Dominican Republic, and Barbados, as well as with Mexico, especially through the well-known Bracero program (1942 to 1964), produced flows of workers.

Today most migrant workers are Hispanics and Blacks. There are also small populations of Central and Latin American immigrants and persons from the Philippines, as well as the newest group of immigrants, the Southeast Asians—Hmong, Thai, and Laotians.

THE EXCLUSION OF FARM WORKERS FROM SOCIAL LEGISLATION

Farm workers have not benefitted from the various pieces of the social legislation that were beginning to be enacted in the 1930s by state and federal governments. Many of these laws were established to improve the lives of hired employees. For example, unemployment insurance coverage established as part of the Social Security Act in 1935 excluded farm workers. It was not until 1976 that most farm workers were granted such benefits. Likewise, farm workers were excluded from the minimum-wage guarantees granted industrial workers under the Fair Labor Standards Act of 1938. Not until 1966 was minimum-wage protection granted to some farm workers. Workers compensation laws are intended to provide individuals with basic protection from injuries incurred at work. There is no federal workers compensation, however; such coverage is established by individual states. As Table 7.1 shows, few states offer farm workers such compensation to the same extent that they cover other workers. The lack of such coverage is all the more critical given the irregular enforcement of Occupational Safety and Health Administration regulations within the farm sector. The ability of farm workers to address employment-related grievances more directly via collective bargaining with employers is hamstrung by their exclusion from the provisions of the National Labor Relations Act that established

Table 7.1

Type of Workers' Compensation Coverage for Agricultural Workers by State, 1986

Agricultural Workers Covered the Same as All Other Workers	Limitations on Coverage for Agricultural Workers	Voluntary Coverage Available for Workers*
Arizona	Alaska	Alabama
California	Delaware	Arkansas
Colorado	Florida	Georgia
Connecticut	Illinois	Idaho
District of Columbia	Iowa	Indiana
Hawaii	Maine	Kansas
Louisiana	Maryland	Kentucky
Massachusetts	Michigan	Mississippi
Montana	Minnesota	Nebraska
New Hampshire	Missouri	Nevada
New Jersey	New York	New Mexico
Ohio	North Carolina	North Dakota
Oregon	Oklahoma	Rhode Island
	Pennsylvania	South Carolina
	South Dakota	Tennessee
	Texas	
	Utah	
	Vermont	
	Virginia	
	Washington	
	West Virginia	
	Wisconsin	
	Wyoming	

Source: Runyan 1989.

*Employers may volunteer to participate in the program, but are not required by law to do so.

the right of workers to unionize and bargain collectively. Such protective legislation has been granted farm workers in just two states, Hawaii in 1945 and California in 1975 (Goldfarb 1981; Runyan 1989).

Moreover, existing farm legislation offers no direct relief of farm worker poverty. The farm programs in effect today provide farmers with some relief from low incomes. These programs, first established by New Deal legislation, were designed to mitigate the effects of commodity surpluses and low farm commodity prices on farmers' incomes, but they contain no provisions for the direct support of farm workers' earnings. Parallel programs enacted under the New Deal that were intended to serve hired farm workers more directly have not endured (Daniel 1981; Majka and Majka 1982; Pfeffer and Gilbert 1989).

The New Deal recovery programs of the 1930s established the precedent of explicitly excluding farm workers from social legislation (Morris 1945; Goldfarb

1981). Although a number of programs administered by the Farm Security Administration, the Resettlement Administration, and other New Deal agencies directly benefitted farm workers, these programs received limited funding and were eventually discontinued. Most appropriations administered by the Department of Agriculture under the New Deal recovery programs went to commercial farmers, distributed via the Agricultural Adjustment Program, the Farm Credit Administration, the Soil Conservation Service, and the Federal Surplus Commodities Corporation. The basic farm programs enacted in the 1930s remain in effect today and include no provisions for the alleviation of poverty amongst farm workers. The architects of the New Deal did not explicitly include farm workers in major farm legislation on the premise that the farm programs would increase aggregate farm income, and farm workers would benefit indirectly as farmers raised wages. It was assumed that farmers would raise wages because of their close personal interest in the economic well-being of their workers (Daniel 1981; Goldfarb 1981; Majka and Majka 1982). This assumption embodied in the farm programs has never been effectively challenged, despite evidence spanning more than fifty years that the benefits received by farmers are typically not translated into improved employment conditions for workers (Daniel 1981; Pfeffer and Gilbert 1989).

Although farm workers in general have historically been excluded from protective legislation as described here, migrant farm workers fare worst of all. Their work at any one farm is typically for a short period of time, and they must travel from place to place in search of employment. Thus migrant farm workers earn less than farm workers employed year-round in one place; even seasonal farm workers living in the locality in which they are employed fare better than the migrants. The seasonal farm workers are able to draw on a network of friends and kin to improve their standard of living. Furthermore, they have the benefit of stable access to educational and health-care facilities (Thomas 1985; Jenkins 1985). Not until 1983, when the U.S. Congress passed the Migrant and Seasonal Agricultural Worker Protection Act (MSAWPA), were some of the special needs of migrant farm workers recognized. This is the first and only legislation geared specifically to the protection of migrant farm workers. This legislation was enacted to protect migrant and seasonal farm workers in terms of pay and working conditions. However, for the most part these protections are guaranteed only to those workers employed by farm-labor contractors, not to those employed directly by the farm owner or operator. Agricultural employers who contract employees only for their own operations are exempt from many of MSPA's provisions (Runyan 1989).

Migrant workers are continually vulnerable, even under the protection of established laws. For example, as recently as 1988, in Wisconsin and in several other states, employers tried to have migrant workers classified as ''independent contractors'' instead of hired farm workers. This would allow employers to ''contract'' with the workers and thus pay neither Social Security, workers compensation, nor unemployment compensation. In other words, employers wanted to evade the requirements of the Federal Fair Labor Standards Act. Migrant workers in Wisconsin obtained assistance from the state's Legal Action. A lawsuit filed by the U.S. Department of Labor, assisted by Legal Action of Wisconsin, resulted in the grower's case being thrown out in the Seventh U.S. Circuit Court of Appeals. The court found that migrant workers were clearly employees of growers and thus were entitled to protection under the Fair Labor Standards Act.

Another example concerned Mexican workers hired by a Wisconsin tobacco farmer in 1989. The farmer housed twenty-two people in one house trailer, which was without electricity, bottled gas, or running water. The situation was revealed when other migrant workers reported the situation to Legal Action. However, under Wisconsin statutes at the time, tobacco was not a crop whose workers were protected under the state's 1977 Migrant Labor Law. Tobacco was not among those products classified as a food or food product, sod, or nursery work, the only types of products included in the law. Thus the farmer's inhuman and unsanitary behavior could not be prosecuted under the state's migrant labor law. Fortunately, this situation was covered by the federal Fair Labor Standards Act and the Agricultural Workers' Protection Act, and the farmer was prosecuted. The next year, a bill was passed in the state legislature to add tobacco to the crops covered by the Migrant Labor Law. The latter law regulates work contracts and compensation as well as housing standards and sanitary conditions.

FARM WORKERS AND AGRARIAN DEVELOPMENT IN THE UNITED STATES

Despite their poverty, migrant farm workers have been excluded from many of the benefits and protections granted to other wage workers. The view of farm workers in American agrarian ideology established an important basis for leaving them out of much farm and labor legislation. Farm work was never held in high esteem in U.S. society. According to the agrarian ideal established early in our history, the work status of the hired farm worker was expected to be temporary. According to this ideal, working for another farmer was considered only as a step toward becoming an independent farm operator. Farm employment was seen as a means for individuals to amass the capital and skills necessary to begin to farm on their own. Farm work was thought of as an apprenticeship whereby one could develop the myriad of skills required to successfully operate a farm. Over time it was expected that hired employees would function with a degree of autonomy similar to that of the farm owner (Schwartz 1945; Daniel 1981; Kloppenburg and Geisler 1985). Depictions of the agrarian ideal typically stressed the homogenizing effect of farm work on the relationships between farmers and their hired employees. Because the worker would soon achieve the same status as his employer, it was assumed that there was little basis for conflicts of interest. Furthermore, because they labored in close personal contact with one another on a daily basis, strong social bonds would presumably be established between the farmer and the worker. Hired workers intent on becoming independent farmers in the locality, it was believed, would also establish social ties via participation in community institutions like churches and schools. Some discussions of the agrarian ideal acknowledged that not all workers would be in a position to become independent farm operators, and that farmers would sometimes have to employ individuals on a more temporary basis during exceptionally busy times like the crop harvest. However, the general consensus was that such workers would not be treated as a class apart, because they were part of an integrated rural community (Coulter 1912; Schwartz 1945; Daniel 1981).

While the extent to which agricultural development in the United States ever actually approximated the agrarian ideal is debatable,[1] it is clear that the interests and possibilities of the rural populace in scaling the agricultural ladder from farm worker to independent farm operator were limited. This fact was borne out in the steady stream of migrants out of rural areas in the latter half of the nineteenth century. In this process the position of hired labor in U.S. agriculture became increasingly marginal, because farmers relied increasingly on machinery as they attempted to expand production and overcome persistent shortages of labor. Consequently, many farms, especially in the Midwest and the Great Plains, were operated with virtually no labor beyond that provided by the farm family (Friedmann 1978; Pfeffer 1983a). In those cases where seasonal or migrant labor was required for the cultivation and harvesting of labor-intensive crops like fruits, vegetables, and tobacco, the hired farm work force was virtually invisible within the sea of family-labor farms.

IDEALIZATION OF THE FAMILY FARM

Although important exceptions to the family-farm model have existed in parts of the South and the West, the bulk of all farms in the United States have been, and continue to be, family operations. This form of organization was hailed as the best approximation of the agrarian ideal developed in the course of U.S. history. The marginal importance of farm workers on family farms meant that the characterization embodied in the agrarian ideal of harmonious employer-employee relations remained unchallenged. This notion became an important legitimating factor for the exclusion of farm workers from social legislation enacted in the 1930s.

As noted earlier, farm workers' exclusion from a variety of New Deal labor legislation was based on the assumption that there was no conflict of interest between farm workers and their employers. This point becomes most clear when one considers the exclusion of farm workers from coverage under the National Labor Relations Act (NLRA). This legislation "provided a legal and institutional framework for industrial conflict, and an environment conducive to the growth of a . . . labor movement that could confront employers directly" (Daniel 1981, p. 173). When pressed to provide a justification for the exclusion of farm workers from coverage under the NLRS, New Deal spokesmen "argued that the interests

Table 7.2
Farms by Amount of Wages Paid, United States, 1987

Annual
Wages Paid ($)   Percentage of All Farms

Annual Wages Paid ($)	Percentage of All Farms
None	60.8
1-999	18.3
1,000-4,999	9.3
5,000-9,999	3.5
10,000-24,999	4.5
25,000-49,999	1.9
50,000-79,999	.8
80,000-99,999	.2
100,000 +	.7
Total	100.0
Number of farms	2,087,734

Source: 1987 Census of Agriculture.

of farm workers . . . would be protected under the Agricultural Adjustment Act, which would provide not only greater aggregate income for the agricultural sector, but also a fair sharing of that new wealth at every level of the farming economy'' (Daniel 1981, p. 174).

The basic assumption at the time was that farm workers were in no need of special protection because of the special character of labor relations in agriculture, that is, the close personal relations between farmers and their employees (Morris 1945; Goldfarb 1981). While this assumption may have been valid for the many farms that employed very little hired labor, those employing large numbers of workers more closely approximated the industrial model of labor organization than the agrarian ideal. Indeed, an enduring characteristic of agricultural employment is its concentration on a relatively small number of large farms nationwide. In 1987 about 1.5 percent of all farms had sales of $500,000 or more and accounted for almost 55 percent of all expenditures for farm labor (Schwartz 1945; U.S. Bureau of the Census 1989a).

AGRICULTURAL EMPLOYERS AND THE
AGRARIAN IDEAL

While family farms have dominated the rural landscape in terms of sheer numbers, farms employing large numbers of workers can also be found. Table 7.2 shows that more than three-fifths of all farms in the United States (60.8

percent) reported no wage labor expenses. On the other hand, a small number of farms reported very large payrolls. For example, 15,150 farms reported paying more than $100,000 in wages annually. Hired labor is most important on farms growing labor-intensive crops like fruits and vegetables, and such employment tends to be erratic during the production season. Workers unable to secure steady employment on any one farm are often required to move from one employer to another. The geographical range of such movement is extended when there is regional specialization in a limited number of crops, because workers are forced to migrate to another location when seasonal employment in the local specialty dries up.

Farms specializing in the production of labor-intensive commodities are found throughout the United States, but the demand for migrant farm workers is especially pronounced in areas where most farms are engaged in the production of labor-intensive crops. In parts of Florida, Texas, and California, farms are typically very large and engage in highly specialized production. Labor relations on such farms bear little resemblance to the agrarian ideal discussed earlier. Observers have long noted that labor relations on large-scale farms are quite impersonal. Workers are viewed abstractly as labor, that is, as a factor of production to be utilized as efficiently as possible in the production process (Daniel 1981).

To minimize the costs associated with employing farm workers, farmers have sought to maximize their control over the work force. Such control is often at odds with the interests of farm workers. For example, farmers have typically attempted to hold down wages, and these efforts have kept workers living in poverty. Farmers have also made an effort to insure that workers are readily available when needed for a particular farm operation and that they remain on the job until the work involved is completed. However, when these workers have been no longer needed on the farm, they have been encouraged to leave the area in search of other work so that any direct or indirect costs associated with their maintenance (e.g., the provision of social services, education, and so on) would be minimized (Jenkins 1985; Pfeffer 1986).

To maintain control of the migrant farm work force, employers of large numbers of farm workers have sought to influence government policy. Part of their strategy is to represent their interests as identical to those of the broader farm sector. In doing so, they have been able to conjure up the agrarian ideal as a means of generating sympathy for their cause. Thus initiatives to improve the lot of farm workers have been portrayed as inimical to the economic survival of all farmers, both large and small. The central argument presented against protective legislation for farm workers is the need to protect family farmers from exorbitant costs. The exclusion of farm workers from protective labor legislation has played an important part in maintaining the powerlessness of farm workers to improve their working conditions (Daniel 1981; Goldfarb 1981).

FARM WORKER POWERLESSNESS

Migrant farm workers enjoy few of the advantages presumed to stem from close personal ties between workers and their employers. As noted earlier, this notion embodied in the agrarian ideal has been used to justify their exclusion from protective legislation granted other workers. In light of this experience, it is not surprising that migrant farm workers have remained an impoverished segment of American society. Moreover, they have been unable to mount successful drives to improve the conditions of their lives.

On the face of things, farm workers hold a strategic position. Given the perishability of many farm commodities, the failure of workers to harvest the crop could prove disastrous for farmers. However, several factors have come together to limit the effectiveness of collective efforts to promote farm worker interests. For one thing, given their impoverished condition, migrant farm workers have lacked a resource base with which to challenge established social structures. For another, migrants have never been a stable part of the agricultural community like the farm workers portrayed in the agrarian ideal. The erratic and seasonal nature of their employment contributes to their exclusion from membership in a stable community and has inhibited the development of social solidarity with other farm workers. This lack of rootedness in a community also makes them ineligible for a variety of social services offered to local residents (Jenkins 1985).

The social marginality of migrants has been reinforced by the active recruitment of ethnic and racial minorities into farm work. Such recruitment has sometimes been justified on account of the unwillingness of Whites to work on farms, given the more desirable working conditions in urban areas. This practice was effective because of racist sentiments of employers and labor unions in urban areas. Racism had the effect of excluding the Chinese, Japanese, Blacks, Filipinos, Mexicans, and others from all but the most menial jobs in urban areas (Schwartz 1945; Pfeffer 1983b). The powerlessness of migrant farm workers was in part due to "the recruitment of a workforce whose estrangement from the social and cultural mainstream was so profound and unalterable as to render it captive economically" (Daniel 1981, p. 27).

The success of the United Farm Workers (UFW) union in California in the late 1960s and the 1970s raised the prospect of a new era for migrant farm workers. For the first time in U.S. history, what appeared to be a stable organization representing the interests of farm workers had come into being. However, the 1980s proved to be a difficult time for the UFW. Membership has declined steadily, and many of the gains won in previous years appear to be in jeopardy. For example, new technologies that permit the field packaging of products like lettuce and broccoli have served to erode the UFW's base of power. In 1977 the UFW and the Teamsters Union reached an agreement on the organization of agricultural workers. Under this agreement the UFW had jurisdiction to organize field workers, and the Teamsters would limit their organizing efforts to workers in packing-shed and postharvest handling operations. But the advent of field packing technologies eroded this distinction, and the Teamsters have been able to negotiate contracts with growers to cover between 5,000 and 6,000 workers involved in such operations. Many of these workers are migrant workers, but of a new sort. They tend to be skilled workers who maintain field packing machines and portable refrigeration units. These workers move with the harvest. For example, those involved with the lettuce harvest will be in the Imperial Valley and Arizona in the winter and in the Salinas Valley in the spring and summer. Unskilled packing workers tend to be local women who do not move with the production. The UFW has made no new efforts to organize workers in about the last ten years. Instead, it has concentrated on representing the approximately 25,000 workers that it has already organized. However, aggressive efforts to organize lettuce workers have been made in recent years by a breakaway group from the Teamsters. Nevertheless, the vast majority of California's farm workers (about 750,000 by some estimates) remain unorganized, and little effort has been made to organize unskilled migrant workers (Villarejo 1990). Thus what the future holds for farm workers in California remains uncertain at best and bleak at worst. Despite some success by the UFW on the West Coast, migrant farm workers in many parts of the United States have not had the benefit of organized and stable representation. For the most part, migrants remain an impoverished group lacking access to stable employment and the benefits and protections enjoyed by workers in other sectors of the economy. We get a better sense of the problems of migrant farm workers by taking a closer look at their attributes and special needs.

THE CURRENT SCENE

Migrant agricultural workers in host states are often an "invisible" population to most year-round residents who do not know when and where migrants work. This invisibility and the varying definitions of "migrant" mentioned earlier have meant that few accurate statistics have been collected on this population. Even though we know little about the characteristics of migrants on a national level (Shenkin 1974), there are a number of local and regional studies that shed some light on this population (White-Means, Chi, and McClain 1989; Rogers 1984; Bleiweis et al. 1977; Barr et al. 1988; Friedland and Nelkin 1971).

Age and Sex

Until recently, the Current Population Survey had a special supplement every two years in December to estimate the farm worker population in the nation. Workers were asked about their employment the previous two weeks. This underestimated seasonal and migrant farm workers because in the cold days of December few of them are employed in agricultural work. In addition, seasonal and migrant farm workers who live in Mexico during the winter are never counted. Thus it is generally agreed that the number of migrant agricultural workers is underestimated. However, if we assume that the characteristics of those who are counted are similar to the characteristics of those who are not counted (this may be a dubious assumption), the following description of migrant workers in 1985 (reported by Oliveira and Cox in 1988) would be appropriate: migrant workers are predominantly male; they tend to be older workers, with a median age of 32; their racial composition is about 46 percent White, 15 percent Hispanic, and 39 percent Black and other races.

Family Status

Each group may work as a family unit, or the adults may travel as "singles," leaving families behind. The specific farm activities in which the migrants are employed often determine whether children and wives are brought along. By and large, it is an advantage to have families harvesting field crops such as green beans, cucumbers for pickles, peppers, and cabbage because families are often paid by the "bushel basket." Children are not useful if migrants work in canneries, where workers get an hourly wage, and husbands and wives often work the same shifts. Mexicans tend to travel in families; labor contracts with other nations are usually for "singles." Even if a husband and wife sign up together, it is likely that they will not be permitted to sleep in the same quarters, because when housing is provided, males and females are usually placed in separate dormitories.

Others found in the migrant population are called "freewheelers" because they roam the country in search of farm work, going where information from their "grapevine" tells them jobs are available. Because of the unpredictability of weather and the difficulty of judging whether a crop is going to be substantial or thin, freewheelers often perform an important service for farmers. However, they usually do not have labor contracts, will often accept wages that are below the minimum wage, and live in housing that is neither inspected nor even defined as "housing," such as abandoned barns or cars or even a blanket under a tree.

Socioeconomic Status

Both national data (Whitener 1984) and in-depth interviews with random samples of migrant workers in Wisconsin (Slesinger 1979a; Slesinger and Ofstead 1990) indicate that the likely annual income of migrants is barely above poverty level. Migrants who travel longer distances each year (over 500 miles) are more likely to be minorities and to receive all their income from migratory farm work (Rowe 1979). For example, in the 1989 Wisconsin study about 46 percent of the workers reported that all of their 1988 income came from migrant work. Another 22 percent supplemented income from migrant agricultural work with unemployment compensation in the winter.[2] Fifty-eight percent of the families qualified for and received Food Stamps, and one-fourth of the families also participated in the Women, Infants, and Children's nutrition program, a program offered only to families with pregnant or lactating women and children under five. Other minor sources of income included other wage work, self-employment, and borrowing from relatives, friends, and banks. Counting all of these sources, their median family income was approximately $7,330 in 1988. On the average, 5.2 persons were dependent upon this income, placing the average household in poverty (Slesinger and Ofstead 1990).

Health Problems

Migrant health and education are two areas of contemporary major concern. Both areas were considered so seriously underserved through the usual state and local governmental and private systems that during the War on Poverty the federal government established national programs to address the special needs of this unusual population. The establishment of migrant health clinics was authorized in 1962 under the Public Health Service Act as part of the Community Health Centers program for the poor and medically underserved population. This meant that throughout the United States, federally funded migrant health clinics were opened where there were sufficient groups of migratory workers. Staffing usually included a physician placed under the National Health Service Corps, as well as physician assistants, nurse practitioners, nutritionists, and outreach workers. Recently, oversight for these clinics was combined with that of the community health centers, the network of centers that were established mostly in poor, urban neighborhoods. Medical services were expanded to include dental care and eye care.

In 1988, however, federal funding for the National Health Service Corps was almost eliminated. The administration also made a strong effort to eliminate the special federal funding of community health centers and fold it into the "block-grant" concept of giving states blocks of money and letting local political powers decide how to divide the pot of money. This was successfully fought by the community health centers and their constituency, so that federal funds still flow directly to these health centers for the poor. However, budgets have barely been maintained and have not increased with inflation. Thus in real dollars budgets have been reduced, and many services have been eliminated.

Given the authors' familiarity with Wisconsin, we can briefly explain what this has meant. In 1984 the Wisconsin migrant health clinic, La Clinica de los Campesinos, had one main location in the state, situated within reasonable reach of about 50 percent of the migrant workers in the state. It also maintained two outstations, one near a set of canneries that employed migrants, the other in a distant area where there was a large area of field work. The outstations were open two long days a week and provided medical and dental services. Three outreach workers from La Clinica traveled to the various housing camps. They identified pregnant women and infants who needed checkups or immunizations;

led small group talks about nutrition; and provided information about the services around the state that were available to migrants.

Recently, La Clinica has had to close the two outstations. For a few years they tried sending a van with a registered nurse to the different locations to conduct blood pressure screening and eye and hearing tests and to provide information about various health conditions. However, the budget was again cut in 1989, and the van sponsored by La Clinica is not in operation. An order of nuns from a nearby city has taken on this role and in the 1989 season visited the camps with a van staffed by two nurses. With only one outreach worker now budgeted by La Clinica, case-finding activities of the clinic have been sharply curtailed.

In the 1989 season Slesinger repeated the migrant health survey that was originally conducted with migrant workers in Wisconsin in 1978. The major health problems identified by migrant workers in the recent Wisconsin survey differed little from those mentioned over ten years earlier (Slesinger 1979b, p. 35). The 1989 problems included back pain, headaches, eye trouble, nervousness, irritability, dental problems, stomach trouble, coughing, shortness of breath, and trouble sleeping (Slesinger and Ofstead 1990). Preventive health care was one of the most serious unmet health needs. Almost 30 percent of the workers had never had a general physical examination, one out of four workers had never been to a dentist, and 43 percent had never had a vision test (Slesinger and Ofstead 1990; Slesinger 1979b, p. 47).

Educational Problems

From the time a child migrates with his or her parents, education suffers. The annual mobility means that the child rarely is registered in only one school each year. Often in the early ages the child is not placed in any school. Once the child is in first or second grade, however, the parents try to keep the child going to school. Once again, using an example of Wisconsin migrant families, this may mean that the child starts school late in September or early October when the family returns to Texas. By the end of March or early April the family starts its annual trek northward. As long as the family is on the move, the child will not be entered into schools along the way (this can be in Arkansas, Missouri, or Minnesota). In late May or early June, when they arrive in Wisconsin, the final receiving state, the "regular" school year is almost completed. With the advent of a summer school program especially conducted for migrant children by the Texas Migrant Council, these children are placed in preschool, elementary-school, or high-school classes with bilingual teachers. The funds to conduct these classes are provided by the 1967 amendment to Title I of the Elementary and Secondary Education Act of 1965, designed to help educationally deprived children.

Not only did this federal act provide funds for hiring bilingual teachers and renting school space in receiving states, it also established the Migrant Student

Table 7.3
Distribution of Children in Wisconsin's Migrant Education Program by Total Number of Schools in which Child Enrolled between September 1, 1982, and August 31, 1983

Number of School Enrollments	Current Migrant Family*	Former Migrant Family
1	14.6	27.6
2	11.4	24.5
3	9.2	21.3
4	12.2	10.3
5	13.1	14.0
6	31.9	0.8
Incomplete Information	7.6	1.5
Total (%)	100.0	100.0
(N)	1,421	658

Source: Cautley, Slesinger, and Parra 1985.

*Current migrant families are those who have been in migrant agricultural work within the past two years. Former migrant families are those who were employed in migrant work two to six years ago.

Record Transfer System (MSRTS) in conjunction with another amendment. This is a computerized system, with educational records of migrant children from all over the United States maintained on a computer located in Little Rock, Arkansas. The purpose of this system is to track the educational records of migrant children. Thus, when a local school registers a migrant child, the office can pull the academic record of that child in order to see what grades the child has completed, what national test scores were recorded, and other basic information about the child. Very often the child returns to the same set of schools year after year. Through this system school officials can see what happened when the child was in his or her home state, and vice versa. However, discontinuities in education still prevail. Table 7.3 presents data from a review of records of children registered in Wisconsin in the MSRTS system for the 1982–83 year. Fifty-seven percent of children in families currently in the migrant work force have had four or more enrollments in one calendar year. This compares with 25 percent of children in families who had been in migrant work, but who had "settled out" of the migrant stream two to six years in the past.

For Mexican and Central and Latin American children, having a bilingual teacher is helpful. Perhaps what is even more important is that there is some appreciation of their cultural heritage and life-style. Dropout rates are still high for children of migrant workers. In the 1989 study 72 married women aged 18–49 in migrant families had produced 307 children, or on average, 4.3 children. Of these, 182, living in 44 families, were age 12 or older and "at risk" of dropping out of school. Twelve of these mothers (27.3 percent) reported that one or more of their children had dropped out of school; approximately 40 percent had dropped out before ninth grade. Many children are forced to drop out because their labor is needed by the family. Some parents feel that children do not need high school if they are to do farm work for the rest of their lives. Some parents do not realize how difficult it is for their children to continue in school when they must leave the classroom before the term is over and start in a class after the term has begun.

Summer programs definitely help this situation. Remedial work is usually stressed in the upper grades. However, to our knowledge, no evaluation of the summer program has yet been conducted. It is hard to keep track of the educational progress of the children registered in the MSRTS program, much less those who are not registered in the program.

FUTURE TRENDS AND POLICY IMPLICATIONS

Looking toward the future of the migrant workers, we identify five national and international trends that will affect their numbers and well-being: (1) biotechnology and genetic engineering; (2) continued mechanization in agricultural production; (3) low-chemical-input or sustainable agriculture; (4) immigration policies and patterns; and (5) federal minimum-wage increases.

First, we are now in the midst of broad applications to agricultural production of genetic engineering and biotechnology. As this is being written, there is much public concern over bovine somatotropin (BST), or bovine growth hormone (BGH) as it is popularly known, and its use on dairy herds. Although milk production and dairy farms rarely employ migrant labor, the replacement of labor by technology remains a concern. Dairy scientists anticipate greater milk production based on fewer cows and less farm labor. However, this technological advance does not target hired hands, but hits the family farm and its idealized place in American tradition, as stated earlier. Instead of hired hands being laid off, some critics of BGH suggest that it is sounding the "death knell" of the family farm.

We cannot say what additional technological and scientific developments may be under the electron microscope. But some possible developments we envision may include pickles that stop growing at three inches; lettuce that will not wilt or bruise; and corn whose sugar content will remain for a week after picking. Should these developments occur, migrant field hands will not be needed to pick and sort cucumbers for size, cut each head of lettuce individually, or work around the clock in canneries canning corn within twenty-four hours of picking.

Second, mechanization has already reduced hand picking in potatoes, grapes, tomatoes, and cherries. It is not unrealistic to expect new machines to be developed to pick apples and cucumbers. Whenever a successful mechanical picker is invented, fewer migrant hands are needed. When migrants do continue to be used after new technology is adopted, as in the case of the mobile packing operations described earlier, migrant work will involve fewer workers and may be transformed from unskilled to skilled workers with better pay.

Third, the call by some farmers, consumers, and environmentalists for the production of agricultural commodities with fewer chemical inputs has received increasing attention in recent years. Historically, chemicals served as a relatively cheap substitute for more expensive labor inputs. Such substitution is especially apparent in the use of herbicides that eliminated the need for manual or machine cultivation to control weeks. However, the negative consequences of such chemical usage are now becoming more apparent. The UFW, in particular, has made a major effort in recent years to educate the public about the perils of agricultural chemicals for farm workers. The development of agricultural practices that allow for the reduction or even elimination of chemicals from farm production may have profound effects on the lives of farm workers. Given the great health risks associated with the use of chemicals, a move toward low-input agriculture might mean improved working conditions for farm workers. It is also possible that low-input agriculture will increase the demand for labor, thereby counteracting some of the trends toward the reduced employment of migrant workers discussed earlier.

Fourth, the erratic history of immigration policies and patterns in the United States will no doubt be repeated in the future. When agricultural producers cry out for minimum-wage farm workers, usually immigrants are the only labor pool available. Yet immigration policies are political, favoring persons from countries whose ancestors are already here, or who are fleeing from political or religious persecution. Occasionally priority is also given to those whose occupations are needed. Unskilled laborers, under the latter category, have lowest priority. Therefore, as in the past, special immigration laws are created to satisfy agricultural labor demands. We anticipate that this patchwork policy will continue.

Finally, we address the minimum-wage legislation. Many critics of poverty policy have noted that marginal poverty families can be raised above poverty level if the minimum wage is raised. There is no doubt that this argument applies to migrant workers. Those who work in canneries or packing houses would get immediate raises in income. Many field workers also earn minimum hourly wages because the "bushel" rate is pegged to the minimum hourly wage.

However, workers and their families who earn only the minimum wage over the planting and harvesting season would still remain in the poverty group, because their annual income is based on their employment during only a portion of the year. For these families, a federal guaranteed annual income plan would be appropriate.

CONCLUSIONS

As we have documented, migrant farm workers as a group are poor and have always been poor. The lack of economic improvement stems from a number of sociopolitical reasons that include the political powerlessness of farm workers, the political influence of agricultural employers, and the marginal status of farm workers in U.S. agricultural development. The number of workers needed in agriculture has been declining and will probably continue to decline, due to developments in mechanization for planting and harvesting and advances in computerization of production lines in canneries and packing plants. At the same time, we anticipate that there will frequently be requirements for large groups of farm laborers for short periods of time as farmers change their crops, depending on world prices. Exemplifying this in Oregon are the thousands of new acres of asparagus fields, a crop that is labor-intensive. Other examples are the "organically grown" fruits and vegetables now being demanded by consumers. These crops often must be hand weeded instead of using applications of herbicides, and this results in sizeable labor requirements. None of these labor needs can be adequately filled by local workers, friends, neighbors, or relatives of the farmers. Migrant workers are and will be sorely needed. But until employers, government officials, organized labor, and others recognize that farm workers have the same rights as employees in other industries, few of the special needs of the politically and economically powerless migrant workers will be met.

NOTES

1. Some have proclaimed the realization of this agrarian ideal with the abolition of slavery at the end of the Civil War (e.g., Cochrane 1979).

2. Unemployment compensation (UC) benefits are difficult for migrants to claim. First, they must have worked for employers who qualify to pay UC. That is, the employer must have paid cash farm wages of $20,000 or more during any calendar quarter or employed ten or more workers in agricultural labor for a minimum of twenty different weeks in this or the previous year. When a migrant is out of work, he or she must file a form on which he or she lists every employer he or she has worked for, no matter where the employer was located. The state then checks these employers to see if they are "covered" employers. If so, the person will receive UC. However, because migrants often work in many states, it is a computer nightmare to check these employers' names, especially since small employers are not covered. UC is also administered by states, so that states differ in reporting periods, qualifying work, and other requirements. It is usually migrants who are employed by large, national companies who are covered by UC, e.g., Green Giant, Del Monte, Heinz, and so on.

Chapter 8

American Indians and Economic Poverty

C. Matthew Snipp and Gene F. Summers

American Indians are one of the smallest minority groups in America. In 1980 they numbered about 1.37 million, or about .6 percent of the total U.S. population of 226 million. The results from the most recent 1990 census are not yet available, but American Indians are still probably fewer than 1.75 million in number. American Indians are also one of the poorest groups in American society. Nearly one of every four families has an income below the poverty level. In 1979 half of all Indian families had an income less than $14,000. During that same year half of the White families in America had incomes of almost $21,000. Even those Indians who are not poor feel the burden of Indian poverty.

American Indians are primarily rural people. Slightly over one-half of all American Indians and Alaska natives reside outside of metropolitan areas, many on reservation lands (see Figure 8.1). There are 278 reservations, and a little over one-third of the Indian population lives on these or other specially designated trust lands under the administration of the Bureau of Indian Affairs (BIA). These lands are commonly referred to by Native Americans as "Indian Country" and are located mostly west of the Mississippi River (see Map 8.1).

In many respects reservations resemble small quasi-sovereign governments located within the boundaries of the United States. They have a unique political and legal status that has evolved over decades of treaty making, legal settlements, court decisions, and policy actions. Today they are governed by tribal officials and have a unique relationship with the federal government that transcends the authority of local and state governments. Poverty policy in Indian Country must work within this legal context.

Reservation residents have the equivalent of dual citizenship, as members of their tribe and as citizens of the United States. Because of past agreements and relationships between their tribal governments and the United States, they have some rights and privileges that are not available to other U.S. citizens. When American Indians leave their reservations, they become subjects of local and

Figure 8.1
American Indian Places of Residence

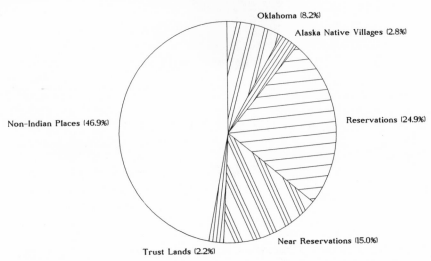

Oklahoma (8.2%)

Alaska Native Villages (2.8%)

Non-Indian Places (46.9%)

Reservations (24.9%)

Near Reservations (15.0%)

Trust Lands (2.2%)

state laws where they reside, like any other U.S. citizen, and they forfeit most benefits of their dual citizenship status. For example, programs of agencies such as the BIA and the Indian Health Service (IHS) operate almost exclusively in Indian Country.

Outside of reservations, American Indians are most heavily concentrated in large cities in the West and the Midwest. Cities such as Los Angeles, San Francisco, Seattle, Minneapolis, Chicago, and Oklahoma City have large populations of urban Indians. Yet urban American Indians enjoy few of the special legal distinctions conferred upon reservation Indians. Consequently, the public policies directed at urban Indian poverty are not very different from those affecting all impoverished urban minority groups.

American Indians comprise a unique ethnic group in the United States. The rural American Indian populations are concentrated on reservations characterized by high levels of poverty. Urban American Indians certainly are not immune to poverty and economic hardship; but very few policy initiatives are aimed at this group that are not directed at other urban groups as well.

In this chapter we provide a brief outline of the historical treatment of American Indians in the United States from colonization up to the present day, placing specific emphasis on the federal government's solution to the "Indian problem." We explore in greater detail the federal government's policies toward poverty among American Indians during the twentieth century, detailing the social and economic conditions facing American Indians today. Finally, we conclude with some general policy recommendations that would contribute to the improvement of conditions facing the Native American population.

PUBLIC POLICY AND AMERICAN INDIANS:
A HISTORICAL OVERVIEW

Since the founding of the United States, public policy for American Indians has been marked by several different eras (Snipp and Summers, 1991). In the earliest days of the nation, the leaders of the new government had little choice except to negotiate as equals with Indian tribes. Limited military and financial resources left the fledgling U.S. government with few options except to deal with the leaders of various Indian tribes on a true government-to-government basis.

This era was short-lived, however, and soon gave way to the removal era (ca. 1830–80), in which thousands of Indians were removed from their tribal homelands, often forcibly, and resettled on reservations or the Indian Territory in what is now the state of Oklahoma. As the U.S. population expanded in numbers and spread across the continent, American Indians were typically perceived as obstacles to national development, an attitude expressed in the doctrine of ''manifest destiny.'' Efforts to remove and isolate American Indians away from new White settlers' advances ushered in a period of widespread and bloody conflict between Whites and Indians. Ultimately, American Indians were resettled on reservations, and by the end of the nineteenth century it was widely expected that American Indians would recede into extinction.

The allotment era followed, and in this period (ca. 1880–1930) the federal government implemented genocidal measures to force Indians to abandon their traditional ways and adopt the practices of White society. The policies of this era were designed to begin the process of a deliberate devaluation of the Native American culture, with the hopes of hastening the assimilation of American Indians into ''mainstream'' American culture. To hasten the assimilation and thereby the disappearance of American Indians as a distinct ethnic group, Indian families were assigned parcels of land (land allotments) and expected to adopt European agricultural practices. Bureau of Indian Affairs boarding schools were established during this period. Indian children enrolled in these schools were to be indoctrinated into ''mainstream'' America with an education that stressed the European heritage of American history. Native American culture and history were neither taught nor allowed as part of the curriculum in these schools.

From the founding of the United States until the early twentieth century, the economic hardships suffered by American Indians did not concern the American public. During its first 130 years the federal government concentrated on dislodging American Indians from their homelands. Their continued existence was regarded as an impediment to national development. By the late nineteenth and early twentieth centuries the extinction of American Indians appeared imminent. Public policy continued to be aimed toward the goal of eliminating the remaining American Indian population, but the strategy was changed from physical extermination and isolation of American Indians to cultural annihilation. It was not until the 1920s that the economic plight of American Indians received serious

Map 8.1
American Indian Lands and Communities

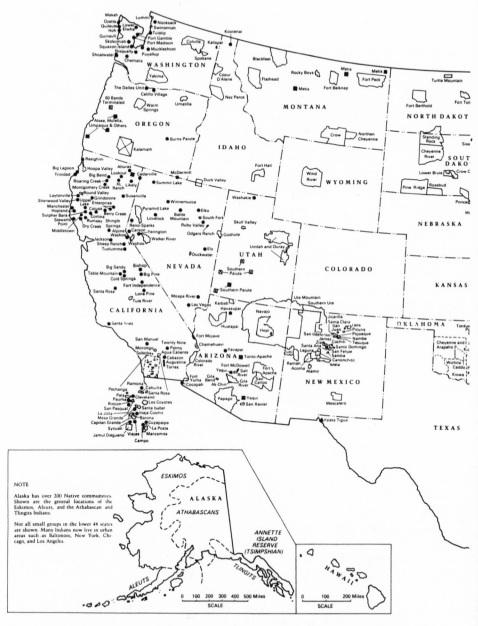

Source: Reprinted from *American Indians*, by C. Matthew Snipp. Copyright © 1989, Russell Sage Foundation. Used with permission of the Russell Sage Foundation.

Red Lake
Nett Lake
Nett Lake
Deer Creek
Grand Portage
Lake Superior
Leech Lake
Red Cliff
Fond Du Lac
Bad River
Ontonagon
L'Anse
White Earth
Keweenaw Bay
Bay Mills
Mille Lac
Lac Court Oreille
Lac Du Flambeau
Mole Lake
Ottawa & Chippewa
Chippewa
Hannahville
Upper Sioux
Prior Lake
St. Croix Communities
Menominee
Stockbridge Munsee
Potawatomi
Ottawa & Chippewa
Lower Sioux
Prairie Island
Oneida
Isabella
Flandreau
Isabella
Yankton
Santee
MINNESOTA
WISCONSIN
Lake Michigan
nnebago
Omaha
IOWA
Sac and Fox
Potawatomi
Lake Huron
Lake Ontario
St. Regis
Mohawk
MAINE
Malecite
Micmac
Passamaquoddy
Pleasant Point
Penobscot
VER.
N.H.
MASS.
Oneida
Onondaga
Seneca
Tonawanda
Cattaraugus
NEW YORK
Nipmuc
Wampanoag
CONN. R.I.
Narraganset
Scaticook
Montauk
Pequot
Mohegan
Paugusett
Shinnecock
Poosepawtuck
Seneca
Alleghany
Cayuga
Seneca
N.J.
Miami
OHIO
INDIANA
ILLINOIS
PENNSYLVANIA
MARYLAND
WEST VIRGINIA
DEL.
Moor
Nanticoke
Rappananock
Upper Mattaponi
Amherst County
Pamunkey
Mattaponi
Chickahominy
VIRGINIA
Person County
Haliwa
Iowa
Kickapoo
Potawatomi
Wyandot
Chippewa
Munsee Delaware
MISSOURI
KENTUCKY
NORTH CAROLINA
Cherokee
Comarie
Lumbee
Catawba
Waccamaw
Quapaw
Modoc
Wyandotte
Seneca
Peoria
Ottawa
Seneca
Kaw
Osage
Cherokee
TENNESSEE
SOUTH CAROLINA
Summerville
Fawnee
kapoo
Land Fox
Creek
Seminole
otawatomi
d Shawnee
Chickasaw
Choctaw
ARKANSAS
MISS.
Choctaw
ALABAMA
GEORGIA
LOUISIANA
Choctaw
Tunica
Coushatta
Choctaw
Alabam-Coushatta
Chitimacha
Houma
Creek
FLORIDA
Brighton
Big Cypress
Miccosukee
Seminole
Hollywood
Seminole

		Federal Indian Reservation
		Former Reservations in Oklahoma
▲		State Reservations
■		Indian Groups Without Trust Land
		Federally Terminated Tribes and Groups

50 0   50 100 150 200 Miles
SCALE

attention, almost as an afterthought in the social reform movement that swept the nation at the turn of the century.

The reform movement reached American Indians in the 1920s and took notice of their desperate economic circumstances. By then it was clear that earlier efforts to exterminate them or culturally assimilate them had failed. Those American Indians who had survived lived in abject poverty, and social reform activists appealed to the national conscience on their behalf.

The years from 1930 to 1950 marked the era of the Indian New Deal policies. These policies are particularly noteworthy for several reasons. First, they were genuinely sympathetic to American Indian problems and represented a marked departure from the hostility of the past. Also, these policies coincided with the rise of the welfare state in America, and thus the Indian New Deal was America's first serious effort to develop public policies for confronting the economic hardships of reservation Indians. From this perspective, the Indian New Deal and the events leading up to it mark the earliest beginnings of antipoverty policies for American Indians.

In 1950 the federal government moved to dissolve its involvement with American Indians by terminating the reservation system; this was the termination era (ca. 1950–75). These policies resurrected earlier ideas about the hastening of the assimilation of American Indians into "mainstream" American society. They differed, however, in the amount of emphasis that was placed on the economic problems facing the American Indians population. Thus these new policies were aimed primarily at improving the economic opportunities available to American Indians, with the assumption that increased opportunity would solve the various social problems facing American Indians as well as facilitate the integration process.

American Indians refused to abandon their culture and communities, however. By the mid-1970s the federal government recognized the commitment of Native Americans to their cultural heritage and ways of life and instituted the current policy of self-determination. The policy was officially inaugurated with the passage of the American Indian Self-Determination and Educational Assistance Act of January 4, 1975. This legislation marked the culmination of a long period of political struggle by American Indians, who had viewed themselves all along as conquered nations. The act restored certain rights of self-government in their communities. The movement for self-determination also has had major implications for economic opportunities in Indian Country.

These eras are convenient for sketching the major public policy developments that have affected the well-being of American Indians. However, a closer look at these policies and their impact is essential for understanding the nature of American Indian poverty and the measures that have been taken against it. Beyond the historical record, quantitative data are virtually nonexistent for assessing the early attempts to deal with American Indian poverty. It is possible, however, to examine data from later years to gauge more recent levels of economic hardship among American Indians. The Indian New Deal is a natural point of departure because this policy initiative set the stage for antipoverty efforts that have continued into the present.

FEDERAL POLICY DURING THE TWENTIETH CENTURY

The Meriam Report and the Indian New Deal

Concern for the poverty facing reservation Indians emerged for the first time in the mid-1920s. As America became more urbanized and prospered in the 1920s, there was growing concern among various reform groups about the dire economic conditions on Indian reservations. In the summer of 1926 the Office of Indian Affairs (a precursor of the BIA) with financial support from John D. Rockefeller, Jr., commissioned a blue-ribbon panel to study reservation conditions. The legwork for this study was undertaken by the Institute for Government Research (a forerunner of the Brookings Institution) and directed by Lewis Meriam, an institute staff member and an attorney by training. The commission's report was submitted to the secretary of the interior early in 1928 and has since become known as the Meriam Report (Prucha 1984).

The Meriam Report was one of the first documents to focus attention on the economic problems on reservations. The report sidestepped the moralistic tone of earlier studies and brought to bear a rigorous, social scientific perspective on American Indian poverty. The Meriam Report was unique because it attempted to generate systematic empirical data about the economic problems in Indian Country. It found that the health and economic well-being of American Indians were abysmally low by even the most rudimentary standards. The Office of Indian Affairs was criticized for being inefficient and generally unsympathetic to the needs of American Indians. Finally, the report recommended a substantial increase in public funds for improving the health, education, and economic welfare of American Indians.

This document also was notable because it was widely acclaimed by Indian reform groups as a genuinely pro-Indian document. Among those organizations hailing the Meriam Report was the American Indian Defense Association, headed in 1928 by John Collier (Prucha 1984). Collier later became the commissioner of Indian affairs in the Roosevelt administration and adopted the Meriam Report as the blueprint for the Indian New Deal (Prucha 1984). Collier served as commissioner throughout the Roosevelt administration, and most historians agree that he was the most influential commissioner in the twentieth century and one of the most notable in the history of Indian and U.S. government relations.

Under the Indian New Deal, the federal government took its first steps in 1933 to bring economic relief to Indian Country. The Indian New Deal, like the New Deal for other Americans, emphasized natural-resource conservation, job creation, and public works. Besides these measures, the Indian New Deal included efforts to improve the educational, health-care, and social welfare systems of reservations (Prucha 1984). Equally important, Collier revised allotment policies that had resulted in the losses of millions of acres of Indian lands. He also supported measures for the preservation of Indian culture and the reconstitution of tribal governments. All of these measures were intended to improve the social and economic viability of reservation communities and especially to improve the material conditions in which reservation Indians lived (Prucha 1984, chapter 37).

The Indian New Deal was profoundly important. It ended the disastrous policies of the allotment era that reduced Indian lands from 138 million acres in 1887 to 52 million acres in 1934 (Prucha 1984, p. 896). It also reversed earlier policies attacking Indian culture and contributed to the passage of the Wheeler-Howard Indian Reorganization Act of 1934. This legislation was particularly important because it reconstituted tribal governments that had heretofore been outlawed.

The Indian New Deal was not an unqualified success, however, and its legacy is the subject of much debate, especially among historians (Philp 1986; Smith and Kvasnicka 1981). For example, a controversial livestock-reduction program was implemented in the interest of soil conservation, but its draconian measures devastated the herds of many Indian farmers, especially on the Navajo reservation. Also, the Indian Reorganization Act forced tribes to model their governments after precepts of American democracy, and these often clashed with traditional tribal authority structures. But the greatest failure of the Indian New Deal was its inability to abate reservation poverty. After ten years of Indian New Deal efforts, at the onset of World War II, poverty among American Indians was still at the same level documented by the Meriam Report.

While there are many explanations for why the Indian New Deal failed to significantly reduce American Indian poverty, lack of sufficient funds was obviously the major cause of failure. It is clear from historical accounts that the Indian New Deal was able to score specific legislative victories, but it was never able to marshal the resources necessary for improving the economic conditions of American Indians (Prucha 1984; Philp 1986). The Indian New Deal showed that Congress was willing to entertain policy proposals sympathetic to American Indians, such as overturning allotment-era policies, but not to commit large amounts of public funds for the sole benefit of American Indians.

Termination and Federal Policy in the 1950s

Collier's reforms in Indian policy, especially his efforts to combat poverty, receded following World War II. At the close of World War II the federal government was loath to continue its special recognition of American Indian tribes. Believing that American Indians should join the mainstream of American society, the federal government moved on several fronts to sever its obligations to Indian tribes. Consequently, the post–World War II years, until 1975, are known as the termination era of federal Indian policy.

The policies of the termination era were three-pronged: (1) to settle all out-standing claims made by tribes against the federal government; (2) to dissolve reservation boundaries and abolish the reservation system; and (3) to relocate reservation Indians to urban areas. In short, the federal government intended to end its recognition of and involvement with all American Indian tribes. Ter-mination was a failure in regard to all three policy goals.

By agreeing to settle outstanding claims, the federal government publicly acknowledged its 150-year record of broken treaties and unfulfilled commitments with Indian tribes. As long as these claims remained outstanding, it would be impossible for the federal government to completely terminate its involvement with Indian tribes. Thus the first step toward termination was to close the books on Indian claims. To expeditiously deal with the large volume of Indian claims, the federal government established the Indian Claims Commission (ICC) in 1946 (Fixico 1986). Within the first five years of its existence, the ICC reviewed 852 cases (Fixico 1986). Legal wrangling extended the commission's work for over thirty years. In 1978 the commission was finally dissolved by Congress, and pending claims were referred to the federal courts (Fixico 1986, pp. 25–31).

The heart of the termination policy was the abolition of the reservation system. After several years of congressional debates the policy was officially adopted in July 1953 with the passage of House Concurrent Resolution (HCR) 108. The resolution attracted little public attention at the time of its passage, but it had far-reaching consequences for American Indians, especially those living on res-ervations.

House Concurrent Resolution 108 was the work of conservative members of Congress seeking to end the special status of American Indians and eventually to sever all relationships between the federal government and Indian tribes. HCR 108 slated thirteen tribes for termination, but Congress implemented termination procedures for only six groups (Fixico 1986, p. 99). In the end, only the Klamath Reservation in Oregon and the Menominee Reservation in Wisconsin were ac-tually terminated. The Menominee tribe was restored to reservation status in the early 1970s; the Klamath Indians are still seeking restoration. Thus the aim of HCR 108 to dissolve the reservation system was virtually a total failure.

The third goal of the termination policy was to relocate reservation Indians to urban areas. The Bureau of Indian Affairs relocation programs were designed to parallel the termination of federal recognition of reservations. Programs such as the BIA's Direct Employment Assistance program were aimed at moving Indians away from the poverty and economic hardship of reservation life and into mainstream urban economies abundant with opportunities, thereby dispers-ing reservation Indians and hastening their assimilation. Efforts to relocate res-ervation Indians began as early as 1951 and continued throughout the 1960s as part of the War on Poverty. Between 1952 and 1972 over 100,000 American Indians were processed through these programs (Sorkin 1978, p. 25).

The relocation programs attempted to promote assimilation by moving Indians to jobs in designated urban relocation centers such as Chicago, Los Angeles,

San Francisco, and Oklahoma City. Once relocated to these cities, Indians participated in job training and counseling in a manner similar to the structure of some programs in the Office of Economic Opportunity or Comprehensive Employment and Training Act (CETA) projects. Through relocation and job training and with the benefit of employment assistance, American Indians were supposed to take their place in urban American society.

From their inception, the BIA relocation programs fell far short of meeting their stated objectives. Relocated Indians often did not find economic security in their new homes, and for this and other reasons, they frequently returned to their reservations (Fixico 1986). Some particularly well qualified American Indians were able to successfully make the transition to urban life, but many other less qualified individuals were not so fortunate (Clinton et al. 1975; Sorkin 1978; Fixico 1986). All too often, relocation programs took poorly educated, unemployed, and poverty-stricken reservation Indians and turned them into poorly educated, unemployed, and poverty-stricken city dwellers (Snipp and Sandefur 1988).

There are several plausible ways of looking at urban relocation as an antipoverty measure. For American Indians with some education, work experience, and familiarity with Anglo culture, the relocation programs seemed to work. Relocation programs gave them an additional boost to facilitate the transition into the urban labor market. However, it is not clear that the relocation programs were essential for the success of these workers. In fact, to the degree that their numbers raised the achievement rates for relocatees, it could be argued that such individuals helped the relocation programs attain the appearance of success, rather than the programs actually helping them.

American Indians with little education and limited work experience and unfamiliar with non-Indian culture benefitted very little from relocation programs. In fact, very few completed the programs or remained in urban areas for any great length of time (Fixico 1986). Records indicate that between one-half and two-thirds of all relocated Indians eventually returned to their reservation homes (Levitan and Hetrick 1971, p. 176). Urban life had been an alienating experience in a hostile environment. There were few employment opportunities for American Indians with little education or work experience. The highly structured, confining, fast pace of urban life is the antithesis of the less structured and slower-paced life-style of reservation communities. For these newcomers, the absence of job opportunities and the omnipresent, alien urban culture were a potent incentive to return to their reservation homes where they could be near family and kin and participate in a more familiar way of life (Hodge 1971; Snipp 1989, pp. 84–88). From this perspective, it is hardly surprising that disadvantaged American Indians might have enjoyed few benefits from relocation, or that they abandoned the relocation programs in large numbers.

The relocation programs also exacerbated the "brain drain" commonly associated with rural-to-urban migration, thus creating another problem for Indian leaders and policymakers concerned with reservation poverty. The relocation programs encouraged the most qualified residents to emigrate from the reservation, while the least productive members of the population were left behind. Educated, experienced persons in their prime working ages left the reservation, while the very young, the very old, and the poorly educated remained.

Reservation emigration also seriously hampered efforts to stimulate economic opportunities on the reservation. By removing the most productive segments of the labor force, the policy reinforced a spiraling process of economic decline. Productive workers emigrate because there are limited opportunities on the reservation, but existing opportunities are reduced further because a productive labor force is unavailable for sustaining economic development.

Tribal Sovereignty and Self-Determination

The social legislation passed in the early and middle 1960s was frequently predisposed toward recognizing the rights of racial and ethnic minorities. This tendency served the interests of American Indian communities in a variety of contexts. At the same time, supporters of American Indians formed task forces and produced studies that harshly criticized past policies, especially those of termination (Prucha 1984).

A decade of American Indian activism in the 1960s and the effects of the civil rights movement contributed to the official close of termination policy with the passage of the American Indian Self-Determination and Educational Assistance Act of 1975. However, the termination policies had declined in popularity nearly a decade earlier. The harmful consequences of these programs, their lack of measurable success, and Indian communities' opposition made them an easy target for critics (Prucha 1984; Gross 1989). The new orientation that emerged encouraged the federal government to deal with American Indian poverty by developing tribal resources, especially those of reservations.

One of President Kennedy's early pieces of antipoverty legislation was the Area Redevelopment Act of 1961. This law targeted Indian reservations, among other poverty-stricken areas, for special treatment. Four years later, the Area Redevelopment Administration (ARA) was succeeded by the Economic Development Administration (EDA). Like the ARA, the EDA focused on job-creation measures on reservations through the development of reservation infrastructure such as roads, bridges, waste disposal, and industrial parks (Levitan and Hetrick 1971; Sorkin 1971; Levitan and Johnston 1975; Prucha 1984).

Between 1965 and 1970 EDA spent nearly $78 million on projects sited on over 107 reservations (Levitan and Hetrick 1971, p. 160). Because these reservations were ill equipped for economic development, over three-fourths of EDA assistance was spent on public works and technical assistance, while less than one-fourth was actually spent on attracting business developments. The EDA claimed to have created 3,000 jobs between 1965 and 1970 in an evaluation, but its report noted that these gains may have reflected the healthy state of the national economy (Levitan and Hetrick 1971, p. 168). Projects in particularly isolated areas and projects such as industrial parks were not notable successes, an observation consistent with studies of similar efforts. These studies indicate that projects such as industrial parks were ineffective measures for abating poverty and unemployment, especially for minorities (Summers et al. 1976).

In 1968 the BIA estimated that $230 million was needed to successfully finance commercial and industrial development; however, only $20 million was available from all sources including the EDA, BIA, Small Business Administration (SBA), and private lenders. In retrospect, many EDA projects provided much-needed community infrastructure, and they were probably temporarily successful in creating employment, especially in construction. However, it is equally clear that they did not have a lasting impact in eradicating poverty and joblessness from American Indian reservations.

The Economic Opportunity Act passed in 1964 also paid particular attention to reservation poverty. This act created the Office of Economic Opportunity, which was an umbrella organization that oversaw the activities of programs such as Head Start, Volunteers in Service to America (VISTA), the Job Corps, and Community Action, along with programs to provide housing assistance, job training, summer youth employment, and small-business loans. In various combinations and organizational forms, virtually all of these programs provided services to American Indians, typically under the auspices of tribal governments, intertribal consortiums, or urban-based Indian centers. In 1968 alone, $22 million was spent on Indian community action programs. However, this sum represented only 5 percent of the total federal budget for American Indians, of which about 79 percent was spent on the Bureau of Indian Affairs and the Indian Health Service (Sorkin 1971; Prucha 1984, pp. 1094–95). That is, most of what was spent on reservations went to purchase health care from the IHS and administrative services from the BIA. Criticism that efforts to improve the material conditions on reservation life were too little and too late were therefore substantiated. This is probably still true today as poverty and unemployment continue to be a persistent problem for most reservations.

Another important development took place in the area of educational policy for American Indians. Dating back to colonial times, schools operated primarily by missionary groups existed for the purpose of Christianizing and "civilizing" Indian children. In the late nineteenth century the federal government became directly involved with Indian education through the creation of BIA boarding and day schools. The ostensible purpose of these schools was to hasten the assimilation of American Indians through a curriculum that heavily emphasized Anglo farming practices, domestic skills for girls, speaking of English and a potpourri course on "civilization" (Hoxie 1984, chap. 6; Prucha 1984).

Changes in educational policies during the 1960s marked a dramatic departure from past practices. These policy shifts were reflected in three ways. First, and perhaps most important, for the first time in history, American Indians assumed a significant degree of influence in the education of their children. For example, legislation mandated that BIA schools form advisory committees consisting of

Indian parents (Prucha 1984). Some tribes such as the Wisconsin Oneida formed their own school districts and school boards, and Navajo Community College was organized under the auspices of the Navajo tribe. Second, school curricula, especially in BIA institutions, adopted a positive view of American Indian culture, implemented programs of cultural and bilingual education, and moved away from the view of education as indoctrination for assimilation into Anglo society. Third, educational programs for American Indians were broadened beyond what had been mainly vocational training to include efforts to stem high-school dropout rates and provide opportunities for higher education.

Unfortunately for the residents of Indian Country, the War on Poverty was short-lived. Soon after the election of Richard M. Nixon, the Office of Economic Opportunity was dismantled, and its constituent programs, such as Head Start, were shuffled into other federal agencies. Although Nixon was a staunch opponent of the War on Poverty, his vision of the "new federalism" was particularly sympathetic to tribal autonomy and principles of self-determination. When legislation such as the Comprehensive Employment and Training Act (CETA) emerged in the place of War on Poverty programs, federal assistance remained a mainstay for jobs, education, and work experience for American Indians, especially on reservations. Tribal governments, for example, were eligible to bid as prime contractors for CETA programs.

With the passage of the American Indian Self-Determination and Educational Assistance Act of 1975, tribal governments assumed major responsibility for administering services in their communities. The legislation was extremely important for tribes seeking greater control over reservation development. Many tribes formed consortiums for operating employment and training programs, while larger reservations such as the Navajo administered their own programs. However, these programs were short-lived, eliminated by the Reagan administration in 1981 and replaced with the vastly scaled-down Job Training and Partnership Act.

SOCIAL AND ECONOMIC CONDITIONS IN 1980

Although the success of efforts to educate and employ American Indians cannot be evaluated precisely, it is clear that American Indians in the 1970s, after the War on Poverty, were better educated and had better employment opportunities than in the years of the preceding decade (Snipp 1989). Income gains and poverty reductions are displayed in the figures and tables that follow.

The statistics in Figure 8.2 show very clearly that American Indians made significant gains in educational attainment between 1970 and 1980. The percentage of American Indians with a high-school diploma more than doubled between 1970 and 1980—from 22 percent to nearly 56 percent. This increase moved American Indians, who lagged behind Blacks in 1970, ahead to a slightly higher level of educational attainment than Blacks in 1980. Nonetheless, Blacks

Figure 8.2
High-School Graduates, 1970 and 1980

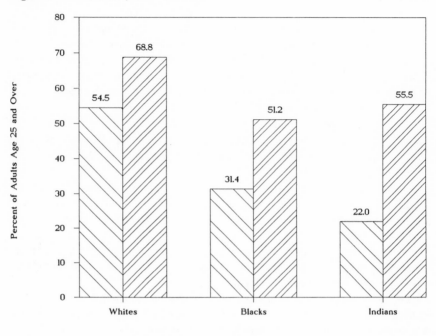

and American Indians have considerably lower levels of educational attainment than Whites.

Virtually the same conclusions can be drawn from the comparisons of college graduates among Blacks, Whites, and American Indians in Figure 8.3. American Indians made impressive educational gains in the 1970s, but they remain far behind the educational attainment of White Americans. Predictably, the economic circumstances of American Indians closely parallel their educational attainments.

In 1969 the median family income of American Indians was 96 percent of the median family income of Blacks and only 59 percent of the median family income of Whites (see Table 8.1). During the 1970s the median family income of Indians increased by 19 percent, pushing them ahead of Black family income, which increased less than 5 percent. By 1980 the relative economic position of Blacks and American Indians was reversed, with the median family income of Blacks being 92 percent of the median family income of American Indians. The economic position of American Indians remained far behind that of Whites. Even with the gains of the 1970s, Indian family incomes were only 66 percent of the family incomes of Whites. The changes in American Indian family income led to parallel declines in poverty.

The seriousness of poverty on reservations is dramatically demonstrated by

Figure 8.3
College Graduates, 1970 and 1980

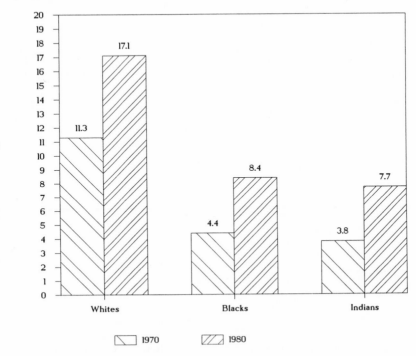

the data in Table 8.2 that show the median family income and percentage of families in poverty on the sixteen most populated reservations. In 1969 the percentage of families living in poverty ranged from 42 percent on the Wind River Reservation to an astonishing 78 percent on the Papago Reservation. Between 1969 and 1979 most of these reservations experienced some reduction in poverty, ranging from 20 percentage points for the Eastern Cherokee to a slight increase at the Pine Ridge Reservation. Even so, one-third to over one-half of all Indian families residing on these reservations still had incomes below the official poverty line in 1979.

Given that most reservations witnessed reductions in family poverty during the 1970s, it might be reasonable to expect that this would be matched by substantial increases in family incomes. However, reductions in poverty did not necessarily result from higher real family income. Changes in family and household structure, such as lower fertility and fewer persons per dwelling, make it possible for poverty rates to decline without significant increases in income levels (see Snipp 1989, chap. 4, 5, and 8). This is evident when we compare changes in median family income with changes in poverty. For example, family poverty declined at the Zuni Pueblo by 12 points, from 56.7 to 44.6 percent, during the 1970s. Yet during the same period real family income at the Zuni Pueblo actually

Table 8.1

Median Incomes and Families with Incomes below Poverty Levels for Blacks, Whites, and American Indians, 1969 and 1979 (1979 Dollars)

	Median Family Income	Median Household Income	Percent of Families Below Poverty
Blacks			
1969	$12,013	9,215	29.8
1979	12,598	10,943	26.5
Whites			
1969	19,723	16,058	8.6
1979	20,835	17,680	7.0
American Indians			
1969	11,547	a	33.0
1979	13,724	12,256	23.7

Source: U.S. Bureau of the Census 1983; U.S. Bureau of the Census 1972b; U.S. Bureau of the Census 1973.

ª Not available.

dipped slightly, from $10,476 to $10,354. The other reservations shown in Table 8.2 experienced income gains that might be expected with lower poverty, but in several cases the gain was only a few hundred dollars. On the other hand, reservations such as the Navajo, Papago, and Blackfeet added more than $2,000 to their median family incomes.

Finally, the last column in Table 8.2 shows the percentage of families receiving BIA public assistance. BIA public assistance is similar to the welfare relief provided by many county and city governments under the title of general assistance. It is not the same as Aid to Families with Dependent Children (AFDC) and usually involves smaller benefits with fewer restrictions than AFDC. Considering the relatively high poverty rates and low family incomes, the level of BIA public assistance on these reservations is surprisingly low (see the last column of Table 8.2). With the exception of the Standing Rock and Fort Peck reservations, 10 percent or less of reservation families receive BIA assistance. Indian families may be receiving aid from other programs such as AFDC or

Table 8.2
Median Family Incomes and Families with Incomes below Poverty Levels for American Indians Residing on the Sixteen Largest Reservations in 1980 (1979 Dollars)

Reservation	1969		1979		
	Family Income	Percent of Families in Poverty	Median Family Income	Percent of Families in Poverty	Percent of Families Receiving BIA Assistance
Navajo[a] (AZ,UT,NM)	6,106	62.1	8,397	50.5	7.0
Pine Ridge (SD)	7,745	54.3	7,942	54.7	10.2
Gila River (AZ)	6,766	58.6	7,955	50.7	8.8
Papago (AZ)	4,950	78.1	7,003	56.2	8.3
Fort Apache (AZ)	8,599	53.3	9,273	47.6	2.5
Hopi[a] (AZ)	6,839	61.8	8,197	50.9	6.3
Zuni Pueblo (NM)	10,476	56.7	10,354	44.6	1.1
San Carlos (AZ)	7,932	62.3	7,986	53.6	3.1
Rosebud (SD)	6,795	62.9	8,868	47.7	9.2
Blackfeet (MT)	8,430	47.8	10,576	33.7	5.9
Yakima (WA)	10,231	45.5	11,324	34.2	9.4
Eastern Cherokee (NC)	8,168	52.2	9,774	32.7	2.3
Standing Rock (ND,SD)	7,231	58.3	8,107	51.3	14.2
Osage[b] (OK)	*	*	16,095	13.9	5.4
Fort Peck (MT)	10,111	46.7	10,864	38.4	20.5
Wind River (WY)	9,241	42.0	10,816	36.0	3.0

Source: U.S. Bureau of the Census 1986; U.S. Bureau of the Census 1973.

[a]Navajo and Hopi Reservations data is not strictly comparable in 1969 and 1979 because of administrative changes in the 1970s.

[b]Osage Reservation data not available for 1970.

Food Stamps, but clearly they do not rely heavily on this type of BIA assistance. Also, the low use may reflect the fact that some Indian families are loath to avail themselves of BIA assistance for reasons of pride and a distaste for encounters with the BIA bureaucracy.

The Osage are clearly an exception to the extreme poverty shown in Table 8.2. Compared to other reservations, they have extraordinarily high family incomes and a low poverty rate. The Osage Reservation residents are better educated and have higher rates of labor-force participation than Indians on other reservations, largely because the Osage Reservation is located within commuting distance of the metropolitan Tulsa labor market, which experienced a major expansion during the Sunbelt growth of the 1970s. In addition, a number of Osage families receive royalties from oil leases. High oil prices during the 1970s stimulated oil production on leases that in earlier years had been too unprofitable to operate. All these factors played a role in raising Osage family incomes to their high level in 1979.

In summary, these data indicate that American Indians experienced a noticeable improvement in their standard of living during the 1970s. The nature of the data makes it impossible to separate the positive effects of public policies designed to promote economic opportunities from those of improved macroeconomic conditions in the national economy. However, we do know that there were improvements in the 1970s and that public policy very likely played an important role in these gains. Nonetheless, poverty continued to be a very serious problem for American Indians as they entered the decade of the 1980s.

FEDERAL RETRENCHMENT

Throughout the 1970s the federal government, cooperating with tribal leaders, played an active part in dealing with poverty and related problems. CETA and the Economic Development Administration underwrote projects for job training and job creation, respectively; and there were other projects for housing, public health, transportation, and natural-resource management, to name only a few. As the principle of self-determination became institutionalized in federal-Indian relations, tribal governments assumed more responsibility in the management of local services. Yet the federal government remains a primary source of support for most tribes.

However, the late 1970s and especially the early 1980s brought another shift in policies for dealing with the economic disadvantages facing American Indians. Sharp cutbacks in federal aid caused some tribal leaders to wonder whether "self-determination" under the Reagan administration really meant a return to the termination policies of the 1950s. Growing tribal autonomy, a cessation of services, and a shrinking federal role in reservation affairs were certainly reminiscent of termination-era policies.

For tribes heavily dependent on federal support for jobs and other assistance, cutbacks in federal spending created significant hardships. On many reservations a large segment of the work force is employed by the federal government; reductions in federal spending sharply increase unemployment and reduce the labor-force participation of these workers (Snipp 1989). For example, unemployment on the Navajo Reservation doubled between 1979 and 1984, and in September 1984, 40 percent of the Navajo work force was jobless (Bureau of Indian Affairs 1985). Although figures are not available, it seems almost certain that reservation poverty also increased during this period.

While the federal government implemented an unofficial policy of disengagement in the 1980s, the official statement of the Reagan administration came in 1984 with the publication of the report of the Presidential Commission on Indian Reservation Economies (PCIRE). In this report the Reagan administration affirmed its commitment to the principle of self-determination. From the standpoint of the commission, a lower level of federal involvement in reservation affairs was desirable as a way of encouraging private initiative. The commission urged private enterprise as the vehicle to lift American Indians out of poverty, suggesting in fact that federal intervention in the past has slowed the growth of enterpreneurial activities on reservations. Suggestions for abating reservation poverty revolved around ways of improving the reservation business climate. It is important to note, however, that the commission did not encourage tribally owned enterprises. From the commission's perspective, private enterprise meant individual entrepreneurship.

The implementation of the doctrine enunciated by the PCIRE took numerous forms. A well-known example was the Job Training and Partnership Act (JTPA), which replaced the much larger and more expensive Comprehensive Employment and Training Act (CETA). Under JTPA employers were offered inducements to provide training and work experience to program participants. The Bureau of Indian Affairs administered a loan and grant program for starting Indian-owned businesses; and tribes, to a lesser extent, continued to receive support for infrastructure development (cf. Ferguson, Hart, and Seciwa 1988).

Making use of what Mary Olson (1988) called "the legal road to economic development," successful business ventures often depend on having sufficient leverage to create or gain access to market niches. The legal road to economic development amounts to a business development strategy that depends on legal decisions to generate market opportunities. For example, the Lummi tribe in Washington State used a court decision upholding their fishing rights to develop a successful aquaculture industry (Olson 1988). The most significant economic changes on reservations in the 1980s were brought about as tribes became involved in gambling and duty-free tobacco sales.

In the case of gambling, most commonly bingo operations, and tobacco sales, legal decisions upholding tribal sovereignty and exempting tribal governments from state jurisdiction have enabled tribes to establish these activities within reservation borders. Tax-free tobacco sales, "Indian smoke shops," began appearing on reservations in the mid–1970s, and the first Indian bingo operation was established by the Florida Seminoles in 1979. The loss of tax revenues and the inability to control these activities have outraged state and local officials and offended others morally opposed to gambling.

The controversies created by gambling and tobacco sales resulted in numerous court cases upholding the rights of tribes to engage in these activities. Since 1979 bingo and other types of gambling have proliferated on Indian lands, including California rancherias as small as the Tuolumne Rancheria, which had 323 acres and 81 residents in 1980. In 1988 Congress passed legislation designed to control Indian gambling operations by regulating the types of gambling permitted and by creating a review board to set policy and provide oversight.

The proliferation of gambling and tobacco sales in Indian Country does not mean that these activities have been universally successful. In fact, no one knows with certainty how much revenue these operations have generated. Anecdotal evidence seems to indicate that some have been spectacularly successful while others have failed to become profitable (Robinson 1989).

Gambling and tobacco sales are not the only viable economic development activities on reservations, though they are typically the most visible and controversial. For the past decade, many reservations have aggressively promoted economic development, and now there are more privately held Indian-owned businesses on reservations, more tribally owned businesses, and more non-Indian firms on reservations than at any time in the past. Examples of Indian-owned businesses include gas stations, auto body repair shops, and construction companies. The Cherokees in Oklahoma own a carpet mill and subcontract with IBM for electronic-component assembly. The Choctaw tribe in Mississippi manufactures wiring harnesses for General Motors. Although anecdotal information is readily available about these industries, there has been no systematic study of how many firms exist and how successful they are. Data for reservation enterprises are virtually nonexistent. With unemployment figures for reservations hovering in excess of 30 percent for most of the 1980s, we do know that these businesses have not made significant inroads toward improving economic conditions on reservations.

It is not clear what future economic development policy for reservations will be developed. President Bush and members of his cabinet, notably Jack Kemp, have embraced the concept of "enterprise zones" as a vehicle of economic development. Declaring reservations as enterprise zones would provide inducements such as tax reductions and labor subsidies to corporations willing to locate in these areas. Whether enterprise zones become a major policy instrument for the Bush administration remains to be seen. Past experience suggests that dramatic new directions in Indian policy are unlikely and that the short-term outlook calls for a continuation of policies from the past decade with small shifts in emphases on specific programs.

CONCLUSION

From a public policy perspective, given existing budgetary constraints and presidential politics, federal policy for dealing with American Indian poverty in the near-term future is unlikely to be very different from what it has been in the past decade. Despite this inertia, there is no shortage of policy options that might be explored.

The policy options available for consideration can be broadly categorized to focus on either labor-force participation or income redistribution. Labor-force-participation strategies attempt to increase access to economic opportunities either by increasing the number of jobs available or by increasing the skills and hence the individual competitiveness of would-be workers. Income-redistribution strategies are typically aimed at the "deserving poor," persons exempt from labor-market participation by virtue of illness, disability, or some other socially acceptable limiting condition.

Tribes may be able to exploit the natural resources of their reservations more efficiently. This will mean more careful conservation of resources, more carefully bargained lease agreements, better exploitation of treaty rights, and, where possible, investment to increase the land base of the reservations. Tribal governments also may wish to consider ways of attracting capital to the reservation. This will require federal assistance to underwrite loans and make grants for business development. Tribes may also consider developing exportable resources in nontraditional activities areas, such as the service sector.

Upgrading workers' qualifications to make them more competitive in the market can be accomplished through a variety of well-known programs. Education and training are obviously important options. Like other rural Americans, Indians have traditionally low levels of education, while jobs being generated in the growing service sector require ever-higher levels of education and skill. Training for business management might be especially beneficial for helping tribes and tribal members deal effectively in the highly competitive American economy.

The role of tribal governments in income redistribution, like that of other local governments, is very limited. The taxation authority of tribal governments is legally ambiguous, and the tax bases of most reservations are very weak. Thus tribes and tribal members can participate in programs for income redistribution such as AFDC, but the impetus for initiating such programs will likely remain in the federal domain for the foreseeable future.

American Indians represent a sizeable number of rural Americans living in poverty. In rural areas there is no question that some of the most persistent and severe instances of economic hardship are found on Indian reservations. Yet for several hundred thousand American Indians, "home" is one of 278 federally entrusted reservations. Since the late nineteenth century these descendants of "the first of this land" have been subjected to changing federal policy aimed at giving them social and economic equality with other Americans. Yet nearly a hundred years later they remain among the poorest of Americans. Without a renewed commitment to deal with the economic deprivation endemic to American Indian reservations, the first of this land will continue to be among the last to share in this nation's riches.

NOTE

This chapter was prepared while C. Matthew Snipp was a fellow at the Center for Advanced Study in the Behavioral Sciences. Financial support was provided by grants from the National Science Foundation (BNS87–00864), the Graduate School of the University of Wisconsin, the University of Wisconsin College of Agriculture and Life Sciences, and the Ford Foundation's Rural Poverty and Resources Program and the Aspen Institute's Rural Economic Policy Program.

Chapter 9

Rural Poverty in the Northeast: The Case of Upstate New York

Janet M. Fitchen

In much of the Northeast, including upstate New York, northern Pennsylvania, and parts of northern New England, one can easily see the physical expressions of rural poverty: worn-down old farmhouses where no farms exist anymore; old trailers in the open countryside, encased in rough-wood additions and surrounded by inoperable automobiles; small clusters of houses, tar-papered shacks, trailers, and made-over school buses grouped together along back roads of an overgrown hilly landscape; and small, run-down villages with vacant stores, decaying old houses now converted to cheap apartments, and abandoned brick factories. Rural poverty is not new in the Northeast; it is a long-standing problem, especially in the more remote areas dependent on extractive industries, such as mining and lumbering, in upland areas where agriculture has long been marginal or has been abandoned, and in small towns where manufacturing has died out. While the rural poverty of the Northeast has not been as pervasive or well known as the endemic poverty of southern Appalachia, it has persisted over the decades. In some parts of upstate New York, where community-level research was conducted in the early 1970s and in the late 1980s, rural poverty appears to have increased recently. Furthermore, major economic, social, and demographic changes in the area have made rural poverty qualitatively worse.

Poverty is unevenly distributed around rural New York and generally remains characteristic of the more remote counties, while being less common in rural counties closer to the state's metropolitan areas. For example, in New York's eight counties classified as the "most rural" (out of forty-four "rural" counties; see Map 9.1), a 16 percent poverty rate in 1980 tied with the New York City metropolitan rate, but was significantly higher than that of the upstate metropolitan areas and rural counties adjacent to them. Those counties that are most rural had an 11.2 percent unemployment rate in 1980, compared to a 6.7 percent rate in the metropolitan counties, and together these eight rural counties earned only 77 percent of the median family income of metropolitan counties (Eberts

Map 9.1
Rural Counties in New York State

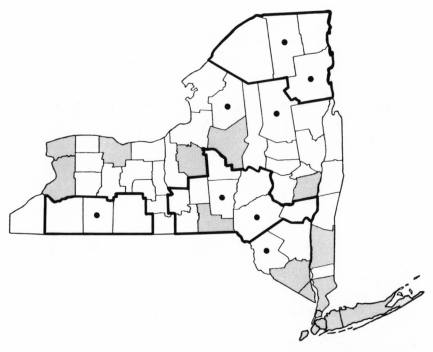

Note: The 18 shaded counties are metropolitan counties. The 44 unshaded counties are officially "rural" counties. ● indicates the 8 counties classified as "most rural" (Eberts and Khawaja 1988). Bold outlined areas indicate the 16 counties where research was conducted.

1984). The net change over the 1980s, despite a deep recession early in the decade and an employment slowdown near the end of the decade, left the state's most rural counties showing some gains in employment and income levels, but lagging even farther behind the metropolitan areas. What had been a $5,000 per capita income gap between the eight most rural counties and the eighteen metropolitan counties in 1981 had grown to nearly a $7,000 gap by 1986, and per capita income in the eight most rural counties had fallen to only 60 percent of the level earned in the metropolitan counties. In 1988 there was a 6.0 percent unemployment rate, on average, in the eight most rural counties, while the statewide rate stood at 4.3 percent (Eberts and Khawaja 1988, pp. 9–11).

In all rural counties the late 1980s saw unemployment rates drop to "unprecedented" lows, for example, down to 5 percent in counties that earlier in the decade had sustained unemployment levels in the teens. As in decades before, the more remote rural counties performed less well, while on the fringes of economically expanding metropolitan areas, some rural counties became significantly less poor, as measured by rising per capita income and falling unemployment rates (Eberts and Khawaja 1988; Economic Development and Technical Assistance Center 1987). For those places that have shown economic improvement, however, it is not at all clear from available statistics whether this represents an improvement in the condition of residents already there or, instead, a population movement, such as an influx of people of higher economic level, an out-migration of people of lower economic level, or a mixture of the two. Thus there is no solid information to indicate what has happened to the economic status of people, only what has happened to places.

Despite a significant decline in rural unemployment and the general recovery of the northeastern economy in the mid–1980s, poverty appears to be growing worse in many rural New York communities as the decade of the 1990s begins. In some rural localities new and growing poverty is being added to the old base of poverty left from the past. At the start of 1990 some rural counties were experiencing major increases in welfare rolls (especially Home Relief) and in households on Food Stamps, an increase that exceeded caseload growth in New York City. For example, while the number of people on Food Stamps rose 5.6 percent in New York City from 1989 (monthly average) to April 1990, the increase in the rest of the state was 13.2 percent. In some rural counties, meanwhile, the number of persons on Food Stamps increased more than 20 percent.

Where unemployment has decreased but poverty has not diminished commensurately or has even increased, people in local institutions, agencies, and governments all express frustration that it is very difficult to obtain adequate and up-to-date quantitative data to measure or "prove" the deteriorating local situation. School districts still have to use the 1980 census in their documentation for the state, knowing full well that the figures are hopelessly outdated. Internally, they cite such indicators as free-school-lunch lists or numbers of children in foster care or in families receiving Aid to Families with Dependent Children (AFDC), but they admit that these are inaccurate indicators. Administrators, supervisors, and caseworkers in welfare departments, specialists in educational and youth programs, counseling centers, and planning offices, as well as volunteers and staff in emergency services, have all mentioned various indicators of worsening poverty: the number of children needing special education has increased markedly; court cases establishing child neglect and abuse are increasing dramatically; teen pregnancy appears to be increasing; and an increasing percentage of program "intakes" fall below 75 percent of the federal poverty level. None of these local indicators is, however, a satisfactory proxy for official income-defined poverty status, and none is adequate to document increasing poverty to the satisfaction of funders and state government. In some places the situation is changing so rapidly that by the time the 1990 census data become available at the disaggregated levels needed for local planning and grant writing, they may already be seriously out of date.

At the same time, rural poverty is also undergoing significant qualitative changes. In fact, change in characteristics and conditions of the rural poor, especially as compared to situations documented in earlier research (Fitchen

1981), has been one of the major findings of several years of a broad-ranging research project carried out in a dozen rural counties in New York State (Fitchen 1991). Changes in rural poverty are now being examined in communities scattered through sixteen counties in three regions of the state: the central area, the north, and the western southern tier (see Map 9.1). The research reported here is based on semistructured in-depth home interviews with rural individuals and families who are poor, observation periods in such places as schools, Head Start centers, and local employment programs, and in-depth interviews with knowledgeable people in local agencies, institutions, and governments, including commissioners and caseworkers in welfare departments, school administrators and teachers, mental health professionals and social workers, employment counselors, probation officers, and many others. Of more than 400 interviews and observations from 1985 to 1990, 150 probed local poverty situations: 30 were with low-income individuals, and the remainder were with representatives of local agencies and schools. In spring 1990 I conducted several additional in-depth interviews and 15 questionnaire interviews, as well as three focus-group sessions with low-income individuals, and collected more documentation from local institutions, programs, and agencies. Although reliable data on the numbers of poor people now living in rural counties are not presently available, this onsite research provides descriptive—and disturbing—evidence that indeed, rural poverty has not been substantially reduced in recent years, and that in some localities it has been growing worse not only in numbers of people affected, but also in the difficulties of their situations and in its impacts on communities.

This chapter focuses on several of the changes observed in characteristics and conditions of rural poverty and indicates some of the causes behind the deteriorating situation. However, since rural poverty is so different from urban poverty and from the standard urban-based images of poverty that shape public perceptions and government policies, it is perhaps useful to begin with a brief description of the physical and social environments in which rural poor people live.

THREE RESIDENTIAL PATTERNS OF RURAL POVERTY

Poverty in rural New York is most commonly found in three different nonfarm residential patterns: open-country clusters of intergenerationally poor families; trailer parks and informal clusters of older mobile homes; and villages or small towns where unwanted single-family houses and vacant store buildings have been converted to low-rent apartments. While poor people are also found on farms, particularly as dairy-farm laborers and migrant crop harvesters, the agriculture-related poor constitute only a minor segment of the state's rural poverty population.

The three predominant residential patterns described here are not types of poverty, however, for each includes some people who are not poor and some who are only occasionally poor. Furthermore, residents may move back and forth from one type of settlement to another. Nonetheless, differentiation among the three residential patterns is important for analytical purposes and for social-program design.

Pockets of Rural Poverty Left from the Past

The oldest and visually most obvious form of rural poverty in the Northeast is the depressed rural neighborhood characterized by a small cluster of a half-dozen to a dozen or so homes. The "dilapidated" housing includes run-down farmhouses, modest, unfinished frame houses with secondhand windows and unmatched roofing materials, very old trailers encased in wooden additions, and shacks made of used lumber and covered in black sheathing material. Many such neighborhoods have existed for at least a generation or two, while others are more recent. Space around the homes is filled with old cars, tires and car parts, building materials, household appliances, snowmobiles, and other recreational objects. There are no nearby stores, schools, or public buildings. People must travel, often twenty miles or more, to towns and small cities where they work, go to school, shop, and tend to official business such as licensing cars, making court appearances, and picking up Food Stamps.

A greater problem than geographical isolation, however, is social isolation (Fitchen 1981). Residents' social life is almost entirely confined to the immediate neighborhood or within a network of similar depressed neighborhoods that are linked by geographic proximity, kinship, marriage, car trading, and shared poverty and stigma. Residents' conceptual separation from the larger urban-based community is revealed verbally: they refer to it as "the outside world." Reciprocally, the people of the rural pockets of poverty are still referred to by the larger community in the same derogatory terms used for decades: "poor white trash"; "people who live like animals"; or the "the shack people" (Vidich and Bensman 1958).

The adults of these depressed neighborhoods had grown up in poverty, either in the same locale or in a similar pocket of poverty nearby, and they remained chronically poor. The twenty households that I had studied over several years hovered just around the official poverty line. Most households had at least one person employed most of the time in the 1970s; but most workers were in the lower-paying jobs on highway and public works crews, on night-shift janitorial jobs, and in small factories. Even workers whose steady jobs generally put their families above the poverty line would fall into poverty when struck by an accident, illness, or loss of job. Women with small children were more likely to stay at home rather than hold a job, but some worked at night while their husbands or mothers took care of the children. People's ability to survive in this poverty depended on a variety of strategies by which they minimized cash outflow and increased income, and on a network of relatives and friends, also poor and usually living nearby (Fitchen 1981, pp. 61–83). People "make do" on their own to the extent they can, using these social resources to substitute for inad-

equate financial resources. Though always short of money and never accumu-
lating a cushion to boost them out of poverty, they tide themselves over from
crisis to crisis, just getting by, but never getting ahead.

Poverty in Trailer Parks and Informal Trailer Clusters

At the edge of villages and along country roads, many rural low-income people
live in trailers (officially "mobile homes"), including individual trailers placed
on privately owned lots and trailers set close together in the less expensive
mobile-home parks. Informal trailer clusters, a smaller and less commercial
arrangement than a trailer park, are also common in many localities, typically
three to six older trailers sitting in the yard next to an old farmhouse.

For rural people of insecure and inadequate income, trailers are "the housing
of choice"—a "choice" severely constrained by low income and low earning
potential. While not all residents of trailer parks are poor, many occupants of
the lower-rent parks and clusters are either below or only slightly above the
poverty line. In one small trailer cluster that appeared recently, two of the four
trailers were rented to young single women heads of households on welfare. For
neither of these women was this a desired form of housing: it was a temporary
stopgap. For the single women, their trailer was the only housing available
within the welfare allowance, the only way they could maintain independence
from parents, previous husbands, or boyfriends. Social isolation and antisocial
behavior are reported by many trailer-park residents as major problems in daily
life. Many residents hope that they can eventually save up enough money to
move their trailer out of a park to their own land in the countryside and eventually
build a real house there; but in most households the income, whether from
earnings or transfer payments, is entirely used up just in everyday living expenses.

For all their shortcomings, and there are many, trailers have the one advantage
of being cheaper to purchase or rent than conventional housing. However, they
are not necessarily cheap in proportion to the income of their occupants. In most
regions even the cheaper parks charge a trailer owner $100 to $150 a month just
for the lot with its sewer and water service and electrical hookup, while charging
at least $350 a month for tenants who rent a trailer. Although used trailers more
than twenty years old can be purchased for $5,000, they are costly to heat and
are extremely hazardous in case of fire; even a small trailer made in the late
1970s, and therefore built in compliance with the first industry standards, may
cost $10,000 to $20,000.

Poverty in Villages and Small Towns

In many of the state's rural counties, there are one or two hamlets or villages
where an increasing number of low-income families are living in rented apartments among the rest of the home-owning residents. This growth in low-income
tenant population in a rural village is a result of both demographic and economic

changes: long-term population loss through exodus of better-educated young and the more affluent elderly, the death of some of the old people, and decline in local industry, commerce, and employment. As general deterioration of the village leaves some houses and commercial buildings vacant, the family heirs or outside investors who own them are unable to sell or rent their buildings for their original purposes, and so they convert them to apartments, which they rent out at rates just low enough to attract people on welfare or earning low wages. A house that once held a single family may now contain two, four, or more rental units; a former store may have been converted to four family apartments. In communities where a significant and noticeable population of low-income tenants lives in such apartments, village residents who are employed in the area's better jobs or commute long distances to work, as well as those who are retired, report that the increase in low-income tenants weakens community solidarity and tarnishes the community's self-image and reputation. Such a community becomes known in the area as a low-income housing area, "slum," "dump," or "welfare community." One such hamlet in the central part of the state had shrunk in the 1970s and early 1980s from about 400 families to about 300, but began gaining residents again after the middle of the decade when some vacant single-family homes were converted to apartments. Several houses in the village now hold two or more rental units, one holds a dozen apartments with over two dozen people, and a few more houses and spaces above stores are currently undergoing conversion to low-rent apartments. The community is known in the area as "a poverty town." In another village of about 1,500 people, one section of the village contained 100 dwelling units, of which 23 units in 12 buildings were rental apartments: most were owned by absentee landlords, and most were classified as substandard.

Rents in these converted village apartments are fairly low compared to those in other villages or small cities nearby, and most of the tenants are poor. The predominant tenant household is a single woman with a child or children and maybe a boyfriend. Men and women with jobs earn low wages, but many are without work and without reliable transportation to get to a job if they had one. On a typical weekday young men are working on cars, small children are at play on front steps, and very young mothers push their babies in strollers along the sidewalks to the convenience store or to the public pay phone by the drugstore. Many households are supported partially or completely by welfare. At the one remaining grocery store in such a village, an estimated 40 percent of customers use Food Stamps. Friendship and informal support networks link some of the tenants; but tension, distrust, and violence among neighbors are common. Turn-over of tenants in these apartments is high, and people often move out in the night, showing up later on in another apartment or another town.

Recent Poverty Trends in Rural Communities in New York

In rural New York all three kinds of rural poverty settlements appear to be growing in size and number, while deteriorating in quality. However, rural poverty is easily overlooked because it occurs in small populations dispersed over an expansive and sparsely populated area beyond the purview of metropolitan residents. Furthermore, the more noticed changes in the rural landscape are the result of other people's affluence: the rapid growth of expensive new vacation homes in scenic areas and the spread of high-priced year-round residential development into rural places near metropolitan centers.

Rural poverty is also hidden by aggregate demographic data and economic indicators. Even at the county level, aggregate statistics on economic conditions may hide or fail to show the existence or worsening of rural poverty, as examples from the sixteen research counties in upstate New York demonstrate. In one county, for instance, the existence of tenacious poverty is statistically overshadowed by a high per capita income reflecting the presence of a small number of very wealthy individuals. Elsewhere, one of the most serious open-country pockets of poverty in the state, in terms of intergenerational longevity and social and economic marginality, lies within a rural county that consistently has one of the state's lowest unemployment rates and one of the higher levels of per capita income. One of the worst situations of village-apartment poverty lies in a county where wealth and land values have greatly increased in recent years. Some of the most crowded and possibly most unsafe trailer parks lie within counties that have strong economies. Several rural counties with median income above the state average contain townships with per capita income under 60 percent of the state level.

The lack of congruence between healthy county-level economic indicators and a significant rural poverty problem is also reflected in changes over time. For example, a reduction in the number of people who are poor and the depth of their poverty may not match improvement in county unemployment rates. One county has now nearly recuperated from job losses in the early 1980s, when major local factories implemented a 50 percent labor-force reduction. Rehirings and new job creations in the county brought unemployment down to under 5 percent in 1988. In autumn 1989 the creation of a record number of new jobs gave the county its largest-ever number of jobs by the end of that year and led to predictions of a labor shortage to come. But at the same time, the number of poor people in the county was also increasing. Thus, at the end of the decade, while the county's business community rejoiced over the recovering local economy, local government and service providers also felt frustrated that poverty, as shown by numbers of people depending on government services, had not dropped commensurately. In 1988 over 20 percent of the population was still receiving some form of assistance from the Department of Social Services each month, and the county had the state's highest rate of public assistance recipients. Welfare rolls in the county did go down slightly just after mid-decade, but then began growing again, slowly at first, then rapidly, with a 12.5 percent increase in public assistance cases from April 1989 to April 1990. This unexpected rise worried the county's commissioner of social services, who claimed that the state's new eligibility levels for AFDC were not sufficient to explain the dramatic growth in caseload. A somewhat similar situation was occurring in certain other counties: the economic woes of the early–1980s recession seemed over and the local economy seemed to be holding its own, but the problem of poverty still existed, and in some places it was growing. In virtually all of the research counties, it appeared that the three kinds of settlements described earlier were increasing in the 1980s, especially in the last few years of the decade.

The tenacious poverty of long-term depressed rural neighborhoods was little changed in 1990 from what it had been in 1970: clusters of kin-related poor people living in substandard housing surrounded by junk cars were still dispersed along back roads, cycling into yet another generation. In several of the localities where I had earlier done interviewing, the same pockets of poverty are still there today—but the number of people, shacks, and trailers in them has grown. Most of the growth appears to be from "natural increase" rather than the arrival of new residents from elsewhere, although there is still some movement within and among nearby depressed neighborhoods. Preliminary inquiries indicate that while a few individuals have broken out of poverty, managing to get on their feet in nearby small cities or even out of state, most who were adults in the 1970s have spent the last decade where they were or have moved around from one pocket of poverty to another. Few have been able to generate enough momentum to rise above their economic and social marginality. The young adults mostly settled close to the parental home, some in trailers placed in the side yard. Some returned home after a brief residence elsewhere, seeking refuge from a larger world in which they were unable to participate effectively. Of the dozens of 1970s-era children observed and tracked in over fifty families, recent follow-up on just a few families revealed that they have grown up to be poor and insecure, both economically and socially. Some became parents very early, and their children are growing up now in these same pockets of poverty, already identified by schools, public health officials, and family courts as children at risk.

Trailer parks and informal trailer clusters also grew through the 1980s in some localities, especially where land values were not yet rising sharply, and where there were neither land-use ordinances nor market disincentives for putting trailers on the land. While patterns of mobile-home growth vary considerably in different localities, both individually placed trailers in the open country and trailers in commercial parks or informal clusters have been increasing, as indicated by inspection and counting in some localities over several years, by interviews with park residents and agency caseworkers, and by county building-permit records. Residents of the trailer clusters and lower-cost parks represent a mixed population of working and nonworking, poor and nonpoor, though few residents are financially secure or much above the margin of poverty: in one isolated trailer park all thirty-nine households were on either AFDC or disability payments. Initial interviewing in some trailer parks indicates that it is simply availability and relatively low cost that draw people to these settlements, and most residents come from nearby areas. There is increasing crowding of trailers within many trailer parks: more trailers are being inserted between each two previous trailers, no more than a car's length from the next; and new loop roadways are being built and more trailers placed along them. At the edge of one village, a trailer park that began a decade ago with only a few trailers now holds a few dozen and is still growing. By the start of the 1990s, however, many parks were full, unable to expand any further. Where not zoned out, new trailer parks are being started. There is also more crowding of people within many of the trailers now, as tenants double up, trying to keep housing costs down or fulfilling their obligations to relatives and friends by providing them temporary shelter.

Most striking of all, though, is growth in the village form of poverty settlement. In some counties more villages are now receiving low-income populations moving into one- or two-bedroom apartments within formerly single-family houses; and more homes within such villages are being divided up and rented out. Research still in progress indicates that the increased poor population of these villages comes from several sources, and that the situation varies from county to county and even among villages within a single county. In some communities most apartment tenants are local people, born and raised within the county or perhaps the adjacent county. Some have only recently fallen into poverty, as is the case with some young parents, married or single, who have set up independent households but find themselves unable to keep up with the rents in the county's larger villages or small city. Others are young adults who have come back to their home counties now that the Sunbelt jobs they found in the late 1970s and early 1980s have dried up: they return with little savings and limited job skills and are unable to obtain adequate employment in the local economy. Still others grew up in poverty in nearby rural depressed neighborhoods and have recently moved into villages to gain "independence," greater social activity, and convenient access to services. The increased number of tenant households in such villages may also reflect an increase in the number of households, especially in counties where the number of households has recently been growing more than twice as fast as the population. Many apartments, for example, contain single mothers living separately from parents and from husbands or fathers of their children.

In other villages, in contrast, the growth of low-income residents is due mostly to in-migration from other areas, and "local" tenants are outnumbered by low-income people who have come from elsewhere. This is the case in certain larger villages, for example, in a few villages that are located within one hundred miles of a metropolitan area and along a bus or train line, and where there is a large stock of old houses ready to be made over into apartments, so that rents are relatively low. The new and rapidly increasing in-migrant population in such villages is related to recent escalation of rents in or closer to metropolitan areas. Urban low-income residents squeezed out by high rents report that they came to rural villages to find cheaper housing and to join relatives or friends who had already made the move.

An example of this latter type of village poverty is one community that experienced a major influx of low-income people starting in 1988. While not all of the in-migrants moving into the converted housing units in the village are poor or on welfare, the poverty dimension of the in-migration becomes quickly apparent in the Department of Social Services and other community agencies providing poor people with services from emergency food to job training. The county has experienced a 50 percent increase in welfare rolls in just over two years, almost all of it within this village of around 5,000 people. In just three months in 1990 there was a 7 percent increase in the welfare caseload, a bulge of new cases entering the system that was only partially explainable in terms of recent changes in eligibility rules. Food Stamp participants not on public assistance rose even more quickly: a 13 percent increase was registered in one month in early 1990. Most of the new service-needy people represent very recent arrivals in the county, and to a large extent they are arriving in an emergency situation: a community action agency reported a 25 percent growth in emergency services in one year and stated that "people are showing up at the door with no money, no food, no housing, and no job." A sampling of 41 new welfare applicants over a few months in this period of high caseload growth revealed that while 11 had been in the county a year or more, 30 were more recent: 7 had been in the county from six months to a year; 11 had been in the county from one month up to six months; and 12 had been in the county less than a month, 5 of them less than a week. Over one-quarter of the welfare "intakes" sampled, 11 out of the 41, listed their last residence as out of state; but of the 30 who had been in the village less than a year, most listed their last previous residence in nearby counties. Local sources and initial interviews suggest that prior to the last place of residence, most new arrivals had originally lived in the New York City metropolitan area.

This village's sudden and dramatic impoverization is only a more extreme case of what has been taking place over many years within many rural counties, in which one or two small communities in the county become the catch-basin for low-income people edged out of the economically healthier communities. But it appears that the number of villages demonstrating this pattern is increasing now; and where the phenomenon is very recent, it has quickly become significant. The pattern is particularly observable in villages where in-migration is from outside the county, from a metropolitan area and the counties adjacent to it: here one finds more conversion of houses to apartments and more lower-income families moving into the village. It should be noted, however, that in other villages or hamlets of rural counties there may be little or no apparent growth of low-income population and minimal conversion of old empty houses into low-quality apartments. In fact, many rural villages appear to have a population that for the most part is economically secure if not well off, and a few are experiencing upgrading in housing connected to an influx of more affluent residents. The factors causing some villages to remain stable or become less disadvantaged while others increasingly become catchment locations for low-income people are complex and not yet researched, but the comment of one county official where the primary village of the county is experiencing significant impoverization by in-migration indicates the main factors: ''In towns where there are no rentals available or where the rents are high because of the ski [resort] areas, we have very few [welfare] cases. It would certainly appear at first glance that 'affordable' and available housing draws people to certain towns. Also, the location of services appears to be an attraction.'' The depressed villages spiraling downward, as well as the cycling of rural depressed neighborhoods into another generation of poverty and the growing trailer parks and clusters, are all part of the general worsening of rural poverty that local county officials, caseworkers, educators, and human-service workers refer to, deal with, and are frustrated about because the poverty problem seems to be getting worse despite their efforts to cope with it.

THE DYNAMICS OF RURAL IMPOVERIZATION: CAUSES AND PROCESSES

Over and over again in rural communities, government officials, social-service workers, educators, and the general public ask why. If unemployment has come down so far and the general economy seemed so much better in 1989 than a few years before, why is there still so much poverty? Why has the long-standing poverty of the past not been overcome? Why does poverty seem to be growing now, both in numbers of people and in the difficulty and severity of their problems? Answers to these questions have begun to emerge from community-based research in the three regions.

The creation of more and worse poverty on top of the poverty that already existed is the result of a complex interweaving of several different situations and processes. Most of the causal factors are neither unique to rural areas nor limited to New York State, but they appear to have become much more prevalent in rural New York in recent years. At the same time, other factors commonly associated with poverty in other regions of rural America, as well as in urban America, such as racial and ethnic characteristics, are not presently significant in rural upstate New York, where, at least until very recently, the state's rural poverty population matched its overall rural population, which is more than 95 percent White, non-Hispanic. In rural New York four closely interrelated causes of impoverization stand out most clearly: inadequate employment, housing problems, changes in family structure and dynamics, and geographical mobility. Each of these contributes directly to poverty, but each also exacerbates and is exacerbated by the others, so that together they produce an effect far greater than their sum.

The Rural Employment Situation Remains Inadequate

In general, the economies of rural counties of New York have been service-oriented or manufacturing dependent, and some are undergoing a further shift to the service sector as local factories have been lost. Here, as elsewhere in rural America, "the severe recession in manufacturing, downsizing of U.S. manufacturing plants, changing occupational mix, and shifting locational patterns in U.S. manufacturing have negatively affected more rural citizens and communities than other economic adjustments in the 1980s" (Deavers 1989b, pp. 33–34). The northeastern states have been especially affected by the extended manufacturing decline. In 1990 the federal Bureau of Labor Statistics reported that seven northeastern states all fell in the bottom ten states nationwide in employment growth in the 1987–89 period (New York ranked forty-fifth in job growth, by percentage, while Vermont did considerably better than its neighbors, and Maine made it into the top ten) (Levine 1990, p. 1). Reflecting national trends, the biggest increase in rural poverty in New York seems to be among the working poor.

In rural New York the low official unemployment rates of the late 1980s, around 5 to 6 percent, masked a significant population of long-term unemployed people, people who have never had a formal job or have not worked in years and are not actively seeking work. They include men on public assistance and disability payments and women supported by a husband's earnings or public assistance. The low rate also hides the men and women who are underemployed. For example, in one county in summer 1987, while there were only 1,400 people officially counted as unemployed, 2,300 people were listed on the computer records of the Private Industry Council as wanting employment. Many of these, according to employment officials, were wanting better jobs than they had, or full-time rather than part-time jobs.

Working rural people are increasingly at risk of being poor. The drop in unemployment after the severe recession in the early 1980s has brought a decrease in AFDC cases in some rural counties as women who had been on welfare have taken jobs. But this decrease has been accompanied by an increase in Food Stamps and Medicaid for people not on public assistance, as the jobs they took have left them still near or even below the poverty line and still eligible for— and desperately in need of—these programs. Many jobs in rural New York are seasonal (especially in the tourist industry and forestry), part-time (especially in retail sales), and temporary (in certain manufacturing industries). Many employers pay no benefits, some lay off workers just before they reach the point of gaining a raise and benefits, and some increase wages very slowly. A typical example of workers caught in this deteriorated employment situation is a man who started work in a factory at $3.25 an hour in early 1987 and by early 1990 was still earning only $4.45 an hour. With two preschool children, one with a serious health problem, his wife is not working. The family is on Food Stamps and Medicaid, but is having real difficulty making ends meet: they have moved frequently as they try to reduce housing costs but then find that their less expensive housing is inadequate.

Available entry-level jobs in these counties in 1989 were mostly at pay near the minimum wage, for example, part-time supermarket checkout jobs at $4.05

an hour. Many of the jobs listed with the local employment service were part-time, and some were temporary, or else required a level of education, skills, experience, and certification beyond what most low-income job seekers could meet. Most of the local jobs within the grasp of the poor are only suitable as a second income in a family and may even be advertised as such; but the people seeking jobs may need to provide the primary family income. For example, one young mother living in a trailer park in a small village is sole provider for herself and her child. The Welfare Department wanted her to get a job, and she herself desperately wanted to get off welfare. The only job she could get was a thirty-hour-a-week job in a supermarket in town at $3.75 an hour, which yielded an income well below the poverty level. She interviewed at a fast-food restaurant for a second part-time job, but found it impossible to combine the shifts of two jobs. Besides, she still would not have had health benefits. She can retain Medicaid, Food Stamps, and partial assistance for a while, but when that runs out, she expects to be much worse off than she was when she had full public assistance. But if she were to quit her supermarket job, she would be "sanctioned" by the Welfare Department, which would require her to wait thirty days before applying again for any benefits. This employment-welfare bind, encountered by poor people virtually everywhere in the United States, appears especially acute in rural areas, where recent employment shifts are toward part-time service-sector work, and where many adults lack skills and experience to get any of the better jobs that may have been created.

Other people in these counties, while not usually below the poverty line, find themselves right on the margin, no matter how hard they work. In one family the husband is working a fairly good job in construction and moonlighting at a part-time janitorial job after hours. As he was unable to do more than barely make ends meet in their crowded trailer, his wife took a job, leaving one child in school, one in Head Start, and the third at a babysitter. When problems developed with the child-care arrangement, they reassessed the situation and came to the conclusion that her working was not good for the child, and that her job did not even make much sense financially, given the cost of babysitting and extra driving. It was also an exhausting routine, since both she and her husband were working about twenty-five miles from home. So she quit, and they remained just at the edge of poverty.

Recent factory closings in rural New York have thrown many blue-collar workers into poverty. One county's fourth-largest employer, a factory producing plastic health-care products, closed down in 1989 to move to Mexico, throwing nearly 500 workers out of jobs. Workers who had started as long as thirty years ago, some of them without finishing high school, had moved up over the years to a point where they were earning eight dollars an hour. Displaced line workers who did get jobs within the first few months almost all suffered a significant pay cut (to five dollars an hour or less), as well as undesirable changes in shift hours, working conditions, and benefits, and a longer commute from home. In this case, as in another plant of the same size in another county that had closed down two years previously, older employees, above age 40 or 45, and those of any age who lacked a high-school diploma had the most difficulty in finding replacement jobs. In a small plant of one hundred workers in yet another county, of the fifteen non-high-school graduates, most of them in their 40s and 50s, only one had obtained a substitute job within three months of being laid off. In all these plant-closing cases, many displaced workers remained unemployed for a year or more and then, in desperation, took a low-paying service-sector job or a job in a new assembly plant paying only $4.50 an hour.

Some people cannot get jobs, even in a time of low unemployment. High rural unemployment of the past decades has taken its toll on a whole cohort of young adults who grew up into joblessness in the late 1970s and early 1980s. In a tight job market marginally educated young people from the rural pockets of poverty were not wanted; and they became even less wanted as their years out of the labor force increased. Despite the recent turnaround in employment, these long-term unemployed people are unwanted now and are labeled "unemployable" by employers and employment personnel. Some job-readiness classes in rural communities are attempting to help men and women overcome barriers to employment, such as physical disabilities, alcoholism, health problems, family problems, and lack of transportation, as well as attitudinal and self-esteem barriers. Helping long-term unemployed people overcome such barriers is a tremendous task, but essential, since getting an "unemployable" person his or her first job cannot lift him or her out of poverty if he or she lacks work-related and basic living skills to keep the job. Even the best employment training, however, does not lift people out of poverty if the jobs pay no more than poverty wages.

The Rural Housing Situation Is Becoming Worse

Substandard housing in rural areas continues to be a problem. The housing of many poor people in rural New York remains seriously substandard, despite recent and effective activity by some local rural housing corporations using state and federal funds for rehabilitation and construction. Much of the housing in the open-country pockets of poverty is structurally unsound, and units lack adequate wiring, running water, or plumbing. In the villages and hamlets, housing may be of no better quality. In several instances, where vacant houses and store buildings have been converted into low-rent apartments, human-service workers have indicated in interviews that these apartments probably could not meet code if there were inspections. Some county Departments of Social Services are now more active in ensuring inspection before clients move into apartments, but code enforcement in many places is lax. In some of the burgeoning trailer parks and the new trailer clusters along back roads, water and sewer systems are unable to meet increased demands or state codes. Tenants claim that they are scared to complain to authorities, although a new state hotline and mobile-home tenants' rights office should help protect them. Local health departments may be slow to inspect housing and enforce codes, although recently a few trailer parks and apartment buildings in rural counties have been forced by the authorities to close down. One of the reasons inspection and enforcement have been limited is that in most counties there simply is no alternative low-cost housing to which people could move.

Poor rural people have always had to put up with poor-quality housing because they could afford no better; many prefer to sacrifice quality of housing as a way to minimize cash expenses and remain independent of welfare, or to stretch a welfare grant where the housing allowance falls far short of the actual rent. But the quality has been deteriorating recently. Several families who have moved frequently in the last few years report inadequacy of a rented apartment or trailer as the reason they moved out, citing such problems as electrical wiring that poses a fire hazard, leaking roofs, ventilation problems, nonfunctional plumbing, and no hot water.

Rural housing costs are rising. However inadequate, housing in rural areas of the state is now becoming considerably more expensive than it was as recently as 1986, largely as a result of greater competition among an increasing number of poor people for a shrinking supply of low-cost homes.

Stricter land-use regulations, building ordinances, and housing codes affecting rural areas now prevent low-income home-owning families from using their traditional strategies to provide cheap makeshift owner-occupied housing for themselves and their extended families. At the state level, for example, a uniform building and fire code prohibits people from occupying a partially completed home and from utilizing used or rough-cut lumber in construction, thus curtailing adaptive strategies poor rural people have traditionally used to build, modify, and extend a house gradually over the years as family needs change and money and materials become available. Tightened local land-use regulations have further circumscribed the strategies open-country people use to provide housing at minimal cash cost. Regulation of trailers on individual lots in the open countryside, for example, restricts poor people's housing options and increases the cost. For instance, a couple may now be prohibited from bringing in a third trailer as a temporary home for a grown daughter just separated from her husband. In some localities trailer parks may soon become casualties of suburban expansion and increasing land values. Owners of trailer parks within commuting distance to employment centers find that they can reap a better return on investment by converting from trailers to condominiums. In some open-country areas rural gentrification has reduced the number of inexpensive old farmhouses available for local people to rent or buy.

In many small towns surplus housing resulting from out-migration has traditionally provided low-cost rural housing, but recently growing demand for cheap village apartments, particularly where low-income people have settled after being forced out of nearby towns or metropolitan areas by escalating rents, has caused small-town rents to rise considerably. In one rural county not far from the outer edge of the New York metropolitan area, a vacancy rate in 1988 of only 1 percent had pushed rents up and caused some people to move to other counties where a stock of old buildings suitable for conversion makes apartments cheaper and more available; but with the growing demand, rents are pushed up in these secondary locations also. In some small towns the recent construction of state prisons has boosted local housing demand, with particular impact on rents: in one such community a woman on AFDC in 1988 could find a two-bedroom apartment for under $250, but a year later there was nothing for less than $350. Because few rural communities have public low-income housing, except for the elderly, young families have little protection against market-driven increases in rents.

Increasingly the rural poor are renters rather than owners of their housing. In the past many rural poor people had the security and limited cash expense of owning a place to live, or having parents who owned a place, even if it was just a crumbling farmhouse or a plywood-sided shack. But because of increased regulation of land uses and tightened housing codes, as well as competition for old houses, opportunity for people with limited income and no savings to own their housing has diminished. People are no longer as free to put their own trailers or shacks on their relatives' property, and fewer of the poor people in rural areas today have either land or relatives with land. The security of ownership is increasingly being replaced by the precariousness of tenancy.

Other trends, including the increase in single-parent households and eroded incomes, exacerbate the difficulty rural poor people have in coping with the necessity of renting and with the escalating rents now occurring in some rural areas. In several of the sixteen rural counties studied, AFDC clients were typically paying rents around $100 above the welfare shelter allowance: in one case, two-thirds were paying more than $100 over their allowance. In one county in 1989, rent allowance for a woman with one child was $229 a month (including heat); but rent for a two-bedroom apartment, the size required by welfare regulations for a mother with one child, was $325 to $350 a month.

The problem with renting is not only that rent payments take up so much income, but that they require a cash outlay on a regular basis. Many of the tenants, particularly in trailer parks and small-town apartments, are single women trying to get off welfare or trying to support a family on a minimum-wage salary from a service-sector job. Many have repeatedly been forced to move out of an apartment because they get behind in their rent. When they can find another place, they face a large up-front cash cost, often at least $700, in security deposit, rent, and installation charges. For single mothers, the rent burden is often the reason they are unable to make it on their own, the expense that sends them to welfare, keeps them on welfare, or makes them return to it.

Family Relationships Are Increasingly Unstable and Insecure

In my earlier ethnographic study of open-country pockets of poverty in the 1970s, I found families with considerable marital strife, often involving violence and temporary separation. It was striking, however, that these married couples basically stayed together. Though difficult and often personally destructive, their marriages endured for many years. Some couples held tenaciously to bitter marriages "for the sake of the children" and expressed a strong belief that their own difficult adulthood reflected a childhood deprived of the security of a two-parent home. There were indeed single mothers with babies, young women who had not yet married and were, in most cases, still living at home with their parents, or perhaps living with the father of the baby. But the expectation, and the eventual reality in most cases, was marriage, though not necessarily to the father of the baby. In the late 1980s my research revealed a substantially changed picture.

Female-headed households are increasing among the rural poor. On the national level "female-headed households" are still less common among the rural poor than among the urban poor, composing only 27 percent of rural poor households as compared to 39 percent of urban poor households (Duncan and Tickamyer 1988, p. 245); but this family form appears now to be rising significantly in rural areas. When I interview long-term married couples and young couples, they talk in terms of long-term commitment to marriage; but when I interview human-service workers, they indicate that long-term marriage is no longer expected and does not seem respected. They believe that the rural poor, particularly young adults, are not staying married as long as they used to. While young mothers talked in interviews of wanting to marry in the future, their assessment of the likelihood of having a stable marriage was low. This was especially true among those poor living in the village apartments and trailer parks.

The growing incidence of one-parent families is also indicated in the records of some agencies and institutions. In any Head Start center many of the children have only a mother listed on school records or have two different parental addresses listed. Records in one rural school with a 20 percent poverty rate indicate that less than 45 percent of its children live in two-parent homes. Among the women enrolled in Extension's Nutrition Education for Low Income Families (ENELIF), as among people in the Federal Supplementary Feeding Program for Women, Infants, and Children (WIC), the population of women includes a high rate of single parents. However, the concept or category of families headed by a single woman is quite misleading for purposes other than program eligibility, for it lumps together a considerable variety of causes and configurations. In reality, as revealed in home interviews, the common rubric "female-headed household" includes two distinct patterns: the very young women who have not been married but have become mothers and the slightly older women who have been legally married and then separated or divorced.

Family arrangements are increasingly temporary. The frailty of many families in rural poverty also appears to be increasing, but again, the unstable reality is seriously understated by our structure-oriented terminology. Because the standard terms "two-parent family" and "single-parent family" have no temporal dimension, they convey more stasis and stability than is the case in actuality. Family histories, on the other hand, reveal that many rural low-income women are living a life of temporary relationships, sometimes on their own without a man, sometimes with a boyfriend, often with a series of boyfriends, whose major instrumental and emotional participation in the lives of women and children, as lovers and as fathers, is virtually ignored in most definitions and enumerations. The family, in these cases, is characterized by instability and flux and by risk of sudden dissolution; and these major disruptions reverberate through relationships of children with parents, stepparents, stepsiblings, and the entire extended family, particularly on their fathers' side. Several women have indicated in interviews that by the time they had two children they had had at least two steady live-in male partners, with intervening periods of living alone. They appear to have bounced rather quickly from one boyfriend to singleness and then to another relationship. But as interviews with caseworkers and counselors in domestic-violence programs indicate, often the next relationship also dissolves or blows up, leaving a woman even more vulnerable than before, in search of a new place to live, a new mate, and a new setting for her children. This temporariness, now common among the rural poor, appears as a significant contrast to the situation in the 1970s.

Destabilization of marriage and family is occurring in a social context that itself is less secure. In contrast to my earlier ethnographic study, preliminary findings now indicate that among the young poor adults, especially those living in village apartments and trailer parks, networks of extended family tend to be less developed and less available. An individual may not be as enmeshed in and protected by a network of relatives who, no matter how poor or "down and out," were always available in the past in the open-country pockets of poverty. Some individuals still do have such networks, which they mobilize especially for securing a temporary place to stay while looking for an apartment of their own, and perhaps for babysitting and transportation, but most appear less anchored among relatives. Reports of social-service caseworkers and a variety of human-service workers, such as counselors in teen parenting programs, workers in community action programs, and Head Start staff, indicate that many clients do not have relatives they can turn to and count on for emergency support. The absence or inaccessibility of relatives makes it harder for young poor parents, especially single mothers, to cope with their situation.

Where relatives are less available as an informal support system, some young adults appear to be substituting networks of peers. A woman may maintain a roster of boyfriends, ex-boyfriends, and their friends, as well as her girlfriends and their friends and a few past or present neighbors. This peer network may function reasonably well for emergencies, but in many cases it lacks the stability, permanence, and resources of the old family-based network, economically impoverished as that may have been. Relationships appear to be instrumental, involving occasional child care, temporary housing in emergencies, transportation, household goods and used appliances, Food Stamps, cigarettes, and advice. Relationships are subject to squabbles and are often short-lived. In some rural communities where drug dealing and drug use have infiltrated (and here I have little concrete information beyond local newspaper reports, interviews with local law enforcement personnel, and some court-monitoring reports), the drugs circulated in peer networks create less durable bonds than the "blood" of extended family networks.

The diminished social support network apparent today among young low-income rural families makes them less able than their parents' generation was to cope with economic and social marginality. The weakened informal support system both contributes to and suffers from a fourth factor in the dynamics of worsening rural poverty, increased geographic mobility.

Geographic Mobility of Rural Poor People Is High and Increasing

All three factors cited earlier interact, and together they contribute to a fourth factor: a high level of residential mobility of rural poor people. Especially in the case of some village apartments and trailer parks, people move frequently from one residence to another, often within the same community and usually within the same county or among adjacent counties. The timing of the move often coincides with changes in family status.

Mobility of young adults with children is especially high. In general, young adults are the most mobile, for they are the ones dealing with the most difficult situations of poverty and stress, trying to support themselves and their children on inadequate employment or meager welfare, dealing with numerous agencies and programs, and seeking to finish growing up and putting their lives together. In some localities young unmarried couples and single mothers from open-country pockets of poverty are moving to villages, making a break with parents, and seeking a livelier social life, often with welfare paying the rent. Once there, they may move frequently within or among several small towns. Moves are often quite sudden and are often interspersed with an interlude of staying with a friend or family member for a few weeks. The most commonly expressed reason for moving is "I got evicted because I got behind in the rent," a point confirmed by landlords. For some households that show a pattern of moving every three to four months, this seems a major contributor, but it is usually not the whole story. Moves result from a combination of the shortfall between available cash and living expenses and the instability of personal relationships. For the increasing number of single mothers, the frequent moves appear to be part of a pattern of "shopping around" for a better life situation, for a larger apartment or for cheaper housing, for a possible job or a better job, for a better place to raise the kids, or a better boyfriend. But in many cases each successive residence is not better, but worse than the one before, and the moves may be frequent. One young single mother had moved seven times in one year since she and her baby had fled from a violent boyfriend, staying temporarily with different relatives in already-overcrowded housing, moving into a condemned building, then into an apartment she could not afford, then living with her girlfriend until the welfare department ruled that out, and eventually ending up in a roadside cluster of trailers. Her case is by no means rare.

A family's mobility may become even greater as time goes on because the lack of strong ties to place, to people, to a home, to a good job, and to local institutions gives people less reason than ever to stay put. If housing and job situations fail to improve, it seems likely that more people will become mobile. Children are helpless victims in this high mobility. Young children of these households have already experienced many moves before they enter school, and as school attendance records reveal, moves of kindergarten and elementary-school children into and out of rural school districts are growing especially rapid and frequent.

Mobility intensifies problems of stigma. Stigmatization of low-income people by name, by residence location, and by the "welfare" label is as effective in small racially homogenous rural communities of upstate New York as skin color is in other regions in limiting a sense of social belonging. Mobility and high population turnover make it even more likely that stereotypes will become substitutes for firsthand knowledge. New residents who are poor may be conspicuous in negative ways in a small community: they may be using Food Stamps in the local grocery store; they may keep the church people busy with emergency food services; their children may hang around the main-street stores and sidewalks because their apartments lack yards; the adults may hang around on the sidewalks or in a local tavern during the day because they are not employed or hold either part-time or night-shift jobs. In general, the older, more comfortably situated families totally avoid the new population of low-income people and often refer to them, as a group, in derogatory terms, most commonly as "transients," revealing both the reality of high mobility and also an unstated hope that they will move on.

Negative attitudes may be especially strong if the new residents are thought to have moved in from elsewhere. Longer-term residents often state that the new people moving into the village apartments have come from a neighboring county "to take advantage of our easy-going welfare department," or from out of state "to take advantage of New York's higher welfare benefits," or from "the city," in which case they are thought to bring with them such urban vices as crime and drugs. Interviews with some low-income newcomers, including some who have simply moved in from the surrounding hinterland and some who migrated out from a nearby city, have picked up a perception of not being wanted and a sense of social marginalization that exacerbates the problems they have in settling into a community and may contribute to their further mobility.

In some rural communities the in-migration of poor people now includes a significant number of people who are racially or ethnically different from the predominantly White non-Hispanic existing population. In these cases racial or ethnic prejudices in the receiving community compound the other negative attitudes toward the arriving low-income people.

The mobility of the low-income population is unsettling to community institutions as well as to the individuals who move. Head Start and elementary-school personnel report that the greatly increased mobility they have seen in recent years is causing problems for their programs. Many schools are finding the mobility serious enough that they are trying various innovative techniques to make new and returning children feel welcome, to expedite record transfer to other schools, and to deal with children's distress and insecurity stemming from impending or recent moves. Schoolteachers and administrators cite children who leave school in the mid-fall and reenter in the spring, children who come, children who go, and children who come and then go. For classroom social dynamics as well as curriculum progress, these moves are disruptive; they also involve considerable testing of children to determine appropriate placement in the new school and require spending extra time to acquaint a child with the particular reading system or math approach used in his or her new school. Teachers express frustration that just when a child is beginning to feel at home and to show improvement, he or she leaves the district. In one rural school district with a 1980 poverty rate of 20 percent, ninety children, representing 14 percent of the entire student body, withdrew during one recent year. Most of these departures were from the lower grades, and they were replaced by a nearly equal number of children entering—some of them actually former pupils subsequently returning to the district. While total enrollment stayed nearly the same, there were many "new" children to be integrated into classrooms during the year. Fully half of the departures were due to parents or a parent moving away, and the next most common reason was family change, including splitting up of mother and partner/ spouse, which often triggers a move. Classroom teachers and principals in this and other rural schools perceive a distinct correlation between mobility of children and lower socioeconomic status of their families, and between both of these and low academic achievement. Although most parents who were interviewed expressed a preference for staying within the same school district, this is often impossible due to a lack of affordable housing, job changes, agency problems, and interpersonal factors.

Other community programs and agencies, besides schools, report the frequent comings and goings of their clients and members and have had to adjust programs and staff assignments in response. Housing-assistance-program personnel in several counties report that some of the individuals whom they help in finding a place to live are repeat cases, people who have moved as frequently as every three or four months, thus consuming a considerable amount of agency time and energy. Some community action programs (CAPs, or community action agencies, the remnant of the Old Economic Opportunity Act) have now assigned staff members not only to help people find housing, but also to help them keep it through financial and management counseling and other proactive problem-solving approaches.

In a broader sense, too, turnover of low-income residents destabilizes the cohesion and organized social life of some small towns. Long-time home-owning residents claim that they do not personally know and never interact with the low-income tenants next door or across the street. Their social groups and institutions, reduced in membership and diminished in functioning, are unable to bridge the economic, status, and life-style gulf between the two local populations.

CONCLUSION: A COMPLEX, DYNAMIC SITUATION

Increasing and worsening rural poverty, in New York or more generally in the Northeast, is a complex, interwoven set of interacting problems. Local-level research in dozens of rural communities leads to four general conclusions about the dynamic situation of poverty in rural places at this time.

First, rural poverty, meaning the poverty of people living in rural places, is a result of two separate processes: rural residents falling into poverty; and people who are already poor moving into a rural place. Second, increased rural poverty includes both impoverization of people and impoverization of communities. Impoverization of communities not only perpetuates the economic marginality of some residents, but may also exacerbate and prolong their social marginality.

Third, factors contributing to or worsening rural poverty have been identified in four realms: employment, housing, family relationships, and geographic mobility. All of these factors operate together, contributing to and compounding the whole complex, troubled situation. As we have seen, problems in the employment sector have the serious effects they do because they are accompanied by increased rural housing costs and by destabilized marital and family structures, and all three of these together contribute to and are in turn affected by heightened geographic mobility. While these causal factors are neither new nor unique to rural poverty, they are much more prevalent among the rural poor now than in the past, and they undermine the traditional adaptations that until recently have enabled rural low-income people to survive and maintain independence despite their poverty.

Fourth, rural impoverization is not a "rural problem" existing freestanding and independent of what is happening in urban America and the nation as a whole. Particularly in the densely populated Northeast, with its many metropolitan areas, what happens in cities has major consequences for poverty in rural localities: rural impoverization is directly tied to changes occurring in urban areas. If metropolitan and urban-fringe housing costs escalate, poor people may disperse outward to rural areas. If metropolitan areas generate affluent people who would rather live or vacation in small towns, then the lower-income residents already in small towns may be displaced by affluent in-migrants and pushed to more remote and less expensive areas. These two trends alone have great significance for rural communities as social systems and for their service and educational institutions; and they exemplify the interweaving of rural poverty with urban-generated forces. By contrast, there is only a rather weak connection between increasing rural poverty and forces of agricultural change in the region. Although the present wave of rural impoverization became evident at the same time as the farm crisis, it is less the result of farm problems than of sweeping changes in the nonfarm economy and of demographic and social changes in rural areas. While indeed some dairy-farm laborers have been displaced by farm loss and farm consolidation and may now be at risk of further economic marginalization, on the whole, this new rural poverty is mostly impoverization of nonfarm people and nonfarm communities.

Overall, although this research is still in process, it seems inescapable to conclude that poverty in rural areas of New York, and probably in much of the rural Northeast, is undergoing major changes in characteristics and patterns. These changes contribute both quantitatively and qualitatively to a worsening of poverty in rural places, and they have serious implications for the future. As research in the 1970s found, when rural people who are economically marginal become socially marginal as well, their poverty is compounded and prolonged, cycling into successive generations. Current research indicates that today we have the continuation, yet another generation later, of this tenacious long-term poverty. But we may also be witnessing the creation of a new wave of rural poverty, composed of people who slip from temporary poverty caused by adverse circumstances into the entrenched poverty and marginalization that become perpetuated. Parents who themselves are victims of circumstances may watch their children spin further downward as victims of poverty. These casualties of adverse rural circumstances are occurring at a time when the traditional informal strategies and supports are weakened, and when communities are less able or less willing to respond. The present situation may indeed be the seedbed of a whole new crop of rural poverty in the future.

NOTE

Part of the research for providing demographic, economic, and social background was supported by a 1988 Summer Research Grant from Ithaca College. Research in 1990 has been supported by a grant from the Ford Foundation's Rural Poverty and Resources Program and the Aspen Institute's Rural Economic Policy Program. I am grateful to these sources. I also acknowledge, with deep appreciation, the input of many people throughout the sixteen counties who have shared so much of their time, insight, and concern during this research.

Chapter 10

The New Poor in Midwestern Farming Communities

Cornelia Butler Flora

This chapter reports the emergence of a relatively new form of poverty in midwestern farming communities, groups of people that are now more at risk of being poor than in previous decades. Most of these new poor are the working poor, laboring in multiple jobs that offer little hope for upward mobility. Other new poor include elderly women, and still others include young families. In the first section of this chapter, I will detail how the class structure and traditional American ideals have created a climate unsympathetic to many of the new poor. This will be followed by an analysis of the characteristics of the new poor and their survival strategies in these communities. Throughout, an emphasis will be placed on how the negative effects of the changing economy in the midwestern farming communities have been exacerbated by low wages and community alienation of the poor.

EFFECTS OF CLASS STRUCTURE AND TRADITIONAL VALUES ON THE NEW POOR

By 1988, 13.6 percent of the nonmetropolitan residents of the North and West fell below the poverty line, compared to 11.8 percent of metropolitan residents (U.S. Bureau of the Census 1989b). Although strictly comparable data for the areas analyzed are not available, 1979 can be characterized as the last "good" year for agriculture in the Midwest, and 1980 was the beginning of the farm crisis (U.S. Bureau of the Census 1982b). Per capita income in farm counties in the middle border states declined between 1979 and 1986 (Strange 1990, p. 9).

As the chapter by Deavers and Hoppe stresses, it is no longer accurate to think of most farmers as poor. The majority of farmers are doing well, in part due to government farm programs. In most cases the poor in farming areas are the wage laborers who work several jobs at low wages, but still have trouble making it. They are young adults with children trying to survive in a changed economy. A few young farmers are also poor. While they resemble the rural poor in Appalachia and the Northeast, in the Midwest they have the additional burden of struggling in a social world that is largely unsympathetic to their plight.

Poverty tends to be hidden in the nation's midwestern farm communities. The ideology of "we're all just folks" serves to hide class differences, and farming-community norms against conspicuous consumption blur what are often substantial differences in wealth and income. Yet even in the most traditionally egalitarian rural communities—the family-farm-centered communities of the Midwest and the Great Plains—increasing income inequality and an increasing proportion of the population in poverty are challenging the myth that a strong work ethic automatically results in financial success. It is especially disturbing to realize that even in communities of hardworking farm families there are many who are having an increasingly difficult time trying to "pull their own weight." Problems began with the farm crisis of the early 1980s. Whereas the Great Depression affected everyone and therefore did not erode community integrity, the hard times of the early 1990s are characterized by growing inequality in rural farm areas, with one group doing quite well and another struggling.

Elites in rural communities often have property or investment income and do not sympathize with those whose only income is in the relatively more visible wage sector. There is still a strong low-wage, low-tax ideology in rural areas that assumes that anyone earning over $2.50 an hour (especially if not doing heavy physical work) is overpaid. Some in rural areas continue to view the poor in their communities as simply those unwilling to work hard enough or forgo enough consumption to "make it."

When people do recognize that their neighbors work hard and still have financial problems, they often can only attribute this breakdown of the "natural" causality of "work equals financial success" to a conspiratorial movement of outside forces. In many parts of the Midwest and middle border region extremist movements, such as the Word, the Sword, and the Arm of the Lord, are growing stronger, reflecting the belief that the current crisis of personal efficacy is caused by an un-American conspiracy engineered from outside the community.

In 1985 Department of Agriculture researchers identified 716 counties in which agriculture contributed an average of at least 20 percent of the total labor and proprietor income for the period 1975–79 (Bender et al. 1985). By the late 1980s the number of farming-dependent communities had declined to 516 counties. As is clear from the definition, even in farming-dependent counties the majority of the population do not earn their living from agriculture, and only a minority are actual farm operators. The recent decline in the number of farms and the increase in farm foreclosures has probably contributed to the increase in the number of poor in farming communities. However, they are probably not the major cause of the increased poverty in these rural communities. Rather, a continuing low wage base underlies the increasing poverty rate in farming-dependent counties in the Midwest. It is not the farmers who are poor; their income improved over the decade of the 1980s. Rather, the new poor in the Midwest are those wage earners who are often holding down several low-wage, part-time jobs.

In the last half of the 1980s farm income increased substantially, almost directly as a result of the crop subsidies authorized by the 1985 Food Security Act. By 1988 the average household income of U.S. farmers was estimated at $41,558. This was more than one-fifth greater than the average income of American households. Farm household income is estimated to have increased even more in 1989 (Kalbacher and Brooks 1990, p. 23). However, the increased movement of capital to agriculture has not resulted in appreciable increases in the standard of living in farming-dependent communities. That capital has gone to reduce debt to mortgage holders, generally outside the community, and much of the capital invested in obtaining new machinery and petrochemical inputs leaves the community almost immediately. Clearly the increase in total farm income has not helped the growing number of poor in these communities.

While agriculture itself declined as a major industry in the United States during the 1980s, many farming-dependent communities were also hit by declines in other natural-resource-based activities, such as timber and mining, occupations that often supplemented farm incomes in those areas. For example, most of the Great Plains farming-dependent counties also had some oil located in them, which provided an additional source of income as well as employment. The fact that petroleum production was providing what little diversification existed in the local economy meant that these communities were especially vulnerable when oil prices fell.

Few families in farming communities depend on a single enterprise or source of employment for support. People engage in multiple self-employed activities, including a variety of sales and service offerings and wage labor that is often seasonal. Many also receive a variety of transfer payments, including Social Security payments. Of course, deficiency payments from farm programs contribute to the income of farm owners and operators, but they are not officially defined as transfer payments.

The poor in farming-dependent counties, with the exception of elderly women living alone, are working poor. The official unemployment rates for farming-dependent counties are well below those of other types of counties in the United States. Many people are self-employed in these farm communities where employment in the formal business and manufacturing sectors is limited. When jobs are not available, would-be workers often withdraw from the job market, rather than look for jobs they know are not there. Local norms discourage receiving welfare benefits even when people are eligible. Consequently, the poor in farming-dependent counties are much less likely to get welfare assistance of any type.

WHO ARE THE NEW POOR?

In the past the poor in farm communities would move on, seeking employment elsewhere when times got tough locally or when they lost their land. Today these circumstances are changing. Four types of new poor are discussed here: nonfarm low-wage workers, young debt-burdened farm operators, farm workers, and elderly women.

Nonfarm Workers

The poor in rural areas are increasingly young adults with no tie to agriculture who are currently employed. They also tend to have young children. Wages in farming-dependent communities are low in part because such communities tend to be located in states with "right-to-work" laws that greatly curtail workers' ability to organize. Further, many farm states have stipulated a minimum wage below the national minimum-wage level. In addition, many jobs in farming-dependent communities fall outside the reach of federal minimum-wage legislation because the number of employees per establishment is so small. An average wage in a farming community can be as little as two or three dollars an hour in both farm-related and service-related activities.

Over the last decade these wages have not increased, and families of the working poor have responded to hard times by relying on two or more members of the household in the labor force. Thus there is an increasing need for day care in these communities. Community leaders have not acknowledged the need for mothers to work, however, largely because they hold "traditional" values. The farmers that control the county budgets recount the economic sacrifices their family made so the wife could remain at home, forgetting that owning one's house and land made the difference between a lower level of consumption and total lack of access to food or housing.

The decade of the 1980s was a time when many nonfarm jobs either evaporated or declined in quality. For example, a recent analysis of farming-dependent Kansas counties showed a decline in quality of jobs in retail trade and in other nongovernmental services in the 1980s (Flora et al. 1990). Manufacturing establishments are becoming smaller, with fewer workers and smaller payrolls per worker. The number of low-wage retail and service jobs has increased, with retail jobs increasingly centralized in service-center chains, such as Wal-Mart, a merchandizing empire that has invaded rural areas throughout the nation. Such chains create fewer jobs than the "mom-and-pop" establishments they put out of business. Since they use part-time help as much as possible, their fringe benefits are no better than those of the smaller establishments they replaced, and workers can only count on working twenty to thirty hours each week.

Farm Operators

High indebtedness pushed many young farmers, particularly those with school-age children, into a new kind of poverty in rural areas. These farm families are "asset-rich," with substantial land and farm machinery that they purchased for top dollar in the inflationary 1970s. Even with the sharp deflation of farm assets in the first half of the 1980s, their net worth is high. But high indebtedness means that they have substantial cash-flow problems. Each time they receive a check for government payments or a crop sale, they must decide how much to pay the bank (that often has a lien on the money), how much to reinvest in the enterprise (which includes investing in the inputs needed for the next year's crop), and how much to invest in supporting the family's basic needs.

Poverty hit this group of landed poor at the same time the Reagan administration mandated cutbacks in federally funded poverty programs such as Food Stamps. Farmers could accept emergency help from farm aid groups, but that did not help the chronic cash-flow problems they faced over time. Their high gross income from farm operations obscures their low net income, which is caused by the high proportion of interest and debt in their current expenditures. Furthermore, according to a study by Public Voice for Food and Health Policy, ignorance of public programs combined with a sense of pride that defines "taking welfare" as moral failure keeps indebted farm families in the Great Plains farming communities off Food Stamp programs (Public Voice 1987).

These farm families, who once were independent producers who hired little labor and made a living from their farm enterprises, now try to combine their diversified farm enterprises with off-farm work. As that off-farm job is the low-wage sector as well as irregular, reflecting economic volatility and seasonal trends, their income is precarious.

Between 1979 and 1985 poverty rates increased at over twice the national rate in such hard-hit farming-dependent states as Iowa, Kansas, Nebraska, and Minnesota (Ross and Danziger 1987). Yet access to poverty programs remained low. In Kansas, for example, one hears much more concern that unworthy recipients might get Food Stamp assistance than that those in need have access to such assistance. Such a focus on "welfare cheaters," rather than on real need, has increased the stigma attached to receiving assistance, particularly in rural areas. Even free school lunch programs are underused by these new poor, in part because the forms to be filled out are not appropriate for self-employed individuals and small-business owners, and in part because parents want to avoid the stigma associated with "asking for a handout."

Farm Workers

Whereas migrant workers have long been a recognized poverty group, farm workers on family farms have traditionally been viewed as an extension of the family enterprise. The "hired man" may not have earned much, but he was assured either room and board year-round or an apprenticeship with the farm operator, who often allowed the hired hands to reinvest their wages and become part owners of the farm they worked. However true the perception of the farm hand in the Midwest was in the past, the growing use of industrial-style farm labor in America's heartland puts farm workers in the group of new poor. The class differences between farm operators and farm workers has increased, even in family-farm areas in the Great Plains and Midwest.

Farm workers in farming communities in the Midwest are primarily White, and they have a good chance of being poor. In 1987, 24.5 percent of the White families employed in farming, forestry, and fishing had incomes below 125 percent of the poverty level. Thirty-seven percent of the White males employed in farming, forestry, and fishing had incomes below 125 percent of the poverty level. Whites employed in farming are nearly twice as likely to be poor as Whites in any other occupation. These statistics contradict commonly held assumptions about the benign conditions for midwestern farm workers.

The "boom" in farming during the 1970s channeled a great deal of capital into agricultural enterprises. That capital was used primarily to buy land, but also to purchase machinery and chemical inputs. Farms became larger, renters became owners, and indebtedness increased markedly. However, in analyzing changes in farm population in farming-dependent counties in the western half of the United States, one can see that farm population did not decline as a portion of the population during the 1970s, despite an increase in farm size (Flora and Flora 1988). Instead, increased capitalization was accompanied by an increasing division of labor in agriculture, with fewer owners doing the management work and more workers doing the day-to-day manual work of farming—usually at below the minimum wage and with few, if any, fringe benefits. These workers are often young, with small children.

Farm operators with only one or two employees are not required to pay minimum wages. In many areas of the Great Plains a full-time "hired man" gets less than $600 a month, which does not include provisions for housing or transportation. Other kinds of employment in farming communities are also low-paying. Further, the low wages are not offset by in-kind provision of subsistence through room and board. According to the 1988 rural and rural farm survey, two-thirds of farm workers live off farm (U.S. Bureau of the Census 1989c).

Farms have increased both in size and division of labor in farming-dependent areas. The farm owner/operator tends to specialize in the book work, which includes marketing, buying of inputs, and selling of the products. This work is both physically and mentally separated from the farm work that is increasingly done by hired laborers. These hired laborers are often hired at below the minimum wage and are sometimes provided substandard housing as an in-kind wage. Anecdotal evidence suggests that these employees and their young families move frequently because they are seeking better wages and living conditions, and thus they are not integrated into the community. Their mobility makes their poverty even less visible to more stable and established community members, who feel that while times are tough, anyone who wants to work can make it.

Elderly Women

Widowhood and divorce have historically plunged women into poverty. For each woman who undergoes the experience, the move into poverty is jarring.

In rural areas elderly women living alone make up a growing number of the rural poor as the population in rural areas ages.

Elderly women living alone tend to own some property, usually the house in which they live. Home ownership in a rural community restricts their mobility because they cannot find housing elsewhere equivalent to the home they own in a farm community for the price they could get if their home were sold. Low property values in rural areas, coupled with high replacement costs for housing anywhere else, keep the elderly women in place. These women subsist on fixed incomes and pay a substantial portion of their cash income for property taxes (although they pay no mortgage or rent). They tend not to participate in community activities because they want to spend as little as possible. Because they are constantly strapped for cash, they hold firmly to a "low-tax" ideology and consistently vote in ways that limit investment in the community that could help other segments of the rural poor, and that could eventually have positive spin-offs for their own well-being.

This group of women remains poor despite the relatively generous increase in Social Security benefits over the last twenty-five years. Because their productive years were spent in activities outside the formal sector (as workers on farms or in family businesses), they are eligible for Social Security benefits only as spouses at the minimum payment level. Their primary economic contribution was to lower expenditures outside the household through gardens, home canning, home sewing, raising chickens, milking cows for milk and cream, and so forth, and thus there was never any special provision for their future security. In most cases their husbands assumed that they were providing for them by reinvesting every cent in the family business.

SURVIVAL STRATEGIES OF THE RURAL POOR

Cheap Housing

Farming-dependent communities do have inexpensive housing. Its availability can be an attraction for individuals who want to have a home in which to raise a family and who are willing to work hard for low wages. There is evidence that more and more houses in farming-dependent communities are run down but occupied. These houses are generally rental units, often owned by elderly people who live in nursing homes or with relatives out of town or by heirs who may live on either coast. These landlords are unable or unwilling to maintain the houses, and their renters are also unable to afford the kind of maintenance it takes to keep the once-neat single-family dwellings in good repair. Thus the problems of low-income families are exacerbated by the problems of increasingly substandard housing, even though it is affordable.

Even landlords who are community residents know little about their tenants, viewing them as outsiders. There is a recognition that there is a growing group of people, generally relatively transient, who must make arrangements for rent to be paid on a weekly rather than a monthly basis due to their severe cash-flow problems.

Home Work

The availability of workers willing to provide the space and labor for manufacturing has led to an increase in "home work." Major manufacturing firms contract out assembly or service work on a piecework basis. This work tends to be done by both farm and nonfarm rural women. Home work means that workers absorb overhead costs in building and equipment, the usual employer costs of benefits, and the "down time" due to irregular demand for the product. Since agricultural work is itself seasonal, fluctuating demand for industrial home labor matches the cyclical, but somewhat more predictable, demand for agricultural labor.

The lack of well-paid jobs in the formal sector makes home work a necessity for many households. Since most work in the formal sector in rural areas does not pay much over the minimum wage, home work is comparatively attractive to women, in that they do not have to invest time or money in travel to work. The legitimacy of home work is reinforced in the rural Midwest, as it viewed as appropriate for women to remain in the home. Until the late 1980s, federal law prohibited home work for a single source, but the recent lifting of the ban on home work will serve to keep wages low in rural farming areas. One consequence of home work is that it further disguises the actual extent of rural poverty in the heartland. As Osha Gray Davidson pointed out, "Home work adds no capital, physical plants, roads or community resources. In the long run, such 'economic development' only institutionalizes rural poverty" (Davidson 1989, p. 90).

Skimping on Health Care

A major problem of the working poor in farming communities is the lack of fringe benefits, especially health insurance. This has been particularly detrimental to the farming population, because during the farm crisis many indebted farmers dropped their health insurance. Thus rural hospitals, already hard pressed by unequal Medicare reimbursements, find themselves unable to cope with the number of charity cases. The result, according to rural health practitioners, is a growing tendency not to seek medical treatment and an increasing incidence of chronic health problems among the children and young adults in these communities.

Home work and small businesses also tend not to provide fringe benefits. Low wages are often paid in cash, with the worker convinced that he or she is better off if "Uncle Sam" does not collect a portion of the paycheck for Social Security or unemployment. Thus lack of attention to chronic illnesses is compounded for the new rural poor when catastrophe strikes. They have no recourse to hospital or medical care and are dependent on whatever care for the indigent the local area can provide once their meager savings are used up.

The Invisibility of the New Working Poor

In rural counties, particularly farming-dependent counties, many individuals work, shop, and live in three different places. This results in unique problems for the poor, as transportation is often necessary to maintain a decent quality of life and is expensive. For the older female segment of the new poor, lack of transportation and dispersed services isolate them from basic services. Similarly, the non-working spouse and families of the working poor are even more anonymous. They cannot afford to move closer to the place of work, and because they are outside the nexus of church, farm, and youth organizations in small-town life, they have limited contact with their neighbors.

Families of the working poor in farming communities tend to have two members in the labor force. This gives them less access to the kinds of expenditure-reducing activities in which household members have engaged in the past. Previously, everything from food to fuel could be provided by family members. Now these must be purchased because the need for cash forces more family members into the labor force. Most families have only one dependable vehicle, so if one member drives to a rural manufacturing job, the other must take a service job closer to home or look to home-work opportunities.

Local Response to Poverty: The Low-Wage Imperative

Local leaders, despite their desire to increase population in farming communities, are concerned about those new arrivals who are attracted by cheap housing. It appears to long-time residents that the new migrants' main social activity is frequenting the local bars. They are socially isolated and do not participate in local organizations and churches. These poor newcomers tend to be employed in the low-paying service and manufacturing occupations and often come to farming communities that open light manufacturing factories. They have lower educational levels than the current residents of farming communities and the in-migrants who buy local businesses or set up their professional offices. They are thus defined as in but not of the community. Even local leaders who pride themselves on knowing everyone in town cannot quite tell you who these people are or what they do. No systematic data exist on this mobile rural population. They come from other rural areas, work in minimum-wage jobs that change often, and do not stay long enough to "count" in public calculations. But these are the people who work for low wages in these communities. Economic development efforts in farming communities tend to stress low-wage employment. When new manufacturing enterprises come into farming counties, local employers pressure these new employers to keep wages down. Our interviews in farming communities have revealed special contracts made with national and multinational corporations who have a companywide wage scale to encourage them to pay below scale in return for other concessions, such as local tax exemptions, cheap utilities, and so on. In one case we found a locally based company that was discouraged from offering more than four dollars an hour because, in the words of the Small Business Administration advisor, "they would raise the wage scale in that part of the state."

As the number of elderly increases, low-wage employment to provide services for them will also increase. The prognosis for future improvement in the income of the working poor in farming communities is still not good. Unless economic development in the rural Midwest can be rephrased from "any job" to "jobs that pay an acceptable basic wage," the working poor will remain poor, mobile, and invisible. The current high unemployment—previously unknown in many areas of the rural Midwest—partly reflects the need for multiple jobs per family. More individuals are recorded as "seeking work." But the kind of jobs available and the systematic efforts of local elites to hold wages down mean that poor families with multiple wage earners can do little to better their economic condition.

CONCLUSION

The new poor in midwestern communities include several distinct groups. One group of these "new poor" is made up of older women with some assets and low, government-guaranteed income who are recognized and respected by their neighbors in their efforts to deal with their decreased economic status that has come with widowhood. But although the farm crisis and resulting bankruptcies have contributed a few "new poor" to farming communities, the major new groups of people living in poverty are those whose employment situation has not changed appreciably as a result of the farm crisis of the early 1980s. These new poor are those whose low wages make them the "working poor," who have less community stability and roots than elderly widows, but who nonetheless have been present in rural communities since their founding. The difference in the last decade of the twentieth century is that they are staying in greater numbers due to limited options in urban areas. These more transient rural poor make decisions based on economic opportunities—the existence of jobs. They have little job security, reflecting the volatile nature of the rural labor market. With the decline of formal-sector manufacturing jobs in the rural heartland, they take on minimum-wage service work or home work. Their wages have held steady while the cost of living has increased. Only their access to low-cost housing and their relative lack of salable skills keep them in rural communities. Meanwhile, their quality of life, measured in the health and educational options for themselves and their children, declines, as such expenses are "luxuries" that can be done without on a day-to-day basis.

While tight volunteer networks of women's clubs and churches may cushion some of the weight of poverty for the rural widow women, no such network of concerned community members exists for the working poor. They are living in the community, but are not integrated into it. Civic leaders view their problems as being of their own making, so there is limited community-based support or local social welfare measures made available.

When rural leaders do struggle with local efforts to improve economic conditions, they tend to think in terms of numbers of jobs created, not job quality. The leaders tend to be self-employed individuals who own their own homes or businesses and have some direct control over their economic well-being, and they have little sympathy for those who must work for others. The minimum wage seems adequate to those who have other sources of income and the security of property ownership. Poverty is still considered to be due to a lack of proper attitude and lack of hard work.

Part III

Policies for the Rural Poor

Chapter 11

Modernization and the Rural Poor: Some Lessons from History

Alice O'Connor

America rediscovered its poverty problem during the 1980s. As in earlier periods of heightened concern, public attention was drawn to certain "new"—and frightening—aspects of poverty. Homelessness, the growth in poverty rates among children, the "feminization" of poverty, and the emergence of an "urban underclass" were all focal points for scholarly research and philanthropic-foundation initiatives throughout the 1980s. As the chapters in the previous part of this volume show, rural poverty also grew worse during the 1980s, though this part of the poverty story seems to have escaped public attention. Rural areas have more than their share of the "new" poverty—people without homes, women heading households, and children. Some even talk of a rural underclass. But rural poverty can also be described in terms of a very old story—of people working at low-wage jobs with few or no benefits, of two-parent families, and of the elderly (Porter 1989; O'Hare 1988). Indeed, from a historical perspective much of current-day rural poverty is not a "new" problem at all.

Important as it is to take note of changing trends in poverty, our tendency to focus on the "new" fails to acknowledge the historical roots of contemporary poverty problems and how history has shaped the way we think about the solutions. In the hope of gleaning some lessons from history, this chapter reviews efforts on the part of social scientists and federal government policymakers to promote modernization as a strategy for fighting rural poverty from the New Deal to the Great Society.

From the 1930s through the 1960s, liberal reformers and social scientists approached rural poverty within the context of sweeping social and economic changes that were making the United States a truly modern society. These interconnected social and economic changes, including industrialization, urbanization, and the creation of the welfare state, were regarded as both the cause of and the potential solution to rural poverty. On the one hand, the modernization process displaced much of the agricultural labor force and spelled an end to traditional and valued ways of life in rural communities. As one sociologist writing in the late 1950s put it, "The death of rural neighborhoods with their country stores, frame churches, and one-room schools is a phenomenon that typifies the great mobility of the American people and the unprecedented growth of an industrial civilization" (Pearsall 1959, pp. 181–82). But observers also believed that modernization offered an answer to the problems of the rural poor in the form of improved farm productivity, economic growth and diversification, migration to the cities, and government social programs.

In the decades after World War II, policymakers became convinced that the advantages outweighed the drawbacks of modernization, and they promoted regional growth, industrialization, and urbanization as the answer to rural poverty. Their policies took the form of mostly uncoordinated efforts to restructure the agricultural economy, provide new job opportunities in other sectors of the economy, train rural people to participate in the industrial work force, and encourage cultural integration with an urbanizing society. As these policies stimulated the economic growth and out-migration that lifted many rural people out of poverty, social scientists began to explain the persistent poverty of those who remained in rural communities as a cultural rather than an economic problem. They argued that the rural poor lacked the values and aspirations essential for success in the modern, urbanized "middle-class" society and thus were unable to benefit from modernization. By the mid-1960s poverty analysts were referring to the rural poor as "the people left behind."

Thus modernization played an important role in determining the fate of America's rural poor from the New Deal to the Great Society, influencing the way social scientists defined the poverty problem as well as the strategies used to combat it. Yet in some ways modernization further marginalized the rural poor. To understand why, it is worth taking a closer look at the ideas and policy strategies informing the modernization approach.

DEFINING THE PROBLEM

During the 1920s and 1930s American social scientists began to write about the vast social and economic changes drawing small towns and independent agrarian communities into the orbit of "outside" commercial and industrial interests. From this perspective, poverty arose from the failure or inability of certain segments of rural society to adjust to the demands of an industrial economy and urbanized ways of life. In attempts to identify what was preventing the necessary adjustments, social scientists came up with three major explanations for rural poverty, each emphasizing barriers to economic and social modernization.

One explanation, originating with Southern sociologists at the University of North Carolina during the late 1920s, described poverty as the product of the South's "colonial" political economy. They urged agricultural reorganization, planned regional industrialization, and political reform in response. A second explanation, found mostly in work by social anthropologists studying rural communities in the United States and abroad, understood poverty as a product of the cultural barriers to modernization in "tradition-oriented" societies. Development economists, who based their conclusions on observations of "underdeveloped" countries after World War II, offered a third explanation that depicted poverty as part of a "vicious circle" of political, economic, and cultural barriers to modernization. In response, they called for comprehensive planning to stimulate industrial growth, political democratization, mass education, and the cultivation of an indigenous class of entrepreneurs to set the development process in motion.

POVERTY AND POLITICAL ECONOMY: THE SOUTHERN REGIONALISTS

In the 1930s the South was both the poorest and the least industrialized region in the United States. Linking the plight of the poor to the region's overall economic backwardness, the Southern "regionalist" sociologists drew attention to rural poverty as part of their crusade to "reconstruct the region" and realize a greater degree of economic, political, and cultural "integration" with the rest of the nation. Led by sociologist Howard Odum, scholars based at the University of North Carolina published research on the South's most controversial problems: race relations, farm tenancy, mill workers' conditions, and the agricultural "allegiance to King Cotton" (Vance 1971). Refusing to blame Southern economic backwardness on the "natural" inferiority of the labor force, the regionalists insisted that the South brought poverty on itself by resisting change, exploiting its labor, and allowing outside industrial interests to take advantage of its wealth of natural resources.

The regionalists emphasized the inefficiency as well as the injustice of poverty in their analysis of the plantation economy. One-crop farming depleted the soil and bankrupted landowners. The farm tenant system created a class of "shifting landless workers" who were "victim[s] of an enforced arrested development" (Raper 1968). In a study of White and Black poor tenants, Arthur Raper and Ira deA Reid concluded:

Farm tenants are expensive to the plantation . . . because they are inefficient. They are not expected to exercise initiative, but to do what they are told to do. They are not supposed to be resourceful; they are supposed to be attentive, obedient, cheerful. They seldom apply themselves to their task with enthusiasm. Their inadequate diet, their submerged status in the community, their subservient relationship to the landlord, and the meager returns for their labor leave them with low vitality and without an economic motive. Here lies the main reason for their listlessness, their improvidence, their hopelessness. Disinherited and defenseless, farm tenants have become resigned to landlessness and chronic dependency. (Raper and Reid 1941, pp. 37–38)

Regionalists were convinced that land-tenure reform was the key to regional economic recovery. New Deal farm policies, which subsidized large landowners at the expense of the landless poor, were only perpetuating the "shadow of the plantation."

Equally important to the regionalist reform cause was the promotion of locally controlled industrialization. The South was a "colonial" economy exploited as a source of natural resources and cheap labor by outside industrial and commercial interests. The colonial analysis became one of the central themes of President Roosevelt's National Emergency Council report on the South, which depicted the South as the victim of a virtual conspiracy to favor Northern industrial interests through government tariff policy and discriminatory freight rates. Southern poverty, the report concluded, would be overcome through national economic planning to foster decentralized industrial growth. Such reform was in the national interest, for the "South is the Nation's greatest untapped market" (National Emergency Council 1938, p. 61).

The regionalists called for economic growth and reform as the engine of change, but their vision of the New South extended to politics and culture as well. The task of restructuring the economy required a new kind of governance, one informed by technical social scientific knowledge and unhampered by local power structures. Endorsing an approach later embodied in the Appalachian Regional Council, Odum called for the creation of regional planning structures that would bypass state boundaries to reflect shared economic needs. The regionalists also argued that the South needed to escape the myth of a "feudal" agrarian past so that it could recognize the strength of its more democratic "folk" tradition. Such a cultural renaissance called for a new realism that recognized, as historian C. Vann Woodward later said, the "generations of scarcity and want [that] constitute one of the distinctive historical experiences of the Southern people" (Woodward 1968, pp. 17–18).

Despite their willingness to criticize the South, the regionalists wanted to overcome the stigma of being labeled the nation's "number one economic problem." In a symposium organized in 1945 to discuss the South as "economic *opportunity* number one," the Southern Regional Council sponsored papers focused on how to achieve economic growth through industrialization (Southern Regional Council 1945). Caught up in what historian George Tindall called the "growth psychology" of New South industrialists (1965), the regionalists' postwar strategy sought rapid modernization "based on the importation of employers" (Danhof 1964, p. 23). Significantly, this strategy was based on a "low-wage philosophy" that reasoned that "any action to raise Southern wages . . . would threaten the region's supreme competitive advantage (its cheap labor), would hamper industrial development, and therefore prolong the very poverty it was supposed to relieve" (Tindall 1965, pp. 466–67). Social and political reform—the other key ingredients of regionalist antipoverty thinking—would follow in the wake of growth.

Over the next two decades many of the regionalists' economic growth goals were realized, while social and political goals lagged behind. Initially responding to demand stimulated by wartime needs, the South began a period of rapid industrialization during the 1940s, and the combination of out-migration, agricultural diversification, the disappearance of the farm tenancy system, and urbanization helped to narrow interregional gaps in per capita income. Looking back over these developments, regionalists could say that the South had shed its "colonial" status and was beginning to "converge" with national standards of economic well-being. "The Mason-Dixon line no longer constitutes an Iron Curtain against the Affluent Society," Vance wrote in 1965. Yet, he added, Southerners continued to show resistance to the "way of the nation": racial segregation, the lack of equal opportunity, and a failure to embrace a more democratic political culture prevented the South from joining the Great Society (1965, p. 222). Poverty, while more contained, still existed in "problem areas" of the South, especially Appalachia.

Writing from the "new regionalist" perspective of the 1960s, Vance suggested the need to look at the noneconomic factors of poverty. Seen in "the context of national development," Appalachia "lagged behind in the processes of population redistribution, of economic and cultural development, and in the equalization of opportunity." Part of the problem, Vance said, was that "attitudes that represented virtues in the early days may become handicaps in the present" (Vance 1962). Writers Harry Caudill, John Fetterman, and others also cultivated a new regionalist perspective on poverty. There was a new kind of economic colonialism at the root of Appalachian poverty, they said, and it had as much to do with attitudes as with political economy. "The dole" had become the basis of the local economy and proved an even more terrible employer than the colonialist coal and textile manufacturers. "Knox County is not primarily in the agriculture business, nor is it in the timber business or the coal business, or the brassiere business. Knox County, like all the counties of Appalachia, is in the welfare business. And business is great," said Fetterman in his book *Stinking Creek* (1967). In *Night Comes to the Cumberlands*, Caudill (1963) held "welfarism" responsible for "the wholesale demoralization of the mountaineers." Sharply critical of federal government initiatives to aid poor rural communities, these writers advocated a revised, intensified form of the older regional strategies. Appalachian poverty called not merely for growth but for "development": investments in human capital, early childhood and youth education, social services, community participation in economic planning, and natural-resource planning to protect the environment—a program, that is, to help the mountaineers help themselves. Caudill made the case for a Southern Mountain Authority modelled on the Tennessee Valley Authority. Vance urged more aggressive efforts to bring the Appalachian birth rate in line with modern standards by encouraging contraception. Though virtually declaring the contemporary generation of adult mountaineers a lost cause, Vance expressed confidence that this comprehensive application of enlightenment and technology would eliminate poverty from the region by the 1980s (Vance 1962). Eliminating poverty was no longer a matter of restructuring the economic and social order. Now it was a matter of bringing the poor into the modern economy and changing their attitudes to conform with a modern outlook.

TRADITIONALISM AND THE "CULTURE OF POVERTY": THE SOCIAL ANTHROPOLOGISTS

In focusing on the attitudes of the rural poor, the regionalists picked up on themes from the work of social anthropologists studying the impact of modernization on traditional ways of life. Albeit more reluctantly, social anthropologists, too, had come to regard modernization as a desirable goal for traditional communities and a strategy for combatting rural poverty. Their research focused on the cultural barriers to modernization and linked the problem of persistent poverty to the persistence of traditional values, institutions, and even personality types in a modern world.

In community studies conducted during the 1920s and 1930s, social anthropologists showed a marked ambivalence—if not antipathy—toward modernization. In *Plainville, U.S.A.*, anthropologist Carl Withers (writing under the pseudonym James West) described the "agony of social and economic reorientation" in a small midwestern farm community hit hard by the Great Depression and "years of bad luck, poor management, and struggling with debts" (1945, p. 50). He generally approved of the objectives of New Deal agricultural reformers who were trying to encourage more scientific farm practices and efficient management as a way of raising community standards of living. But he also recognized the loss that the new ways would bring and wrote almost wistfully of the past. "The greater problem for all 'backwards' and 'poor' communities like Plainville is one which doubled or even tripled income will not solve. For better or for worse, they are doomed as 'traditional' communities. As their ancient value systems crumble under the blows of a new 'tradition' imposed from outside, their problem is to learn to participate more fully in the cultural rewards of the greater society" (Withers 1945, pp. 225–26).

The Plainville tradition Withers described was forged during the nineteenth century on the American frontier, where extended family bonds were strong, self-sufficiency was the economic ideal, and Jeffersonian democracy was the basis of the communal ethos ("This is one place where ever'body is equal. You don't find no classes here" was a favorite local saying [Withers 1945, p. 115]). But in the 1920s the frontier closed, the automobile arrived, and new technology opened up new economic opportunities: "migration, machinery and money" brought Plainville into the modern world (Withers 1945, p. 206). Though the locals denied it, a class system appeared in the form of a rigid line between "prairie" people who knew how to profit in the cash economy and the "hill" folk who remained immersed in the subsistence way of life (Withers 1945, p. 136).

The Great Depression and recovery threatened to exacerbate class divisions:

prairie people were in a position to benefit from a commercializing agricultural sector; hill folk were in danger of being left out. Withers ended on a note of uncertainty about whether modernization and prosperity would be worth the loss of the democratic traditions of the frontier.

In the postwar decades a new generation of social anthropologists participated in applied research projects designed to stimulate economic growth, education, and improved health conditions and otherwise bring the amenities of modern life to "underdeveloped" countries in Asia, Africa, and Latin America. Described by President Eisenhower as "our most effective countermeasure to Soviet propaganda and the best method by which to create the political and social stability essential to lasting peace," technical assistance to promote modernization became an official component of U.S. foreign-aid policy in the Act for International Development of 1954 (Eisenhower 1954). Moreover, from all appearances modernization had brought prosperity to American farm communities without the class divisions predicted by Withers. In a restudy of Plainville conducted during the 1950s, sociologist Art Gallaher found a thriving commercial agricultural center divided only by mild status distinctions. In response to the remaining problem of "substandard" family farms, Gallaher urged a course of "industrialization and concentrated management," "reorientation of farm policy in line with technological advances and national and international needs," and "social planning" to help those not yet adjusted to modern economic realities. Far from being a threat to democracy, these policies were wholly consistent with democratic values (Gallaher 1961, p. 258).

As they came to regard modernization in a more favorable light, anthropologists adopted a decidedly antiromantic tone in portraying the culture of traditional societies. In several studies of "underdeveloped" countries, traditional culture was identified as a source of resistance to social and economic modernization. Revising scholarly assessments of traditional rural culture in the United States, historian Richard Hofstadter questioned whether the ideal of frontier agrarian democracy had ever existed at all. "In a very real and profound sense . . . the United States failed to develop . . . a distinctively *rural* culture" (1955, p. 43), Hofstadter said in *The Age of Reform*.

If rural culture means an emotional and craftsman-like dedication to the soil, a traditional and pre-capitalist outlook, a tradition-directed rather than career-directed type of character, and a village community devoted to ancestral ways and habitually given to communal action, then the prairies and plains never had one. (1955, pp. 43–46)

Similarly concluding that the agrarian values of rural "Springdale" were based in myth, sociologists Arthur Vidich and Joseph Bensman warned that the locals' attempts to cling to mythical values could

become the basis for a backlash against the full sweep forward of American history as it develops in the present and the future. Populism gone sour could become the source of an antidemocratic, quasi-totalitarian reaction which in spite of its origins in an earlier democratic ideology would turn against the new cultural lifestyles evolving in our society. (1958, p. 346)

Traditionalism had come full circle in the social scientific mind.

In 1959 anthropologist Oscar Lewis published *Five Families: Mexican Case Studies in the Culture of Poverty*, a book based on the results of life-history interviews and psychological tests of families living in rural Mexican villages and Mexico City (Lewis 1959). Here he introduced the concept of the culture of poverty, a concept that linked many of the cultural and psychological traits associated with rural traditionalism to the persistence of poverty among certain subgroups in modernizing societies. In explaining this connection, Lewis made an important distinction between what he believed to be the simple cultural "backwardness" of peasants living in "well-integrated" societies where everyone was poor and the culture developed by rural and urban poor people living in capitalist, class-stratified societies. The former were poor by modern standards but not by the standards of their own subsistence economies. In contrast, the poor in industrial capitalist societies were fully aware of their own relative deprivation and felt a profound sense of alienation from the rest of society. In response to their deprivation, the poor developed habits and psychological adaptations that put them at odds with modern capitalist culture: they showed no signs of middle-class ambition, sought gratification when and where they could find it rather than planning for the future, felt powerless over their own destinies, and frequently indulged in "deviant" social and sexual behavior. What was more, they were passing these traits on to their children. The culture of poverty isolated the poor from the rest of modern society.

In his study of the "mill village subculture" of textile workers in the Piedmont area of North Carolina, anthropologist Kenneth Morland showed a similar inclination to associate features of cultural traditionalism with persistent poverty. In Morland's depiction the typical adult villager was enmeshed in a kind of "premodern" worldview that left him "resigned to his lot . . . more noncompetitive than competitive, more dependent than independent, more submissive than dominant . . . hostile toward outsiders but loyal and devoted to his kindred group" (Morland 1958, p. 251). These attitudes left the mill workers poor and powerless in the competitive world of industrial capitalism. Like Lewis, Morland believed that efforts to help them would have to include political organizing and education to help overcome the cultural attributes that tended to perpetuate their disadvantages.

Other writers, less sympathetic than Morland and Lewis, used culture as an explanation of why economic and development strategies would not work in poor rural areas. In studies of "Coaltown" and "Little Smoky Ridge" Herman Lantz and Marion Pearsall described the same complex of personality traits social scientists now associate with underdeveloped areas: resignation; fatalism; antagonism to change; "explosive individualism"; and resistance to the "clock-regulated" demands of an industrial work force (Lantz 1971). The products of isolation, scarcity, and "childhood experiences within the traditional family system," these traits had become an entrenched way of life that, as Lantz put it, "is basically at odds with industrialization." "As presently constituted," he continued, "the pattern of life and working habits plague any stable industry that wants to move in" (1971, pp. 207–8).

In his influential book *Yesterday's People*, Presbyterian minister Jack Weller said that the "lower class mountain culture" was a "pathological, problem-creating" way of life. Unable to help themselves, the mountaineers would also resist outside help: "No matter what the proposal, the dead hand of traditionalism always has life enough to slap it down" (Weller 1965, p. 100). The mountain poor were developing a subculture actively antagonistic to the middle-class mainstream.

As popularized during the 1960s, the culture-of-poverty theory was used to justify a wide range of policy strategies. Though convinced that nothing short of socialist revolution could alleviate the "mass" poverty in developing countries, Lewis urged poverty warriors to employ individualized counseling and social-work services in the United States (Lewis 1969). Others, mostly pinning their hopes on future generations, suggested early childhood education and training programs to overcome the cultural and social "deprivation" suffered by poor children and youth. Still others, like Lantz and Weller, used cultural analyses to suggest that government intervention in poor rural communities was an exercise in futility. By the 1970s the culture of poverty was almost entirely associated with a conservative argument against the welfare state—and remains so today. The culture-of-poverty concept has had far more significance for the politics of antipoverty policy than for program design (Leacock 1971; Valentine 1968).

THE VICIOUS CIRCLE: RURAL POVERTY AS A DEVELOPMENT PROBLEM

As social scientists began to take note of the disparities between isolated "pockets" of rural poverty and the growing affluence of the rest of America, they concluded that what they were seeing was analogous to the situation of poor countries in a growing worldwide economy. The field of development economics was an outgrowth of World War II and what Gunnar Myrdal called the "challenge of world poverty": the fate of "underdeveloped countries" in a "postcolonial" era (Myrdal 1970). In their efforts to spur rapid growth in predominantly agrarian economies of the third world, development economists became increasingly convinced that political democracy, an achievement-oriented culture, and local entrepreneurship were also essential "preconditions" for modernization (Hirschman 1958; Rostow 1971). The problem seemed to be that no one of these ingredients could be created without reinforcement from the others. Third-world poverty was embedded in what economist H. W. Singer called "a system . . . of interlocking vicious circles" in which economic, political, and cultural deficiencies fed on one another. Reversing the circle called for comprehensive change (Singer 1949).

Writers who applied the vicious-circle analogy to the "pockets" of poverty in the United States were careful to draw distinctions between "our" poverty, which existed in isolated "pockets," and "third-world" poverty, which was a product of political and economic "backwardness." In *The Affluent Society* economist John Kenneth Galbraith distinguished between the "mass" poverty of underdeveloped countries and the "minority" poverty of America in the 1950s. Further, "case" poverty could be explained by individual circumstances such as temporary unemployment or disability. "Insular" poverty, on the other hand, was a fact of life in Appalachian communities and required more comprehensive solutions (Galbraith 1984). The Appalachian poor were but one among several subgroups living in Michael Harrington's "other America." Harrington likened them to "an underdeveloped nation in our midst." Caught in a "vicious circle," they were "internal aliens" living "within the most powerful and rich society the world has ever known," said Harrington. "The poor are not like everyone else. They are a different kind of people. They think and feel differently; they look upon a different America than the middle class looks upon." The vicious circle was being drawn more tightly: people were poor because they were powerless, and people were powerless because they were poor (Harrington 1962 pp. 16, 18, 146, 184).

The vicious circle was the prevailing image of poverty adopted by the small group of policymakers and activists urging Americans to wage a "war on poverty" during the 1960s. Though it was borrowed from the development perspective, the analysis did not always translate into the kind of comprehensive economic and social reform envisioned in overseas development projects. For his part, Harrington called for political change, "a vast social movement, a new period of political creativity to empower the poor and penetrate the wall of pessimism and despair that surrounds the impoverished millions" (Harrington 1962, pp. 183–84). While the language of empowerment was contained in War on Poverty community action programs, these programs did not mandate the more fundamental reforms Harrington called for. Instead, the key for the more practical-minded social scientists and administrators who designed the War on Poverty was to find strategic points of intervention in the vicious circle.

Cautioning against "going to the extreme of declaring that nothing can be done if everything is not done," sociologist S. M. Miller made the case for using manpower development as a "starter mechanism" for a broader economic development process in Appalachia (Miller 1966). Others thought of breaking the vicious circle in more individualistic terms and lauded the remedial benefits of interventions such as Head Start and the Job Corps. Applied in the U.S. context, the "vicious circle" became a rationale for remedial interventions rather than comprehensive economic and social reform.

As an intellectual framework, modernization offered three distinctive explanations for rural poverty that featured important common points. All three started out with a focus on the economic and social barriers to modernization facing the rural poor. However, in the midst of a growing economy and rising standards of living following World War II, social scientists began to narrow their focus almost exclusively to the "deficiencies" of the poor themselves and paid little attention to the economy and culture of the larger society in explaining poverty. In this narrow focus analysts failed to look beneath the surface of economic prosperity and "middle-class culture" to draw attention to the inequitable distribution of the benefits of modernization. Similarly, as the next section will discuss, government policies were primarily aimed at fixing the deficiencies of the poor, treating poverty as a problem apart from its larger social and economic context.

THE POLICY FRAMEWORK

As a strategy for eliminating rural poverty, modernization does not represent a coherent ideology so much as a loose set of policies to strike at the root causes rather than just the symptoms of rural poverty: reorganizing the agricultural economy to promote greater efficiency and farming as "a business, not a way of life"; maintaining steady economic growth and full employment in the non-agricultural sector; directing migration of surplus labor to follow new job opportunities; and providing education and services to help people adjust to change. Beginning in the 1930s, there was broad agreement among policymakers on the goals envisioned by this strategy. However, there was little agreement about how it should be implemented.

The more conservative approach suggested that "free-market" economic growth was the best remedy, reflecting the assumption that rural poverty would "wither away" in the "adjustments" accompanying economic diversification (Patterson 1986). Though also relying heavily on economic growth, liberals advocated active government participation in every step of the modernization process: planning economic growth, maintaining full employment, directing migration flows, retraining people for new industrial jobs, promoting equal opportunity for the minority poor, and helping poor migrant families adjust to more urban ways of life. In reality, rural antipoverty policy fell somewhere in between these two extremes: largely unregulated economic growth was seen as the driving force of modernization, and loosely coordinated programs would help raise the skills and education levels of the rural poor so they could adjust to economic change. At no point did these programs amount to the comprehensive antipoverty strategy suggested by the liberal modernization framework.

In order to understand the limited thrust of rural antipoverty policy, it is useful to look at the history of three separate attempts to establish comprehensive rural antipoverty programs. During the New Deal the Resettlement Administration and the Farm Security Administration represented efforts to address the needs of the poorest farmers in the midst of government-stimulated changes in t'~ agricultural economy. Twenty years later the Area Redevelopment Adminis' tion was established to address poverty in "depressed" rural and urban communities by stimulating the kind of targeted economic development Southern regionalists had advocated in their earlier writings. In the War on Poverty the architects of the Economic Opportunity Act of 1964 included what they considered a comprehensive set of proposals for addressing the problems of the rural poor who had been "left behind" by economic growth. As reform proposals, all three efforts entailed elements of economic reform and, to a lesser extent, political empowerment for the rural poor. Their proponents faced strong political opposition from congressional conservatives and representatives of more "established" agricultural and business interests (Finegold 1988). The reformers were also constrained by certain features of the U.S. welfare state: the limited range of interventions policymakers were willing to use to stimulate economic growth, the fragmentation of responsibility for individual programs across several administrative departments, and the administrative and political distinctions between policies to address the needs of the poor and policies to achieve economic growth. Particularly after the New Deal, liberal reformers were very tentative in their attempts to change the economic conditions facing the rural poor and instead focused on changing the poor themselves.

THE NEW DEAL

With the passage of the Agricultural Adjustment Act of 1933, New Deal planners launched the major component of farm recovery policy, the restructuring of the agricultural economy through a combination of price supports, more efficient land use, and long-range policy planning to link production goals with national consumer needs (Kirkendall 1966). In response to pressure from groups urging more fundamental land reform on behalf of poor farmers, President Roosevelt established the Resettlement Administration (RA) by executive order in May 1935 to provide "rural rehabilitation and relief in stricken agricultural areas." Under the direction of Rexford Tugwell, the RA pursued an eclectic and often-controversial set of experimental programs including government acquisition of marginal land; resettlement of displaced farmers in model rural or suburban "greenbelt" communities; loans and educational and technical assistance to improve productive capacity; and relief through cash and in-kind assistance. Tugwell advocated an approach that put priority on land reform and industrial job opportunities for tenant farmers. Other liberal reformers in the RA envisioned the creation of small self-sufficient family farms that could take advantage of new agricultural technology by organizing in larger cooperative units (Baldwin 1968; Kirkendall 1966).

Such "visionary" proposals as large-scale land reform proved hard to administer and politically controversial. By the fall of 1935 the bulk of RA activities were focused on "rehabilitation"—through loans and technical assistance—rather than reform. Tugwell was the target of animosity from conservatives suspicious of his "socialistic" leanings, and the press gave unfavorable publicity to the more experimental RA programs. Tugwell resigned at the end of 1936, and at his recommendation the RA was subsumed within the Department of Agriculture (Baldwin 1968).

RA's brief and controversial life was a prelude to congressional efforts on behalf of the farm poor. With impetus from a report issued by Roosevelt's Special Commission on Farm Tenancy—to which sociologists Howard Odum and C. S. Johnson contributed—Congress passed the Bankhead-Jones Farm Tenancy Act of 1937 authorizing the Farm Security Administration (FSA) (United States Special Committee on Farm Tenancy 1937). The FSA had a far more restricted mandate than the RA and was considered by many to be an inadequate response to the core problems of rural poverty. Proceeding "with caution" in the wake of the RA experience, FSA administrators emphasized the more "orthodox" goals of rural rehabilitation, not reform (Baldwin 1968). Land-purchase loans and education in management techniques comprised the major component of FSA programming, along with more limited efforts to establish agricultural cooperatives for low-income farmers.

For the most part, the disfranchised, landless, and minority rural poor were not reached by these programs. Nevertheless, the FSA administrators were perceived as a challenge to the status quo; they were in government to represent the interests of poor people. For this they earned the enmity of commercial farm and business interests, powerful national organizations such as the American Farm Bureau, and congressional conservatives on the lookout for political subversives in the New Deal. Following years of challenges to its authority, FSA faced its "final showdown" beginning in 1943. Congress diminished the agency's responsibilities, reduced its appropriation, and authorized a special committee chaired by known FSA opponent Harold D. Cooley of North Carolina to investigate its activities. The FSA's programs were reduced and its leadership was replaced as a result of these hearings, and the FSA was finally abolished by legislation creating the Farmer's Home Administration in 1946.

The FSA was under constant pressure from its conservative opponents and clearly suffered as the "poor people's" agency in the government agricultural establishment. The FSA experience illustrates what has become a persistent dilemma in federal antipoverty programs since the New Deal. On the one hand, without a separate agency the needs of poor farmers were unrepresented in agricultural recovery policy. On the other hand, the separate agency uncoupled antipoverty policy (defined as relief and rehabilitation) from structural economic change. Relief and rehabilitation were targeted; economic growth was for the good of everyone.[1] As its short life and limited appropriations suggest, FSA and the needs of the people it represented were deemed subordinate to agricultural economic growth.

THE POSTWAR YEARS

The "second-tier" nature of antipoverty programs became more apparent in postwar social welfare policy. The more liberal program, reflected in the recommendations of Roosevelt's National Resource Planning Board (NRPB), was to consolidate and expand many of the New Deal's programs. The NRPB recommended an active government role in economic planning, full-employment policies that would include job creation, national health insurance, expanded social insurance coverage, and national standards for welfare beneficiaries. Preventing poverty, the report argued, was an integral component of postwar economic growth strategy. The course chosen by Congress was in fact just the opposite: New Deal jobs programs were dismantled, and the Employment Act of 1946 fell far short of liberal goals for economic planning and full employment (Amenta and Skocpol 1988). For the next two decades the poverty problem was treated with "benign neglect" as liberals and conservatives alike put their faith in economic growth as a panacea for social problems (Patterson 1986).

There were problems beneath the surface of America's postwar prosperity, however, that became evident as the economy went through a series of recessions in the 1950s. Deteriorating urban areas felt pressure from the inflows of unskilled Black and White rural migrants in search of job opportunities. These migrants seemed to be forming a "structural unemployment" problem that was left unaddressed in the unregulated labor market. Meanwhile, out-migration from rural communities skimmed off the young and the educated while the elderly and dependent stayed put. To the dismay of long-time residents—and their congressmen—once-thriving communities were threatened with wholesale poverty.

To redress the problems of poverty in "depressed" rural and urban communities, the federal government undertook a limited experiment in planned economic development in the early 1960s. Originally proposed in 1956 by Senator Paul Douglas of Illinois, the Area Redevelopment Act was designed to help urban and rural communities that for a variety of reasons, such as an untrained labor force, inadequate infrastructure, or remote location, were not in a position to benefit from economic growth. In an approach reminiscent of Southern regionalist strategies, the government would help the communities by encouraging local development planning and providing loan assistance to attract new industries. In brief, the idea was to bring "jobs to people, not people to jobs" (Levitan 1964). Congress passed the Area Redevelopment Act in 1961.

Although lengthy negotiations left the original bill diminished in scope, the Area Redevelopment Act did retain the bare bones of a development strategy to address poverty in depressed areas: with federal assistance, communities would put together comprehensive development plans contingent on their ability to attract new industries; the federal government would offer low-interest loans to help draw the businesses into communities designated as eligible for assistance; grants from a public-works fund would be made available to build up infrastructure; and government would also provide a limited amount of worker retraining assistance (Levitan 1964). Responsibility for the program rested in the Area Redevelopment Administration (ARA) housed at the Department of Commerce, but program administration was scattered across several agencies. The loan program was administered by the Small Business Administration, rural development plans were monitored by a special office in the Department of Agriculture, and retraining was administered by the Departments of Labor and Health, Education, and Welfare.

From the very beginning this controversial program was closely scrutinized by friends and opponents alike. The ARA made some crucial errors that cost the "fledgling administration" key support early on. Its first loan was to a nonunion shirt factory in Arkansas, and later an ARA-funded shoe factory in Indiana refused to hire Blacks (Sundquist 1968). Bowing to pressure from members of both parties, the ARA designated many more areas eligible for assistance than its limited funds could possibly reach (Levitan 1964). But as the program's chief evaluator, Sar Levitan, pointed out, the problems with the ARA were more fundamental. Taking what Levitan called a "trickle-down" approach to development, the program was not equipped to address the basic economic problems of depressed communities. Most of the aid was directed at the businesses rather than the communities, and communities were given no leverage for regulating wage scales, benefits, or job quality. Rural communities in particular were in the same old position of having to lure businesses through offers of cheap labor and tax breaks, undermining improvements the bill was designed to provide. National labor-market conditions were not favorable for the ARA; with unemployment rates relatively high, employers did not have much need to go to isolated depressed areas in search of skilled labor.

In 1965 Congress declined to renew ARA's appropriation but did not entirely give up on its limited economic development strategy. The Economic Development Act (EDA) of 1965 took a more selective approach to designating aid-eligible areas, building projects around "growth centers" rather than individual communities. The bill also authorized the secretary of commerce to designate regional planning bodies along the lines of the Appalachian Regional Council. The ever-popular public-works provisions were renewed and expanded in the new legislation. On balance, EDA invested more in rural public infrastructure projects than anything else. The development aspect of depressed-areas legislation was diminished in favor of its more politically popular components.

As realized in the form of the ARA and EDA, federally administered rural development policy represented a very limited departure from the status quo. To some extent ARA's efforts were also undercut by the federal government's failure to coordinate different social welfare programs. Thus ARA was working to bring jobs to people without providing the necessary retraining to equip local residents to take industrial jobs. Meanwhile, new Department of Labor training programs created by the Manpower Demonstration and Training Act of 1962 did offer training to people in their communities, but did not have the capacity to create the jobs. Such lack of coordination meant a missed opportunity for a more comprehensive approach to the recognized job and human-capital problems of poor rural communities. Residents of rural communities found themselves caught in the difficult choice of whether to stay and make something of what limited opportunities they had, or to leave what for many was a valued way of life, a choice labeled by some as the "flight or fight" dilemma.

THE WAR ON POVERTY

While the fate of the ARA was being decided in Congress, President Johnson was mobilizing the resources of his administration to fight an "unconditional war on poverty." Professing faith in the nation's capacity to eliminate the pockets of poverty in places like Appalachia, Johnson appointed chief Peace Corps administrator Sargent Shriver to head an interagency task force that brought together representatives from the Departments of Labor, Agriculture, and Health, Education, and Welfare. Their job was to draft legislation that would amount to a comprehensive approach to the poverty problem. The result was the proposed Economic Opportunity Act of 1964 (EOA).[2]

The "total" strategy proposed by the task force included several components. The first was to stimulate economic growth and create job opportunities, objectives the administration would pursue through sizeable tax cuts but not, as some advisors pleaded, through direct job creation (Weir 1988). The other components were contained in the major titles of the proposed EOA: youth employment and training; community action in rural and urban areas; and the establishment of a separate agency, the Office of Economic Opportunity, to oversee the poverty programs and act as an advocate on behalf of the poor in the federal government. Proposals of particular interest for the rural poor were contained in Title III, "Special Assistance to Rural Families." Title III was designed to address the needs of the estimated one million farm families headed by the aged, handicapped, and undereducated (less than eighth grade), referred to in Department of Agriculture background literature as "boxed-in" families because they were seen to be incapable of relocating to urban areas. Its provisions reflected a strategy of relief, rehabilitation, and, to a lesser degree, land reform on behalf of the poorest farmers: $1,500 capital grants would finance farm improvements; $2,500 low-interest loans would contribute toward the purchase of farms or the start of new home enterprises; loans to low-income farmers' cooperatives would improve their position in local markets; and a Family Farm Development Corporation would be authorized to make loans and grants to nonprofits for purchasing large tracts of land that would then be developed into small units appropriate for subsistence farming and sold below cost to low-income farmers. For the "boxed-in" families, such assistance would provide an alternative to ending up on the welfare rolls in the cities. At the same time, their children would be benefitting from youth and early childhood education programs provided through other aspects of the Economic Opportunity Act. This was a comprehensive effort to break the circle of poverty in rural farm families (U.S. Congress, Senate, 1964).

Congressional hearings on the EOA aired considerable skepticism about Title III provisions, much of it questioning the wisdom of "prolonging the agony" of poor farmers rather than helping them to relocate (U.S. Congress, Senate, 1964, pp. 88–89). But it was not until the floor debate on the bill that significant changes were made in the rural title. The proposed amendments were accompanied by warnings from Senator Strom Thurmond and others that Title III amounted to nothing less than an attempt to resurrect the ghost of Rexford Tugwell and other "subversives" associated with the Farm Security Administration. Thurmond even quoted from the Cooley Committee investigation of FSA, during which the agency had been called an "experiment station of un-American ideas and economic and social theories of little or questionable value." Turning next to the poverty task force's recommendation to create the Family Farm Development Corporation, Thurmond declared, "In point of fact, this program appears to come directly out of our foreign aid programs for Latin America. It looks as if we are now going to impose some of those same socialistic devices on our own people that we have tried so hard to ram down the throats of our Latin American neighbors" (*Congressional Record* 1964, pp. 16704–6). Though Thurmond's statements did not necessarily represent the majority view, they helped diminish already-flagging support for the land-reform component of Title III. The final legislation eliminated the Family Farm Development Corporation, changed grant provisions to loans, and cut the appropriation by fifteen million dollars. The new legislation did contain, however, provisions for the health and welfare of migrant farm workers.

It is difficult to judge "what might have been" had Congress passed Title III of the EOA as originally proposed. Even its supporters admitted that its provisions amounted to only a limited "first step" toward alleviating farm poverty, let alone the larger problem of rural poverty (Shriver 1964). On the other hand, the family-farm development program would have introduced the principle of reform into rural antipoverty programming and might have helped to establish more of an institutional concern with the farm poor within the Department of Agriculture. As it turned out, the war on rural poverty consisted of much safer rehabilitative and relief measures: loans to poor farmers, youth employment, and the variety of interventions contained in rural community action programs. Many of these programs were very successful in helping individuals escape poverty and establishing important community social welfare networks in rural areas. However, they did little to address the economic and political inequities at the root of rural poverty. These shortcomings were acknowledged in a report issued by President Johnson's Advisory Commission on Rural Poverty in 1967, in which the rural poor were significantly referred to as "the people left behind" (U.S. President's National Advisory Commission on Rural Poverty 1967).

RETHINKING MODERNIZATION?

The concepts and policies associated with modernization offered at best a limited framework for addressing the needs of the rural poor from the New Deal to the Great Society. Economic growth, industrialization, and migration to urban areas did offer many an escape route out of poverty. But centered as they were around the postwar "growth psychology" and "middle-class" cultural norms, these same processes were used to create a new rationale for maintaining low wage structures, failed to address the problems of subsistence farmers, and left the rural poor as powerless as ever. Moreover, modernization concepts were often based on overwhelmingly pejorative—and unsubstantiated—ideas about the "backwardness" of rural culture. In depicting the poor as the "other" Americans, social scientists and activists perpetuated the notion that poor people are not "people like us" and gave credence to the idea that the rural poor were incapable of adjusting to the demands of the modern world.

Living as we do in a "postmodern" age, it is tempting to conclude that modernization was simply a flawed strategy from the start. But to reject the modernization framework wholesale would be to overlook some of its important positive elements. As articulated by Southern regionalists and New Deal reformers, the modernization framework offered a socioeconomic explanation for rural poverty and envisioned comprehensive economic and social development as its solution. Equally important, the modernization framework implied that poverty was not an "intractable" social problem but could be redressed through purposeful social action. In contrast, today's deficit-driven legislative agenda has little room for development strategies, and thoughts of eliminating poverty are deemed hopelessly naive.

To summarize, there are three major lessons that might be helpful in efforts to rethink the modernization approach to rural poverty. First, poverty concepts based on supposedly distinct cultural characteristics—whether the culture of poverty or the underclass—stigmatize the poor, perpetuate false stereotypes, and only widen the political gap between "us" in the middle class and "them" in poverty. Second, economic growth is no panacea for poverty. To the contrary, economic growth without broader development—without education, training, and political change to give poor communities a voice in their own future—has too often occurred at the expense of the rural poor. Third, it is possible to break out of the narrow, deficit-induced framework within which legislators define rural antipoverty measures today. But to think more expansively about policy requires facing up to another lesson gleaned from historical experience: the real barriers to meeting our antipoverty goals are not economic or cultural but political, and they may be the hardest of all to break down.

NOTES

This chapter is part of a research project supported by the Rural Policy Fellowship Program, a program sponsored by the Ford Foundation's Rural Poverty and Resources Program and the Aspen Institute's Rural Economic Policy Program and administered by the Woodrow Wilson National Fellowship Foundation.

1. Significantly, as Finegold (1988) points out, farm laborers were even prevented from participating in the one universal social welfare program based on universal prin-

ciples—Social Security; until 1954 they were left out of coverage. For a discussion of the politics of universal versus targeted programs, see Heclo 1986.

2. Much of what follows is based on insights from a conversation with James Sundquist, who was deputy under secretary of agriculture and the representative to the War on Poverty task force in 1964.

Chapter 12

Empowerment and Rural Poverty

Steve Suitts

While the number of poor people vastly increased during the 1980s, public policy on poverty in the United States suffered from social fatigue, ideological deadlock, and the politics of incrementalism. Gone were the days of the 1960s and early 1970s when community efforts and general public discourse explored how government could reduce poverty in fundamental ways. During the last decade Congress considered only modest adjustments in the system of welfare, which both liberals and conservatives attacked as ineffective. Although the federal Family Support Act was passed in 1988 as welfare reform, its implementation during the early years was sluggish and half-hearted, and its modest statutory changes embody more aspirations than realities of change. Clearly the federal government has had a decidedly puny response to the ominous trends of rising poverty (see, for example, Cottingham and Ellwood 1989; Danziger and Weinberg 1986).

Nowhere have discourse and public policy been more inert than on issues of rural poverty. The debate about poverty and government has centered on the central cities, where social scientists, historians, and researchers dispute the nature and causes of persistent poverty and an urban underclass. In comparison, the scholarship on rural poverty has been sparse, and seldom has the discourse on policy appreciated the unique aspects of rural poverty (Gramlich 1986; Katz 1989).

One emerging theme in the recent debate about urban poverty, nonetheless, resonates with traditions among the rural Southern poor for bringing about change. At the end of the 1980s, conservatives began to promote the empowerment of the poor as a useful strategy for change (Butler 1990; Scanlon 1990; Woodson 1990). This new definition of empowerment borrows heavily from the consumerism of Adam Smith (giving the poor more choices as consumers), whereas the nation's authentic tradition of empowerment among poor Blacks and Whites lies in the collective struggle for democratic change in the rural

South. Today, as yesterday, control of political and economic institutions serving the poor can be a meaningful strategy for reducing poverty, improving local conditions, and enlivening the national public policy on poverty across the nation. We recognize that working for control over institutions that involve the poor is an opportunity because of an understanding of past movements among the Southern rural poor and an appreciation of how democratic control of institutions can vitally influence practices and policies at all levels.

HISTORY OF POLITICAL AND ECONOMIC EMPOWERMENT IN THE RURAL SOUTH

Strategies to empower the rural poor as a group have their origins in the American South more than a century ago and have reappeared in more recent times. Beginning in the Populist movement of the late 1800s, poor farmers in the South and the West organized buying and selling cooperatives for self-help and to mount a political campaign for alternative economic programs. Helping its members solve immediate, practical problems, the Farmers Alliance stirred a new kind of collective self-confidence, establishing an effective instrument of recruitment for the Populist cause and helping to educate its members about economic issues. In doing so, the cooperative movement developed a new democratic vision of how to address poverty (Goodwyn 1978; Hahn 1983; Hackney 1969).

Because of provincialism and racial divisions the movement failed. Yet it demonstrated that profound change might be possible through empowering people collectively. According to historian Lawrence Goodwyn, "In their institutions of self-help, Populists developed and acted upon a crucial democratic insight: to be encouraged to surmount rigid cultural inheritances and to act with autonomy and self-confidence, individual people need the psychological support of other people. The people need to 'see themselves' experimenting in new democratic forms" (Goodwyn 1978, pp. 295–96).

Forty years later, another cooperative movement developed among the poor in the South and the West. As a part of the New Deal for rural areas, two federal agencies, the Farm Security Administration (FSA), an agency created to assist small, low-income farmers, and the Rural Electrification Administration (REA), designed to extend electricity into rural areas, undertook to create cooperatives controlled by local citizens throughout poor, rural areas. The FSA helped to establish more than 25,000 poor people's cooperatives—mostly in the South—to lease land, create buying and marketing associations, purchase farm machinery and services, offer health care, and provide water and other necessities. REA financed the development of hundreds of utility cooperatives covering most of rural America in order to build power lines and to carry electricity and telephone service to isolated communities, creating jobs along the way (Baldwin 1968; Mertz 1978; Marshall and Godwin 1971).

During the Roosevelt era the U.S. Department of Agriculture had a firm belief in the democratic participation of local farmers in the operations of government farm programs. By one count, in 1939, almost 900,000 people—over whom federal officials exercised no direct control—were sitting on boards and attending meetings where decisions were made about the allocations of resources and the administration of federal programs in rural areas (Baldwin 1968; Mertz 1978).

Conditions in the South, however, reflected the prevailing political culture of segregation. Blacks were excluded from participation in almost every aspect of the federal government's grass-roots democracy. Rather than using these democratic processes as a means of challenging prevailing conditions, the cooperatives and elective committees in the Department of Agriculture were kept segregated to make the agency's work more acceptable to established local interests. As a result, the REA co-ops were organized only by White farmers—and often not the poor White farmers—and the other democratic processes of the New Deal's agricultural program also were reserved usually for Whites only (Baldwin 1968; Mertz 1978).

The exceptions to this rule of segregation were found in the work of the Farm Security Administration. FSA-sponsored co-ops included some that were all Black, such as a settlement established for one hundred destitute African Americans in Wilcox County, Alabama, where the federal agency purchased a large White plantation and provided funds for housing, equipment, and community improvements. In others, Blacks and Whites worked together on equal terms despite the opposition of racist politicians and other White community leaders. According to one commentary, "Hundreds of thousands of poor people in the rural South received valuable assistance from the FSA and other New Deal anti-poverty programs" (Marshall and Godwin 1971, p. 33).

Some FSA administrators envisioned the agency's co-ops as more than experiments in self-help; they attempted to prompt local mass action and solidarity among the Black and White poor in the Populist tradition. Indeed, political scientist V. O. Key observed that "the New Deal affected the masses of the South as had no political movement since the Populist uprising" (1949, p. 645). It showed poor Whites that politics could deliver more than oratory on preserving the Southern way of life and poor Blacks that the federal government cared about their welfare. Yet the power of segregated politics (and a poll tax that kept poor Whites out of the political system) doomed this cooperative movement. There was no political power to sustain and enlarge this economic empowerment. By 1946 small Black and White farmers—failing to join forces—lacked the political clout to preserve the Farm Security Administration. (It was replaced by the Farmers' Home Administration as a result of the lobbying of large farmers.) REA continued to finance electrical and telephone service, but the utility cooperatives remained segregated, virtually abandoning their role as an antipoverty effort in order to serve often the interest of large landowners (Key 1949; Baldwin 1968).

Efforts to empower the rural poor emerged once again in the 1960s as a part of the civil rights movement in the South. To combat the control of local White elites, local Black leaders established a wide range of cooperatives—including credit unions, farming productions, handicrafts, and sewing bees—creating job-related income independent of the local White economy. These cooperatives attempted to empower poor Black people through democratic participation. Father A. J. McKnight, founder of the Southern Cooperative Development programs, recognized in southern Louisiana during the late 1950s that poor Blacks suffered from a "poverty of the spirit worse than that of the body" (Marshall and Godwin 1971, p. 39). By encouraging participation in an independent democratic process that had a practical effect, the cooperatives helped to free Blacks from a history of fear and intimidation and to build the promise of an improved economic life. Like the Populists before them, these cooperatives promoted a program of political change. Cooperative leaders were a vital part of the movement for the economic and political empowerment of the rural Black poor (Chestnut and Cass 1990).

As a part of the civil rights movement, the Federation of Southern Cooperatives was founded in 1967 to nurture a growing number of poor people's cooperatives throughout the region. The federation and its 10,000 local members have continued to function, but the cooperative movement has not profoundly reduced rural poverty. Like the movements before them, the cooperatives as economic institutions suffered from problems of modest financing, inexperience with marketing, and, at times, poor management; moreover, they became divorced from their mission to stimulate broad rural economic reforms and public policies that address the deeply entrenched causes of poverty (Marshall and Godwin 1971).

None of the three movements to empower the rural poor achieved its primary goals, but the cumulative effects of their activities is evident in some local communities. In Gee's Bend (Wilcox County), Alabama, where the FSA enabled the establishment of a Black cooperative settlement in the 1930s, grew the Freedom Quilting Bee, one of the earliest Black women's cooperatives, in the 1960s. The quilting bee originated a wide range of antipoverty efforts in the county, and the community was the home of the first Black elected officials in the county. Gee's Bend also provided leadership to the local civil rights movement, challenging segregated and racist practices throughout the 1950s and 1960s. The quilting bee continues to operate today (Callahan 1987).

In Holmes County, Mississippi, the local leadership of the civil rights movement in the 1960s came out of the same community where the Farm Security Administration had assisted several hundred Black farmers in acquiring land and starting cooperatives in the 1930s. These independent farmers led the Blacks to challenge segregated schools and barriers to Black voter registration in the county.

Throughout the region, the independence of Black co-op leaders from the White economy has been essential for political change, beginning in the 1960s. These leaders were in a position to challenge local racist practices without fear of direct economic reprisals. Many were also free to register to vote because they were least likely to suffer from the direct economic retaliation of White employers and local White landowners. Although other forms of employment (especially funeral homes and Black insurance agencies) also provided independence, cooperative leaders often were the political leaders and, later, some of the Black elected officials who have helped to change Southern politics (McLeod 1990).

RECENT POLITICAL EMPOWERMENT OF THE RURAL POOR

Since the work of co-op leaders and other civil rights workers in the 1960s, the increase in the number of Black elected officials in the South has been phenomenal. In 1965, 87 Blacks held elected political office in the South. In 1989 more than 4,000 were in elected offices. These changes were made possible by dismantling legal disenfranchisement, by nonpartisan efforts to register and turn out Black voters, and by the passage and the enforcement of the federal Voting Rights Act of 1965. In recent years enforcement of the act has slowed local White resistance and eliminated the use of election schemes (such as voting countywide instead of in local districts) that fence out the influence of growing Black registration and turnout.[1]

Because Black elected officials have become the standard proxy for measuring political change in the South, research too seldom examines the actual changes in public policy and practices that occur as a result of poor Blacks' political empowerment. Although the limits of local government are substantial in the rural South, social scientists with the National Research Council (NRC) in 1989 found a real impact of Black empowerment on local hiring and municipal expenditures. Having a Black mayor increases the Black share of the municipal work force and improves the delivery of local services such as police and fire protection, trash collection, and road repair to Black residents.

The NRC's Committee on the Status of Black Americans also found that Black representation is correlated with increased local spending on health care and, possibly, on housing and education. "Black representation at the municipal level seems to have the greatest leverage on delivery of basic city services, which can improve the quality of life for Black constituents in very straightforward (and relatively non-controversial) ways. The major share of the benefits from Black local governance may have helped produce the new Black middle class" (Jaynes and Williams 1989, p. 251).

The benefits of changing political power in the rural poor South have not been limited to the local government. The clearest evidence is found in the transformation of congressional support for antipoverty efforts over the last twenty-five years by U.S. representatives from the South's Black Belt, where the nation's largest concentration and population of rural Black poor are located. The Black Belt stretches across the deep South where the large plantation existed during slavery and goes upward near the coast of the Southern states on the Atlantic

Table 12.1
Voting Record on Poverty Issues: Ratings of Support for New or Expanded Antipoverty Programs, 1965–89

	1965-1977	1978-1989
Alabama	4%	17%
Arkansas	38	82
Florida	12	55
Georgia	15	50
Louisiana	8	33
Mississippi	3	61
North Carolina	8	61
South Carolina	16	36
Virginia	5	7
Black Belt	11%	41%

Source: "Rural Poverty and Empowerment," working paper of Jay Stewart. Work based upon analysis of "key votes" identified by the *Congressional Quarterly Almanac* for the years 1965 through 1989 from the U.S. House of Representatives. "Black Belt districts" include congressional districts that have encompassed most of the rural counties that had a majority Black population during the early part of the century and continue to have a Black population of more then 30 percent. See Steve Suitts and Jay Stewart, *Rural Poverty and Political Change* (Southern Regional Council, forthcoming).

Ocean. It is a subregion of the South where the empowerment of poor Blacks has met with the most persistently hostile response.

From 1965 through 1989 the U.S. House of Representatives cast thirty-eight significant votes relating to establishing or expanding federal antipoverty programs. Examining the votes of members of Congress representing most of the Black Belt counties within two periods—from 1965 through 1977 and from 1978 through 1989—reveals a radical change in voting behavior among these House members. From 1965 through 1977 the Black Belt congressional delegation in the South supported antipoverty programs with only 11 percent of its vote on twenty-six important roll calls. From 1978 through 1989, however, Black Belt congressional support enlarged to 41 percent on twelve significant roll calls (see Table 12.1).

The most significant changes in voting on poverty were in Black Belt districts in Arkansas, Florida, Georgia, Mississippi, and North Carolina. In Mississippi, for instance, support for antipoverty programs skyrocketed from 3 percent in the early period to 61 percent in the more recent time. Fundamental gains in support for antipoverty efforts were realized in the Black Belt of every Southern state and almost every Black Belt congressional district.

This shift represents a significant change in the outcome of proposed antipoverty legislation. For example, the key roll call on the Family Support Act (modest as it is) in the U.S. House of Representatives resulted in passage by only seven votes. Legislation providing emergency loans to long-term unemployed homeowners in 1983 passed the House by only twenty votes. Increases in Medicare funding in 1982 passed by only thirty-two votes. In each of these decisions fewer than seventeen votes changed the outcome, and in each case the change in voting behavior of members of Congress representing Black Belt had a decisive effect in the final tally.

By the same measure, if political changes in the Black Belt had occurred earlier, some different outcomes might also have been possible. In 1967, for example, the decision of the U.S. House of Representatives to slash the budget of the Office of Economic Opportunity could have been prevented by a swing of sixteen votes. In 1972 a substantially higher minimum wage could have passed the House had five votes from the Black Belt supported the more generous legislation.[2]

These political changes over the last three decades have ushered in a new era of Southern politics, one that has deepened the region's political support for civil rights and concern for the poor through government action. The changes represented a growing concern for policies and resources for the poor among government officials at a time when, in general, the government was diminishing its commitment and initiative to address poverty. In this respect these changes in political power among the rural Black poor created one of the few instances where government officials in the 1980s became more willing to address poverty than they were in the 1960s.

Despite this progress, the changes in the South's Black Belt remain ongoing, part of a quiet, unfinished political revolution. Reliable precinct data in Southern states strongly suggest that Blacks in the Black Belt continue to have one of the lowest rates of voter registration and turnout, a pattern generally correlated with low levels of education and income for all races. Although there are more Black elected officials, the rural South remains substantially underrepresented. According to a survey of the rural South in 1985, 89 percent of 176 municipalities with less than 2,000 persons and a Black population of 50 to 64 percent had no Black mayor. Sixty-three percent of the Southern small towns had no Black mayor if their Black population ranged from 65 to 79 percent (see Table 12.2). Most of these towns are in the South's Black Belt.

This pattern of lingering underrepresentation is reflected in county governments as well. In 1985, among the eighty-two majority Black counties in seven Southern states (primarily Black Belt counties), local governments were headed by Whites in sixty-one counties; twenty-three had only one Black county commissioner; and in fifteen others all county commissioners were White (McDonald 1989).

RECENT ECONOMIC EMPOWERMENT OF THE RURAL POOR

Unlike the recent gains in political empowerment, democratic participation by the Southern rural poor in their own economic institutions since the 1960s

Table 12.2
**Municipalities of Less Than 2,500 Population without Black Mayors by Racial
Composition of Population in the South, 1985**

Percent Black Population:

Population of Municipality	50-64%	65-70%	80-99%
Less than 2,500	89%	63%	25%
(Number)	(176)	(78)	(84)

Source: Adapted from William O'Hare, "Racial Composition of Jurisdictions and the Election of
  Black Candidates," *Population Today*, June 1986, pp. 6–8.

and early 1970s has been unimpressive. Many rural cooperatives created by the
poor in the 1960s have remained viable, but most have had little growth and
retain only a limited capacity to go beyond the necessities of survival. Moreover,
the crucial role of independent co-ops in providing freedom from the local White
economy and as a vehicle for solidarity has diminished as desegregation in the
workplace and marketplace has spread to the Black Belt. Farming and production
cooperatives have continued to provide some economies of cooperation, allowing
small Black farmers and others to earn modest incomes. Yet, at best, the farm
cooperative movement today is a holding action among the rural poor.

In contrast, utility cooperatives financed by the Rural Electrification Administration have grown since the 1930s to be powerful and resourceful institutions
throughout rural areas. In 1988 rural electric and telephone co-ops had more
than $65 billion in assets and more than $1.4 billion in net income; they owned
and maintained more than 40 percent of the electric distribution system and 15
percent of the phone systems in the country; and they were often the largest
single business organizations in their communities. They continue to serve the
vast majority of the rural areas, including areas with many rural poor.[3]

Although the assets of utility co-ops have enlarged, the principles of democracy
have not. Their "Whites only" origins have persisted in many parts of the rural
South. According to an internal memorandum of the National Rural Electric
Cooperative Association, the boards of directors of the utility cooperatives were
virtually segregated until the 1970s, when REA undertook modest efforts to
increase the number of Blacks in governance. In 1969, for example, only 3
Blacks were among more than 6,000 members of the boards of directors of the
nation's electric cooperatives. By 1975 the number of Blacks had increased to
67, and by 1979 the number was 101. If other minorities are added, primarily
American Indians and Hispanics in western states, only 273 non-Whites were

among 8,739 members of the boards of directors of both telephone and utility co-ops in rural areas.

In 1979 the co-op boards of directors in the South showed very few Blacks. In Georgia only 15 of 323 members of the co-op boards were Black; moreover, in service areas where Blacks were a majority of the households, several utility co-ops' boards had no Black members at all. Black representation on such boards in Alabama was no greater, and in Mississippi none of the 174 members of the electric co-op was Black in 1979.

Among rural telephone cooperatives minority representation appeared even smaller. In the South, only in Texas, South Carolina, North Carolina, and Arkansas did telephone cooperatives have any minority members on the boards of directors in 1980. The grand total throughout the South was 9 Black members.[4]

Over the course of the 1980s the level of participation of Blacks in the utility co-ops' decision making appears to have improved only marginally. In 1982 Blacks constituted less than 5 percent of the total membership of the rural electric co-op boards in the South, a level of representation that apparently has inched forward in more recent years (Southern Regional Council 1990).

Even these modest gains of Blacks on the co-ops' boards may be an exaggerated proxy for real democratic participation. The files of the Rural Electrification Administration suggest that many Blacks who serve on boards were originally handpicked by all-White boards. For example, in 1974 the manager of the Prince George Electric Cooperative in the Black Belt of Virginia submitted the minutes of a recent meeting of his board of directors with these comments: "Mr. Charlotte is a Negro (colored man) and has been a member of the Prince George Electric Cooperative for approximately twenty five to thirty years. We feel he will make an excellent board member." Charlotte continued to sit on the co-op board as of 1989.[5]

Generally, the election procedures in most Black Belt cooperatives have the same characteristics that have allowed local political institutions to remain exclusionary, at least until the enforcement of the federal Voting Rights Act. Most have at-large elections with a slate of candidates who are proffered by a majority White nominating committee selected by the majority White board of directors. In most cooperatives, it appears, nominations from the membership require prior notice and more than a few signatures from members. These procedures have the same generic elements and the same effect as the discriminatory election schemes that have frustrated Black political empowerment (Southern Regional Council files 1990).

Some utility cooperatives in the South, however, have not failed to enlarge "grass-roots democracy"; rather, they have abandoned democratic governance altogether. In Alabama, Mississippi, and Texas, especially, several electric co-ops did not hold any valid elections during the late 1970s and early 1980s, according to REA records. For example, data from about twenty electric cooperatives in Mississippi from 1975 through 1983 indicate that almost half failed to hold a valid election during any of these years. In effect, the governing boards abandoned democratic participation in favor of self-perpetuation.[6]

THE DELTA ELECTRIC POWER ASSOCIATION AND ABANDONED DEMOCRACY

A recent example of both the abandonment of the democratic process and blatant hostility toward poor Black participation among the electric cooperatives is found in the Delta Electric Power Association (EPA), which provides electricity to several rural majority Black communities in the Mississippi Delta. The Delta EPA serves portions of eight counties in the Mississippi Delta. Each has at least a 50 percent Black population. Personal income in the areas is very low; poverty is high; and unemployment is structural and deep. Farming remains the predominate industry, and most of it is done on large plantations owned by White families who have controlled the land in the counties for more than a century. These farming operations offer relatively few jobs since much of the process has become mechanized.

Members of the governing board of the Delta Electric Power Association have always been chosen from among the prominent White farmers in the area. They are also some of the largest consumers of electricity. The board governs an operation with standing assets of more than $42 million, and in 1988 the co-op showed a net income of $3 million. It serves 19,000 customers, including almost 1,500 irrigation operations on the farms. In fact, Delta sells more total electrical power for irrigation than for any other category of service except residential.[7]

Based on data from the early 1980s, the rate structure of Delta has been very regressive. The cost per kilowatt hour (kwh) of power for the small residential user was more than twice as high as the cost per kwh for large users in 1981. Compared to eight other electric utilities in Mississippi, including an investor-owned utility and other member-owned operations, Delta had the highest rate for small users and the lowest rate for large users of electricity.

The co-op employs a staff of ninety-four full-time employees and more than twenty part-time workers. During the 1970s and early 1980s Delta had around thirty Black employees, virtually all in positions of unskilled laborers or janitorial work. At the same time, the co-op held stock in two local segregated country clubs.[8]

From 1971 (the earliest available records) until 1983 the Delta co-op held no valid election. Instead, its board members called for an election each year, established the time of the election in the middle of a weekday, and announced that members should appear for its annual meeting and election. Since the board usually designated the conference room of the local chamber of commerce (with a capacity of about forty people) as the site of the annual election for its 19,000 members, the board presumably did not expect to hold an election. Instead, it declared the absence of a quorum of members and reappointed itself to serve until a valid election could be held. Each year, perhaps for decades, the board of directors followed this self-perpetuating, antidemocratic ritual—until 1983.

In early 1983 local Black community leaders began work in the Delta EPA area to inform member-consumers of their opportunity to participate in the co-op elections. They identified the places where most Black EPA members lived, developed a campaign to educate them, and began a process to select an alternative slate of candidates to nominate for the board of directors. According to co-op rules, three members of the board of directors would be elected at the annual meeting on April 12, and each co-op member present could cast one vote and three proxy votes.

Community leaders also began efforts to secure needed information concerning the co-op's operations and procedures. A request under the Freedom of Information Act (FOIA) for data concerning the co-op's past operations was filed at the Rural Electrification Administration. Locally, the co-op manager denied that a list of co-op members existed and refused a request to send to all members a mailing outlining the alternative candidates' platforms. Later, he claimed that there were only index cards that had members listed on them and that these were impossible to duplicate. (A membership list without addresses was finally produced the day after the April 12 election.) The co-op also took days before it honored a request for a current copy of the bylaws. When the alternative candidates requested a copy of a sample ballot that would be used at the annual meeting, the co-op again delayed for days and finally produced a ballot that was inconsistent with the just-released report of the co-op's nominating committee (*Delta Democrat-Times* September 1983; *Greenwood Commonwealth* March 1983).

Delta's original notice of election to its members stated that three positions on the board of directors would be filled; however, the nominating committee presented twelve nominations for membership on the board. The sample ballot produced by the co-op showed that only three people were to be elected. The confusion was finally cleared up on the eve of the election. At that time, REA information arrived in Mississippi, showing that the co-op had not had a quorum for more than a decade and that the present board of directors had perpetuated itself in office over that time. Facing a challenge for the first time, the co-op's management attempted to forestall a complete takeover of the co-op by illegally changing the number of members to be elected from twelve to only three.

The co-op management undertook other maneuvers to assure that the challenge to its control would be unsuccessful. With little notice, it changed the time of the meeting on April 12 from two o'clock in the afternoon to ten o'clock in the morning. This change presented real problems for challengers since it made it very difficult for people in outlying areas to attend. In order to arrive and be registered before 10:00 A.M., cars or buses had to begin picking up people in half of the EPA's counties as early as 6:00 A.M. (most had no automobiles of their own.) Moreover, those with work had to choose between a day's pay or participation in the co-op's election. For those who chose to come from the outlying counties, attendance also meant setting aside a complete day.[9]

On April 12, 130 Black people did attend the Delta annual meeting, and most of them carried three proxies. At promptly 10:00 A.M., while people were being registered slowly by the co-op employees, the head of the co-op convened the meeting and quickly recognized a member of the board of directors who questioned whether a quorum existed. At this point the co-op manager ruled that no quorum existed and attempted to adjourn the meeting. Members of the incumbent board left the conference room. Afterwards, the self-perpetuating board issued a notice that it had met and changed its bylaw provisions concerning a quorum. Now the co-op would permit an unlimited number of proxies to be voted by any one person and required proxies to be filed with the co-op office five days in advance of the election. Visitors would not be allowed at the annual meeting unless they were approved in advance by the board of directors. (Staff members of the Southern Regional Council had attended the earlier election meeting as observers.)

After the announcement the self-perpetuating board and the co-op's White professional staff actively began to solicit proxies from members. White EPA staff members apparently worked days, nights, and weekends using co-op vehicles to collect proxies for the special June 14 election. (They also may have been paid overtime by the co-op.) In co-op uniforms the repairmen and other staff members discouraged Black customers from giving proxies to the challenge group.

Delta's general manager vehemently denied allegations of racial bias, justifying the co-op's self-perpetuating history with explanations that echoed the sentiments of past racist voter registrars in the South: "I think the fact that people don't come out is a vote of confidence in the board. They must be satisfied with the way we are running things" (*New York Times* March 1984). In 1983 Delta hired the first Black to work inside its main office in Greenwood. Yet it held a second election with staff-collected proxies, reelecting its old White board members, who remained adamant in preventing an elected Black consumer to join them. Delta continues to have no Black board members (*Greenwood Commonwealth* April 1983; *Jackson Clarion Ledger* June 1983).

PROSPECTS FOR EMPOWERMENT OF THE RURAL POOR

Because poor Blacks remain without power in many places, the concepts of empowerment of the poor in rural America have a strategic future role in the work to reduce poverty. In the rural South—and in other poor rural areas in the nation—effective efforts to empower the rural poor in political elections will have a central and essential role. In the Black Belt political change already has begun to redistribute opportunities for existing government services and available jobs to poor African Americans. It has also had a dramatic effect on the voting behavior of members of Congress representing most Black Belt counties on issues of poverty.

These changes in behavior, resources, and policies represented the only significant political movement during the 1980s toward enlarging the capacity and the collective will of government to reduce poverty. Although this movement was not enough to reverse the trends of increasing poverty or the government's inclination to make only minor adjustments in existing programs during the 1980s, the full potential for political change in this growing movement has not been realized. Until full empowerment of poor Blacks in political institutions in the Black Belt is a reality, the nation will be without some decisive voices, votes, and ideas from the rural Black poor.

To establish a movement to bring about fundamental change to address rural poverty that can succeed where other movements have failed, the democratic control of rural economic institutions must be a part of the strategy to change. In rural places like the Black Belt the existing utility cooperatives are one of the first and most important economic institutions that the poor can help control. They are relatively rich in resources and influential in local areas, and they appear to have very little democratic control in many rural poor communities.

Utility co-ops are also a good place for the rural poor to gain power because they encompass the cooperative decision making that is vital to both the welfare of rural areas and the process of movement building. They are economic institutions that locally provide for the needs of the whole community and, therefore, require communitywide cooperation and decision making. Both electric and telephone cooperatives are critical parts of the infrastructure of rural areas, and their policies can have a great impact on the nature of local economic development. They provide a basic necessity to the poor and have a system of organization that can provide other essential services to the poor. Utility co-ops are also a growth industry, providing services that are at the core of the information age.

Equally useful, the co-ops have opportunities and methods for effective local community participation and education on matters of local and national policy. Their magazines, mail billings, meetings, service routes, and local offices offer remarkable networks of communications in communities, so that democratic participation goes beyond only casting ballots.

Of course, the empowerment of the poor in the rural South, alone, will not be enough to transform entirely the development of public policy on poverty in the United States beyond the limitations of the 1980s. Yet the nation has never had the benefits of full democracy in the South, nor has the region ever experienced full economic and political empowerment of the poor. The progress of past movements suggests that the potential of these changes could be profound.

Despite the lingering effects of racism and poverty, the American South represents a region where profound change has occurred. It is significant that this change has been unleashed in the past by movements where the poor empower themselves. Strategies that encourage empowerment embrace democratic principles and thus are essential if the nation is to seriously address poverty.

NOTES

1. Joint Center for Political Studies, 1989; *Southern Changes*, November 1981; United States Commission on Civil Rights, 1981; *Extension of the Voting Rights Act*, Hearings before the Committee on Civil and Constitutional Rights of the Committee on the Judiciary, House of Representatives, 97th Cong. 1st sess. 1981.

2. Congressional Quarterly 1988, 1984, 1983, 1968, 1973. Generally, the literature has correlated changes in voting behavior only with urban Black congressional districts. See Whitby 1987. Also on voting rights changes, see Parker, 1990.

3. See Rural Electrification Administration 1989a, 1989b; Doyle 1979.

4. See Richard Larochelle, Memorandum on Minority Participation in Rural Electric Cooperatives, July 17, 1984; Office of Equal Opportunity, 1981, pp. 108–9.

5. Frank M. Remorenko, Jr., to Joe S. Zoller, Letter of September 27, 1974, "Equal Opportunity—Prince George Electric Cooperative, Waverly, Virginia," Rural Electrification Administration files; Virginia, Maryland, and Delaware Association of Electric Cooperatives 1990, p. 29.

6. Rural Electrification Administration files, 1975–1982; Southern Regional Council files, 1990.

7. "A Comparison of Delta EPA Kwh Rates to Those of Six West Mississippi EPAs and Those of Mississippi Power and Light Company, 1981," Working Paper, Southern Regional Council files.

8. "Employment Data—Delta Electronic Power Association," 1975 and 1981, Form 15, REA files; Form 7-A, 1976, REA Files.

9. Form 7-A, 197–1983, REA files; Southern Regional Council files.

Chapter 13

Policies to Alleviate Rural Poverty

Robert Greenstein and Isaac Shapiro

When most Americans think about poverty programs, they envision programs for people in the inner city. There is often little appreciation of the extent of poverty in rural areas or the impact some antipoverty policies can have there. In fact, certain policies could help the rural poor even more than the urban poor. To identify these policies, it is helpful first to analyze the characteristics of the rural poor.[1]

CHARACTERISTICS OF THE RURAL POOR: HOW THEY DIFFER FROM THE URBAN POOR

Three characteristics of the rural poor stand out. They are more likely than the urban poor to be employed, living in two-parent families, and elderly.

Rural Workers

In 1987 nearly two-thirds—65 percent—of all rural poor families had at least one worker. In urban areas this figure was lower—54 percent. Moreover, many of the rural poor who do not work are elderly, disabled, or ill. In 1987 some 70 percent of the rural poor family heads who were not ill, disabled, or retired did work, and nearly one in four worked full-time year-round. More than six of every seven poor heads of rural two-parent families who were not ill, disabled, or retired were people who worked (Shapiro 1989).

Of those who were not ill, disabled, or retired and did not work, nearly one-third looked for work in 1987 without success. Many of the remainder were single parents caring for young children. Furthermore, even among single parents, the degree of work was high. More than half of the poor single parents in rural areas who were not ill, disabled, or retired worked in 1987.

If work effort is higher in rural than in urban areas, why are overall poverty rates higher in rural America? One reason is that wages are lower in rural areas; those who do work are much more likely to be poor in rural than in urban locations. A family in which the household head works is about twice as likely to be poor in rural as in urban settings. This ratio holds for both Whites and Blacks and for both full-time and part-time workers.

As Lucy Gorham's chapter indicates, some 42 percent of all rural workers earned a wage too low to lift a family of four out of poverty, even with full-time, year-round work. By contrast, 29 percent of urban workers earned a wage this low. Similarly, nearly one of every three rural workers paid by the hour— 32 percent—earned less than $4.35 an hour in 1987. Some 22 percent of urban workers who were paid by the hour received a wage below $4.35 (Hendrickson and Sawhill 1989).

In short, many of the rural poor work but remain poor because their earnings are low. If their earnings could be increased, progress could be made in alleviating their poverty.

Two-Parent Families

Of all rural poor people living in families in 1987, some 61 percent lived in two-parent families. Just 39 percent lived in a family headed by a single parent (Porter 1989). This contrasts sharply with the figures for urban areas and especially for central cities. In the nation's central cities only 42 percent of poor people living in families were members of a two-parent family. Some 58 percent lived in single-parent families.

These findings have two implications. Since most poor two-parent families include at least one worker, these data underscore the importance in rural areas of policies to aid the working poor. Second, these findings indicate that those aspects of the welfare system that discriminate against two-parent families are particularly adverse for rural residents.

The Elderly

In 1987 some 13 percent of all rural poor people were 65 and over, while 10 percent of the urban poor were elderly. Poverty rates are especially high among rural elderly Blacks. In 1987, nearly half—46 percent—of Black elderly people living in rural areas were poor. By contrast, 30 percent of the Black elderly in urban areas were poor that year.

GENERAL POLICY IMPLICATIONS

These findings ought to bode well for efforts to alleviate rural poverty. Many Americans tend to regard low-income people who either work or are elderly and who are married or widowed as the "deserving poor." This suggests that efforts to assist these groups should have a better chance of generating political support.

Yet while there has often been broad support for efforts to assist the elderly poor (as compared to poor families with children, for example), this has not always been the case for the working poor or poor two-parent families. In the past these groups have often been neglected.

There are indications, however, that changes are occurring in the policy climate. In particular, proposals to assist low-income working families are attracting more support than only a few years ago. As a result, prospects for making a significant dent in rural poverty are brighter than in some time. In fact, Congress enacted some important policy reforms in 1990 that should be of considerable help to the rural working poor. The remainder of this chapter focuses primarily on policy initiatives that could aid rural working poor families, low-income elderly people in rural areas, and rural poor two-parent families.

POLICIES TO ASSIST THE RURAL WORKING POOR

In fashioning policies to assist the working poor, a basic goal can be established: if a parent works full-time, the family should not have to live in poverty. The goal is to make work pay enough that a family with a full-time worker will not be poor. This goal should be consistent with the basic work ethic and values of this country.

Attaining this goal entails a series of changes in federal and state tax and wage policies. One of the most important policy areas involves the earned income tax credit (EITC).

Earned Income Tax Credit

The federal earned income tax credit is a "refundable" tax credit for low-income working families with at least one child living at home. For tax year 1990, the credit applied to families with earnings and adjusted gross incomes up to $20,264, and the maximum benefit was $953.[2]

A key feature of the credit is its refundability. This means that if a family's credit exceeds its income tax liability, the family receives a check from the Internal Revenue Service for the difference. For example, if a family has income too low to owe federal income tax but qualifies for a $600 EITC, the IRS will send the family a check for $600. The refundable aspect of the credit initially was designed to offset the high burden posed by the regressive payroll taxes that low-income working families pay. The credit is widely regarded as both "pro-work" and "profamily." Families without a working parent do not qualify. Similarly, absent parents are not eligible.

The EITC was established in 1975 and enlarged by the Tax Reform Act of 1986. It is emerging as one of the federal government's major sources of support for low-income working families. In tax year 1988 more than eleven million families with children—far more than received any other means-tested benefit—received EITC benefits of $5.9 billion.

The EITC is especially well suited to rural working families. Since wages are lower on average in rural than in urban areas, and since more of the rural poor than of the urban poor are employed, the rural poor are overrepresented among the EITC's beneficiaries. The EITC has other advantages for the rural poor as well. There are no geographic access problems, since eligible families need not travel to a government office to apply. They simply file a federal income tax return. Similarly, there is no stigma associated with EITC benefits, which come in the form of an IRS check indistinguishable from any other tax refund check.

The positive attributes of the EITC have led to significant expansions of the credit both in the Tax Reform Act of 1986 and in the 1990 budget agreement.[3] In the more recent of these two expansions, Congress included a $13-billion expansion of the EITC (over five years) in the large package of budget changes and deficit-reduction measures passed in the fall of 1990. The new legislation will increase EITC benefits more than 70 percent when the expansions are phased in fully. By 1995 many families will receive annual EITC benefits in the $2,000 range (in 1995 dollars). The legislation also includes provisions to ensure that benefits in other programs—such as Aid to Families with Dependent Children (AFDC), Supplemental Security Income (SSI), Food Stamps, Medicaid, subsidized housing, and rural housing—are not reduced when a family receives its EITC payment. The new legislation, while making substantial improvements in the EITC, leaves two issues not fully addressed, however: the need to vary EITC benefits by family size and the need to enable more families to receive EITC payments throughout the year rather than in a lump-sum tax refund after the year is over.

The proposal to adjust EITC benefits by family size has received widespread support among poverty analysts and policymakers from across the political spectrum. Family needs increase with family size, and the poverty line rises with family size as well. Welfare benefits also rise with family size. But wages do not. The result is that as family size increases, low-wage work leaves families further and further below the poverty line. Moreover, low-wage work becomes less competitive with welfare as family size grows.

The legislation enacted in 1990 takes a step toward addressing this problem by setting up a two-tier EITC benefit: one benefit for a family with one child and a slightly higher benefit level for families with two or more children. While this is a step in the right direction, it does not go far enough. The difference in the benefit levels is only about $150 a year, far below the difference in the poverty line (or in welfare benefits) for an additional family member.

Moreover, the lack of a third tier in the new EITC benefit structure for families with three or more children is problematic. Sixty percent of all children in working poor families live in families with three or more children. In addition, the poverty rate among working families with three or more children is 20 percent, while it is less than 10 percent for working families with one or two children. These findings underscore the importance of an additional adjustment in the EITC for families with three or more children.

Another problem with the EITC is that more than 99 percent of its beneficiaries receive their benefits in the form of a tax refund after the end of the tax year. The EITC would likely be more effective both in meeting ongoing household needs and as a work incentive if it were provided as part of the regular paycheck throughout the year. If the EITC payments are provided to a family in its regular paychecks, they will better match the family's need to pay bills such as rent. In addition, the EITC is likely to be more effective in making work more attractive than welfare if it is received in the regular paycheck, because a family may compare its potential take-home pay to its monthly AFDC check.

For some time, federal law has permitted workers to receive the EITC in their regular paychecks, but few employers or low-income working families seem to be aware of this option. (This option is known as the "advance payment" option.) Some employers may be declining to inform their workers of the option because they believe that it would involve too much paperwork.

The 1990 legislation mandates a study by the General Accounting Office of why the advance payment system does not work more effectively and how it can be improved. The study is due in November 1991. The results of this study will deserve careful examination to see if they can help guide efforts to make the EITC advance payment system more effective.

For the EITC to be fully effective, strengthened outreach efforts are also necessary to ensure that families eligible for benefits actually receive them. The Tax Reform Act of 1986 eliminated federal income tax liabilities for most working poor families with children. Many of these families now receive a W-2 form at the end of the year showing that no income tax was withheld from their paychecks. As a result, many of these families may conclude that there is no reason to file a tax return. If they do not file, they lose the refundable EITC benefits they have earned. If the EITC is to encourage work and reduce poverty, working families too poor to owe income tax must know of its existence and the need to file a federal tax return to receive it.

Some significant EITC outreach efforts were launched in 1989. These efforts involved public officials (including leaders of business, labor, religious, and charitable organizations). However, much of the activity has been concentrated in metropolitan areas and especially in cities. More extensive outreach efforts are needed in rural areas as well.

Furthermore, due to passage of the new EITC legislation in 1990, outreach efforts will be more important than ever in the years after 1991. This is true because the new law makes a major change in how to file for the EITC: for the first time in the EITC's history, families will have to file a separate tax schedule to receive it.

Until now, families filing the standard 1040 or 1040A forms did not need to complete any other forms. In fact, if they failed to complete the EITC line on the form, the IRS would generally compute their benefits for them and send them a check. That will now change. To reflect the new EITC expansions and to reduce errors in the EITC, Congress made a series of technical changes in the credit. These changes make it impossible to include the EITC on the regular tax form. Starting with the tax filing season for the 1991 tax year, families claiming the EITC will need to file a separate schedule along with their 1040 or 1040A form, just as families claiming itemized deductions must file a separate schedule.

This new requirement demands a major enlargement in outreach efforts to inform low-income working families of the need to file this new, separate schedule to receive the EITC benefits they have earned. Given the large proportion of poor rural families that contain an employed member, such outreach efforts will be particularly important in rural areas.

Minimum Wage

The earned income credit has enjoyed support across the political spectrum. Indeed, some seem to regard the EITC as a panacea—the principal or only major policy change needed to respond to the poverty of low-income working families.

For example, in recommending policy directions for the Bush administration, the conservative Heritage Foundation called for increasing the EITC enough that a family of four with a full-time minimum-wage worker could be brought to the poverty line (Heatherly and Pines 1989). Yet even after the minimum wage is raised in 1991, and even when the recent EITC expansion is fully implemented, the combined effect will fall short of the goal of ensuring that full-time minimum-wage workers and their families are not poor. Full-time minimum wage work will fall $4,100 below the poverty line for a family of four before payroll taxes are subtracted and $4,800 below after payroll taxes are taken out. To reach the poverty line through EITC enhancement alone would require a credit equal to more than 60 percent of earnings. Such an EITC benefit structure would cost tens of billions of dollars and create unacceptably high marginal tax rates, rendering it politically infeasible.

To enable both rural and urban working families to reach the poverty line if they work full-time, both the enlarged EITC and an increased minimum wage are needed. A higher minimum wage would be especially significant to the rural working poor, since a large fraction of the rural work force is employed at or near the minimum-wage level.

In November 1989 legislation raised the federal minimum wage in two steps to $4.25 an hour by April 1991. This legislation makes up only about two-fifths of the ground lost to inflation during the 1980s, when the minimum wage remained frozen for more than nine years while the Consumer Price Index rose more than 40 percent.

This erosion in the minimum wage is significant. Throughout the 1960s and 1970s full-time work at the minimum wage generally lifted a family of three out of poverty (before payroll taxes were subtracted). In 1991 it will leave such a family several thousand dollars below the poverty line.

While most minimum-wage workers are not poor, a majority of the poor who work have earnings at or near the minimum-wage level. In 1987 nearly three of every five poor workers paid by the hour earned $4.35 an hour or less. This is particularly significant since $4.35 is approximately the level the minimum wage would have reached in 1987 had it kept pace with inflation during the 1980s.

These data suggest that a large share of poor workers would be aided by restoring the minimum wage to its level of the 1960s and 1970s. A restoration along these lines was recommended by a blue-ribbon panel convened by the Ford Foundation to recommend social welfare policies for coming years.[4] Restoring the purchasing power of the minimum wage would affect an especially large fraction of low-paid workers in rural areas, since nearly one in three rural workers paid by the hour received wages at or near the minimum wage in 1987.

Furthermore, such a restoration of the minimum wage would mesh nicely with the EITC. If the minimum wage were restored to its average level of the 1960s and 1970s, it again would lift a family of three with a full-time minimum-wage worker to the poverty line. The enlarged earned income tax credit could help ensure that minimum-wage families of more than three people also could be lifted to or near the poverty line, particularly if a third tier (for families with three or more children) were to be added to the EITC.

In short, to assist the working poor more effectively, a group heavily overrepresented in rural areas, tax and wage policies should work in tandem. Only a combination of a strengthened EITC and minimum-wage enlargement appears able to ensure that full-time work lifts a family from poverty. As poverty analyst David Ellwood has commented, without a joint EITC minimum-wage approach, "it is virtually impossible to guarantee that work will pay enough to keep families out of poverty" (Ellwood 1988, p. 112).

FACTORS THAT CAN PUSH RURAL WORKING FAMILIES BACK INTO POVERTY

Even with an expanded EITC and a restored minimum wage, many poor rural families with a full-time worker may effectively remain poor because other costs push them back below the poverty line. This is especially true if a family's employer fails to provide health insurance and the family must purchase an expensive individual family policy, if the family incurs significant child-care costs, if the state in which the family resides taxes the family back into poverty, or if a shortage of affordable housing requires the family to pay so much of its income for housing that insufficient income remains for other needs. Policy reforms in these four areas are needed as part of a comprehensive strategy to address poverty among the rural working poor.

Lack of health insurance coverage is a particular problem for rural working poor families. While many of the nonworking poor qualify for Medicaid because they receive AFDC benefits (families on AFDC are automatically enrolled in Medicaid), a much smaller proportion of working poor families have either Medicaid or private health insurance.

In 1986 nearly half—or 48 percent—of all poor children living in households in which the head worked full-time year-round lacked any public or private health insurance. By contrast, fewer than one-third—31 percent—of poor children living in a household in which the head did not work lacked health insurance (Chollet 1988). A breakdown of these figures on an urban/rural basis is not available, but with the working poor being overrepresented in rural areas and underrepresented in urban settings, it seems likely that this problem affects rural families most severely.

In recent years both the federal and state governments have taken steps to extend Medicaid coverage to pregnant women and children from low-income working families that are not on AFDC. In November 1989, for example, legislation was enacted extending Medicaid to pregnant women and children through age 5 who live in families with incomes up to 133 percent of the poverty line. The budget legislation passed in 1990 requires state Medicaid programs to cover children aged 6 through 18 in families with incomes below 100 percent of the poverty line. This requirement is phased in over twelve years by extending coverage through the nineteenth birthday to poor children born after September 31, 1983. Thus, on October 1, 1991, state Medicaid programs will have to cover poor children up to their eighth birthday. By October 1, 2002, poor children up to their nineteenth birthday will be covered. These legislative actions are likely to have a disproportionately large effect in rural areas, where more poor families work, wages are lower, and AFDC participation also tends to be lower.

In the years ahead the federal and state governments could build on the actions of the late 1980s. For example, the federal government could give states the option to extend Medicaid coverage to all children in poverty before the year 2002. Speeding up expansion of Medicaid coverage would benefit rural areas. The federal government could also give states the option of expanding coverage to children with incomes up to 185 percent of the poverty line, an option states already possess for pregnant women and infants. State-level initiatives to make health-care coverage available to uninsured people at affordable costs would also be particularly relevant to low-income rural residents.

Child-care costs pose another problem for working poor families. A family that otherwise has lifted itself out of poverty may see its disposable income plunge several thousand dollars below the poverty line because of the cost of child care.

The 1990 budget legislation took several positive steps in this area as well. Major child-care legislation was incorporated into the final budget package. Two new programs of grants to states for child-care services were established. The larger of the two programs, the Child Care and Development Block Grant program, is designed to increase the availability, affordability, and quality of child care. The second program will provide child-care services for low-income families that are not on AFDC but that need child-care assistance to work and are at risk of becoming welfare recipients if they do not receive such assistance.

These new programs will improve efforts to provide affordable quality child care, especially if the initiatives receive full funding at both the federal and state levels (a matter that is now open to some question). One other important child-care reform was not enacted, however. Earlier in 1990 the Senate had approved a measure to make the federal dependent care tax credit refundable. This provision was not included in the final package that was approved in the fall of 1990; it deserves to be resurrected. Consideration should also be given to making state dependent care credits refundable.

In effect, dependent care tax credits are subsidies provided through the tax code that reduce the child-care costs of working families. The federal credit provides a subsidy equal to between 20 percent and 30 percent of the first $2,400 per child in annual child-care costs, for up to two children.[5]

Yet the federal credit and most of the eighteen state dependent care credits fail to assist the very group that needs child-care assistance the most—working poor families. The credit does not help these families because it is not refundable. Working families with incomes too low to owe income tax receive no tax credit payment. This means that nearly all of the child-care subsidies provided by the credit, the federal government's principal source of child-care assistance, go to middle- and upper-income families (Isensee and Campbell 1987; Shapiro and Greenstein 1990). An Urban Institute analysis found that only 3 percent of the child-care subsidies provided through the credit went to families in the bottom 30 percent of the income distribution (Barnes 1988). This problem can be addressed by making the dependent care credit refundable, like the earned income credit. This would help those working poor families that incur child-care expenses but earn too little to owe income tax.

A third area needing attention is state income tax policy. The Tax Reform Act of 1986 advanced the principle that working poor families should not be taxed deeper into poverty by eliminating federal income tax burdens on these families. In the years since 1986 a number of states have followed suit. As of mid–1990 some seventeen of the forty-one states with state income taxes did not impose such taxes on four-person families with incomes below the poverty line. Yet the remaining twenty-four states with state income taxes do tax their working poor families further into poverty. Eighteen of these states levy income tax on two-parent families of four with income below 75 percent of the poverty line, while seven tax families of four with incomes below half the poverty line.[6]

Since so many of the rural poor work, state revenue policies that extract income tax from working poor families affect rural residents disproportionately. Nevertheless, rural states are more likely than urban states to impose this tax on working poor families. Of the eighteen states that impose income tax on families below 75 percent of the poverty line, fourteen have a higher-than-average proportion of rural residents.[7]

As had been demonstrated by many of the states that eliminated income tax burdens on working poor families, removing these families from state income tax rolls usually can be done in a targeted manner entailing only small revenue losses. Moreover, these revenue losses often can be offset with some modest loophole-closing or other base-broadening measures. Such a combination of measures—removing income tax burdens on low-income working families and financing this step by base-broadening revenues that principally affect more affluent households—is particularly beneficial to rural areas.[8]

A final area needing attention is housing policy. Rural working households whose wages and earned income tax credits lift them out of poverty can still face difficulty if housing costs consume an inordinate share of their income. Under standards set by the U.S. Department of Housing and Urban Development (HUD), housing is considered affordable for a low-income household if it does not consume more than 30 percent of the household's income. Yet census data show that in 1987 (the latest year for which these data are available), nearly three of every four poor households in rural areas paid more than this for housing, with nearly half (45 percent) spending at least 50 percent of income for housing.[9]

These high housing-cost burdens are related to a growing shortage of affordable rental housing in rural areas. In 1970 there were 500,000 more low-rent housing units in rural areas than there were low-income renter households. By 1987 there were 1.3 million fewer low-rent units in rural areas than low-income renter households.[10]

Yet while most poor rural households face housing costs outside HUD's affordable range, relatively few receive any form of housing assistance. Fewer than one in every three poor renters in rural areas receive any kind of federal, state, or local rent subsidy or lives in public housing. Providing rental assistance to a larger proportion of poor rural households appears to be the key to making progress here. The need and costs for additional housing assistance are so large that expansion of both federal and state efforts in this area is likely to be necessary.[11]

If these various steps were taken—wage and tax policies to lift full-time working families to the poverty line, state tax policies that do not tax these families back into poverty, and policies that provide access to decent child care, health care, and housing at prices these households can afford—major progress would be made in alleviating poverty among the rural working poor. However, one other segment of the rural working poor also needs attention: those who cannot work full-time year-round because they have been laid off for part of the year.

UNEMPLOYMENT AND UNEMPLOYMENT INSURANCE

Since 1980 rural workers have been more likely than urban workers to be unemployed during a year. During this same period unemployment insurance coverage has dropped sharply. In 1988 only 31.5 percent of the unemployed workers nationwide received unemployment insurance benefits in an average month. This constituted a record low. Moreover, in the most rural states coverage tends to be even lower. In the ten states with the highest proportions of rural residents, 29 percent of the unemployed received benefits in an average month of 1988.

Of particular concern are the difficulties faced by rural residents of high-unemployment areas. In 1988 fewer than one in every thirty-five people in the urban labor force—2.8 percent—resided in a county with a double-digit unemployment rate. By contrast, nearly one of every seven people in the rural labor force—13.4 percent—lived in a county with an unemployment rate of 10 percent or more (Shapiro 1989).

Residents of depressed rural areas are among those who have been most severely affected by the contraction of the unemployment insurance program. One of the major changes made in this program in 1981 as part of that year's large federal budget cuts was to curtail the extended unemployment benefits program. The extended benefits program is designed to provide an additional thirteen weeks of benefits to jobless workers who live in high-unemployment areas, have been out of work for at least six months, and are still looking for employment. The 1981 budget cuts, however, greatly restricted the circumstances under which a state can qualify to provide extended benefits. In 1988 only one state—Alaska—qualified to provide these benefits. Nine other states with unemployment rates of 7 percent or more—including West Virginia, with a 9.9 percent rate that year, and Mississippi, with an 8.4 percent rate—failed to qualify. These nine states included some of the most rural states in the nation.

To address these problems, consideration could be given to modifying the criteria for determining when extended benefits are paid. This could be done both by broadening the criteria for determining where states can provide these benefits and by establishing additional criteria on a "substate" basis. Currently, extended benefits are provided only if an entire state qualifies. Substate criteria would enable regions of a state with very high unemployment to pay extended benefits to jobless workers, even if the entire state did not qualify. This would be of particular benefit to hard-pressed rural areas.

POLICIES TO ASSIST THE ELDERLY

Elderly people who are poor are generally in this condition because the benefit levels they receive from government programs are too low to lift them from poverty. (The elderly poor are generally not in a position to supplement their income from other sources.) This problem is particularly acute in rural areas.

The federal government's principal cash assistance program for the aged and disabled poor is the Supplemental Security Income program (SSI). While SSI benefits are substantially higher than AFDC benefits in most states, they leave many SSI beneficiaries well below the poverty line.

The basic federal SSI grant was $386 a month for single individuals in 1990 and $579 for couples. These payment levels equal 75 percent of the poverty line for an elderly person living alone and 89 percent of the poverty line for an elderly couple. For those SSI recipients who also receive modest Social Security payments, the situation is only a little better. For these people, combined federal SSI and Social Security payments equal $406 a month for individuals and $599 for couples.

To bring elderly and disabled SSI recipients closer to the poverty line, many states supplement the federal SSI benefits with state benefit payments. But these SSI state supplements tend to be small. In all except four states, combined federal and state SSI payments still do not reach the poverty line. Moreover, nearly half the states fail to provide SSI state supplements. Most of the states failing to provide these payments are rural states.

Only seven of the fifteen most rural states supplement federal SSI benefits, while twelve of the fifteen most urban states do. Furthermore, among those highly rural states that do pay SSI state supplements, the average supplement was just $38 a month in 1987. This is much lower than the average payment in the twelve highly urban states that provide these supplements; in these states the average monthly SSI supplement was $98 (Shapiro and Greenstein 1988). In addition, of the twenty-four states that provide no SSI supplement at all, twenty are states in which the proportion of residents living in rural areas exceeds the national average.

The strategies for addressing poverty among the rural elderly poor are not mysterious. They include raising the basic federal SSI benefit to the poverty line—or in the absence of such action at the federal level, establishing state SSI supplements in states now lacking them and increasing the size of the supplemental benefits in many states now providing them.

Outreach programs and efforts to improve access to SSI also are needed. It is estimated that only 50 percent to 60 percent of those eligible for SSI actually participate (ICF Incorporated 1988; Coe 1985; Leavitt and Schulz 1988). Increasing this rate could have significant effects on low-income rural elderly people.

TWO-PARENT FAMILIES

The rural poor are much more likely to be members of two-parent families than the urban poor are. Traditionally, two-parent families have been discriminated against in the U.S. welfare system. Until 1990, for example, states had the option of denying AFDC benefits to poor families with children in which both parents are present. Some twenty-three states, including many of the most rural states, declined to cover two-parent families.

The Family Support Act of 1988 altered this situation. Since October 1, 1990, all states have been required to cover two-parent families under AFDC. However, those states that did not cover two-parent families in the past can elect to provide benefits to such families for only six months in a twelve-month period. If a two-parent family is still impoverished after six months and continues to meet all other AFDC eligibility criteria, the state may cut off the family's benefits.

Twelve states have decided to limit AFDC benefits for two-parent families to six months; four of these states are among the ten most rural states in the nation. Furthermore, in the other eight states that selected six-month coverage, a highly disproportionate number of the families that could be cut off after six months are likely to be families residing in rural communities where unemployment remains high and jobs are not readily available.

OTHER POLICY INITIATIVES

In addition to the policy changes discussed earlier, several other policy initiatives would be of value. The federal minimum wage is unlikely to be restored fully to its purchasing power of the 1960s and 1970s. In fact, minimum-wage supporters may have a battle on their hands just to keep the $4.25-an-hour wage standard from eroding after 1991. As a result, it is unlikely that federal action alone will set the EITC/minimum-wage combination at a level sufficient to assure that families with a full-time minimum-wage worker are not poor.

State action is likely to be needed to attain this goal. States can help by establishing their own earned income credits—by the end of 1990, five states had done so—and by setting state minimum-wage levels above the federal wage standard. As of April 1990, ten states and the District of Columbia had minimum wages above the federal level of $3.80 an hour.

In addition, states can seek to "maximize" the federal dollars that come into their states through the SSI and Food Stamp programs by using outreach strategies to increase participation. As noted, only 50 percent to 60 percent of those eligible for SSI participate. In the Food Stamp program the overall participation rate is higher (about 60 percent of the eligible households are estimated to participate), but participation among the elderly and working poor is much lower. Some 37 percent of eligible low-income working households and 39 percent of eligible elderly households are estimated to participate (Doyle and Beebout 1988).

Rural areas have much to gain from increasing participation in the SSI and Food Stamp programs because the groups with the lowest participation rates— the low-income elderly and the working poor—are disproportionately rural. Effective outreach, including efforts to improve access and remove barriers to program participation, can be of particular benefit to rural residents.

Moreover, effective since July 1989, the federal government provides 50 percent matching funds for state Food Stamp outreach efforts, including outreach activities that states contract with nonprofit organizations to perform. This makes it less costly for states to engage in these activities.

There are also a number of other policy initiatives that, while largely beyond the scope of this chapter and not disproportionately rural in focus, would be beneficial. These range from better education, job-training, and basic-skills-improvement programs to expanded early intervention programs for poor children, such as Head Start. Increases in basic AFDC benefit levels, which have eroded badly in most states over the past two decades, also would benefit a sizeable number of poor rural single-parent families.

DISTRIBUTIONAL ISSUES

Finally, broad policy decisions affecting the distribution of income and resources among various income strata have significant consequences for the rural poor and for rural economies in general. Census data show that wealthy people are significantly underrepresented in rural areas, while poor people are overrepresented. This suggests that broad tax and transfer policies that redistribute income upward tend to cause a net outflow of income from rural areas.

Census data reveal that in 1988 only 11 percent of all rural households were in the top fifth of the U.S. income distribution, while 26 percent fell into the bottom fifth and 51 percent were in the bottom two-fifths. Looked at another way, only 12 percent of all households in the wealthiest fifth of the U.S. income distribution were households that lived in rural areas. By contrast, 29 percent of the households in the bottom fifth were rural residents (Barancik 1990). Given these figures, it is not surprising that as income disparities have widened in recent years between rich and poor U.S. households, income disparities between urban and rural residents have grown as well (Barancik 1990).

MOVING TOWARD THESE GOALS: SUPPORT FROM RURAL POLICYMAKERS?

Moving toward the policy goals presented here will require support from rural policymakers and opinion leaders. In the past such support often has not been forthcoming. There appears to be a substantial gap between the perceptions many policymakers have about the poverty population and poverty programs and the reality reflected in the data on these issues. Too often, poverty is seen by both rural and urban observers as an urban and primarily an inner-city phenomenon. Poverty policies and programs are assumed by many rural policymakers to be primarily urban in orientation.

This need not be the case. Various policies and programs to aid the working poor, the low-income elderly, and two-parent families—such as earned income credit outreach programs, elimination of state income tax burdens on working poor families, extension of health insurance to more adults in working poor families, increases in SSI benefits, and full-year AFDC eligibility for impoverished two-parent families—would disproportionately help the rural poor. Initiatives in these areas could make significant dents in rural poverty and would channel more resources into rural economies at the same time.

NOTES

Research on which this chapter is based was supported by the Ford Foundation's Rural Poverty and Resources Program and the Aspen Institute's Rural Economic Policy Program. The chapter draws heavily on several reports of the Center on Budget and Policy Priorities, including Shapiro and Greenstein 1990; Shapiro 1989; Porter 1989; Lazere, Leonard, and Kravitz 1989; and Barancik 1990.

1. In this chapter the term "rural" is used to refer to nonmetropolitan areas and residents as defined by the Census Bureau, while the term "urban" refers to metropolitan areas and residents.

2. For tax year 1990, an eligible family received a credit of fourteen cents for each dollar earned up to $6,810. At that level, a family qualified for the $953 maximum credit. The credit remained at $953 until earnings surpassed $10,730. The benefit then phased out at a slow pace, falling ten cents for each additional dollar of income until the credit reached zero at income of $20,264.

3. The Center on Budget and Policy Priorities initiated and helped coordinate the 1989 campaign to publicize the credit and the need for low-income working families to file a federal income tax return. The center added a rural component to the campaign in 1990. Efforts are needed on a much larger scale, however.

4. Ford Foundation 1989, p. 55. The panel recommended restoring the purchasing power of the minimum wage to its 1981 level. This is slightly below its average purchasing power in the 1970s.

The principal argument raised against a minimum-wage increase is that by raising the cost of labor, it decreases demand for labor and hence employment opportunities. Because of these labor-market effects, the task for policymakers is to set the minimum wage at a level that strikes the appropriate balance between positive income effects and negative employment effects. The adverse effects of restoring the minimum wage to its level of the 1960s and 1970s are likely to be modest, in part due to today's tight labor markets and the reduced number of youths projected to enter the labor market in the 1990s. For an analysis of the effects of the minimum wage on job opportunity, see Shapiro 1988.

5. Families with incomes up to $10,000 qualify for a 30 percent credit. The credit percentage then phases down as income rises, until income reaches $28,000. Families with incomes above $28,000 qualify for a 20 percent credit.

6. This discussion of state income taxes is drawn from Shapiro and Greenstein 1990. It is based on work by Frederick Hutchinson, state tax analyst at the Center on Budget and Policy Priorities.

7. Of all fifty states, thirty-three have a higher-than-average proportion of rural residents.

8. This combination of measures is beneficial to rural areas not only because working families are overrepresented in rural locations but also because upper-income families are underrepresented there. See Barancik 1990.

9. These data are from the American Housing Survey, 1987, which was conducted by the Census Bureau. The survey data contain separate breakouts for "nonmetropolitan" and "rural" households. Consistent with the practice used throughout this chapter, the term "rural" here refers to "nonmetropolitan" as defined by the Census Bureau.

10. Low-income renter households are defined as households with incomes below $10,000, as measured in 1987 dollars. A low-rent unit is a unit that rents for no more than 30 percent of the income of a household making $10,000 a year—that is, for no more than $250 a month, measured in 1987 dollars.

11. A fuller discussion of rural housing data can be found in Lazere, Leonard, and Kravitz 1989. This study shows that the housing-cost burdens faced by poor households are somewhat higher in urban than in rural areas, but that poor rural households are more likely to live in substandard housing than their urban counterparts.

References

Adams, Terry, and Greg J. Duncan. 1988. "The Persistence of Urban Poverty and its Demographic and Behavioral Correlates." Mimeo, Ann Arbor: Survey Research Center, University of Michigan.

Agee, James and Walker Evans. 1941. *Let Us Now Praise Famous Men*. Boston: Houghton-Mifflin.

Allen, Joyce, and Cynthia Rexroat. 1989. "Economic Recovery and the Economic Status of Southern Black Families Headed by Women: A Nonmetro/Metro Comparison." Unpublished research proposal to the Aspen Institute, Washington, D.C.

Amenta, Edwin and Theda Skocpol. 1988. "Redefining the New Deal: World War II and the Development of Social Provision in the United States." Pp. 81–122 in *The Politics of Social Policy in the United States*, edited by Margaret Weir, Ann S. Orloff, and Theda Skocpol. Princeton: Princeton University Press.

Arnow, Harriette. 1963. Review of Harry Caudill, *Night Comes to the Cumberlands*. *New York Times Book Review*, July 21, 1963, 25.

Auletta, Kenneth. 1982. *The Underclass*. New York: Random House.

Baca Zinn, Maxine. 1987. *Minority Families in Crisis: The Public Discussion*. Research Paper No. 6. Memphis: Center for Research on Women, Memphis State University.

Baca Zinn, Maxine, and Bonnie Thornton Dill. 1990. *Race and Gender: Re-visioning Social Relations*. Research paper no. 12. Memphis: Center for Research on Women, Memphis State University.

Baldwin, Sidney. 1968. *Poverty and Politics: The Rise and Decline of the Farm Security Administration*. Chapel Hill: University of North Carolina Press.

Ball, Richard A. 1968. "A Poverty Case: The Analgesic Subculture of the Southern Appalachians." *American Sociological Review* 33:885–95.

Balliett, Lee. 1978. "A Pleasing tho' Dreadful Sight: Social and Economic Impacts of Coal Production in the Eastern Coalfields." A Report to the Office of Technology Assessment, U.S. Congress.

Bane, Mary Jo. 1986. "Household Composition and Poverty." Pp. 209–31 in *Fighting Poverty: What Works and What Doesn't*, edited by Sheldon H. Danzinger and Daniel H. Weinberg. Cambridge, Mass.: Harvard University Press.

Bane, Mary Jo, and David Ellwood. 1986. "Slipping Into and Out of Poverty: The Dynamics of Spells." *Journal of Human Resources* 21 (1):1–23.

Barancik, Scott. 1990. *The Rural Disadvantage: Growing Income Disparities between Rural and Urban Areas.* Washington, D.C.: Center on Budget and Policy Priorities.

Baratz, Morton S. 1955. *The Union and the Coal Industry.* New Haven: Yale University Press.

Barnes, Roberta Ott. 1988. *The Distributional Effects of Alternative Child Care Proposals.* Washington, D.C.: Urban Institute.

Barr, Donald J., A. Demarco, C. H. Feuer, and R. L. Whittlesey. 1988. *Liberalism to the Test: African-American Migrant Farm Workers and the State of New York.* Ithaca, N.Y.: Department of Human Service Studies, Cornell University.

Beaulieu, Lionel J., ed. 1988. *The Rural South in Crisis.* Boulder, Colo.: Westview Press.

Becketti, Sean, William Gould, Lee Lillard, and Finis Welch. 1988. "The Panel Study of Income Dynamics after Fourteen Years: An Evaluation." *Journal of Labor Economics* 6(4): 472–92.

Bellah, Robert N., Richard Madsen, William S. Sullivan, Ann Swidler, and Stephen M. Tipton. 1985. *Habits of the Heart: Individualism and Commitment in American Life.* Berkeley: University of California Press.

Bellamy, Donald S., and Linda M. Ghelfi. 1989. "Southern Persistently Low-Income Counties: Social and Economic Characteristics." Pp. 51–61 in *Rural Development Issues of the Nineties: Perspectives from the Social Sciences,* edited by Thomas T. Williams, Walter A. Hill, and Ralph D. Christy. Proceedings of the 46th Annual Professional Agricultural Workers Conference, December 4–6, 1988. Tuskegee University, Tuskegee, Alabama.

Bender, Lloyd D., Bernal L. Green, Thomas F. Hady, John A. Kuehn, Marlys K. Nelson, Leon B. Perkinson, and Peggy J. Ross. 1985. *The Diverse Social and Economic Structure of Nonmetropolitan America.* Rural Development Research Report no. 49. Washington, D.C.: Economic Research Service, U.S. Department of Agriculture, September.

Beneria, Loudes, and Gita Sen. 1981. "Accumulation, Reproduction, and Women's Roles in Economic Development: Boserup Revisited." *Signs: Journal of Women in Culture and Society* 7(2):279–98.

Bixby, Ann Kallman. 1989. "Public Social Welfare Expenditures, Fiscal Year 1986." *Social Security Bulletin* 52(2):29–39.

Blee, Kathleen M., and Dwight B. Billings. 1986. "Reconstructing Daily Life in the Past: A Hermeneutical Approach to Ethnographic Data." *Sociological Quarterly* 27, no. 4 (Winter):443–62.

Bleiweis, Phyllis R., R. C. Reynolds, L. D. Cohen, and N. A. Butler. 1977. "Health Care Characteristics of Migrant Agricultural Workers in Three North Florida Counties." *Journal of Community Health* 3(1):32–43.

Bloomquist, Leonard E. 1987. "Performance in the Rural Manufacturing Sector." In *Rural Economic Development in the 1980's: Prospects for the Future,* edited by David L. Brown, J. Norman Reid, Herman Bluestone, David A. McGranahan, and Sara M. Mazie. Rural Development Research Report no. 69. Washington, D.C.: Economic Research Service, U.S. Department of Agriculture.

Bloomquist, Leonard E., Leif Jensen, and Ruy A. Teixeira. 1988. "Too Few Jobs for Workfare to Put Many to Work." *Rural Development Perspectives* 5(1):8–12.

Bluestone, Barry, and Bennett Harrison. 1982. *The Deindustrialization of America*. New York: Basic Books.

———. 1988. "The Growth of Low-Wage Employment 1963 to 1986." *Papers and Proceedings of the American Economic Review* 78(2):124–28.

Bradbury, Katharine. 1986. "The Shrinking Middle Class." *New England Economic Review*, September/October, 41–54.

Brown, Charles C. 1988. "Minimum Wage Laws: Are They Overrated?" *Journal of Economic Perspectives* 2(3):133–46.

Brown, David L., and Kenneth L. Deavers. 1987. "Rural Change and the Rural Economic Policy Agenda for the 1980's." In Agriculture and Rural Economy Division, *Rural Economic Development in the 1980's*. Washington, D.C.: Economic Research Service, Department of Agriculture.

Brown, David L., and Mildred Warner. 1989. "Persistent Low Income Nonmetropolitan Areas in the United States: Some Conceptual Challenges for Development Policy." In *National Rural Studies Committee: A Proceedings*, edited by Emery Castle and Barbara Baldwin. Eugene, Oreg.: Western Rural Development Center, Oregon State University.

Brown, James S. 1972. "Migration: Take It or Leave It." Pp. 130–44 in *Appalachia in the Sixties: Decade of Reawakening*, edited by David S. Walls and John B. Stephenson. Lexington: University Press of Kentucky.

Bureau of Indian Affairs. 1985. *Local Estimates of Resident Indian Population and Labor Force Status*. Mimeo. Washington, D.C.: U.S. Department of Interior.

Burnham, Linda. 1986. "Has Poverty Been Feminized in Black America?" In *For Crying Out Loud: Women and Poverty in the United States*, edited by Rochelle Lefkowitz and Ann Withorn. New York: Pilgrim Press.

Butler, Stuart M. 1990. "No Truce in the War on Poverty." *New York Times*, August 12.

Callahan, Nancy. 1987. *The Freedom Quilting Bee*. Tuscaloosa: University of Alabama Press.

Caudill, Harry. 1963. *Night Comes to the Cumberlands: A Biography of a Depressed Region*. Boston: Little, Brown.

Cautley, E., D. P. Slesinger, and P. Parra. 1985. *Children of Migrant Agricultural Workers in Wisconsin*. Department of Rural Sociology, University of Wisconsin, Madison.

Chestnut, J. L., Jr., and Julia Cass. 1990. *Black in Selma*. New York: Farrar, Straus, and Giroux.

Children's Defense Fund. 1988. *Vanishing Dreams: The Growing Economic Plight of America's Young Families*. Washington, D.C.: Children's Defense Fund.

Chollet, Deborah. 1988. *Uninsured in the United States: The Nonelderly Population without Health Insurance, 1986*. Washington, D.C.: Employee Benefit Research Institute.

Clark, K. B. 1965. *Dark Ghetto: Dilemmas of Social Power*. New York: Harper and Row.

Clinton, Lawrence, Bruce A. Chadwick, and Howard M. Bahr. 1975. "Urban Relocation Reconsidered: Antecedents of Employment among Indian Males." *Rural Sociology* 40:117–33.

Cobb, James C. 1982. *The Selling of the South: The Southern Crusade for Industrial Development, 1936–1980.* Baton Rouge: Louisiana State University Press.

———. 1984. *Industrialization and Southern Society, 1877–1984.* Lexington: University Press of Kentucky.

———. 1990. "Somebody Done Nailed Us on the Cross: Federal Farm and Welfare Policy and the Civil Rights Movement in the Mississippi Delta." *The Journal of American History* 76:912–36.

Cochrane, Willard W. 1979. *The Development of American Agriculture: A Historical Analysis.* Minneapolis: University of Minnesota Press.

Coe, Richard C. 1985. "Nonparticipation in the SSI Program by Eligible Elderly." *Southern Economic Journal* 52:891–97.

Colclough, Glenna. 1988. "Uneven Development and Racial Composition in the Deep South, 1970–1980." *Rural Sociology* 53:73–86.

Coles, Robert. 1971. *Migrants, Sharecroppers, Mountaineers: Vol. II of Children of Crisis.* Boston: Little, Brown.

Collins, Patricia Hill. 1990. *Black Feminist Thought.* Boston: Unwin Hyman.

Commercial Appeal. 1987. "Attitudes of Regions Studied." Thursday, November 12.

Committee on Federalism and National Purpose. 1985. *To Form a More Perfect Union.* Washington, D.C.: National Conference on Social Welfare.

Congressional Quarterly. 1968. *Congressional Quarterly Almanac 1967.* Washington, D.C.: Congressional Quarterly.

———. 1969. *Congressional Quarterly Almanac 1968.* Washington, D.C.: Congressional Quarterly.

———. 1973. *Congressional Quarterly Almanac 1972.* Washington, D.C.: Congressional Quarterly.

———. 1974. *Congressional Quarterly Almanac 1973.* Washington, D.C.: Congressional Quarterly.

———. 1983. *Congressional Quarterly Almanac 1982.* Washington, D.C.: Congressional Quarterly.

———. 1984. *Congressional Quarterly Almanac 1983.* Washington, D.C.: Congressional Quarterly.

———. 1988. *Congressional Quarterly Almanac 1987.* Washington, D.C.: Congressional Quarterly.

Congressional Record. 1964. July 23, 16704–6.

Corbin, David Alan. 1981. *Life, Work, and Rebellion in the Coal Fields: The Southern West Virginia Miners, 1880–1922.* Urbana: University of Illinois Press.

Corcoran, Mary, Rodger Gordon, Deborah Laren, and Gary Solon. 1987. "Intergenerational Transmission of Education, Income, and Earnings." Mimeo. Ann Arbor: University of Michigan.

Cottingham, Pheobe H., and David T. Ellwood, eds. 1989. *Welfare Policy for the 1990s.* Cambridge, Mass.: Harvard University Press.

Coulter, John L. 1912. "Agricultural Laborers in the United States." *Annals of the American Academy of Political and Social Science* 48(2):30–44.

Daberkow, Stan G., and Herman Bluestone. *Patterns of Change in the Metro and Nonmetro Labor Force, 1976–82.* Rural Development Research Report no. 44. Washington, D.C.: Economic Research Service, U.S. Department of Agriculture.

Danhof, Clarence. 1964. "Four Decades of Thought on the South's Economic Problems."

Pp. 7–68 in *Essays in Southern Economic Development*, edited by Melvin L. Greenhut and W. Tate Whitman. Chapel Hill: University of North Carolina Press.

Daniel, Cletus E. 1981. *Bitter Harvest: A History of California Farm Workers, 1870–1941.* Berkeley: University of California Press.

Danziger, Sheldon, and Peter Gottschalk. 1985. "How Have Families with Children Been Faring?" Report to the Joint Economic Committee. Washington: D.C.: U.S. Congress.

Danziger, Sheldon H., and Daniel H. Weinberg. 1986. *Fighting Poverty: What Works and What Doesn't.* Cambridge, Mass.: Harvard University Press.

David, Martin, and John Fitzgerald. 1988. *Measuring Poverty and Crises: A Comparison of Annual and Subannual Accounting Periods Using the Survey of Income and Program Participation.* SIPP Working Paper no. 8805. Washington, D.C.: U.S. Bureau of the Census, July.

Davidson, Osha Gray. 1989. "Doing Home Work down on the Farm." *The Nation* 249:87–90.

Deavers, Kenneth L. 1989a. "Rural Development in the 1990's: Data and Research Needs." Paper prepared for the Rural Social Science Symposium, "New Directions in Data, Information, and their Uses." American Agricultural Economics Association Annual Meeting, Baton Rouge, Louisiana.

———. 1989b. "Scope and Dimensions of Problems Facing Rural America." Pp. 33–42 in *Rural Development Issues of the Nineties: Perspectives from the Social Sciences.* Proceedings of the 46th Annual Professional Agricultural Workers Conference, December 4–6, 1988, Tuskegee University, Alabama.

Delta Democrat Times. 1983. "McLaurin Seeks Post." September 4.

Development Associates. 1983. *Final Report: The Evaluation of the Impact of the Part A Entitlement Program Funded under Title IV of the Indian Education Act.* Arlington, Va.: Development Associates.

Dill, Bonnie Thornton. 1988. "Female-Headed Families in the Rural Mid-South." Unpublished research proposal to the Aspen Institute, Washington, D.C.

Dillman, Caroline. 1988. *Southern Women.* New York: Hemisphere Publishing Co.

Doyle, Jack. 1979. *Lines Across the Land.* Washington, D.C.: Environmental Policy Institute.

Doyle, Pat, and Harold Beebout. 1988. *Food Stamp Program Participation Rates.* Washington, D.C.: Mathematica Policy Research, Inc. and Food and Nutrition Service, U.S. Department of Agriculture.

Duncan, Cynthia M. 1985. "Capital and the State in Regional Economic Development." Ph.D. diss., University of Kentucky.

Duncan, Cynthia M. 1987. "Public Policy for Good People in a Bad Economy and Bad Politics." Proceedings of the October, 1986, conference *The Land and Economy of Appalachia*, Lexington.

Duncan, Cynthia M., and Ann R. Tickamyer. 1988. "Poverty Research and Policy for Rural America." *American Sociologist* 19(3):243–59.

Duncan, Greg J. 1983. "The Implications of Changing Family Composition for the Dynamic Analysis of Family Economic Well-Being." In *Panel Data on Incomes*, edited by A. B. Atkinson and F. A. Cowell. London: London School of Economics.

Duncan, Greg J., Richard D. Coe, Mary E. Corcoran, Martha S. Hill, Saul D. Hoffman, and James N. Morgan. 1984. *Years of Poverty, Years of Plenty: The Changing*

Economic Fortunes of American Workers and Families. Ann Arbor, Mich.: Institute for Social Research.

Duncan, Greg J., and Daniel H. Hill. 1989. "Assessing the Quality of Household Panel Survey Data: The Case of the PSID." *Journal of Business and Economics Statistics* 4:441–51.

Duncan, Greg J., and Willard Rodgers. 1987. "Single-Parent Families: Are Their Economic Problems Transitory or Persistent?" *Family Planning Perspectives* 19(4):171–78.

Eberts, Paul. 1984. *Socioeconomic Trends in Rural New York State: Toward the 21st Century.* Albany: New York State University Press.

Eberts, Paul and Marwan Khawaja. 1988. "Changing Socioeconomic Conditions in Rural Localities in the 1980s: Experiences in New York State." Ithaca, NY: Cornell University Agricultural Experiment Station, Bulletin No. 152.

Economic Development and Technical Assistance Center, 1987. *1986 Population Estimates and 1985 per Capita Income Estimates for Subcounty Areas of New York State.* Plattsburgh, N.Y.: Economic Development and Technical Assistance Center.

Eisenhower, President Dwight D. Message to Congress, June 23, 1954

Eller, Ronald D. 1982. *Miners, Millhands, and Mountaineers: Industrialization of the Appalachian South, 1880–1930.* Knoxville: University of Tennessee Press.

Ellwood, David T. 1986. *Targeting Would-be Long-Term Recipients of AFDC.* Princeton, N.J.: Mathematica Policy Research.

———. 1988. *Poor Support: Poverty in the American Family.* New York: Basic Books.

Erikson, Kai. 1976. *Everything in Its Path: Destruction of Community in the Buffalo Creek Flood.* New York: Simon and Schuster.

Falk, William W., and Thomas A. Lyson. 1988. *High Tech, Low Tech, No Tech: Recent Industrial and Occupational Change in the South.* Albany: State University of New York Press.

Farm Tenancy. 1937. *The Report of the President's Committee on Farm Tenancy.* 1937. Washington, D.C.: U.S. Government Printing Office.

Feagin, Joe R. 1989. *Race and Ethnic Relations.* 3d ed. Englewood Cliffs, N.J.: Prentice-Hall.

Ferguson, T. J., E. Richard Hart, and Calbert Seciwa. 1988. "Twentieth Century Zuni Political and Economic Development in Relation to Federal Indian Policy." Pp. 113–44 in *Public Policy Impacts on American Indian Economic Development,* edited by C. M. Snipp. Albuquerque: Institute for Native American Development, University of New Mexico.

Fetterman, John. 1967. *Stinking Creek.* New York: Dutton.

Finegold, Kenneth. 1988. "Agriculture and the Politics of U.S. Social Provision: Social Insurance and Food Stamps." Pp. 199–234 in *The Politics of Social Policy in the United States,* edited by Margaret Weir, Ann S. Orloff, and Theda Skocpol. Princeton, N.J.: Princeton University Press.

Fitchen, Janet M. 1981. *Poverty in Rural America: A Case Study.* Boulder, Colo.: Westview Press.

———. 1991. *Endangered Spaces, Enduring Places: Change, Identity, and Survival in Rural America.* Boulder, Colo.: Westview Press.

Fixico, Donald L. 1986. *Termination and Relocation: Federal Indian Policy, 1945–1960.* Albuquerque: University of New Mexico Press.

Flora, Cornelia Butler, and Jan L. Flora. 1988. "Public Policy, Farm Size, and Community Well-Being in Farming-dependent Counties of the Plains." Pp. 76–129 in *Agriculture and Community Change in the U.S.: The Congressional Research Reports*, edited by Louis E. Swanson. Boulder, Colo.: Westview Press.

Flora, Cornelia B., and Sue Johnson. 1973. "Discarding the Distaff: New Roles for Rural Women." In *Rural U.S.A.: Persistence and Change*, edited by Thomas Ford. Ames: Iowa State University Press.

Flora, Jan L., Cornelia B. Flora, Yu-Ching Cheng, Dwight Dickson, Mohammad Amin ul-Karim, and Yun-Ji Qian. 1990. "The Changing Structure of Communities in the 1980s: The Kansas Case." Pp. 89–99 in *Sustainable Rural Communities in Canada*, edited by Michael E. Gertler and Harold R. Bake. Saskatchewan: Canadian Agriculture and Restructuring Group.

Ford Foundation. 1989. *The Common Good: Social Welfare and the American Future*. Project on Social Welfare and the American Future, Policy Recommendations of the Executive Panel. New York: Ford Foundation.

Frederickson, Mary. 1989. "Working Women." In *Encyclopedia of Southern Culture*, edited by Charles R. Wilson and William Ferris. Chapel Hill: University of North Carolina Press.

Friedland, William H., and Dorothy Nelkin. 1971. *Migrant Agricultural Workers in America's Northeast*. New York: Holt, Rinehart and Winston.

Friedmann, Harriet. 1978. "World Market, State, and Family Farm: Social Bases of Household Production in an Era of Wage Labor." *Comparative Studies in Society and History* 20:545–86.

Fuguitt, Glenn, and Calvin Beale. 1984. "Changes in Population, Employment, and Industrial Composition in Nonmetropolitan America." Paper presented at the Annual Meeting of the Population Association of America, Minneapolis, Minnesota, May.

Galbraith, John K. 1984. *The Affluent Society*. 4th ed. Boston: Houghton Mifflin.

Gallaher, Art. 1961. *Plainville Fifteen Years Later*. New York: Columbia University Press.

Galston, William A. 1985. *A Tough Row to Hoe: The 1985 Farm Bill and Beyond*. Washington, D.C.: Roosevelt Center for American Policy Studies.

Garnick, Daniel H. 1984. "Shifting Balances in U.S. Metropolitan and Nonmetropolitan Area Growth." *International Regional Science Review* 9(3):257–73.

———. 1985. "Patterns of Growth in Metropolitan and Nonmetropolitan Areas: An Update." *Survey of Current Business* 65:33–38.

Garnick, Daniel H., and Howard L. Friedenberg. 1982. "Accounting for Regional Differences in Per Capita Personal Income Growth, 1929–79." *Survey of Current Business* 62:24–34.

Getz, Virginia K., and Robert A. Hoppe. 1983. "The Changing Characteristics of the Nonmetro Poor." *Social Development Issues* 7(1):29–44.

Goldfarb, Ronald L. 1981. *Migrant Farm Workers: A Caste of Despair*. Ames: Iowa State University Press.

Goodwin, H. L., Jr., and Lonnie L. Jones. 1986. "The Importance of Off-Farm Income in the United States." *Rural Sociologist* 6(4).

Goodwyn, Lawrence. 1978. *The Populist Moment: A Short History of the Agrarian Revolt in America*. London: Oxford University Press.

Gorham, Lucy, and Bennett Harrison. 1990. *Working below the Poverty Line: The*

Growing Problem of Low Earnings across the United States. Washington, D.C.: Aspen Institute for Humanistic Studies.

Graebner, William. 1974. "Great Expectations: The Search for Order in Bituminous Coal, 1890–1917." *Business History Review* 48(1):49–72.

Gramlich, Edward. 1986. "The Main Themes." Pp. 341–57 in *Fighting Poverty: What Works and What Doesn't*, edited by Sheldon H. Danziger and Daniel H. Weinberg. Cambridge, Mass.: Harvard University Press.

Greenstein, R. 1987. Unpublished proposal to Aspen Institute, Washington, D.C., for a project on rural poverty issues.

Greenwood Commonwealth. 1983a. "Blacks to Seek Utility Posts." March 29.

———. 1983b. "Black Groups Challenge Delta Electric." April 13.

Gross, Emma. 1989. *Contemporary Federal Policy Toward American Indians.* Westport, Conn.: Greenwood Press.

Hackney, Sheldon. 1969. *Populism to Progressivism in Alabama.* Princeton, N.J.: Princeton University Press.

Hahn, Steven. 1983. *The Roots of Southern Populism.* London: Oxford University Press.

Hall, Jacqueline Dowd. 1979. *Revolt against Chivalry: Jessie Daniel Ames and the Campaign against Lynching.* New York: Columbia University Press.

Hansen, Niles. 1979. "The New International Division of Labor and Manufacturing Decentralization in the United States." *Review of Regional Studies* 9:1–11.

Harrington, Michael. 1962. *The Other America: Poverty in the United States.* New York: Penguin Books Ltd.

———. 1984. *The New American Poverty.* New York: Holt, Rinehart and Winston.

Harris, Fred R., and Roger W. Wilkins, 1988. *Quiet Riots: Race and Poverty in the United States.* New York: Pantheon.

Heatherly, Charles L., and Burton Yale Pines. 1989. *Mandate for Leadership III: Policy Strategies for the 1990s.* Washington, D.C.: Heritage Foundation.

Helco, Hugh. 1986. "The Political Foundations of Anti-Poverty Policy." Pp. 312–40 in *Fighting Poverty: What Works and What Doesn't*, edited by Sheldon H. Danziger and Daniel H. Weinberg. Cambridge, Mass.: Harvard University Press.

Hendrickson, Susan E., and Isabel V. Sawhill. 1989. *Assisting the Working Poor.* Changing Domestic Priorities Discussion Paper. Washington, D.C.: The Urban Institute.

Henry, Mark, Mark Drabenstott, and Lynn Gibson. 1986. "A Changing Rural America." *Economic Review* 7/8:23–41.

———. 1987. "Rural Growth Slows Down." *Rural Development Perspectives* 6:25–30.

Hill, Martha S., and Greg J. Duncan. 1987. "Parental Family Income and the Socioeconomic Attainment of Children." *Social Science Research* 16:39–73.

Hill, Martha S., and Heidi Hartmann. 1988. *The Employment of Mothers and the Prevention of Poverty.* SIPP Working Paper no. 8826. Washington, D.C.: U.S. Bureau of the Census.

Hill, Samuel S. 1989. "Civil Rights and Religion." In *Encyclopedia of Southern Culture*, edited by Charles R. Wilson and William Ferris. Chapel Hill: University of North Carolina Press.

Hirschman, Albert. 1958. *The Strategy of Economic Development.* New Haven, Conn.: Yale University Press.

Hodge, William H. 1971. "Navajo Urban Migration: An Analysis from the Perspective of the Family." Pp. 346–391 in *The American Indian in Urban Society*, edited by Jack O. Waddell and O. Michael Watson. Boston, Mass.: Little, Brown.

Hofstadter, Richard. 1955. *The Age of Reform*. New York: Vintage Books.

Hoppe, Robert A. 1985. *Economic Structure and Change in Persistently Low-Income Nonmetro Counties*. Rural Development Research Report no. 50. Washington, D.C.: Economic Research Service, U.S. Department of Agriculture, October.

———. 1987. "Shifting Income Patterns: Implications for Nonmetro America." *Rural Development Perspectives* 2:2–5.

———. 1988. "Two Types of Poverty, Two Types of Policy." Paper presented at the symposium "Toward Rural Development Policy for the 1990s: Enhancing Income and Employment Opportunities." Washington, D.C.

Hoppe, Robert A., and William E. Saupe. 1982. *Transfer Payments in Nonmetropolitan Areas*. Staff Report no. AGES820827. Washington, D.C.: Economic Research Service, U.S. Department of Agriculture.

Horan, Patrick M., and Charles M. Tolbert II. 1984. *The Organization of Work in Rural and Urban Labor Markets*. Boulder, Colo.: Westview Press.

Hoxie, Frederick E. 1984. *A Final Promise: The Campaign to Assimilate the Indians, 1880–1920*. Lincoln: University of Nebraska Press.

ICF Incorporated. 1988. *Rates of Participation of the Elderly in the Supplemental Security Income Program*. Baltimore, Md.: Commonwealth Fund Commission on Elderly People Living Alone.

Isensee, Lynne Crofton, and Nancy Duff Campbell. 1987. *Dependent Care Tax Provisions in the States: An Opportunity for Reform*. Washington, D.C.: National Women's Law Center.

Jackson Clarion-Ledger. 1983. "Electric Coops Seat an All-White Board." June 15.

James, David R. 1988. "The Transformation of the Southern Racial State: Class and Race Determinants of Local State Structure." *American Sociological Review* 53(2):191–208.

Jaynes, Gerald David, and Robin M. Williams, Jr, eds. 1989. *A Common Destiny: Blacks and American Society*. Washington, D.C.: National Academy Press.

Jenkins, J. Craig. 1985. *The Politics of Insurgency: The Farm Worker Movement in the 1960s*. New York: Columbia University Press.

Jensen, Leif. 1987. "Rural Minority Families in the United States: A Twenty-Year Profile of Poverty and Economic Well-Being." Paper presented at the 1987 Meetings of the Rural Sociological Society. Washington, D.C.: Economic Research Service.

Johnson, James P. 1979. *The Politics of Soft Coal: The Bituminous Industry from World War I through the New Deal*. Urbana: University of Illinois Press.

Joint Center for Political Studies. 1989. *Black Elected Officials: National Roster*. Washington, D.C.: Joint Center for Political Studies.

Jones, G. C. 1985. *Growing Up Hard in Harlan County*. Lexington: University Press of Kentucky.

Jones, Jacqueline. 1985. *Labor of Love, Labor of Sorrow*. New York: Basic Books.

Kalbacher, Judith Z., and Nora L. Brooks. 1990. "Farmers Are Part of American Mainstream." *Choices* 5:22–23.

Kasarda, John. 1989. "Urban Industrial Transition and the Underclass." Pp. 26–47 in *The Ghetto Underclass: Social Science Perspectives*, edited by William J. Wilson. Annals of the American Academy of Political and Social Science, vol. 501. Newbury Park, Calif.: Sage Publications.

Katz, Michael B. 1989. *The Undeserving Poor: From the War on Poverty to the War on Welfare*. New York: Pantheon.

Kentucky Coal Association and the Governor's Office for Coal and Energy Policy. 1989. *Kentucky Coal Facts, 1989–90 Pocket Guide*. Lexington: Kentucky Coal Association.

Key, V. O. 1949. *Southern Politics in State and Nation*. New York: Knopf.

Killian, Lewis M. 1970. *White Southerners*. New York: Random House.

Kirkendall, Richard S. 1966. *Social Scientists and Farm Politics in the Age of Roosevelt*. Columbia: University of Missouri Press.

Kloppenburg, Jack R., and Charles C. Geisler. 1985. "The Agricultural Ladder: Agrarian Ideology and the Changing Structure of U.S. Agriculture." *Journal of Rural Studies* 1(1):59–72.

Kornblum, William. 1984. "Lumping the Poor: What Is the 'Underclass'?" *Dissent* 31(3):295–302.

Lantz, Herman. 1964. "Resignation, Industrialization, and the Problem of Social Change: A Case History of a Coal-mining Community." In *Blue-Collar World*, edited by Arthur B. Shostak and William Gomberg. Englewood Cliffs, N.J.: Prentice-Hall.

———. 1971. *People of Coal Town*. Carbondale: Southern Illinois University Press.

LaRochelle, Richard. 1984. "Minority Participation in Rural Electric Cooperatives." Memorandum, July 17. Washington, D.C.: Rural Electrification Administration, U.S. Department of Agriculture.

Lazere, Edward B., Paul A. Leonard, and Linda L. Kravitz. 1989. *The Other Housing Crisis: Sheltering the Poor in Rural America*. Washington, D.C.: Center on Budget and Policy Priorities and Housing Assistance Council.

Leacock, Eleanor Burke. 1971. *The Culture of Poverty: A Critique*. New York: Simon and Schuster.

Leavitt, Thomas D., and James H. Schulz. 1988. *Time to Reform the SSI Asset Test?* Washington, D.C.: Public Policy Institute, American Association of Retired Persons.

Lefkowitz, Rochelle, and Ann Withorn, eds. 1986. *For Crying Out Loud: Women and Poverty in the United States*. New York: Pilgrim Press.

Lemann, Nicolas. 1986. "The Origins of the Underclass." *Atlantic Monthly* 6:31–55; 7:54–68.

Lerner, Gerda. 1972. *Black Women in White America*. New York: Pantheon Books.

Levine, Richard. 1990. "After Gains of the 80s, Northeast Is Lagging in the Growth of Jobs." *New York Times*, April 25.

Levitan, Sar A. 1964. *Federal Aid to Depressed Areas*. Baltimore, Md.: Johns Hopkins University Press.

———. 1985. *Programs in Aid of the Poor*. 5th ed. Baltimore, Md.: Johns Hopkins University Press.

Levitan, Sar A., and Barbara Hetrick. 1971. *Big Brother's Indian Programs with Reservations*. New York: McGraw-Hill Books.

Levitan, Sar, and William B. Johnston. 1975. *Indian Giving: Federal Programs for Native Americans*. Baltimore, Md.: Johns Hopkins University Press.

Levitan, Sar, and Isaac Shapiro. 1987. *Working But Poor*. Baltimore, Md.: Johns Hopkins University Press.

Levy, Frank. 1987. *Dollars and Dreams: The Changing American Income Distribution*. New York: The Russell Sage Foundation.

Lewis, Oscar. 1959. *Five Families: Mexican Case Studies in the Culture of Poverty.* New York: Basic Books.

———. 1969. "The Culture of Poverty." Pp. 187–220 in *On Understanding Poverty,* edited by D. P. Moynihan. New York: Basic Books.

———. 1971. "The Culture of Poverty." In *Poverty in America: A Book of Readings,* edited by Louis A. Ferman, Joyce L. Kornbluh, and Alan Haber. Ann Arbor: University of Michigan Press.

Lichter, Daniel T. 1988. "Race and Underemployment: Black Employment Hardship in the Rural South." In *The Rural South in Crisis,* edited by Lionel J. Beaulieu. Boulder, Colo.: Westview Press.

———. 1989. "Race, Employment Hardship, and Inequality in the American Nonmetropolitan South." *American Sociological Review* 54(3):436–46.

Light, Ivan H. 1972. *Ethnic Enterprise in America: Business and Welfare Among Chinese, Japanese, and Blacks.* Berkeley: University of California Press.

Lyson, Thomas. 1988. "Economic Development in the Rural South: An Uneven Past—An Uncertain Future." In *The Rural South in Crisis,* edited by Lionel J. Beaulieu. Boulder, Colo.: Westview Press.

———. 1989. *Two Sides to the Sunbelt.* New York: Praeger.

Majchrowicz, T. Alexander, and Linda M. Ghelfi. 1988. *Employment and Earnings in Nonmetro Industry, 1979–86.* Economic Research Service, U. S. Department of Agriculture, Agriculture Information Bulletin no. 552. Washington, D.C.: November.

Majka, Linda C., and Theo J. Majka. 1982. *Farm Workers, Agribusiness, and the State.* Philadelphia: Temple University Press.

Manufacturers Record. 1913. "Development or Exploitation?" 63 (April 17).

Marshall, Ray, and Lamond Godwin. 1971. *Cooperatives and Rural Poverty in the South.* Baltimore, Md.: John Hopkins University Press.

Martin, Philip L. 1988. *Harvest of Confusion: Migrant Workers in U.S. Agriculture.* Boulder, Colo.: Westview Press.

McClanahan, Sara, and Irwin Garfinkel. 1989. "Single Mothers, the Underclass, and Social Policy." Pp. 92–104 in *The Ghetto Underclass,* edited by William J. Wilson. Newbury Park, Calif.: Sage Publications.

McDonald, Laughlin. 1989. "The Quiet Revolution in Minority Voting Rights." *Vanderbilt Law Review* 42:1249–97.

McGranahan, David A. 1987. "Rural Workers in the National Economy." In *Rural Economic Development in the 1980's: Prospects for the Future,* edited by David L. Brown, J. Norman Reid, Herman Bluestone, David A. McGranahan, and Sarah M. Mazie. Rural Development Research Report no. 69. Washington, D.C.: Economic Research Service, U.S. Department of Agriculture.

McLeod, Jay. 1990. *Mind Stayed on Freedom.* Lexington, Miss.: Rural Organizing and Cultural Center.

Mertz, Paul. 1978. *New Deal Policy and Southern Rural Poverty.* Baton Rouge: Louisiana State University Press.

Miernyk, William. 1979. *Coal: Problems and Prospects in the 1980s.* Reprint Series 10(9). Morgantown: Regional Research Institute, West Virginia University.

Miller, S. M. 1966. "Appalachia Invents Its Future." Unpublished paper delivered at conference on "Manpower in Appalachia," West Virginia University.

Mines, Rick. 1990. Research Director, National Commission on Agricultural Workers. Personal communication. Washington, D.C.

Morland, Kenneth. 1958. *Millways of Kent*. Chapel Hill: University of North Carolina Press.

Morris, Austin P. 1945. "Agricultural Labor and National Labor Legislation." *California Law Review* 54(1):1939–89.

Morrissey, Elizabeth S. 1985. *Characteristics of Poverty in Nonmetro Counties*. Rural Development Research Report no. 52. Washington D.C.: Economic Research Service, U.S. Department of Agriculture.

Mountain Association for Community Economic Development, Inc. (MACED). 1986. *Coal and Economic Development*. Volumes 1–6. Berea, Ky.: MACED, Inc.

Moyers, B. 1986. "The Vanishing Black Family." CBS News Special Report.

Moynihan, D. P. 1965. *The Negro Family: The Case for National Action*. Washington, D.C.: Office of Policy Planning and Research, U.S. Department of Labor.

———. 1986. *Family and Nation*. New York: Harcourt Brace Jovanovich.

Munnell, Alicia H. 1987. "Lessons from the Income Maintenance Experiments: An Overview." *New England Economic Review*, May/June: 32–45.

Murray, Charles. 1984. *Losing Ground: American Social Policy, 1950–1980*. New York: Basic Books.

Myrdal, Gunnar. 1970. *The Challenge of World Poverty*. New York: Pantheon.

National Emergency Council. *Report to the President on the Economic Conditions of the South*. 1938. Washington, D.C.: U.S. Government Printing Office.

New York Times. 1984. "Electric Co-ops Facing Challenges on Racial Make-up of Boards." March 5.

Office of Equal Opportunity. 1981. *Equal Opportunity Report, U.S.D.A. Programs in 1980*. Washington, D.C.: U.S. Department of Agriculture.

O'Hare, William P. 1988. *The Rise of Poverty in Rural America*. Washington, D.C.: Population Reference Bureau.

Oliveira, Victor J., and E. Jane Cox. 1988. *The Agricultural Work Force in 1985: A Statistical Profile*. Economic Research Service, U.S. Department of Agriculture, Agricultural Economic Report 582. Washington, D.C.: U.S. Government Printing Office.

Olson, Mary B. 1988. "The Legal Road to Economic Development: Fishing Rights in Western Washington." Pp. 77–112 in *Public Policy Impacts on American Indian Economic Development*, edited by C. M. Snipp. Albuquerque: Institute for Native American Development, University of New Mexico.

Orshansky, Mollie. 1963. "Children of the Poor." *Social Security Bulletin* 26(7):3–13.

Osterman, Paul. 1990. "Welfare Participation in a Full Employment Economy: The Impact of Family Structure and Neighborhood." Unpublished manuscript. Cambridge, Mass.: Massachusetts Institute of Technology.

Parker, Frank R. 1990. *Black Votes Count: Political Empowerment after 1965*. Chapel Hill: University of North Carolina Press.

Parker, Glen L. 1940. *The Coal Industry: A Study in Social Control*. Washington, D.C.: American Council on Public Affairs.

Patterson, James T. 1986. *America's Struggle against Poverty, 1900–1985*. Cambridge, Mass.: Harvard University Press.

Pearce, Diana M. 1978. "The Feminization of Poverty: Women, Work, and Welfare." *Urban and Social Change Review* 11:28–36.

Pearce, Diana, and Harriette McAdoo. 1981. *Women and Children: Alone and in Poverty.* Washington, D.C.: National Advisory Council on Economic Opportunity.

Pearsall, Marion. 1959. *Little Smoky Ridge.* Tuscaloosa: University of Alabama Press.

Pfeffer, Max J. 1983a. "Social Origins of Three Systems of Farm Production in the United States." *Rural Sociology* 48(4):540–62.

———. 1983b. "Industrial Farming." *Democracy* 3(2):37–49.

———. 1986. "Immigration Policy and Class Relations in California Agriculture." Pp. 252–86 in *Studies in the Transformation of U.S. Agriculture,* edited by A. E. Havens, Gregory Hooks, Patrick H. Mooney, and Max J. Pfeffer. Boulder, Colo.: Westview Press.

Pfeffer, Max J., and Jess Gilbert. 1989. "Federal Farm Programs and Structural Change in the 1980s: A Comparison of the Cornbelt and the Mississippi Delta." *Rural Sociology* 54(4):551–67.

Philp, Kenneth R., ed. 1986. *Indian Self-Rule.* Salt Lake City, Utah: Howe Bros.

Plotnick, Robert D., and Felicity Skidmore. 1975. *Progress against Poverty: A Review of the 1964–1974 Decade.* New York: Academic Press.

Porter, Kathryn H. 1989. *Poverty in Rural America: A National Overview.* Washington, D.C.: Center on Budget and Policy Priorities and Housing Assistance Council.

Portes, Alejandro. 1985. "The Informal Sector and the World-Economy: Notes on the Structure of Subsidized Labor." Pp. 53–62 in *Urbanization in the World-Economy,* edited by Michael Timberlake. Orlando, Fla.: Academic Press.

Presidential Commission on Indian Reservation Economies (PCIRE). 1984. *Report and Recommendations to the President of the United States.* Washington, D.C.: U.S. Government Printing Office.

President's National Advisory Commission on Rural Poverty. 1967. *The People Left Behind.* Washington, D.C.: U.S. Government Printing Office, September.

Prucha, Francis Paul. 1984. *The Great Father.* Vol. 2. Lincoln: University of Nebraska Press.

Public Voice for Food and Health Policy. 1987. *Profiles of Rural Poverty: Facing Barriers to the Food Stamp Program.* Washington, D.C.: Public Voice for Food and Health Policy, July.

Raper, Arthur. 1968. *Preface to Peasantry.* 2d ed. New York: Atheneum.

Raper, Arthur, and Ira deA. Reid. 1941. *Sharecroppers All.* Chapel Hill: University of North Carolina Press.

Reimund, Donn, and Mindy Petrulis. 1987. "Performance of the Agricultural Sector." In *Rural Economic Development in the 1980's.* Washington, D.C.: Economic Research Service, U.S. Department of Agriculture.

Rexroat, Cynthia. 1989. "Economic Transformation, Family Structure and Poverty Rates of Black Children in Metropolitan Areas." *American Economic Review,* 79: 67–70.

Ricketts, Erol R., and Isabel V. Sawhill. 1988. "Defining and Measuring the Underclass." *Journal of Policy Analysis and Management* 7(2):316–25.

Robinson, Bert. 1989. "Horse Betting: New Game Plan for State Tribes." *San Jose, California Mercury News,* October 2.

Rogers, Kenneth A. 1984. *Health Status and Economic Productivity of Migrant Farm Workers in Orange County, New York.* Community Services Research and Development Program. Buffalo: State University of New York at Buffalo.

Rosenbaum, James E. and Susan J. Popkin. 1989. "Employment and Earnings of Low-

Income Blacks Who Move to Middle-Class Suburbs.'' Paper presented at a conference on ''The Truly Disadvantaged,'' Northwestern University, Evanston, Illinois.

Ross, Christine M., and Sheldon Danziger. 1987. ''Poverty Rates by State, 1979 and 1985: A Research Note.'' *Focus* 10:1–5.

Ross, Peggy J., and Elizabeth S. Morrissey. 1987. ''Two Types of Rural Poor Need Two Types of Help.'' *Rural Development Perspectives* 4(1):7–10.

———. 1989. ''Rural People in Poverty: Persistent versus Temporary Poverty.'' In *National Rural Studies Committee: A Proceedings*, edited by Emery Castle and Barbara Baldwin. Eugene, Ore.: Western Rural Development Center, Oregon State University.

Rossi, Peter. 1989. *Without Shelter*. New York: Priority Press Publications.

Rostow, Walter W. 1971. *The Stages of Economic Growth*. 2d ed. Cambridge: Cambridge University Press.

Rowe, Gene. 1979. *The Hired Farm Working Force of 1977*. Agricultural Economic Report no. 437. Washington, D.C.: U.S.D.A. Economics, Statistics, and Cooperative Service.

Ruggles, Patricia. 1989. *Measuring the Duration of Poverty Spells*. SIPP Working Paper no. 8909. Washington, D.C.: Bureau of the Census, May.

Runyan, Jack L. 1989. *A Summary of Federal Laws and Regulations Affecting Agricultural Employers*. Agriculture Information Bulletin no. 550. Washington, D.C.: Economic Research Service, U.S. Department of Agriculture.

Rural Electrification Administration (REA). 1989a. *Rural Electric Borrowers*. REA Bulletin no. 1–1. Washington, D.C.: U.S. Department of Agriculture.

———. 1989b. *Rural Telephone Borrowers*. REA Bulletin no. 3–4. Washington, D.C.: U.S. Department of Agriculture.

Rural Electrification Administration Files. 1974. Frank M. Remorenko, Jr., Letter to Joe S. Zoller, September 27, 1974. ''Equal Opportunity—Prince George Electric Cooperative, Waverly, Virginia.''

———. 1975–1982. ''Report of Compliance and Participation.'' *Participation Reports for Southern Coops*. Washington, D.C.: Rural Electrification Administration, U.S. Department of Agriculture.

Sawhill, Isabel. 1988. ''Poverty in the U.S.: Why Is It So Persistent?'' *Journal of Economic Literature* 26(3):1073–1119.

Scanlon, John. 1990. ''People Power in the Projects: How Tenant Management Can Save Public Housing.'' *Backgrounder*, no. 758. Washington, D.C.: Heritage Foundation.

Schiller, Bradley, R. 1984. *The Economics of Poverty and Discrimination*. 4th ed. Englewood Cliffs, N.J.: Prentice-Hall.

Schwartz, Harry. 1945. *Seasonal Farm Labor in the United States*. New York: Columbia University Press.

Seltzer, Curtis. 1985. *Fire in the Hole: Miners and Managers in the American Coal Industry*. Lexington: University Press of Kentucky.

Sessions, James. 1989. ''Civil Rights and Religion.'' In *Encyclopedia of Southern Culture*, edited by Charles R. Wilson and William Ferris. Chapel Hill: University of North Carolina Press.

Sewell, W. H., and R. M. Hauser. 1975. *Education, Occupation, and Earnings: Achievement in the Early Career*. New York: Academic Press.

Shapiro, Isaac. 1988. *The Minimum Wage and Job Loss*. Washington, D.C.: Center on Budget and Policy Priorities.

————. 1989. *Laboring for Less: Working But Poor in Rural America*. Washington, D.C.: Center on Budget and Policy Priorities.

Shapiro, Isaac, and Robert Greenstein. 1988. *Holes in the Safety Nets: Poverty Programs and Policies in the States*. Washington, D.C.: Center on Budget and Policy Priorities.

————. 1990. *Fulfilling Work's Promise: Policies to Increase Incomes of the Rural Working Poor*. Washington, D.C.: Center on Budget and Policy Priorities.

Shenkin, Budd N. 1974. *Health Care for Migrant Workers: Policies and Politics*. Cambridge, Mass.: Ballinger.

Shriver, Sargent. 1964. Statement before the Select Committee on Poverty of the Committee on Labor and Public Welfare, July 23.

Simon, Richard M. 1981. "Uneven Development and the Case of West Virginia: Going beyond the Colonialism Model." *Appalachian Journal* 8(3): 165–86.

Singal, Daniel J. 1982. *The War Within: From Victorian to Modernist Thought in the South, 1919–1945*. Chapel Hill: University of North Carolina Press.

Singer, H. W. 1949. "Economic Progress in Underdeveloped Countries." *Social Research* 16: 1–11.

Slesinger, Doris P. 1979a. *Migrant Agricultural Workers in Wisconsin*. Population Note no. 8. Madison: Department of Rural Sociology, University of Wisconsin, Madison.

————. 1979b. *Health Needs of Migrant Workers in Wisconsin*. Madison: Department of Rural Sociology, University of Wisconsin, Madison.

Slesinger, Doris, P. and E. Cautley. 1988. *Estimation of Migrant and Seasonal Agricultural Workers in Iowa, Kansas, Missouri, and Nebraska*. Madison: Department of Rural Sociology, University of Wisconsin, Madison.

Slesinger, Doris P., and Cynthia Ofstead. 1990. *Migrant Agricultural Workers in Wisconsin, 1989: Social, Economic, and Health Characteristics*. Madison: Department of Rural Sociology, University of Wisconsin, Madison.

Smith, Jane F., and Robert M. Kvasnicka. 1981. *Indian-White Relations: A Persistent Paradox*. Washington, D.C.: Howard University Press.

Smith, Lillian. 1949. *Killers of the Dream*. New York: W. W. Norton.

Snipp, C. Matthew. 1988. "Public Policy Impacts and American Indian Economic Development." Pp. 1–22 in *Public Policy Impacts on American Indian Economic Development*, edited by C. M. Snipp. Albuquerque: Institute for Native American Development, University of New Mexico.

————. 1989. *American Indians: The First of this Land*. New York: Russell Sage Foundation.

Snipp, C. Matthew, and Gary D. Sandefur. 1988. "Earnings of American Indians and Alaska Natives: The Effects of Residence and Migration." *Social Forces* 66:994–1008.

Snipp, C. Matthew, and Gene F. Summers. 1991. "American Indian Development Policies." In *Rural Policy in the 1990s*, edited by James A. Christenson and Cornelia B. Flora. Boulder, Colo.: Westview Press.

Sorden, L. G., E. Long, and M. Salick. 1948. *The Wisconsin Farm Labor Program, 1943–1947*. Madison: Agricultural Extension Service, University of Wisconsin.

Sorkin, Alan L. 1978. *The Urban American Indian*. Lexington, Mass.: D. C. Heath.

────. 1971. *American Indians and Federal Aid*. Washington, D.C.: Brookings Institution.

Southeast Women's Employment Coalition. 1986. *Women of the Rural South*. Lexington, Ky.: Southeast Women's Employment Coalition.

Southern Changes. 1981. "Save the Voting Rights Act." November.

Southern Regional Council. 1945. "The South: America's Economic Opportunity Number One." Atlanta: Southern Regional Council.

Southern Regional Council Files. 1990. Atlanta: Southern Regional Council.

Stack, Carol. 1974. *All Our Kin*. New York: Harper and Row.

Strange, Marty. 1990. *Half a Glass of Water: State Economic Development Policies and the Small Agricultural Communities of the Middle Border*. Walthill, Neb.: Center for Rural Affairs.

Summers, Gene, and Kristi Branch. 1984. "Economic Development and Community Social Change." *Annual Review of Sociology*, 141–66.

Summers, Gene F., Sharon D. Evans, Frank Clemente, E. M. Beck, and Jon Minkoff. 1976. *Industrial Invasion of Nonmetropolitan America: A Quarter Century of Experience*. New York: Praeger.

Sundquist, James L. 1968. *Politics and Policy: The Eisenhower, Kennedy and Johnson Years*. Washington, D.C.: Brookings Institution.

Survey Research Center. 1984. *User Guide to the Panel Study of Income Dynamics*. Ann Arbor, Mich.: Interuniversity Consortium for Political and Social Research.

Swanson, Louis E. 1988. "The Human Dimension of the Rural South in Crisis." In *The Rural South in Crisis*, edited by Lionel J. Beaulieu. Boulder, Colo.: Westview Press.

Thomas, Robert J. 1985. *Citizenship, Gender, and Work: The Social Organization of Industrial Agriculture*. Berkeley: University of California Press.

Thurow, Lester. 1987. "A Surge in Inequality." *Scientific American* 256(5):30.

Tickamyer, Ann R., and Cynthia M. Duncan. 1984. "Economic Activity and the Quality of Life in Eastern Kentucky." *Growth and Change* 15:43–51.

────. 1990. "Poverty and Opportunity Structure in Rural America." *Annual Review of Sociology*, 67–86.

────. 1991. "Work and Poverty in Rural America." In *Rural Policy for the 1990s*, edited by J. Christenson and C. Flora. Boulder, Colo.: Westview Press.

Tickamyer, Ann R., and Janet Bokemeier. 1988. "Sex Differences in Labor Market Experiences." *Rural Sociology* 53:166–89.

────. 1989. "Individual and Structural Explanations of Nonmetropolitan Men and Women's Labor Force Experiences." In *Research in Rural Sociology*, vol. 4, edited by W. Falk and T. Lyson, Greenwich, Conn.: JAI Press.

Tickamyer, Ann R., and Cecil H. Tickamyer. 1988. "Gender and Poverty in Central Appalachia." *Social Science Quarterly* 69(4):874–91.

Till, Thomas E. 1981. "Manufacturing Industry: Trends and Impacts." In *Nonmetropolitan America in Transition*, edited by Amos H. Hawley and Sara Mills Mazie. Chapel Hill: University of North Carolina Press.

Timberlake, Michael, Bruce B. Williams, Bonnie Thornton Dill, and Darryl Tukufu. 1991. "Race and Economic Development in the Lower Mississippi Delta." Working paper. Memphis, Tenn.: Center for Research on Women.

Tindall, Georgy. 1965. "The 'Colonial Economy' and the Growth Psychology: The South in the 1930s." *South Atlantic Quarterly* 64:465–77.

Tolbert, Charles. 1989. "Labor Market Areas in Stratification Research: Concept, Definitions, and Issues." In *Research in Rural Sociology*, edited by W. Falk and T. Lyson, vol. 4. Greenwich, Conn.: JAI Press.

Tolbert, Charles and Molly Killian. 1987. *Labor Market Areas for the United States*. Technical Report for Agricultural and Rural Economics Division. Washington, D.C.: Economic Research Service, U.S. Department of Agriculture.

U.S. Bureau of the Census. 1952. *U.S. Census of Agriculture: 1950*. Vol. II, *General Report, Statistics by Subjects*. Washington, D.C.: U.S. Government Printing Office.

———. 1953. *U.S. Census of Population, 1950*. Vol. 2, *Characteristics of the Population*, Pt. 1, *United States Summary*. Washington, D.C.: U.S. Government Printing Office.

———. 1964. *U.S. Census of Population, 1960*. Vol. 1, *Characteristics of the Population*, Pt. 1, *United States Summary*. Washington, D.C.: U.S. Government Printing Office.

———. 1972a. "Characteristics of the Low-Income Population: 1970." *Current Population Reports*, ser. P-60, no. 81. Washington, D.C.: U.S. Government Printing Office.

———. 1972b. *1970 Census of Population, General Social and Economic Characteristics, United States Summary* (PC-1-C1). Washington, D.C.: U.S. Government Printing Office.

———. 1973. *U.S. Census of Population, Subject Report: American Indians* PC(2)–1F. Washington, D.C.: U.S. Government Printing Office.

———. 1982a. Census of Population and Housing, 1980. Summary Tape File 3, Technical Documentation. Washington, D.C.: U.S. Department of Commerce.

———. 1982b. "Characteristics of the Population Below the Poverty Level: 1980." *Current Population Reports*, Ser. P-60, no. 133. Washington, D.C.: U.S. Government Printing Office.

———. 1983. *1980 Census of Population*. Vol. 1, *Characteristics of the Population*. Chapter C, *General Social and Economic Characteristics*. Part 1: *United States Summary* (PC80-1-C1). Washington, D.C.: U.S. Government Printing Office.

———. 1985. "Characteristics of the Population Below the Poverty Level: 1983." *Current Population Reports,* Ser. P-60, no. 147. Washington, D.C.: U.S. Government Printing Office.

———. 1986. *American Indians, Eskimos, and Aleuts on Identified Reservations and in the Historic Areas of Oklahoma (excluding urbanized areas)* (PC80–2–1D). Washington, D.C.: U.S. Government Printing Office.

———. 1987a. "Money Income and Poverty Status of Families and Persons in the United States, 1986." *Current Population Reports, Consumer Income*, Ser. P-60, no. 157. Washington, D.C.: U.S. Government Printing Office.

———. 1987b. "Poverty in the United States, 1985." *Current Population Reports, Consumer Income*, ser. P-60, no. 158. Washington, D.C.: U.S. Government Printing Office.

———. 1988. "Estimates of Poverty Including the Value of Noncash Benefits, 1987." Technical Paper 58. Washington, D.C.: U.S. Government Printing Office.

———. 1989a. *1987 Census of Agriculture*. Vol. 1: *Geographic Area Series*, pt. 51, *United States: Summary and State Data* (AC87-A–51). Washington, D.C.: U.S. Government Printing Office.

———. 1989b. "Poverty in the United States, 1987." *Current Population Reports*, ser. P–60, no. 163. Washington, D.C.: U.S. Government Printing Office.

———. Jointly with the Department of Agriculture. 1989c. "Rural and Rural Farm Population: 1988." *Current Population Reports*, ser. P-20, no. 439. Washington, D.C.: U.S. Government Printing Office.

U.S. Census Bureau. 1989d. "Transitions in Income and Poverty Status: 1984–85." *Current Population Reports*, ser. P-70, no. 15-RD-1. Washington, D.C.: U.S. Government Printing Office.

U.S. Congress. House. Commission on Civil Rights. 1981. "Extension of the Voting Act." *Hearings before the Committee on Civil and Constitutional Rights of the Committee on the Judiciary. 97th Cong., 1st sess., ser. no. 24, pts. 1–4.*

U.S. Congress. House. 1989. *Background Material and Data on Programs within the Jurisdiction of the Committee on Ways and Means.* WMCP 101–4. Prepared for the Committee on Ways and Means by its staff. 101st Cong., 1st sess. Washington, D.C.: U.S. Government Printing Office.

U.S. Congress. Office of Technology Assessment. 1986. *Indian Health Care.* Report OTA-H–290. Washington, D.C.: U.S. Government Printing Office.

U.S. Congress. Senate. 1988. *Wages of American Workers in the 1980s.* Washington, D.C.: U.S. Government Printing Office.

U.S. Congress. Senate. Select Committee on Poverty of the Committee on Labor and Public Welfare. 1964. *Hearings on S2642, The Economic Opportunity Act of 1964.* 88th Cong. 2d sess. Washington, D.C.: U.S. Government Printing Office.

U.S. Country Life Commission. 1975. "Report of the Country Life Commission." In *Agriculture in the United States: A Documentary History*, edited by Wayne D. Rasmussen, Vol. 2. New York: Random House.

U.S. Department of Agriculture. 1935. *Economic and Social Problems and Conditions of the Southern Appalachians.* Miscellaneous Publication no. 205. Washington, D.C.: U.S. Government Printing Office.

———. 1987. *Rural Economic Development in the 1980s.* Washington, D.C.: Department of Agriculture, Economic Research Service.

U.S. Department of Commerce. Bureau of Economic Analysis. 1989. Local Area Personal Income, 1969–87. Tape file. Prepared by the Bureau of Economic Analysis. Washington, D.C.

U.S. President. 1989. *Economic Report of the President.* Transmitted to the Congress January 1989 together with the Annual Report of the Council of Economic Advisors. Washington, D.C.: U.S. Government Printing Office.

U.S. President's Special Committee on Farm Tenancy. 1937. *The Report of the President's Committee.* Washington, D.C.: U.S. Government Printing Office.

Valentine, Bettylou. 1978. *Hustling and Other Hard Work.* New York: Free Press.

Valentine, Charles A. 1968. *Culture and Poverty.* Chicago: University of Chicago Press.

Vance, Rupert B. 1932. *Human Geography of the South: A Study in Regional Resources and Human Adequacy.* Chapel Hill: University of North Carolina Press.

———. 1962. Introduction and "The Region's Future, A National Challenge." In *The Southern Appalachian Region: A Survey*, edited by Thomas Ford. Lexington: University of Kentucky Press.

———. 1965. "Beyond the Fleshpots: The Coming Culture Crisis in the South." *Virginia Quarterly Review* 41:217–30.

———. 1971. "Oral History." New York: Columbia University Oral History Project.

Vidich, Arthur J., and Joseph Bensman. 1958. *Small Town in Mass Society: Class, Power, and Religion in a Rural Community.* Princeton, N.J.: Princeton University Press.

Villarejo, Don. 1990. Personal Communication. California Institute for Rural Studies, Davis, California, April 26.

Vinje, David. 1988. "Economic Development on Reservations in the Twentieth Century." Pp. 38–52 in *Overcoming Economic Dependency.* Occasional Papers in Curriculum Series, no, 9. Chicago, Ill.: Newberry Library.

Virginia, Maryland, and Delaware Association of Cooperatives. 1990. *Membership Directory.* Washington, D.C.: Rural Electrification Administration, U.S. Department of Agriculture.

Wacquant, Loïc and, William J. Wilson. 1989. "The Cost of Racial and Class Exclusion in the Inner City." Pp. 8–25 in *The Ghetto Underclass: Social Science Perspectives,* edited by William J. Wilson. Annals of the American Academy of Political and Social Science, vol. 51. Newbury Park, Calif.: Sage Publications.

Washington State Employment Security Department. 1990. *Farm Labor in Washington State.* Pullman, Wash.: Labor Market and Economic Analysis, Economic and Policy and Agricultural Statistics Units, February.

Weir, Margaret. 1988. "The Federal Government and Unemployment: The Frustration of Policy Innovation from the New Deal to the Great Society." Pp. 149–90 in *The Politics of Social Policy in the United States,* edited by Margaret Weir, Ann Shola Orloff, and Theda Skocpol. Princeton, N.J.: Princeton University Press.

Weller, Jack. 1965. *Yesterday's People.* Lexington: University Press of Kentucky.

Whitby, Kenny J. 1987. "Measuring Congressional Responsiveness to the Policy Interest of Black Constituents." *Social Science Quarterly* 6, no. 2 (June): 367–77.

White-Means, Shelly, P.S.K. Chi, and J. McClain. 1989. *Health Status and Economic Productivity of Migrant Farm Workers in Orange County, New York.* Final Report to Milbank Memorial Fund. Ithaca, N.Y.: Department of Consumer Economics and Housing, Cornell University.

Whitener, Leslie A. 1984. "A Statistical Portrait of Hired Farm Workers." *Monthly Labor Review* 107(6):49–53.

Williams, Terry and Williams Kornblum. 1985. *Growing Up Poor.* Lexington, Mass.: Lexington Books.

Wilson, Charles R. 1989. "Bible Belt." In *Encyclopedia of Southern Culture,* edited by Charles R. Wilson and William Ferris. Chapel Hill: University of North Carolina Press.

Wilson, William J. 1987. *The Truly Disadvantaged: The Inner City, the Underclass, and Public Policy.* Chicago: University of Chicago Press.

———. 1989. "The Underclass: Issues, Perspectives, and Public Policy." Pp. 182–92 in *The Ghetto Underclass: Social Science Perspectives,* edited by William J. Wilson. Annals of the American Academy of Political and Social Science, vol. 501. Newbury Park, Calif.: Sage Publications.

———. 1990. "Social Theory and Public Agenda Research: The Challenge of Studying Inner-City Social Dislocations." Presidential Address, Annual Meeting of the American Sociological Association, Washington, D.C., August 12.

Withers, Carl (James West, pseud.). 1945. *Plainville, U.S.A.* New York: Columbia University Press.

Woodson, Robert L., Sr. 1990. *Is the Black Community a Casualty of the War on Poverty?* Heritage Foundation Lecture, no. 245. Washington, D.C.: Heritage Foundation.

Woodward, C. Vann. 1968. *The Burden of Southern History.* Baton Rouge: Louisiana State University Press.

Wright, Gavin. 1986. *Old South, New South: Revolutions in the Southern Economy since the Civil War.* New York: Basic Books.

Index

About the Editor and Contributors

TERRY K. ADAMS is Senior Research Associate at the Survey Research Center of the University of Michigan. His research interests include the informal economy systems for child support orders.

KENNETH L. DEAVERS serves as Director of the Agriculture and Rural Economy Division, Economic Research Service (ERS), U.S. Department of Agriculture. At ERS since 1977, he has written extensively about policy issues related to rural development, including rural poverty policy. He also dealt with rural development in previous positions at the Congressional Budget Office and the Economic Development Administration. He earned an M.A. in economics from the University of Chicago.

BONNIE THORNTON DILL is Professor of Women's Studies at the University of Maryland. She was Professor of Sociology and founding Director of the Center for Research on Women at Memphis State University. She is currently conducting research on race, poverty, and gender in the rural South. Dill has published in such journals as *Signs*, *Journal of Family History*, and *Feminist Studies* and is currently editing a book entitled *Women of Color in American Society*.

CYNTHIA M. DUNCAN is Assistant Professor of Sociology at the University of New Hampshire. She is currently conducting a three-year comparative study of social mobility in diverse remote rural communities. Prior to joining the university, she worked on rural poverty and development issues as Research Director of the Aspen Institute's Rural Economic Policy Program in Washington, D.C. and as Research Director of the Mountain Association of Community Economic Development in Berea, Kentucky.

GREG J. DUNCAN is a Program Director of the Survey Research Center and a Professor of Economics at the University of Michigan. He is codirector of the Panel Study of Income Dynamics, with research interests in the economics of poverty and welfare transitions.

JANET M. FITCHEN is Associate Professor and Chair of the Department of Anthropology at Ithaca College in Ithaca, New York. Over the last two decades she has conducted ethnographic research on poverty and on rural America in upstate New York. She is the author of *Poverty in Rural America: A Case Study* (1981) and *Endangered Spaces, Enduring Places: Change, Identity, and Survival in Rural America* (1991).

CORNELIA BUTLER FLORA is Professor and Head of the Department of Sociology at Virginia Polytechnic Institute and State University. She received her Ph.D. from Cornell University and has published widely on community development and change, particularly regarding the structure of agriculture and community well-being, in the United States and developing countries.

LUCY GORHAM is a doctoral candidate in the Department of Urban Studies and Planning at the Massachusetts Institute of Technology. Her doctoral research explores the impact of international trade on the earnings and labor-force participation of high-school dropouts and high-school graduates in the United States. She currently works for the Joint Economic Committee of the U.S. Congress.

ROBERT GREENSTEIN is the founder and Director of the Center on Budget and Policy Priorities. A former administrator of the Food and Nutrition Service in the U.S. Department of Agriculture, he has written extensively on poverty in the United States.

ROBERT A. HOPPE is an economist at the Economic Research Service (ERS), U.S. Department of Agriculture. Currently he is ERS senior specialist in policy research on income levels, poverty, and income support programs in rural areas. Before coming to ERS in 1978, he worked for the Department of Agricultural and Applied Economics, University of Minnesota. He received an M.A. in agricultural economics from Washington State University and a B.A. in economics from the University of Minnesota.

ALICE O'CONNOR works on poverty policy issues at the Social Science Research Council. She received her doctorate in American history from the Johns Hopkins University. Her dissertation, which received a Rural Policy Dissertation Fellowship from the Woodrow Wilson Foundation, is titled "The Meaning of Poverty in the Affluent Society: Poverty and American Social Science, 1930–1970." She was formerly Assistant Director of the Ford Foundation Project on Social Welfare and the American Future.

MAX J. PFEFFER is a sociologist in the Department of Human Ecology at Rutgers University. His current research focuses on household economic strategies, including how low-income households use marginal types of employment like casual farm work as part of an economic coping strategy, and research on how farm families overcome management and labor constraints to the adoption of farm practices that reduce chemical inputs.

ISAAC SHAPIRO is a senior research analyst at the Center on Budget and Policy Priorities. He specializes in employment-related issues and is the coauthor with Sar A. Levitan of *Working But Poor: America's Contradiction* (1987).

DORIS P. SLESINGER is Professor of Rural Sociology, University of Wisconsin, Madison. She is trained in medical sociology and demography. Her research and teaching interests include topics relating to rural health, migrant agricultural workers, and sociodemographic trends among Wisconsin minority populations.

C. MATTHEW SNIPP is Associate Professor of Rural Sociology and Sociology at the University of Wisconsin, Madison. He received his Ph.D. in sociology in 1981 from the University of Wisconsin. He has been a Research Fellow at the U.S. Bureau of the Census and was a Fellow at the Center for Advanced Study in the Behavioral Sciences in 1989–90. Snipp has published numerous works on American Indian demography, economic development, poverty, and unemployment and continues to work on these issues as well as on the spatial organization of U.S. labor markets and on American Indian ethnicity. His most recent book is titled *American Indians: The First of This Land*.

STEVE SUITTS is the executive director of the Southern Regional Council, Inc., the oldest interracial organization in the American South that promotes democracy, opportunity, and social justice through research and technical assistance.

GENE F. SUMMERS is Professor of Rural Sociology at the University of Wisconsin, Madison. His major publications include *Attitude Measurement, Industrial Invasion of Nonmetropolitan America*, *Nonmetropolitan Industrial Development and Community Change*, *Technology and Social Change in Rural Areas*, "The Welfare State in the Community," *Rural Sociology* (1981) (with Matthew Snipp), "Cash Transfers and the Export Base of Small Communities," *Rural Sociology* (1982) (with Thomas Hirschl), and "Organization of Production and Community Income Distributions," *American Sociological Review* (1982) (with Leonard Bloomquist).

STEPHEN SWEET is a research associate with the Youth and Opportunity

Project at the Institute for Policy and Social Science Research at the University of New Hampshire, where he is currently working on a doctorate in sociology.

ANN R. TICKAMYER is Professor of Sociology in the Work, Gender, and Inequality Program at the University of Kentucky and holds a joint appointment in Rural Sociology. In addition to her work on poverty and rural labor markets, she has done extensive research on gender and race differences in labor-market experiences. She currently is part of a Rural Sociological Society task force on rural poverty, heading a working group on poor rural women.

BRUCE B. WILLIAMS received his Ph.D. in 1979 from the University of Chicago. His areas of expertise are comparative race and ethnic relations, economic development, and social change in urban and rural areas. Williams is currently an Associate Professor at the University of Mississippi in the Department of Sociology and Anthropology. He is the author of *Black Workers in an Industrial Suburb: The Struggle against Discrimination* (1987).